Students, Values, and Politics

A Crosscultural Comparison

Otto Klineberg
Marisa Zavalloni
Christiane Louis-Guérin
Jeanne BenBrika

THE FREE PRESS
A Division of Macmillan Publishing Co., Inc.
NEW YORK

Collier Macmillan Publishers
LONDON

The Free Press
A Division of Macmillan Publishing Co., Inc.
866 Third Avenue, New York, N. Y. 10022

Collier Macmillan Canada, Ltd.

Library of Congress Catalog Card Number: 77-94082

Library of Congress Cataloging in Publication Data

Main entry under title:

Students, values, and politics.

    Includes bibliographical references and index.
    1. Students--Political activity. 2. Students--
Attitudes. I. Klineberg, Otto
LB3610.S85   378.1'98'1   77-94082
ISBN 0-02-916770-1

Printed in the United States of America

printing number

1 2 3 4 5 6 7 8 9 10

Contents

Preface

The protests of university students were the point of departure of this inquiry. From about 1965 we witnessed a series of revolts in the universities of many countries; there were riots, fights, confrontations and collisions with the police, and sometimes fatalities. In some cases the revolt was limited, localized; in others, as in the events of May 1968 in France, it came close to leading a whole country into revolution.

In the past students had been criticized for their noticeable political apathy, especially in Europe and North America; suddenly apathy was replaced by activism, often accompanied by violent protest. How can we explain this phenomenon, which was striking, unexpected, disturbing, and widespread?

Many attempts have been made to understand it. Publications have multiplied, and, as we shall see later, a whole series of theories have been suggested, some mutually contradictory, some complementary. Research projects have been undertaken about the origins, education, and characteristics of the activists, for example, and about their motives, the claims made by students against society in general, and so forth. These research projects were often conceived and conducted with care and intelligence, using the best available methodology, but it seemed to us that almost all this research suffered from one limitation. It usually involved only the students of a *single country*, and sometimes even of a *single university*. It was therefore impossible to generalize these conclusions to all activists and still less to all students.

A great deal has been said, for instance, about *youth culture*. In a document on young people prepared by UNESCO (1968) for its Fifteenth General Conference in October–November 1968 it was suggested that this culture is truly international. The English version of this document was published in September 1969 in the first issue of the review *Youth and Society* under the title "Youth in Contemporary Society" (UNESCO, 1969). In it we find the following sentence:

> The young around the world appear to have created a sort of international culture, specifically of youth, in opposition to the adult culture, still fixed in the traditional patterns [p. 10].

We are told in the same document that two fundamental views have been considered in this connection. The first insists on the fact that problems differ from one country to another and that there is little resemblance, analogy, or correlation among them. The second theory, in contrast, tends to the view that the phenomenon of activism was global. Further, this theory holds, its near universality was based on the feeling that humanity is undergoing a crisis in a world threatened by chaos, and indicates the existence of a youth culture which is truly international. The position taken in the UNESCO text is clearly in favor of this second theory.

It seemed necessary and important to obtain data as objective and as international as possible before reaching a conclusion on this question. It was therefore decided to prepare a questionnaire which could be applied to students of several countries, in order to determine whether there was general agreement in youth attitudes or if the agreement was limited to certain domains. With the help of our colleagues in various countries, agreement was reached on the questions to be asked, and the answers were sought from a student sample as varied and representative as possible. The results are based on answers obtained in eleven countries.

We decided not to limit ourselves to a study of leftist activists. If a youth culture really exists—at least in the universities—it should appear not only among the "radical" extremists but also among those occupying other positions in the spectrum of political attitudes. It is possible that a conflict exists, not only and not necessarily between generations, but rather between different sectors of the same generation. In this connection we were especially interested in the attitude of young people toward international relations. The UNESCO document quoted above states, for example:

> Although there are some nationalist youth movements, the young are the most generous partisans of international understanding [p. 17].

Our own results bring us to rather more finely shaded conclusions on this aspect of youth culture, and on other dimensions as well.

Insofar as youth culture is concerned, we might be reproached, first, for having studied only university students. If we really wish to speak of young people in general, we have no right to neglect those who are workers, farmers, soldiers, and many others. We limited our inquiries to students, first because they were more accessible, also because it was primarily their actions which most clearly raised the issue of differences, if not conflict, between generations, as well as of the development of a culture apparently specific to young people. We admit this limitation to the range of our study; we would be happy to see a parallel investigation conducted on young people outside the universities. A second possible reproach is that we did not really obtain a representative sample of students. We shall discuss this criticism below, and shall try to show that we did not do too badly in this regard. We admit, however, that the representative character of our sampling cannot be proved conclusively, and our inferences on the attitudes of young students in general must therefore be considered as probable rather than as definitive conclusions.

We are on firmer ground when we come to the second goal of our study, which was to determine the relation between attitudes and political identification. Our questionnaire required students to define their political membership or preference. This permitted us to compare the attitudes of the French "extrême gauche," for example, with American or British "leftists" or "radicals." In this case we do not need to show that the proportion of "extrême gauche" or "radicals" in our sample corresponds to that in the university population of the various countries. Our comparison is valid for those who so defined themselves. We shall see later that this self-characterization corresponds to a whole series of attitudes connected with a political position—left, center, right, etc.—which permits us to conclude that for the most part our subjects answered our questions honestly and consistently.

Our third goal was to submit to an international test certain conclusions obtained in the course of research, often interesting and important, which was based on a sample studied in a single country. Would these conclusions be valid elsewhere? To take an example, in the case of the problem of the conflict between generations and more particularly of the conflict between the young and their own parents, several American studies suggest that activists are not at all hostile toward their parents. On the contrary, the students accept their parents' "liberal" principles but try to go further in the same direction, seeking to realize the ideals that the parents were unable, or did not really wish, to attain. We have tried to find out whether this same relationship exists in other countries.

Before discussing the findings of our study, we ought to reply to certain questions which the reader might ask:

The students were questioned in 1969–70. Several years have passed since then. Has the study lost any of its contemporaneity or its pertinence? Have students during the interim become as apathetic as they were years ago? Of course we regret that the results of the study took so long to be published, but our limited means and personnel, plus our desire to study the interrelations among the attitudes and opinions expressed, permitted us no alternative. Our study is not a simple poll, but an analysis, with all that that implies concerning statistics and the evaluation of certain hypotheses raised by the researchers.

Concerning the contemporary nature of the problem, we need only read the newspapers. During the time of the preparation of this publication there were student protests in France, Greece, Egypt, and Spain; more recently they have occurred in Italy, the United Kingdom, Turkey, India, and Thailand—and the list is not complete. No, apathy has not entirely replaced rebellion. Situations have changed, but the desire of young people to play a role in determining the nature of these changes is still present.

We have attempted, however, to give a more direct even though partial answer to the question as to what changes in attitudes of students have occurred. During 1976 and 1977 the questionnaire was applied to students in two countries, France and the United States, and comparisons were made of the answers obtained from the new and the original samples. In view of the small size (about 100 students in each country) of the more recent groups, we suggest that these results be regarded only as hypotheses, although we have tried to indicate whenever possible which conclusions appear to us to be plausible. We feel so strongly that it is important to repeat investigations of this kind in order to determine the degree of permanence and change of attitudes that we thought it worth while to perform this supplementary comparison in spite of the limitations of our new sample.

Is not a questionnaire always suspect? How can we know that students replied honestly and sincerely? We certainly would have preferred to interview the students, to ask them supplementary questions, and to let them explain the reasons for their choices and thus to tap some of their underlying attitudes. The questionnaire had to be used for practical reasons, but we have considerable confidence in the veracity of the results obtained. This confidence is based in particular on the coherence of the responses. In all countries, for example, students defining themselves as on the "far left," in the "center," or on the "right" could be clearly differentiated so regularly that our findings cannot be due to simple chance. There are always exceptions, of course, but the general tendencies are clear and convincing. This conclusion is confirmed by the generally favorable reactions of the students to the questionnaire itself, as they had ample space to write in their comments or criticisms.

Is it possible to have a truly international study? Do the questions have the same meaning in the different national contexts? We admit this is a difficult problem. We attempted to solve it at least in part by inviting colleagues from the various countries to participate in the formulation of the questions, to indicate all those questions which did not apply to their country, and those which had to be eliminated because translation into their language was difficult or impossible. After a series of pilot tests, a second meeting of researchers led us to modify and rewrite ambiguous questions and to add new ones which seemed useful or indispensable. The final questionnaire was therefore an international product, which we and our colleagues did our best to make internationally applicable.

Acknowledgments

The authors express their sincerest thanks to the following organizations and individuals:

to the Aquinas Fund for its generous financial support of the research undertaken;

to UNESCO, the International Union of Psychological Sciences, the International Social Science Council, and CORDES (Commissariat Général du Plan, France) for helpful financial contributions; it is important to add that the views expressed in this volume are not necessarily those of the national and international organizations listed;

to the Ecole des Hautes Etudes en Sciences Sociales, the Aquinas Fund, and the International Social Science Council for continuing support for the International Center for Intergroup Relations, Paris, which served as headquarters for this investigation;

to the international group of colleagues who participated in the planning sessions, held in Paris and London, and cooperated in the formulation of the questionnaire: H.G. Ornauer from Austria, Aniela Ginsberg from Brazil, H. Touzard and J. Zarka from France, U. Christiansen from West Germany, T. Tentori and F. Crespi from Italy, A. Chalmers, H. Himmelweit, and M. Jahoda from the United Kingdom, G. Lesser and Stephen L. Klineberg from the United States, and M. Jezernick from Yugoslavia;

to these and so many other colleagues who applied the questionnaires in the various countries included in this study, and who will forgive us, we hope, for not listing all their names;

to A. Thauront for her aid with the factorial analysis;

to Walt Lemke for his help in preparing the first draft of the English version of the text;

to Lynn Kari Petrich for her translation from the French of technical portions of the manuscript;

to Brigitte Vidé for her services as secretary;

to Charles E. Smith and Elly Dickason of The Free Press for their aid in the preparation of the final version;

and last, but far from least, to the thousands of students in many countries and universities who answered our questions.

Chapter 1

The Student Movement: Suggested Explanations

Introduction

In spite of the proliferation of literature on students and protests, there exist few concrete data on the ideological attitudes of students or on their positions taken vis-à-vis the university, the political and social system, and cultural and moral values. Nor have many research efforts been undertaken on the role of the student as a dynamic force in the changing of education and politics. Touraine (1968b) thinks that the more modern and scientific the university becomes, the more it will be actively concerned with politics and ideologies. The number of young people in universities will grow, and this growth will be accompanied by greater and more frequent protests. According to him, the university will engender continuous protests, and revolutionary ferment will develop unceasingly.

A report by UNESCO (1969) on youth in contemporary society indicates that between 1960 and 1965 the total number of young people in the world who are taking advanced studies jumped from 11,174,000 to 16,015,000. This rise of 61 percent in five years demonstrates that students represent a special category in rapid expansion—a force which will increasingly exercise considerable influence. And obviously this rise has continued. If we consider students as the elite and as the potential high-grade staff of society, their opinions and their attitudes could well be the "sextants of the future," to repeat the expression of Finley and Simon (1972). Wright (1963), as a sociologist, insists on the necessity to study this new generation of intellectuals in the world as the real agents of historic change and, speaking of the politics of the students, to proceed to detailed, comparative studies.

Undertaken in eleven countries, the present research permits us, among other things, to proceed to a comparison of students of diverse political orientations in the same country, but also to establish another comparison on the level of a particular political segment from one country to another.

The few concrete studies about the attitudes of young people in 1950s, particularly the work of Gillespie and Allport in 1955, that of Goldsen et al. in 1960, that of Jacob in 1958, and that of Stoetzel in 1953, generally show young people who are sensible, who are principally preoocupied by their own familial and professional futures, and who only rarely manifest interest in the sociopolitical life of the country. These studies reflect the image of a group of young people relatively apathetic in politics. Certain key questions used in our study were borrowed from these previous research efforts in order to establish the nature of changes which have occurred since the 1950s, in particular changes in professional aspirations and in the sources of satisfaction in life.

Differences observed between generations seemed weak before 1960; there apparently existed, in the majority of cases, a kind of continuity between age classes. Then, with the sudden emergence of student agitation in underdeveloped as well as in industrialized countries, what characterized only a few marginal groups became a widespread phenomenon. Of course young people in industrialized countries do not have the same preoccupations as those in developing countries; if the former partially reject a society of abundance, the latter are concerned with the modernization and development of their country. In general, however, youth accepts less and less passively the ideas of its elders and wishes to participate actively in the social and political life of its society—this often expressed in the desire to introduce drastic social changes.

In industrialized countries some research projects show that many young people continued to identify largely with the values and traditions of the past (Converse and Schuman, 1970). It is no less apparent, however, that something fundamental and irreversible seems to have occurred. A new culture emerged, sketched in the work of Marcuse and of many others, which denounced the absurdity of contemporary civilization. Thus, in the United States in the report of the President's Commission on Campus Unrest (1970), we read:

> Race, the war, and the defects of the modern university have contributed to the development of campus unrest, have given it specific focus, and continue to lend it a special intensity. But they are neither the only nor even the most important causes of campus unrest. Of far greater moment have been the advance of American society into the postindustrial era, the increasing affluence of American society, and the expansion and intergenerational evolution of liberal idealism. Together, these have prompted the formation of a new youth culture that defines itself through a passionate attachment to principle and an equally passionate opposition to the larger society. . . . It rejects what it sees to be the operational ideals of American society: materialism, competition, rationalism, technology, consumerism, and militarism. This emerging culture is the deeper cause of student protest against war, racial injustice, and the abuses of the multiversity. . . . Over time, more and more students have moved in the direction of an ever deeper and more inclusive sense of opposition to the larger society . . . [pp. 52–53].

Studies by Yankelovich (1972, 1974) tend to show that the war in Vietnam coincided with and was in part responsible for the emergence of new value systems which modified the attitudes of young people in the United States. These values, which at first characterized only a minority of students, were little by little assimilated by the majority of young Americans, especially once the war in Vietnam had ended. Holtzman et al. describe this situation (1975):

> Religion, patriotism, and the belief that hard work always pays off are no longer seen as very important values by the majority of young Americans. At the same time, there has been a return to traditional career aspirations and a search for economic security. Two motivations are implied by the new set of postaffluent values, desire for personal self-fulfillment and a new vision of what a just and harmonious society might be [pp. 337–338].

In France, Touraine (1968b) also stresses the fact that student uprisings question the objectives and the goals of society and of culture. In May 1968, we found on the walls of the Sorbonne slogans like "We refuse a world in which the certitude of not dying from hunger has been replaced by the risk of dying of boredom" and "We are inventing a new, original world." In the underdeveloped countries, as Lipset (1966) has noted,

> Their [young people's] concern is, from a nationalist standpoint, with the modernization of their country, which would permit it tó take its place with the leading countries of the modern world. . . . it was the retrograde position of their own country in comparison with one of these countries [Great Britain, France, Germany, the models of modernity] or with a vague composite image of all of them which provided the point of departure for the radical criticism of their own countries [p. 138].

In some regions, such as the communist countries of Europe, protesting students object, above all else, to a political structure which is judged too coercive and insist upon freedom of expression for everyone.

It seems that in the majority of countries protest movements, whatever their form and nature, reflect a malaise related to a real need for change. Ideologies, intimately tied to aspects of the society which saw them develop, conserve for a long time a certain national color. It is natural, therefore, that the causes and the forms of young people's protest will vary according to the type and the level of development of the country. We felt that an international comparison would permit us to determine in what measure different cultures and political traditions played a part in determining the variations in student attitudes, as well as the significance that could be attributed to the notion of a worldwide youth culture.

What is the nature of the "revolt"? Who are these "activists"? What do we understand by "protest"? The literature which treats these problems comes mainly from Western countries, and it is certainly the United States which offers the greatest number of studies based on empirical research. We have thus taken generally as our major sources American authors, but also others who have treated particular aspects of student revolt specific to their country or to other countries.

The eleven countries in this study include five countries in Western Europe (France, Italy, Great Britain, Spain, and Austria), one socialist European country (Yugoslavia), two African countries (Tunisia and Nigeria), one country in America (the United States), one in Oceania (Australia), and one in Asia (Japan).

Student Protest: Analysis and Explanation

We have attempted in the section which follows to summarize the various explanations of student activism which have been proposed, particularly in Western, industrialized countries. We have grouped them into several major categories, with the understanding that the categories are not entirely disparate and will necessarily overlap. The categories we found useful are the psychological portrait of the protester; the generation conflict; the power conflict; and the student protest as a new type of social movement (Marxist perspective).

THE PSYCHOLOGICAL PORTRAIT OF THE PROTESTER

A certain number of studies, conducted principally in the United States, seek to explain student protest by concentrating on the "social actor" in the movement, and compare the activists to nonactivist control groups. The leftist activist has been described as follows: he comes from a relatively comfortable socioeconomic background, studies at one of the most prestigious universities and is found among the more brilliant students (Lyonns, 1965; Somers, 1965; Westby and Braungart, 1966). The protesters may indeed be considered "privileged" (Trent and Craise, 1967). Flacks (1967) shows that American activists refuse conventionally institutionalized roles and rarely choose careers in the natural sciences, industry or politics. Their courses, rather, are oriented toward social science and arts and letters. Their relationships with their parents are excellent. These studies also indicate that the activists tend to come from highly educated families belonging to traditionally progressive religious groups, such as liberal Protestants and Jews. However, in other countries, particularly France, Austria, and Italy, where there is a long socialist and communist tradition with a strong working-class base, leftist students often come from less privileged backgrounds (Lipset, 1968).

Many writers, however, continue to speak of the young European protesters as "privileged," "middle-class children," "blousons dorés" (gold shirts) (Boudon, 1970a; Stéphane, 1969; Mendel, 1969), this description either deriving from the American research, or generalizing to the whole group the socioeconomic characteristics of certain leaders or more conspicuous members. As a matter of fact, the leaders often do come from a comfortable, intellectual background, but this is not the case for most of the activist "followers."

In addition, the American research shows that the protesters come from families with a humanist tradition and attitudes—if not leftist, at least liberal, a bit to the left of middle-class conventions (Keniston, 1968; Flacks, 1970). The protesting students, in this perspective, seeking an alternative to existing traditional values, would seem merely to be warming up the social and political ideals either abandoned or set aside by their parents. Keniston (1967), however, makes a distinction, to which we shall return, between the "culturally alienated," who are relatively unadapted to contemporary society and whose revolt is characterized by nonconformist attitudes, and the "activists," extremely politicized and involved, who are fighting within the existing structures of society. The activists are described as having strong personalities and as being successfully socialized, while the alienated have psychological problems due to difficult interpersonal relationships during their childhood within the family. In this perspective—and the idea is also developed by Flacks (1967)—the activists, their parents' spiritual and ideological heirs, are said to be continuing rather than opposing the work of their parents, and there is little generation conflict. The alienated, however, are in clear conflict with their families, adopting a cultural conduct clearly different from that of their parents.

It is very important, as our data will show, not to perceive the students as a homogenous group. We would also caution against the tendency of many writers to catalogue all the protesters as pathological deviants. Thus Bettelheim (1970) refers to the generation of protesters as emotionally ill and paranoiac. For Hook (1970), the protesters are young totalitarian fanatics. Farnsworth (1969) considers that certain of their aggressive acts are completely incomprehensible to the observer accustomed to the habitual standards of adult behavior. Many other opinions could be cited, but such sweeping judgments must be questioned in view of their bias and lack of objectivity. However, if we consider that the militant response is one way of reacting to a rapidly changing political, social, and economic environment, it may be possible to propose, as certain sociologists have done, a typology as a function of the protesters' various responses.

We have already seen that Keniston distinguishes activists (who wish actively to provoke changes in the style of political and social life) from alienated students, who are more oriented toward a personal search for new experiences. More than twenty years ago, Merton (1957) made a distinction between different modes of acceptance or rejection of cultural goals and institutionalized means of realizing them. More recently, Smith, Haan and Block (1970) also developed a typology of orientation of students toward socio-political action. These authors distinguish three types of involved American students—"constructivists," "dissidents," and "activists"—plus two other groups relatively uninvolved, those who are simply "inactive" and those who conform to conventional mores, the "conventionalists." These latter two groups are characterized by the lack of interest they demonstrate in social and political affairs.

The first three groups interest us particularly. The "constructivists," if they are implicated in social and political affairs, remain very conformist in not rejecting traditional values. Like the inactive group and the conventionalists, the constructivists strongly identify with the social and political values of their parents. On the other hand, the "activists" and the "dissidents" reject traditional values and revolt against the sociopolitical system. The activists might be seen as altruists fighting for a more equitable society, while the dissidents are clearly more politicized and center their energy on protesting against well-established institutions and the politics which direct them. The dissidents appear more rebellious against the political and social ideologies of their parents than do the activists.

Later we shall compare these findings with those of the present study including different countries.

THE GENERATION CONFLICT

A second explanatory approach is centered on the theme of the generation conflict. This is a concept which has been widely discussed and to which are attached explanations with sociological, psychological and psychoanalytic aspects, and even ethnological and biophysiological ones. Few of these analyses have an empirical basis; for the most part they rely on speculative hypotheses.

Touraine (1972) also emphasizes the ambiguity of the term "generation conflict." "Either it is rather a separation than a conflict of the generations that is involved," he says, "or it is a conflict that does not so much oppose one generation against another as the powerful against the helpless, who cannot be adequately described in terms of their age" (p. 198). Three major explanatory themes appear in the literature concerned with this problem. The first describes the conflict between the generations as a consequence of the acceleration of social changes; the second is based on an analysis exclusively from a psychoanalytic perpective; and the last sees the conflict as basically a conflict of power.

THE GENERATION CONFLICT AS A RESULT OF RAPID SOCIAL CHANGE

Although their nature differs as between the industrialized and the developing countries, the effects of scientific and technological advances, of urbanization and modernization, of living conditions and communication are the reasons offered by many authors as an explanation of protest. For these writers "generation conflict" usually means a divergence between youth values and the dominant values of the surrounding society—more specifically, those of the parents. This divergence in values between young people and adults is attributed to a rapid social change that has created a gap between their respective formative experiences. According to Birnbaum (1969), "Generational dissidence and revolt are not a perpetual social problem, but assume acute forms only under conditions of extreme dissonance between generational experiences" (p. 148). Mitscherlich (1969), Mendel (1969), and Mead (1970) believe that the process of identification indispensable to the maintenance of tradition is seriously disturbed by the lack of understanding and insufficiency of social contact between generations. From this comes a lack of love and respect for parents and old people, and therefore a loss of the authority of adults in the eyes of young people.

Mead (1948, 1970), in connection with the relation between social change and the divergence of values between generations, has stressed the importance of peer roles in the process of socialization. According to her, the transmission of culture through parents worked in the past in a cultural system which changed slowly. The child could, if given time, take his parents as models and adapt his own life style to theirs. Once social change becomes very rapid, however, this pattern is impossible, Mead indicates, because the child, when he becomes an adult, cannot belong to the same culture which was represented by his father in his own youth. At this point the socializing function of the peer group becomes more important. No longer do omnipotent parents transmit their norms and values; this role is assumed by peers.

As Davis (1940)[1] suggested years ago, the generation conflict occurs, not because the young and poorly socialized are incapable of adapting themselves to the values and dominant symbols of society, but, on the contrary, because the young are the natural agents of modernization. In fact, Davis believes, it is harder for the parents to modernize their points of view because they are the product of specific experiences lived at a certain moment of historic development, while the young are open to all the new experiences. According to Musgrove (1969), the contrast between the experiences of the generations is growing in modern societies. Young people have received in the aggregate a better formal education. The extremely important expansion of the mass media has also contributed to widening the gap between the young and the old. In addition, whereas the preceding generation has in many cases spent its youth in communities "on a human scale," the expansion of urbanization and the rapid growth of schools, universities, and industrial organizations in number and complexity have put the experiences of the young on an entirely different scale from those of their parents, and the texture of human relations has been changed profoundly as a result.

If these authors agree on the role of social change in the student protest movement, they show marked divergence in evaluating the consequences. In fact, for some the change is extremely negative, as it prevents good socialization and leads to a weakening of traditional values. On the other hand, for others the change has a dynamic and positive effect to the extent that it permits a constant renewal of values.

---

[1]In Coser, ed. (1964).

These explanations of the student revolt in terms of generation conflict in fact do not explain the sporadic nature of protest movements and why some students fight against the system and others do not. If we consider the studies already cited which were made during the fifties in Western countries (Gillespie and Allport, 1955; Jacob, 1958; Goldsen et al., 1960), the data obtained reveal no strong rebellion against the family and still less a rejection of the system of existing values. And in the recent events not all students were engaged in protest; the majority were still conforming to the dominant values. Thus we are obliged to ask the following question: if the same causes—accelerated change and the growing influence of the peer group—are as likely to produce conformity as revolt, what importance can we grant them? This notion of the generation conflict as "social change," together with the psychoanalytic perspective, which we shall consider below, in any case contradict the data of Flacks (1967) and Keniston (1969). Their findings indicated that at least in the United States the activists were not engaged in a generation conflict. Their orientations came from their own families, since the young protesters were reactivating the ideas of their parents.

THE GENERATION CONFLICT AND PSYCHOANALYSIS

The psychoanalytic perspective explains most specifically the revolt of youth in wealthy countries. It finds that change, in weakening authority, reveals the deep mechanism of hate toward the father (Feuer, 1968; Stéphane, 1969; Mendel, 1969; Mitscherlich, 1969). The psychological root of the student revolt would thus be the Oedipus complex. According to Feuer (1968), who has done considerable research on the various important movements of revolt in history, all student movements include an inevitable tendency to violence, inspired by a mixed desire for regicide, parricide, and suicide. A decline of respect for the law occurs, and a general erosion of institutions (family, church, school, and country) provokes movements of youth revolt. The forces that arouse this are obscure and subconscious, going back to early childhood. They express the desire to kill the father, and are accompanied by a feeling of guilt and self-hatred produced by the presence of such desires.

Feuer suggests that the center of the conflict is not directly the family, but has widened to larger objectives like the older generation in general, the university, and the government. The functioning of such a displacement is to channel the hostility against the father toward an object that does not inspire the same feelings of guilt.

For Stéphane (1969), the student protest is characterized by the rejection of reality. The middle-class youth of today, students and protesters, are not in revolt against the father; rather, they refuse to recognize the role of the father. Stéphane describes this defense mechanism, which he calls the avoidance of Oedipus, as follows: The adolescent seeks to escape conflict with the father, a defensive avoidance defining the psychic make-up of the protester. The personality of the protester is dominated by narcissism, self-admiration, and intolerance, which characterize the phases of sexual development preceding the Oedipus complex. But there can be no revolution founded on a refusal of reality. For Stéphane, the true revolutionary spirit leads the protester to take the place of the father, rather than to flee from him; it consists in becoming his own father, rather than in suppressing (in imagination, of course) the parental relationship. This suppression takes us back to the pre-Oedipal universe, that is, to a world entirely dominated by the mother, who is at the same time both good and bad, generous and frustrating, the prototype of the society of consumption, of whom we demand everything while desiring to kill her.

Mendel (1969), in a sociopsychoanalytic perspective,[2] thinks on the contrary that the adolescent does not escape or avoid the Oedipal conflict, but faces it without being able to get beyond it, thus causing regression. This impossibility of going beyond the Oedipal conflict has its origins in society. Referring to profound changes introduced by the technical and industrial revolution, Mendel suggests that transmission by society of sociocultural institutions from one generation to another no longer takes place, but that the former value system has not yet been replaced by a new one.

We must note two important points mentioned by Mendel regarding the discontinuity of the process of transmission of values between generations. First, there occurs the weakening of authority, in particular that of the father. Like Mitscherlich (1969), the author sees in the fact that the father no longer works directly in front of the child one of the causes of the weakening of the father image.[3] Mendel also stresses the important role played by the distortion or the near extinction of sociocultural institutions:

> Rites of passage or of initiation, in all known societies, assure the person in puberty the passing from the biological state of the adolescent to the social state of manhood. By these rites society takes the individual in charge at the most crucial age (and the most difficult) of his existence and helps him make this adjustment. In the same way the integration to social life and the perpetuation of traditions could be achieved, by an alliance and an identification of the adolescent with his elders, who transmit the cultural acquisitions of the past [p. 128].

The consequence of this rupture with the older generations and the weakening of sociocultural institutions is that society is vulnerable to the antisocial tendencies of the adolescent, who experiences great difficulty in integrating himself into the world of adults. Mendel introduces a new concept, the "generation crisis," to describe the contemporary, adolescent phenomenon, which he distinguishes from the classical generation conflict. The latter refers to the Oedipal conflict at puberty. It is understood as the adolescent's conscious or subconscious desire to take the place of the father and to enjoy the latter's prerogatives. The "generation crisis," in contrast, is the contemporary refusal of the adolescent to identify himself with the model proposed by the father, adults, and society. Above all, the adolescent does not wish to become like them. He challenges the heritage of the past (or what remains of it) and wishes to destroy it so that nothing of it remains.

These various interpretations of student protest by means of the Oedipal conflict are tempting insofar as they permit us to understand all student movements by means of one general theory. But if we accept the universality of this complex, as the psychoanalysts propose, we find the same methodological weakness as that in the theory of social change. Neither theory explains the sporadic nature of the movements. Besides, we might wonder why, as Keniston has pointed out for the protesting students in the United States, certain students, especially those from liberal

---

[2]Mendel (1969) thus defines this discipline: "It tries to underline its values on the social order by the notion of an unconscious dynamic, while still remembering other forces which are in play on the social level" (p. 13).

[3]This is nothing very new, however, and it is difficult to discover recent changes in the social structure in this respect which would render this idea relevant.

middle-class families, are more prone to revolt than others, generally from poor or working-class families. To make the explanation more acceptable, it would be necessary to modify the hypothesis that bases revolt on the Oedipus complex so as to indicate an exceptionally serious Oedipus complex involving unconscious and unresolved feelings of hatred, particularly strongly felt toward the fathers of the rebellious students. We now know enough, however, about the life and the background of these protesters, in any case in the United States, to be sure that the theory so modified is not confirmed. On the contrary, it seems that most of the student protesters in the United States are relatively close to their parents, that the values they defend are usually those learned at the family dinner table, and that their parents generally tend to be very cultured, liberal or leftist, and politically active. In addition, the psychological studies of radical students in the United States show that they are no more disturbed or neurotic than the nonradicals. Indeed, most of the research indicates that they are better integrated and show better psychological development than the politically inactive students. In general, the studies of American protesters show that there is an "intergeneration solidarity" rather than an Oedipal revolt.

These differing explanations of student protest, mainly that which posits the revolt as the symptom of hostility against the father or elders in general, tend to freeze the student in the role of an object, denying him autonomy and responsibility. Most protesters themselves strongly reject the thesis: "The concept of generation conflict should be dropped entirely. It is only a disguise in the struggle for power" (from a tract, "Nous sommes en marche," 1968). Why could not the youth revolt be interpreted with equal plausibility as a mechanism of self-defense against the will of the "father" to kill the "son" who wants to take his place?

THE CONCEPT OF THE POWER CONFLICT

A great many writers on the problem of youth protest have in a way upheld the protesters' point of view as illustrated by the tract "Nous sommes en marche" quoted above. Thus we find that Musgrove (1969) considers that the generation conflict is only a *power conflict*. He follows Dahrendorf (1959) in postulating that each society is based on the coercion of certain of its members by others. Conflict and change, therefore, are universal traits of social life. Adults try not only to impose their culture but also to keep the young away from decision making in order to keep as much power for themselves as possible. An inquiry made in France by the French Institute of Public Opinion (IFOP) in 1968 shows that 56 percent of the French felt that students should limit themselves to complaints about the university, without trying to play a role in social life and politics.[4] According to these adults, the questioning of contemporary society by the young should not go beyond theoretical discussions.

Musgrove shows that in English history the power of young people from 13 to 20 years of age has continued to decline for two reasons: (1) The population structure has changed. The "age pyramid" has disappeared as the number of people from 40 to 50 years of age has doubled in three centuries. This phenomenon blocks the access of youth to power. (2) The economic structure has been modified, so that fewer inter-

---

[4]Other polls undertaken by IFOP indicate that this percentage increased with "antisocial" events; that is to say, when the students became more threatening to law and order, more French people wanted to limit young people's complaints to the domain of the university.

esting jobs are open to the young. According to this writer, demographic and economic changes have profoundly altered the balance of power between the young and their elders. By devious means young people are kept as long as possible outside society, without any responsibility. According to Musgrove, theories have been elaborated with the approval of teachers in the areas of adolescence, education, and work in order to explain and justify this exclusion. Such theories become ideological tools to maintain the status quo. Between the young and their elders there is not only a barrier of communication or a gap between the generations, but a real conflict of interest. Those institutions whose existence is justified as necessary to socialization, such as the schools with their apparatus of control, seem like forces of a colonial power directed against the native population. In the colonies, the coercive destruction of the traditional culture was rationalized as a well-meaning effort for the good of the people, to improve their standard of living, to give them a better life and more opportunities. Musgrove goes so far as to say that in our Western societies, socialization would be a comparable systematic suffocation of individual alternatives for the benefit of a social conformity that would profit the adults in power.

PROTEST AS A NEW POLITICAL FORCE

A quite different approach to the problem of protest—to accept the student movement as the affirmation of a new political and social force—is upheld by Marcuse, Touraine, and others. In contrast to official Marxism, which considers the students as a force auxiliary to the revolutionary movement of the workers, Marcuse (1964, 1968, 1969) thinks that in a modern industrial country the students represent a major force of protest. In the stage of advanced capitalism, it is up to those who are not directly involved to act, following the revolutionary example of the Third World. Touraine (1968a) compares the contemporary student movements with the worker unrest of the past century:

> If it is true that knowledge and technical progress are the motor forces of the new society, as the accumulation of capital was for the preceding society, does not the university replace the great capitalist enterprise, and does not the student movement have in principle the same importance as the workers' movement in the preceding era?

It seems, therefore, that the protest is seen not merely as a reaction of discontent with the socioeconomic problems of Western society but also, as Touraine emphasizes, as the manifestation of the new themes and new class conflicts of our society.

In this perspective, the wave of student radicalism and opposition would not be the result of a generation conflict, but would represent the rudimentary struggles of a new developing class. Some young people, then, are revolting against a system which seems to them to maintain social, racial, and economic injustice. They fought against the Vietnam War, and they denounce social conformity. They want a radical redistribution of political power and fundamental changes in the quality of life (Denitch, 1970). The emergence of youth as a social body able to take its place in the forefront of such a struggle before the working class was even organized, as Mury (1969) mentions, is fairly well known. We have seen this phenomenon in Russia, in China, in Latin America, etc.

THE COUNTERCULTURE

It is necessary to mention an original movement specific to industrial societies which has gained many followers and whose influence cannot be denied. Roszak (1969) calls this movement the counterculture because, according to him,

> What makes the youthful disaffiliation of our time a cultural phenomenon, rather than merely a political movement, is the fact that it strikes beyond ideology to the level of consciousness, seeking to transform our deepest sense of the self, the other, the environment [p. 49].

He defines the counterculture as

> a culture so radically disaffiliated from the mainstream assumptions of our society that it scarcely looks to many as a culture at all, but takes on the alarming appearance of a barbaric intrusion [p. 42].

This author says of the counterculture:

> It is something in the nature of a medieval crusade: a variegated procession constantly in flux, acquiring and losing members all along the route of march. Often enough it finds its own identity in a nebulous symbol or song that seems to proclaim little more than "We are special . . . we are different . . . we are outward-bound from the old corruptions of the world" [pp. 48–49].

This movement is seen as a consequence of technology, which is the apogee of the organizational integration of industrialized society.

The particular essentials of the counterculture are a lack of politics or antipolitics (e.g., the Woodstock Festival in the United States) and an orientation toward the present which has been termed "the cult of immediacy." Opposing our industrialized societies as oriented toward the future, the counterculture aspires to live intensely the experience of the present (Myerhoff, 1969), and its adherents, "the now generation," have as a slogan "Quality resides in the present."

Another theme connected with the counterculture is a concern with nature and the environment. Numerous sects arise, combining ecology and mysticism: they eat macrobiotic foods, they practice Zen, etc. If industrial society considers nature as a resource to be exploited or an obstacle to be mastered, the counterculture is concerned with man's place in nature and the problems of pollution created by rapid progress. Success is envisaged not in material terms, but as personal development. All the traditional values tied to the work ethic, such as competition, success, money, and social status, are rejected in favor of honesty between individuals, mutual aid, and unrestricted personal relations and physical sensations. The counterculture represents in a way a profoundly hedonist culture opposed to middle-class values. The introduction of play and sensuality to enhance daily life is echoed in certain writings of Marcuse (1955, 1964, 1969). The counterculture in fact has borrowed numerous themes from Marcuse. Even if he did not always have the importance which the new countercultural movement confers on him, he is nonetheless, with the Frankfurt school, one of the precursors of the rupture with orthodox Marxist theory after Lenin and of the return to the critical tradition of Marxism.

What the students have retained above all from this philosopher, who presents an original analysis of social reality combining Marxist and Freudian concepts, is that he denounces the repressive character of advanced capitalist society. He emphasizes the oppression that is no longer open and violent but diffused through the interiorized culture and reproduced by the very people who suffer from it. The lack of possessions and wealth has in the past produced a repressive civilization, but today this lack no longer exists. We must go back to intrinsic human qualities not yet perverted by the external environment, to which man has had to adapt. An instinctual freedom of primitive impulse and the dissolution of social and familial institutions would give birth to a new man, incarnating the most fundamental values of humanism—laws, liberty, justice, reason, and truth.

Marcuse, like the countercultural movement that wants to change man, believes that the individual is something which remains to be created and that instinctual and intellectual liberation is actually a political issue. The means for such creation and liberation envisioned by Marcuse are simple ones: to realize, taking into account established behaviors, another kind of practice—that is, to make manifest in the eyes of the majority the possibility of a different form of existence and the rejection of the established network.

If the parallel movement of continental European counterculture does not have the same importance as in the Anglo-Saxon countries, especially in the United States, we find nevertheless a whole anarchist current converging on the same objectives as the counterculture. We have seen the appearance of many groups more or less organized and often ephemeral, whose ideology, although tinged with Marxism, is very informal and is based on the utopian socialist tradition. For example, we can cite the "situationists" in France, "Kommune I" in Germany, the "provos" in the Netherlands, and the antiauthoritarian and "student power" movements in Italy and in Austria. These movements, which we may call utopian in their rejection of the model both of existing socialist societies and of capitalistic societies, seek new forms of social organization. The original contributions of all these movements are their focus on the freedom of the individual and their refusal of all centralized authority and organization.

Fischer (1970), an Austrian communist philosopher, emphasizes the aspirations of young people toward freedom: if the new left insists on the term "cultural revolution," this means precisely that the revolution will presumably not only bring a modification of the benefits of production, of the division of power, and of social structures, but will overturn our whole way of life, will facilitate self-determination for everyone, and will eliminate every form of the domination of man by man (p. 9). Similarly Vaneigem, a French "situationist" writer, suggests in his treatise *Traité du savoir vivre à l'usage des jeunes générations* (1967) that the purpose of the proletariat is no longer to acquire power, but to put an end to it once and for all [p. 226]. Well before May 1968 Vaneigem had begun to elaborate the "critique de la vie quotidienne," taking up the title of a famous work of Lefebvre (1945). The "situationist" international group's most influential work, *De la misère en milieu étudiant* of 1967, had already formulated precisely the theory of alienation, saying it was partially a result of the "fetishization of merchandise." "Changer la vie" (Let us change our lives) was the slogan of this movement.

If social conditions must be changed, the first prerequisite is a mental revolution accompanied by a drastic change in behavior patterns. Vaneigem speaks of a radical restructuring of our ways of life and thought. According to Gombin (1972), the "situationist" vision of the revolutionary process that will produce the complete man is to extend the limits of the old class struggle. This perspective—foreign to Marxism—

finds its sources in the surrealists and the nineteenth-century poets termed "maudits" (for example, Baudelaire). According to the "situationists," individual liberty will result in collective liberty. They are opposed to orthodox Marxism, since it would bring about a generalized uniformity of life. It is to this movement that we owe the most successful slogans of May 1968 in France.

To the degree to which changing the world implies first changing a way of life, some young people have started by changing their own lives. And, as in the United States today, it may be that we shall see various communes flourish in capitalistic European countries. This dream of communes is part of living anarchist tradition, in which man is purified by contact with the natural environment. According to Lande (1972), these young people reject the sheeplike crowd and the "trilogy" denounced in May 1968—"subway, job, bed"—desiring to realize an elective microsociety within which it may be possible to express deep desires censured by the society. This movement is convinced that only the transformation of the individual can change the world.

These various anarchist currents, like the Anglo-Saxon hippy movement and counterculture, have in common an acute consciousness of oppression by the state and of the loss of individual freedom. Contrary to Marxism, which emphasizes the interdependence of the individual and society, the new left is inspired rather by existentialism, which makes of the individual an end in himself, claiming for each person the right to develop his uniqueness and to affirm himself. But this strictly existentialist revolt has been replaced by a broader revolution of a cultural type, uniting the individual and the social.

The countercultural movement has been important and influential in the evolution of behavior patterns. However, in many cases the hippies, "flower children," or "new humanists," as Myerhoff (1969) has called them, cannot be typed as true protesters. Many observers, in fact, have indicated that a large number of young and not so young people follow this movement more because of fashion, snobbism, or self-interest than from a sincere revolutionary conviction. Certain themes, especially those derived from folklore, of the counterculture have been adopted and reintegrated into the social system (e.g., the development of songs, films, magazines, etc., of the underground).

The typically Anglo-Saxon character of the counter-culture and of the alternative it offers to traditional values should also be noted. In fact, if at all times and in all countries there have been marginal people whose life style and ideas have been clearly in opposition to the dominant status quo, it is only in the United States and, to a lesser degree, in Great Britain that the phenomenon has attained such scope and has had a truly profound influence on youth. In other Western countries the counterculture remains a very minor movement, subject to virulent criticism from traditional leftists, especially in France and Italy. For Touraine (1972) the slowness of the penetration into France, Japan, and Germany of the parallel culture, compared with its rapid diffusion in Great Britain and the United States, may be explained by the fact that the "French, Japanese, and German students are still more tied to their university discipline and their families than are students in the United States. The former students are less 'culturally mobile' and more dependent" (p. 203).

The protesting students do not form a unidimensional group. Keniston's distinction (1965, 1967) between the political activists and those who are passive but culturally alienated takes into account a certain reality. This distinction between the activists and the nonactivists tends, however, to neglect the possible existence of a new form of militancy. In fact it was precisely among the "alienated" students that the counter-culture came into being as a new system of values and normative structure in opposition to those of industrial societies.

It might thus be argued that the group described by Keniston as apathetic really constituted the true innovators. The "activists," interested only in politics and differing little in norms from their families, are conformists fighting in the grand tradition, populist or Marxist, to improve the standard of living and to reduce injustice. These impulses are nothing new and would not explain in themselves the breadth of the phenomenon of protest. Leary (1973) and other experimenters have expressed rather similar ideas. According to them, the activists are simply individuals who, concerned with politics, adhere to the system, while the "acid-heads"[5] and hippies try to break completely with the system.

This countercultural movement, which goes against many of the basic values of our society, provokes strong opposition, as much from the "modernists" who put all their hope in technical progress and directly or indirectly favor technocracy as from those who extol socialized collectivism, refusing individual experiences which lead to a disordered anarchism and sap revolutionary strength. In the first group, Bell (1968) considers this "humanist" and "romantic" current not truly revolutionary, but rather *counterrevolutionary*, and feels that the tactics employed "are never the mark of a coherent social movement, but the last gasp of a romanticism soured by rancor and impotence" (p. 100). For him, certain students still attached to outmoded or old-fashioned values are unadapted to the new age dominated by technology, where the true leaders are the computer specialists, the analysts, and the technobureaucrats. These students subconsciously feel that they have no place in a postindustrial world. It might, however, be asked whether technocracy, as Bell seems to think, represents an ideal for all qualified people. The second group thinks that the counterculture represents only the decadence and philistinism of a bourgeois and capitalist world.

The Marxist Protest

Although we hear a good deal about countercultural protest, drugs, and communes, they still constitute a localized phenomenon found especially in Anglo- Saxon countries (although the use of drugs is increasing elsewhere as well). In fact, in certain European countries in particular, where there is a strong Marxist tradition, the student struggle is not very innovative and continues to make use of language and practice borrowed from Marxism.

Lipset and Schaflander (1971) emphasize the difference between the protest movements in Latin and Anglo-Saxon countries. In the former, the revolutionary groups are extremely politicized, whereas among the Anglo-Saxons there is a mixture of hippy philosophy and a type of Marxism which is often superficial.

In Latin countries, as Gombin also notes (1972), the protest reveals a strong influence of political currents from the beginning of the century, which are influential not only in their methods of revolution but also in the model of the society they propose to construct. Thus in Europe, especially in France, Italy, and Germany, the stu-

---

[5]"Acid-head" describes a person who takes LSD. We must note that Leary was the guru of LSD and organized experimental groups in universities. He was one of the founders in 1963 of the International Federation for Internal Freedom, which proposed to encourage research and experimentation with psychedelic drugs.

dents of the extreme left, heirs of a legally institutionalized left, continue to see themselves as the champions of the poor workers against bourgeois oppression. In the United States, on the other hand, where the left has always been weak, this lack of "approved" rhetoric becomes a positive advantage, for there are no ideological conceptions derived from the past. This permits great flexibility and more experimental research of means and goals, thus completely renewing the content of revolutionary perspectives.

Protest which borrows its themes from Marxism-Leninism poses the problem of the university's appropriation of knowledge and orientation. In this perspective, the students wish to participate not only in the teaching but also in the management of the university. Certain experiments along these lines have been pushed rather far in many universities.

For many revolutionary students, the university represents the instrument of power which from the exterior seems to function as a machine to produce knowledge but as seen from within causes political and social oppression and seeks the introduction of young people into existing society (Schnapp and Vidal-Naquet, 1969). Certain revolutionary students want to go further and make of the university a point of departure for transformation of the system (cf. *Libro bianco*, 1968), changing the university radically to put it under the control and at the service of the people. These students are trying to apply Lenin's plan, according to which the essential task consists in imposing the people's truth as a counterweight to middle-class truth. Class, in general, is seen as bringing up the young generation according to its own conception of the world and its own political convictions in order to train its successors and consolidate its domination.

For many protesting students Soviet communism has become a "reactionary" movement, and a large proportion of militant revolutionaries belong to movements described as Trotskyist or Maoist. These two currents have in common an opposition to the strict obedience of Soviet communism but differ in their revolutionary analysis. The Trotskyites think that the socialist revolution cannot develop in a single country and call for a permanent international revolution. They preach the necessity of a spontaneous democratic organization against bureaucracy. On the other hand, the Maoists, inspired by the activist and anti-bureaucratic philosophy of the Chinese cultural revolution, reproach the Soviet-type communists for their emphasis on obedience and the Trotskyites for their spirit of reform and nonviolence. In addition to the economic and social revolution, the Maoists add the cultural dimension. It must, however, be noted that they reject violently the ideas of the philosopher Marcuse. The revolutionary avant-garde is not at all the student movement (considered to be lower middle class), but rather the proletariat, which remains the oppressed class.

We find, as in the Trotskyist movement, various orientations in the Maoist movement borrowing ideas from "Fidelism" or "Guevarism" and adding more arguments to the already numerous internal quarrels between these different movements. According to Duprat (1968), there are eighteen pro-Chinese parties in Great Britain. To these numerous revolutionary movements, born more or less directly from Maoism and Trotskyism, may be added a group of other subsidiary movements, appearing and disappearing as a function of events. It is certain that this pluralism does more harm than good to the student struggle, in part because these sectarian movements are often very isolated and have little relation with one another, and in part because their ephemeral character does not permit the elaboration of a truly efficacious revolutionary theory and so leads to "adventurist" actions easily controlled by the system.

The large majority of people hardly recognize the differences (either doctrinal or tactical) between these various groups, and most of them are unaware of the existence of these fragmentary parties, except when a sudden outburst brings them to public attention. The press and all those who are against the student agitation tend to group together all these opposing movements of young people more or less politicized and supporting very different ethics under the rubric "radicals." Some even assimilate into this rubric—always for convenience—all imaginable forms of deviance. This simplistic distortion contributes greatly to giving the public a very negative image of protest movements.

This survey of the relevant literature is far from complete, nor does it do justice to the complexity of the issues raised and of the arguments presented. We hope, however, that it does give some idea of the wide range of theoretical and empirical attempts at an understanding of the student movement of a few years ago. At a number of points we feel that our results are relevant to a critical appraisal of the suggested explanations, and we turn now to an account of our own investigation.

Chapter 2

The Study: Background and Methodology

The practically simultaneous appearance in many countries of student movements, the explanations and writings which they evoked and which were often applied to protest as a whole and not only to what was specific to one country, and in particular the sparsity of comparative studies on this theme all led us in 1969 to undertake an international investigation of student attitudes. Our goal was not only to study and to compare student protesters but also to include students of different political tendencies from various parts of the world.

The problems which young people were raising were varied and complex. As we have indicated above, a wide range of publications identified many different facets of the phenomenon. One general formulation was made by Ronko Petkovic concerning the desires of angry students (as cited by J. L. Brau, 1968):

> Without regard to the various motives tied either to university conditions or to the general political situation, student movements have a common denominator, as far as their causes and fundamental aspirations go: they express a refusal of conservative social and political structures, whether one speaks of capitalism or socialism, of parliamentary democracy or of dictatorship. It is not a question of identifying with the systems (or not understanding the differences of these systems) but rather, in each case, to some degree and under well defined aspects, it is a question of the necessity to realize certain changes and to drag certain situations out of their conservatism [p. 274].

We asked ourselves these questions: Who does question society? Are society's critics localized in one political segment, like the extreme left, or are they present in all student groups? What is questioned most in each country? The sociopolitical situation? The university? The culture? Do the diverse student movements, in the majority of cases sympathizing or affiliated with the extreme left, represent an avant-garde of attitudes typical of youth in general, or are they restricted to a "band of thugs so removed from normal life that they seem to wage another battle," as the president of the National Student Union in Great Britain, Trevor Fisk, (1970) believes (p. 78)?

Are the demands and tactics of protesters drastic in comparison with those of their elders, or is this only a renewed version of traditional social differences and of political idealism characteristic of young people? Is there a truly international youth culture, or is this a myth, a facile generalization? Are there shared points of view, and if so, what are they? Would we find similar attitudes in the "same" political

17

group ("left," "right," "center") in all these countries, or is it necessary, for example, to differentiate the students on the right in Spain, France, and the United States?

It is clear that no one instrument, relatively simple and short enough to be practicable, could possibly permit us to answer all these questions. We did attempt to approach those political themes which seemed to be of primary importance, with full awareness of the limitations and constraints we had to impose upon ourselves.

The Questionnaire

The final questionnaire was established after a series of pilot studies had been conducted simultaneously in different countries and after several meetings in Paris and London of the researchers from the participating countries. On the basis of the results of these pilot studies, questions were modified whenever doubt arose as to their clarity or their applicability in the various countries, or when there was difficulty in finding equivalences in different languages. These issues were discussed fully at a final meeting attended by an international group of social scientists, and the decisions reached represented the general consensus.

The questionnaire first includes classical questions concerning professional and familial aspirations, sources of satisfaction in life, etc., borrowed in particular from Gillespie and Allport (1955), in order to make longitudinal comparisons possible, but the questionnaire also contains a whole series of "declarations" taken from the writings of protesting authors like Hayden, Cohn-Bendit and others, from different "gurus" of the counterculture, from theses expounded by Marcuse and other theoreticians of the new role of students, plus the opinions of those who opposed the student movement.

A second series of specific questions seeks to determine to what degree students agree with the ideology proposed by the various movements involving political and cultural revolt. The questionnaire also includes a number of scales for indicating a range of opinions, thus allowing more precise comparisons among groups and among countries. There are also some open-ended questions, offering the students the opportunity to explain in a free and unrestricted fashion their opinions of society in general, of the university system, of prevailing cultural norms, and of protest movements. Various questions also deal with the sociopolitical environment of the university and the cultural environment of the students.

The following major themes were analyzed

ORIENTATION AND POLITICAL OPINIONS

One part of the questionnaire dealt with the problem of the relevance of political definitions as understood by the students themselves. The comparisons between countries were of help throughout this study in determining the meaning of each political concept (e.g., degree of radicalism). We also attempted to determine the relationship of various social and university variables to the political orientation of students, as well as the various influences recognized by students as having played a part in their own political development.

PROFESSIONAL ASPIRATIONS AND UNIVERSITY CHOICES

Other questions treat more particularly the professional and familial future of the students, their fears, hopes, and aspirations: what they expect from a university education and how they envision the functioning of the university within the framework of their society.

SOCIOCULTURAL OPTIONS

Here we approach more general problems, such as students' opinions on war, nationalism, internationalism, discrimination, and immigration. Some questions deal with what the students think of several of society's principal concerns and institutions (morality, religion, democracy, censorship, and family) and the very specific choices they make concerning the relationships between men and women, birth control, and drugs. Finally, other questions present the problem of the reality of the conflict of generations at the social level and, more personally, that of the relationship between the student and his parents. This last point is examined by looking at the affective, moral, and political proximity to the parents and at the differences and the similarities between them.

PROTEST

A whole series of questions allows us to define the attitudes of students in regard to the protest movement, both at the level of its causes (in terms of values) and at the level of its goals, its means of action, and its probable future.

THE IDEAL SOCIETY

Since the domain of utopia appeared important, the questionnaire asked for a definition of the ideal society in which the students wished to live and how it could be created.

The Investigation

The research was conducted during the year 1969–70 with students who had completed at least one year at the university so that they already had a certain knowledge and understanding of the university system. As already noted, the study included five countries in Western Europe (France, Italy, Spain, Austria and Great Britain), one American country (the United States), one in Oceania (Australia), one in Asia (Japan), one socialist European country (Yugoslavia), and two African countries (Tunisia and Nigeria).[1]

[1]The research was also undertaken in three other countries—Colombia, Canada (both French- and English-speaking), and West Germany. In these countries it was impossible, however, to attempt data-

The size of the samples in the various countries differs, depending mainly on the facility or difficulty encountered in collecting the data.

COUNTRY	NUMBER OF STUDENTS
Australia	966
Austria	504
France	856
Great Britain	625
Italy	1,000
Japan	519
Nigeria	395
Spain	895
Tunisia	191
United States	693
Yugoslavia	1,100

The sampling is diversified and includes just about every discipline and whenever possible various types of university.[2]

Profile

AGE

The majority of students are between 19 and 22 years old. There are few under 18. In Nigeria the students are somewhat older; 61 percent are 25 or older and 90 percent are 21 or older. Austria and Tunisia follow, with 63 percent of the students older than 21. In contrast, 23 percent of the students from the United States are 18 or younger, and 87 percent are below 22 years old. Japan and Great Britain, with 82 percent under 22, are also in the group of countries where the student population is young. Australian and Spanish students are also relatively young: 63 percent and 60 percent, respectively, are less than 22 years old. In Italy, France, and Yugoslavia the age of the students is similar, with relatively few under 19 years old.

SEX

In Austria, Italy, Tunisia, Great Britain, France, and Yugoslavia the proportion of men and women is relatively equal. Men are in the majority in Spain, the United States, and Australia. Our samples include very few women in Japan (5 percent) and in Nigeria (10 percent).

---

based analyses because of small sample sizes (Colombia, 84 students, English-speaking Canada, 88; French speaking Canada, 111). In the case of West Germany the data were sent to and analyzed in the United States by Professors K. and G. E. Lang (State University of New York at Stony Brook), but the analysis did not include all the questions. The results obtained in these countries are cited as the situation permits.

[2]In Australia the work was done at the University of New South Wales (Kensington) and the University of Sydney; in Austria at the University of Vienna; in Spain at the universities of Madrid, Barcelona, Santiago de Compostela, Seville, Valencia, and Salamanca; in the United States at private colleges and universities (Radcliffe, Northwestern, Vassar, Cornell, Dartmouth, Princeton, Harvard, Columbia, Wesleyan, Boston, Moorhead, and Haverford) and at state and municipal universities (University of California at Los Angeles, City University of New York, Rutgers, University of Pittsburgh, University of Illinois); the British component included universities situated in Wales (University College of South Wales, Cardiff), in Scotland (Glasgow, University of Strathclyde), and in England (Durham, Universi-

RELIGION

A majority of students in Spain, Italy, Austria, and France are Catholic; a majority are Protestant in Australia, Nigeria, and Great Britain; a majority are Muslim in Tunisia.[3]

EDUCATIONAL BACKGROUND OF PARENTS

In the United States both fathers and mothers of the students reached a level of education higher than in the other countries studied: 54 percent of the mothers and 67 percent of the fathers had finished college. In Japan (51 percent), in Spain (45 percent), and in Yugoslavia and in France (41 percent), about half of the students came from families in which only the father was a university graduate. One mother out of four, at the most, had pursued university level courses. Students with one parent who had studied at the university in Tunisia and Nigeria were quite rare; there was a high proportion of parents who had received only a rudimentary education. In Nigeria 38 percent of the mothers and 23 percent of the fathers had no formal instruction in the Occidental sense. The percentages for Tunisia are 25 percent for the mothers and 9 percent for the fathers.

DISCIPLINE CHOSEN

The majority of students included in most countries were studying social sciences, literature or the sciences rather than medicine, law, business, or engineering. The students in Japan, Yugoslavia, and Spain are the exceptions. In fact, in Japan 36 percent of the students were studying law and 36 percent engineering or business. In Yugoslavia we find 28 percent of the students in law and 27 percent in technology and architecture. In Spain 21 percent were studying law and 29 percent business or engineering.

Few of our students were studying medicine; the highest number is found in Austria (17 percent). Students in Nigeria and in Italy frequently took courses in the humanities (40 percent and 31 percent respectively). Students in the social sciences were found mainly in the United States and in Great Britain (34 percent each).

TYPE OF LODGING

We can divide the students into three groups: those who live with their families, those who are in university housing, and those who have independent lodging.

---

ty of Manchester) and in London itself (University College of London, Kings College of London); in France the universities were in Paris (Nanterre, Halle aux Vins, Vincennes, Sorbonne, Faculté de Médecine, Paris V, Dauphine, Faculté d'Orsay, Beaux-Arts) and in the provinces (Montpellier, Tours, Toulouse, Lille, Nice, Strasbourg, Bésançon, Rouen); other universities were in northern Italy (Milan, Turin, Parma, Siena, Florence) and in central or southern Italy (Rome, Bari, Palermo, Salerno); in Japan, one state university (Todai, which is also known as the University of Tokyo) and one private university (Waseda); in Nigeria, the University of Ibadan; in Tunisia, at Tunis; and in Yugoslavia, at Ljubljana in Slovenia.

[3]We have no information on the religion of students in Japan, in Yugoslavia, and in the United States.

Spanish (73 percent), Australian (66 percent), Italian (59 percent), and Japanese (52 percent) students live with their families. Nigerians and Americans (82 percent and 59 percent respectively) live mostly in university housing. British students (59 percent) live for the most part in private rooms or hotels off campus.

STUDENT WORKERS

Only a minority of students work full-time in addition to their studies (less than 10 percent in each country) or part-time (about 25 percent), except in Japan, where 62 percent of the students have a job. In the two African countries almost all students devote themselves to their studies; only 9 percent work part-time.

Methodology

PROBLEMS OF CROSSCULTURAL COMPARISONS

We have witnessed in the last few years a steady growth in international, comparative research studies on differences in orientations and in values in various societies. This type of work necessitated a tuning up of methodological techniques, demonstrating in particular the pitfalls to be avoided. A careful analysis of the problems involved has been made by Rokkan et al. (1969).

One of the positive aspects of intercultural studies is that they enlarge the field of observation. The information obtained makes it possible to establish more precisely the factors and the conditions which determine the appearance of any given phenomenon and contributes to the analysis of subjective cultural variables in various contexts (Triandis et al., 1973). However, the difficulty of inferring similarities and/or differences among societies on the basis of the results obtained becomes more and more clear as a consequence.

In their crosscultural research on values, Gillespie and Allport (1955) insist on three fundamental requirements in conducting this type of study: (1) utilizing an instrument which is uniform and comparable and which, even when translated, retains the same meaning for all groups of subjects; (2) having comparable samplings with regard to age, sex, and status; and (3) having competent and informed researchers who have a background in the social sciences, are objective in their points of view, and are careful to follow standardized instructions. We now consider the first two of these rules in the light of recent discussions of intercultural methodology.

THE COMPARABILITY OF MEANINGS

Many authors, and notably Frijda and Jahoda (1966), have underlined the difficulty in securing an instrument for crosscultural research whose significance is not deformed by translation. How can we be sure that the contents of the questionnaire which is given to students from various cultures will have the same meaning?

In more technical terms this is the problem of the equivalence of indicators. The plausibility of inferences derived from crosscultural data would require an ideal situation in which we control all factors that could alter their comparability and equivalence. Such a situation is rarely possible since we do not know in advance what are the particular features of the context and of the situation that may affect the results. These features, however, may be discovered *a posteriori* by a careful analysis of observed differences, sorting out what may account for these differences.

The problem, which involves an understanding of the range of individual responses as well as their social and cultural context, is difficult to resolve. At this stage our most realistic knowledge suggests that we should attempt to determine the nature of these cultural differences when the study is in the phase of analysis rather than at the beginning of the investigation (Zavalloni, 1969). We could thus consider both the situational determinants and the attitudinal responses as possible hypotheses (interdependent or competitive). This implies that when we discuss the results, we must always be aware that two possible explanations exist, one giving more weight to the situation, the other to individual factors, without neglecting their possible reciprocal influence.

Studies which systematically examine the relationships between the social context and individual responses are rare. We may perhaps deduce from this that the empirical mastery of what might be considered as one of the fundamental theoretical problems of the social sciences is not yet possible.[4]

In part, it is precisely because we do not know how to resolve this difficulty that we must look at this type of research as mainly exploratory. Ideally, research projects would have as their central theme "preliminary" or "ambiguous" results gathered from different studies, our own included. Their goal would be not to gather a new mass of data to be studied, but to present the results as a "problem." Rokkan (Rokkan et al., 1969) takes a position quite similar to our own. According to him, the argument widely held in favor of representative studies is that it is necessary to establish the structural elements before attempting precise investigations of strategic sectors of the population. The fact that we already possess a mass of information should permit us to develop archives of data for secondary analyses. The more we know about the results of studies already completed, he believes, the easier it will be to plan new research projects and to decide in particular which strategic groups would necessitate further study.

We do not think, however, that secondary analysis will provide a definitive response to our questions, since such an analysis would depend for its principal parameters on the results of the study. Such results should be utilized not as conclusions, but as productive of hypotheses. We need to study more fully strategic subsamples of the population with instruments and approaches which are yet to be defined, but which should make clearer the relationships between structural variables and individual responses.

Confronted with the problem of comparability in the meaning of the questions presented in this study, we adopted a practical position, which is also traditional, by using the following strategy. Several of the researchers responsible for the national research projects had a first meeting to discuss the attitudinal dimensions which we hoped to include in the questionnaire. A second meeting centered on a discussion of the results of the pilot studies, with the goal of comparing the different formulations of the questions.[5] The questionnaire in most cases was never literally translated from

[4]For more detailed analysis of the difficulties which exist in determining individual values versus the situational context in comparative studies, see Keller and Zavalloni (1964) and Zavalloni (1969).

[5]In some cases the researchers were not able to undertake responsibility for all the phases of the study. Once the preliminary stages were completed by them (formulation of the questionnaire, etc.), they

one language to another. The French, American, Italian, British, and Slovenian participants worked together to establish an instrument which could be used in all these countries, and in others in which one of these languages could be used. There were two exceptions: the Spanish and Japanese questionnaires were prepared entirely under the direction of Professor Marcos de la Fuente (Spain) and Professor Donald Wheeler (Japan).

THE COMPARABILITY OF THE SAMPLES

The second condition required in crosscultural research involves the comparability of the samples. As noted above, Gillespie and Allport (1955) enumerate three criteria for this: sex, age, and status. This present study, including (with few exceptions) only students between 18 and 25 years of age, controlled by sex, responds well to these criteria of comparability.

For longitudinal comparisons, the fact that the population studied by these two authors is similar to ours (university students) and that some of the questions which we ask are borrowed from their questionnaire allows us to proceed to a comparison in time, but requires also that we first examine carefully these criteria of comparability. Our results show that the political orientation of the student plays a role which is extremely important in attitudinal domains like the style of family life which one prefers, professional options, and other areas not directly related to political orientation. The different disciplines in which students specialize also intervene, as we shall see, in important ways. Thus, in several of the countries studied, the students in law or in medicine tend to have conservative political and cultural opinions, in contrast with students in the social sciences. At this point sex, age, and status, the three criteria of Gillespie and Allport, appear insufficient to establish intercultural differences. The results indicated that the responses obtained were linked to the political orientation of the students. We would suggest that the list of criteria Gillespie and Allport propose is not exhaustive enough and does not fully permit us to compare national groups, even in a universe as relatively homogeneous as that of university students.

THE 1977 SURVEY

In order to determine the persistence and change in values, a survey was conducted on a minor scale in France and the United States in 1977.[6] In each country approximately 100 students were tested. The criterion followed in the selection of the sample was to maintain the same proportion of the disciplines obtained in 1970 and the same variety in the universities represented.

---

were occasionally replaced by other researchers from the same country who conducted the actual study.

[6] In France the questionnaire was applied at the universities of Montpellier, Reims, Nancy, Lille, Rouen and in Paris (Creteil, Sorbonne, Nanterre, Vincennes, and Ecole Polytechnique), and in the United States at the universities of Pittsburgh and Vermont and Rice, Columbia, and Princeton.

Chapter 3

Political Orientation

This research was undertaken in 1969–70, that is, shortly after the most striking manifestations of student revolt. The contemporary nature of this problem naturally led us to accord a special (although not exclusive) place to protest and to politics. The primary question was to discover how political attitudes become an integral part of the general system of attitudes. In other words, does the fact of having adopted a particular political orientation correspond to a pattern of attitudes, whether in relation to the university, career, cultural values, or politics in general?

Political Self-Definition

The political orientation of the students was determined by the following open question:[1] "How would you describe your own political position?" In their responses the students indicated either a precise political party—for example, Republican in the United States, Labor in Great Britain, UDR (Democratic Union of the Republic) in France; or a more general political label such as "middle of the road," "left"; or, finally, the responses might express an ideology or attitudes without precise political identification, such as "I am against the capitalist system" or "The present disorder comes from the weakness of a too liberal government."

These latter responses—often difficult to code—have been classified as carefully as possible by several researchers who know the situation in each country. Each researcher coded these responses individually, independently of the others. When ambiguities remained as to the meaning of the underlying political orientation, the response was eliminated as unclassifiable.

An international code differentiating as much as possible the various ideological orientations of the student responses was employed by each of the researchers in the different countries (except Yugoslavia) to classify the responses according to a continuum from the far right to the far left.

Although the classification of right-left political tendencies can be made in all of the countries except Yugoslavia, the results naturally remain specific to each country. To be a Republican in the United States, for example, does not have the same connotation as being on the right in France or in Nigeria. In each country, however,

[1]In two countries, Austria and Yugoslavia, political orientation was determined by a forced-choice question.

the fact of being a Republican or on the right implies attitudes more conservative on the whole than to classify oneself as belonging to the left, etc. In each country there exist political forces more or less conservative which can be distinguished from the more liberal or revolutionary movements. The present study attempted to determine in what way tendencies defined as conservative in one nation would be similar to those defined as conservative in other countries.

In order to render the political spectrum of the different samples easier to compare, the categories identified in the international code were combined as follows:

Political spectrum of the different countries (new scale)

Australia
Austria
Great Britain } right—center—left—far left—apolitical
Spain
Tunisia

United States: Republican-right—Democrat-center—Liberal—left—far left—apolitical

France: right—center—left—communist—far left—anarchist—apolitical

Italy: far right—right—center—left—communist—far left—apolitical

Japan: center—left—far left—apolitical

Nigeria: right—progovernment—left—criticizes the system—far left—apolitical—describes the system

In all the countries studied the *far right* (1)[2] was regrouped with the *right* (2), except that in Italy the recent revival of neofascism led us to keep these two categories separate.

The category *liberal* (3) was regrouped with the *center* (4). Only in the United States were these two categories kept separate, since large segments of the student population in this country identified themselves as liberal.

In Japan the category *center* includes the liberals, those who identified themselves with the Liberal Democratic party, and the few cases (about 1 percent) who identified themselves with the right.

The category *left* (5) was unchanged. However, in Japan it includes a particular group of students who declared themselves to be against the capitalist system and inequality (10 percent).

In France and in Italy, *communist* (6) students (respectively 7 percent and 13 percent) were kept as a separate category, as the French Communist party and the Italian Communist party represent in these two countries an important political force sharply distinguished from what may be called the extreme left (Marxist-Leninist, Trotskyist, Maoist, etc.). Also, in France the *anarchists* (8) constitute a separate category. This group played an imporant role in the events of May 1968. In the other countries this category was practically absent (less than 3 percent).

The communist (6) and anarchist (8) categories were regrouped with the *far left* (7) in all the other countries studied except Yugoslavia.

The categories *opportunist* (10), *religious* (11) and *don't know* (12) were regrouped with the category *apolitical* (9). And the category *others* (14), including unclassifiable answers, was regrouped with the category *no answer* (15).

The category labeled *against present system* (13) had obviously a different meaning in each of the countries studied. Whenever additional information was available,

---

[2]See Table 3.1: The numbers in parentheses correspond to the international code's numbers.

TABLE 3.1.

	INTERNATIONAL CODE*	NEW SCALE
1. Far right	Neo-Nazi, neofascist, any specific movement of the far right	Right
2. Right	Conservative, right; progovernment in Spain, Republican in the US, Conservative party, etc.	
3. Liberal	Liberal	Center
4. Center	Middle of the road, in between; Democrat in the US, Christian Democrat in Italy and Austria, Liberal Democratic party in Japan, Democratic Union of the Republic in France, Bourguibist in Tunisia, etc.	
5. Left	Moderate left, noncommunist left; socialist, labor party, Social Democrat, etc.	Left
6. Communist	Communist party	Far left
7. Far left	Radical, revolutionary; Trotskyist, Maoist, etc.	
8. Anarchist	Against any form of government; situationist, "socialisme et barbarie," socialist libertarianism, etc.	
9. Apolitical	Refuses politics, dislikes politics, etc.	Apolitical
10. Opportunist	Individualist, independent, "for any government which gives me good opportunities," etc.	
11. Religious	Christian, believer in God, member of religious sect, etc.	
12. Don't know	"Don't know where I am," "still looking," etc.	
13. Against present system	(Without any other specifications)	No answer
14. Others	Unclassifiable	
15. No answer		

*In Austria the same alternatives (1, 2, 3, 4, 5, 6, 7, 8, 9, 12) were provided but as forced choices.

answers in this category were assigned to relevant alternatives. Otherwise they were assigned to the category *others* (14) or classified as *no answer* (15) in the new scale.

In Nigeria the political scale was slightly modified to stay as close as possible to the type of answers found in this country. Many students (40 percent) did not answer this question concerning their political tendency at all or gave answers that were difficult to classify as a political tendency. Indeed, some students described the present situation of their country but not their own political attitudes:

It's a military government.
All factors have created discontent in Nigerian universities.
University students should be more involved in governmental actions and matters concerning them.

These responses are somewhat beyond the expected range of the question and pose a problem of interpretation. It is obvious that some students felt that the political situation of the country was asked for in the question. This could mean that these students were not politically involved, at least not in the Western sense, or that they had not had time to obtain perspective with regard to recent events and changes in their government which the students were still experiencing; it is of course possible that some considered this question too sensitive. As a consequence, in addition to

right, left, far left, and apolitical identifications, we established three further particular categories: *Describes the system* includes those answers which described the situation of the country. *Progovernment* includes those answers which reflected a positive evaluation of the government: "I think we have a good government," " I am in
favor of our system," etc. *Criticizes the system*, on the contrary, includes those
answers reflecting a negative evaluation of the government or of the present system:
"not satisfactory," "oppressive system," etc.

The number of *no answers*[3] concerning the question varies from one country to
another. The smallest proportions were found in the United States (4 percent) and in
Great Britain (7 percent). The proportion was comparatively higher in Spain (17
percent), Japan (15 percent), France (13 percent), Italy (12 percent), and Australia
(11 percent). The most *no answers* occurred in Nigeria and Tunisia. In effect, 24 percent of the Tunisian students and, as already noted, 40 percent of the Nigerians did
not give their political opinion or gave unclassifiable answers. Lipset (1966) indicates
that in developing countries one finds a large number of students who are not greatly interested in politics in a Western sense, their major concern being with the modernization of the country.

DISTRIBUTION OF THE STUDENTS BY POLITICAL TENDENCIES

In all the countries studied the majority of the students can be found in the noncommunist left or the center.[4]

The group of apoliticals is also relatively popular in almost all the countries
studied, the right and the far left constituting a minority everywhere (Figure 3.1).[5]

In *Australia* the most popular tendencies are the center (36 percent) and the left
(31 percent), followed by the apolitical (23 percent). Only 5 percent of the students
identified themselves either as right or far left.

In *Austria* also the center (32 percent) and the left (28 percent) are the most popular tendencies, followed by the right (17 percent) and the far left (15 percent), 8 percent of the students being apolitical.

French students are comparatively the most left-oriented of the samples studied.
The moderate left (socialist) represents 28 percent of the respondents, the various
groups of the far left 24 percent (communist, 7 percent; far left, 13 percent; anarchists, 4 percent). In France 23 percent of the respondents identified themselves as
apolitical and 19 percent as centrist; the right is represented by only 6 percent of the
respondents.

In *Great Britain* also the moderate left (33 percent) is the most popular tendency,
followed by the apolitical (24 percent), the right (15 percent), the center (15 percent)
and the far left (12 percent).

In *Italy* the political distribution is similar to the French pattern. The left (27 percent) and the far left (23 percent)—if we combine the communists (13 percent) and

[3]Factor analysis of the *no answers* in each country on political questions indicates that this category
regroups many heterogeneous opinions which are, on the whole, rather moderate. These nonrespond-
ing students do not represent a specific subgroup, since for different reasons (politics, censorship, etc.)
they may have voluntarily hidden their political opinions.

[4]The percentage is based on the total number of anwers classified under the political categories, the *no
answer* being excluded.

[5]Figure 3.1 presents in detail the different political categories from the far right to the far left. As
indicated before, these categories have been regrouped into a new scale (see Table 3.1). The following
percentages correspond to this new scale.

Figure 3.1. Distribution of Political Tendencies by Country (Percent).

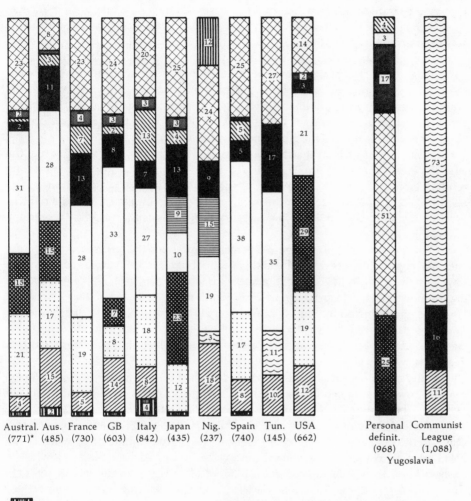

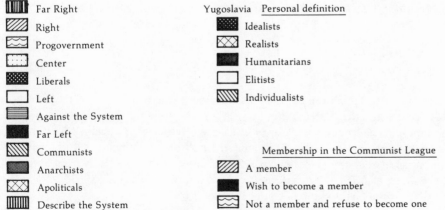

*These numbers correspond to those individuals who replied to the question asking for "self-definition of political orientation." Those giving no response were excluded from this analysis.

the extreme left (10 percent)—are the most popular tendencies, followed by the apolitical (20 percent), the center (18 percent), and the right (8 percent). The far right, kept as a separate category in this country, represents only 4 percent of the students.

In *Japan*, since the category *right* represented only 1 percent of the students, it was regrouped with the center (36 percent)[6], the most popular tendency, followed by the apolitical (25 percent), the far left (20 percent), and the left (19 percent).

In *Nigeria* the distribution along the modified political spectrum is the following: the apolitical (24 percent), the left (19 percent), and the right (18 percent) were the most frequent categories, followed by *criticizes the system* (15 percent), *describes the system* (12 percent), and far left (9 percent); 3 percent of the students expressed opinions favorable toward the government (progovernment).

In *Spain* the majority of the students identified themselves with some form of the left, 38 percent the moderate left and 17 percent the far left. This is an interesting result in view of the fact that Spain at the time of the study was ruled by Franco. The apolitical constitute 26 percent of the sample, the center 11 percent and the right 10 percent. It should be noted that the category *right* included those who favored the government.

In *Tunisia*, as in Spain, the left (35 percent) represents the largest segment of the students' population interviewed and the most popular tendency in the country, followed by the apolitical (27 percent) and the far left (17 percent). The center, including the Bourguibists (11 percent), and the right (10 percent), are the least popular. For some, the ruling Bourguibist National party is associated with a socialist orientation. In order to see whether the students who identified themselves as socialist-left were close to those identifying themselves as Bourguibists or progovernment, we kept these two categories separated.

Finally, in the *United States* the liberal identification is the most popular (29 percent), followed by the left (21 percent) and the center, including the Democrats (19 percent). The apolitical (14 percent) and the right, including the Republicans (12 percent), are less numerous. Concerning the liberal identification, it was thought interesting to determine whether these students are more similar in their opinions to the Democrats or to those identifying themselves as left or socialists (see below). The proportion of far left or radical students (5 percent) is very small in this country. They represent with the Australian far left (5 percent also), the smallest proportion, compared with the other countries studied.

COMPARISONS OF POLITICAL DISTRIBUTION OF THE AMERICAN, FRENCH, AND ENGLISH SAMPLES: A TEST OF REPRESENTATIVENESS

The extent to which the political distribution of the three samples from France, Great Britain, and the United States may be considered representative was evaluated by comparing the frequency of the political "self-definitions" obtained with the figures from three opinion polls—in France the poll of the French Institute of Public Opinion taken at Nanterre-Lettres in 1970; in Great Britain the study *New Students' Politics at Essex in the United Kingdom* (F. Rudd and E. Rudd, 1968); and in the United States the Gallup Poll on College Students (1970).

We find (Table 3.2) for these three countries a relatively high degree of similarity between the political distribution in our study and those in other investigations.

[6]As noted, the center includes the students who identified themselves with the Liberal Democratic party, the party in power.

When we compare our French data with those of the IFOP poll in 1970, we see that the proportion of students on the left is 28 percent in our study as compared with 29 percent in the IFOP poll. That of the extreme left, including the communists and anarchists, is 24 percent in both studies. Students from the right and from the center are 25 percent of our sample and 29 percent of the IFOP poll sample, and the apolitical group is 22 percent in our study, compared with 18 percent.

TABLE 3.2. **Political Representativeness of the American, French, and English Samples (Percent):**

POLITICAL ORIENTATION	FRANCE		GREAT BRITAIN		UNITED STATES	
	Present study (856)	IFOP 1970	Present study (625)	Essex 1968[4]	Present study (693)	Gallup 1970
Right	6 } 25	29[1]	15	15	12	15
Center	19 }		15	13	19 } 40[5]	40[5]
Liberal	–	–	–	–	29 }	
Left	28	29[2]	33	28	21 } 30[5]	30[5]
Communists	7 } 24	24[3]	13 }	5	5	7[6]
Far left	17 }					(4)
Apolitical	23	18	24	31	14	6

* In all tables, the figures enclosed in parentheses represent the number of respondents.
1. Students satisfied with the present regime or desiring to perfect it without changing its nature.
2. Students wishing to change the nature of the regime but using existing institutions.
3. Students ready to proceed to a violent revolution.
4. This study is representative of only one university, Essex.
5. The students were to situate themselves on a scale from the extreme right to the extreme left.
6. The percentage of the far left (7%), as it is specified, in fact includes only 4% of students truly defining themselves as radicals.

In Great Britain, the results of the present study are very similar to those obtained by Rudd and Rudd at Essex in 1968 concerning the right and the center. However, the percentages of students on the left (33 percent versus 28 percent) and on the far left (13 percent versus 5 percent) are larger in the present study. The apolitical students are, in contrast, less numerous (25 percent versus 31 percent).[7]

Finally, in the United States the proportions of rightist (12 percent as compared to 15 percent) and on the opposite side radical students (5 percent and 4 percent) are roughly similar in the present study and in the Gallup poll. The categories *center* and *left* in the Gallup poll are not easy to compare with those in our study, since we kept the liberal identification as a separate category whereas in the Gallup poll liberal students were asked to classify themselves either as middle of the road (center in our study) or left. However, if these categories are combined, almost the same percentages appear in the present study and in the Gallup poll (69 percent and 70 percent respectively). The apolitical position is somewhat more frequent in our study (14 percent) than in the Gallup poll (6 percent).

These comparisons allow us to consider the political variable in the present study as reasonably representative of student political tendencies in these three countries at least. For the other countries we were not able to obtain comparable data. However, the justification of our political scale may be seen *a posteriori* in the internal consistency of the analyses themselves. In fact, as we shall see, there exists in all these countries a considerable degree of consistency in the attitudes within political

[7] The poll conducted by Rudd and Rudd was realized at the beginning of the students' protest in the United Kingdom. This could explain the large percentage of apolitical students found in contrast to the small number of far left students.

groups. Thus students on the left will always (as a group) have more innovative attitudes than conservatives. This holds true not only for attitudes toward the university and sociopolitical systems but also for cultural values.

We must emphasize, therefore, that the limitations of our sampling do not undermine the validity of the analytical relationships between variables; our analysis is of the type recently termed a "theoretical sampling" (Glaser and Strauss, 1967) designed to establish comparisons between subgroups which are essential for the comprehension of the phenomenon. In any case our goal is not to present an exhaustive or definitive survey of the ideas and attitudes of the majority of students, but rather to indicate general tendencies within each national group and to consider these in an international context. Our samples are for the most part sufficiently large and varied so that when differences between countries are substantial, they may be regarded as having a high degree of probability.

THE 1977 SURVEY

The comparison of political tendencies of the respondents between 1970 and 1977 indicates that in France there is no appreciable change in the percentage defining themselves as on the right (6 percent versus 7 percent), as on the far left (17 percent) and as apolitical (23 percent versus 22 percent). In contrast, the moderate left has increased (28 percent to 38 percent) at the expense of the center (19 percent to 11 percent) (Figure 3.2). This situation can be related to the political situation in France, where the left has gained some popularity at the polls.

Conversely, in the United States the shift indicated by the 1977 data is toward conservatism. There is an increase of the right among the students. The Republicans (12 percent versus 25 percent) and the center Democrats (19 percent versus 26 percent) gain at the expense of the liberals (29 percent and 23 percent) and even more of the left (21 percent and 8 percent). The proportion of the far left remained essentially unchanged (5 percent versus 4 percent), as did that of apoliticals (14 percent versus 15 percent).

Similar results appear also in a poll conducted in 1973 by Yankelovich (1974). It will be interesting to see whether this shift toward conservatism in general political orientation is reflected in attitudes and opinions toward sociocultural issues.

POLITICAL DISTRIBUTION IN YUGOSLAVIA

In Yugoslavia, the political orientation of the students was determined through a multiple choice question which read:

With which group would you identify yourself with respect to your professed political beliefs? (Circle only one answer).
   I place myself among:
A-1. Those who are ready to fight for a society in which there is absolute material and class equality.
A-2. Those who believe that absolute material and class equality among people is an idle dream and a utopia, but who, on the other hand, believe that society should offer equal opportunity of access to all of its members.
A-3. Those who believe that the former and the latter, that is, material and class equality among people and a society with equal opportunity, are an idle dream and a utopia.

Figure 3.2. Political Tendencies, 1977 (Percent).

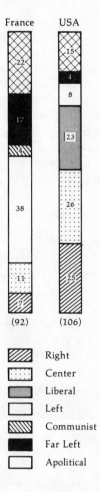

Right

Center

Liberal

Left

Communist

Far Left

Apolitical

Everybody should make his own way as best he can, according to his abilities, whereas society should help those who lack the necessary strength and ability.

A-4. Those who believe in neither utopia nor interference of society in behalf of those who lack ability. Everyone should make his own way as best he can, according to his abilities. Society, however, should help only those whose abilities are above average. It is self-evident that only a society led by an elite can prosper.

A-5. Those who believe in neither utopia nor any kind of interference of society in the lives of its members. Everybody should look after himself as best he can.

A-6. I do not know.

The alternatives were identified as follows: (A-1), idealist; (A-2), realist; (A-3), humanitarian; (A-4), elitist; (A-5), individualist.

The majority of respondents in Yugoslavia (Figure 3.1)[8] placed themselves in the first three groups, all of which well represent, with variations, the socialist ideology of egalitarianism and collectivism. Among the Yugoslavian respondents who accepted one of these choices, 25 percent are what we termed idealists, 51 percent realists, and 17 percent humanitarians. The elitists (3 percent) and the individualists

[8]See page 29.

(4 percent) reflect more the ideology of Western capitalism and are few in number. There are 12 percent of "no answers." Indirectly, these results show that Yugoslav students for the most part accept the political ideology of their country. Whatever the nature and the motives of their protests, they do not seem to question the basic socialist principles as these function in Yugoslavia.

The second criterion concerning Yugoslav politics was membership or nonmembership in the Communist League. The question was: "Are you a member of the Communist League?" The students could choose among the following alternatives: "Yes," "No, but I wish to join," and "No, I refuse to join."

When we consider the official prestige and the power of the Communist League, we are struck by the lack of enthusiasm which the Communist League inspires in so many of the students questioned. The majority (73 percent) has never been affiliated with the Communist League and do not wish to be. Other students either have been members of the Communist League for three years (7 percent) or more (4 percent) or wish to join (16 percent) in the near future (Figure 3.1). The students' attitudes vis-à-vis the League may depend largely on the family milieu, on its position with regard to this organization and on the role the family played in the struggle for national liberation.

It is interesting to note (Table 3.1a)[9] that a majority of students belonging to the League or wishing to become a member have a father (70 percent and 50 percent respectively) and often a mother (42 percent and 25 percent respectively) who are themselves members. Comparatively few students among those who refuse to join this organization have a father (25 percent) or a mother (14 percent) who are already members of the League. Parents of those students who have joined the League or wish to do so were, on the whole, much more active during the struggle for national liberation than the parents of students opposed to this organization (Table 3.1b).

The nature of these activities differs, especially for the men. The participation of fathers of students who are members of the Communist League is of an official nature: many were in the armed forces, while the fathers of the nonmember students and of those who do not wish to join tended to be active in the clandestine resistance.

Family influence seems to play, therefore, an important role in the attitudes of students toward the Communist League. Children of families affiliated with the League and/or which participated in the national struggle as members of a structured and official organization will more probably become members and will be more favorably disposed to the Communist League than children coming from a family which does not belong to the League or did not fight for Yugoslav liberation, or did so but in a clandestine manner.

Other reasons may also influence students to refuse to join the Communist League. A multiple choice question permitted them to make their feelings more precisely known (Table 3.1c). The motives most frequently voiced concerned the lack of efficiency of the Communist League (32 percent), the opportunism of its members (29 percent), and the unsatisfactory nature of interpersonal relationships in the League (20 percent). Some students justified their refusal to join the Communist League by giving more ideological reasons: rejection of its program and its philosophy (18 percent); the lack of freedom of expression (17 percent); and antipathy toward a tendency to form cliques (16 percent). Also, some students judged this

[9]Tables 3.1a–3.1c are on page 54. (Tables with numbers and letters conclude chapters.)

organization as out-of-date (15 percent), while others simply stated they did not yet have enough time for participation (15 percent).

Evaluation of the Popularity of One's Political Outlook

The question "What percentage of university students do you think would share your general political orientation?" had two objectives. The first was to learn how students perceived the popularity of their own political orientation and to find out to what extent they felt themselves to represent a majority (50 percent or more) or a minority (less than 50 percent) in their university. Precision with regard to the opinions of others may certainly be regarded as an important element in social interaction. "It is clear that social interaction is often conditioned by the climate of conditions which characterize the situation. It is not the 'objective' attitudinal climate which is the key factor, but rather the attitudinal climate which one thinks exists" (G. Korte, 1972, p. 576).

The second objective was to see if accurate judgment of the popularity of one's political orientation was related to one's position as a radical or as a conservative and/or was dependent on the specific situation in one's country. In some countries the protest phenomenon was the object of much publicity, as the mass media or the university milieu made value judgments regarding the "liberal" or "radical" position taken. It might be expected that the positions on the left and the far left, seen as dominant, would become subject to a numerical overestimation by those who support these views. On the other hand, according to Korte (1972), conservative or moderate students who disagree with the left will less often reveal their opinions, as they are presumed to be those of a minority group.[10]

In fact our results do not confirm this hypothesis. In general moderate students have a tendency to consider themselves in the majority in the university, while those on the extreme left, in most countries, see themselves as in the minority. The precision, however, with which the students judge the degree of popularity of their opinions seems to depend more on the political situation in their country than on identification with a specific political tendency.

We find also (Table 3.3—page 36) that in countries where only party is in control, as in Nigeria, Tunisia, and Spain (at the time of our study) or even in Anglo-Saxon countries where the two-party system exists, the students have a tendency to overestimate the size of their own political group, when compared to students in Italy, France, Austria, and Japan. This can best be explained by the political structure in the latter countries, as a consequence of which estimates can be made more accurately.

The overestimation of one's own political party is especially evident in Australia and the two African countries in the study, particularly Nigeria. In Nigeria all of the political groups, from the right to the extreme left, think they represent the majority tendency at the university. We find the same phenomenon to a lesser degree in Tunisia, where only the apolitical students consider themselves in the minority. It would seem that in these two countries more than anywhere else there is a tendency toward

---

[10]We shall see apropos of the freedom of expression at the university that the moderate students often feel bullied by the extremists, who ridicule their conservatism.

TABLE 3.3. Evaluation of One's Own Political Orientation as Shared by 50 Percent or More of Fellow Students in Each Country (Percent).

	AUSTRAL.	AUS.	FRANCE	GB	ITALY	JAPAN	NIG.	SPAIN	TUN.	USA
Far right	—	—	—	—	(31)	—	—	—	—	—
	—	—	—	—	44	—	—	—	—	—
Right	(40)	(80)	(39)	(88)	(64)	(156)	(41)	(60)	(13)	(77)
	63	72	40	58	34	51	79	57	60	43
Center	(269)	(151)	(131)	(90)	(144)		(6)	(119)	(16)	(128)
	69	47	57	63	49		83	69	69	60
Liberal	—	—	—	—	—	—	—	—	—	(194)
	—	—	—	—	—	—	—	—	—	73
Left	(234)	(136)	(197)	(197)	(221)	(44)	(35)	(275)	(47)	(136)
	53	23	39	59	39	43	94	53	43	46
Communist	—	—	(48)	—	(108)	—	—	—	—	—
	—	—	8	—	33	—	—	—	—	—
Far left	(36)	(69)	(94)	(72)	(72)	(125)	(19)	(82)	(25)	(26)
	83	15	19	11	32	40	76	19	76	19
Anarchist	—	—	(32)	—	—	—	—	—	—	—
	—	—	3	—	—	—	—	—	—	—
Apolitical	(184)	(44)	(130)	(146)	(169)	(106)	(49)	(174)	(30)	(90)
	50	29	41	63	41	49	66	64	36	41
Total	(763)	(480)	(671)	(593)	(809)	(431)	(221)[1]	(710)	(131)	(651)
	57	36	37	56	40	46	76	55	61	55

1. Includes the category *describes the system* (28), not presented in this table.

competition among the various groups opposing the university, in particular by those students close to the government and those of opposing forces, especially the left in Nigeria and the far left in Tunisia.

In Yugoslavia (Table 3.4) more than half of the students, whether they are members of the Communist League or not or wish to become a member, judge themselves to be in the majority in their university. Student members of the League and those aspiring to become members clearly overestimate their numbers the most, since, as already indicated, student members of the League represent only 11 percent and those aspiring to party membership only 16 percent, while nonmembers constitute 73 percent of the sample.

TABLE 3.4. Evaluation of One's Own Ideological
Orientation and Affiliation as Shared by 50 Percent
or More of Fellow Students in Yugoslavia (Percent).

A. Ideological Orientation

Idealist	(242)	60
Realist	(495)	59
Humanitarian	(163)	59
Elitist	(26)	62
Individualist	(42)	71

B. Affiliation To the Communist League

Member	(119)	53
No, but desire to be	(176)	63
No, and refuse to be	(793)	64

The political groups with which Yugoslav students identify do not vary greatly in their evaluation of their own popularity. Approximately 60 percent see themselves as in the majority at the university, whether they are socialists, idealists, realists, humanitarians, or even elitists—the last group only slightly represented in our sample. The individualists, that is, those who think they are capable of shifting for themselves and of doing what they want, also believe that their opinions are shared by the majority at the university.

In the other countries (Table 3.3) we also find an overestimation of one's own political group, but for some groups the judgments are based on political realities. The students who place themselves beyond the moderate left (i.e., communists, far left, anarchists) for the most part see themselves as in the minority at the university. On the other hand, moderate students and apolitical students believe that they represent the opinions of the majority at the university. In Spain and also in Anglo-Saxon countries (especially Great Britain and Australia) a large number (more than half) of students on the noncommunist left judge that their ideas are shared by the majority.

This is scarcely surprising in Great Britain and in Australia, where conservative and labor governments alternate. In the case of Spain there is also an underevaluation of opposing forces, which may be explained by the fact that they are not well known. In the United States several groups (Republicans, Democrats, and especially liberals) think they reflect the majority tendency in universities. A clarification of the data would require a more precise analysis of the opinions which these various political groups include, in particular for the liberals and the left. We shall attempt this analysis throughout this study, not only for the United States but for other countries as well.

The results described here show that students who belong to the so-called "silent majority" are not only conscious of their power but even have a tendency to overestimate it. On the other hand, in many countries (Great Britain, Spain, the United States, France, Austria, and Japan), students on the far left recognize that they constitute a minority.

THE 1977 SURVEY

In France the results of the 1977 survey indicate an interesting change in where the respondents believe other students are situated politically. The students who define themselves as moderate—or conservative—are much less likely, as compared with 1970, to believe that their opinions are shared by at least 50 percent of the students (right, 17 percent as compared to 40 percent in 1970; center, 22 percent versus 57 percent; apolitical, 21 percent as compared to 41 percent). A similar diminution characterizes the far left (7 percent as compared to 19 percent). On the contrary, the percentage of the students who define themselves as of the moderate left and consider their views shared by at least 50 percent of the students remains unchanged (40 percent and 39 percent) (Table 3.5).

TABLE 3.5. Evaluation of One's Political Orientation as Shared by 50 Percent or More of Fellow Students in 1977 (Percent).

	FRANCE	UNITED STATES
Right	(6)	(26)
	17	63
Center	(10)	(28)
	22	50
Liberal	—	(24)
	—	67
Left	(35)	(8)
	40	25
Communist	(4)	—
	0	—
Far left	(15)	(4)
	7	(2)*
Apolitical	(20)	(16)
	21	38
Total	(90)	(106)
	25	63

*When the number is so small, no percentages have been calculated. This practice has been followed throughout the text.

In the USA the opposite is true. In 1977 it is those on the right that feel much more frequently that they are part of the majority (63 percent as compared to 43 percent in 1970). Correspondingly, the left sees its influence dwindling on campus (25 percent as compared to 46 percent). This change in the perceived popularity of one's position corresponds in a general way to the increasing popularity of the right in the USA and of the moderate left in France in the second survey.

Political Influences

Numerous studies have underlined the preponderant influence of parents on the ideological evolution of their children. In fact, most of the research on political socialization, particularly in the United States, shows that children are most likely to have the same political preferences as their parents. Political orientation appears to be acquired during childhood and to remain more or less unchanged throughout life (Goldsen et al., 1960; Converse and Dupeux, 1962; Hyman, 1959). There would seem to exist, therefore, a great stability of political preferences and a continuity in the type of involvement from one generation to another. At the same time, familial influence is clearly rivaled not only by the growing influence of peers but also by other agents of socialization outside the family, such as schools, teachers, and mass communications.

The students were asked who (friends or peers, parents, teachers, politicians, ideologues, authors, journalists) had most influenced their political evolution. The result (Table 3.6) indicates that in most countries studied, the family plays a minor role as a perceived source of one's political orientation.

TABLE 3.6. Perceived Sources of Political Orientation by Country (Percent).[1]

	AUSTRAL.[2] (753)	AUS.[2] (466)	FRANCE (818)	GB (597)	ITALY (762)	JAPAN (421)	NIG. (233)	SPAIN (689)	TUN. (142)	USA (651)	YUG.[3] (1,018)
Friends[4]	36	31	63	47	41	39	57	58	60	51	4
Family	19	30	27	23	22	8	11	19	16	29	29
Professors	5	2	15	4	8	12	11	4	20	14	7
Ideologists	31	33	52	50	40	38	63	31	68	35	17
No One	10	–	2	–	6	4	1	3	–	–	42

1. The percentages often go beyond 100, as the students frequently mentioned more than one influential source.
2. In Australia and Austria, students were asked to select only one source of influence.
3. In Yugoslavia, students were asked to select three sources of influence, in descending order. We have noted here only the first choice.
4. To facilitate the presentation of the results, we have grouped under "friends" friends and young people of the same age, and under "ideologists" politicians, journalists, authors, etc.

Almost all students realize that they have undergone some sort of outside influence in their political maturation. It is only in Yugoslavia that we find a high percentage (42 percent) of students who believe that no one has influenced their opinions.

The first remark to be made on these results concerns the importance of the peer group (friends, students) in contrast to that of the family and of teachers. Teachers were assigned only a minor role in the political evolution of the students. We find also that ideologists and the media have a perceived influence as important as that of the peer group, except in the United States and in Spain. Indeed, in these two countries[11] the peer group (respectively 51 percent and 58 percent) is more often mentioned as having been influential in the political evolution of students than were ideologists and the media (respectively 35 percent and 31 percent). In Austria alone

[11]This is also the case in West Germany, where the data have been analyzed only partially.

do the students recognize an essentially equal influence of their parents (30 percent), their friends (31 percent), and ideologists and the media (31 percent).

In Yugoslavia the students had to give three answers in descending order. Those who recognized having undergone influence exterior to themselves listed their family first, then ideologists, and finally professors and friends. If we set aside Austria and Yugoslavia—where the family was mentioned as frequently as or more than friends or the media—in general the majority of students from all the countries studied do not attribute to the family a great role in their present political position, but do recognize the role of friends and of the media (in which we have included ideologists).

These results differ somewhat from the conclusions reached in studies made in the United States and in Great Britain and from what is frequently suggested regarding the influence of the family on the political orientation of young people. Wright (1962), for example, remarked that young people in England identified more often with their parents than with their friends. More recently, Musgrove (1967), in research on the reference group or on the "significant others" for British students, found that 67 percent mentioned as the most important people in their lives members of their own families, especially their parents; only 19 percent mentioned their friends. In the United States, Hollingshead (1949), Goldsen et al. (1960), Kahl (1953), etc., found that young people identified largely with the political orientation of their parents. In France also, studies on electoral behavior do not show any marked discontinuity between the attitudes of young people and those of their parents (cf. Boudon, September 1970; Lancelot, 1969).

Is the fact that students in practically all the countries included in this study recognize more political influence from outside of the family the consequence of a real change in the socializing function of the family? Have the peer group and the mass media become more important? Or is this only a false impression—for example, did the interviewed students wish to seem independent and autonomous of their families and thus experience more difficulty in seeing their families as having considerable influence on their own political attitudes?

We must note that the protest events truly demonstrated that young people, as a social group, frequently represented an avant-garde position. Most studies on the transmission of political preference from parents were completed before 1968–1970, the years when student movements were the most widespread.

The analyses made as a function of the political tendency of the students show (Table 3.6a—page 55) that, in general, students on the left and particularly on the far left least frequently mention the family as a source of influence. Moderate students, those on the right and in the center and those who are apolitical, mention the role of their family much more frequently (three times more often on the average).

The differences between moderate and radical students are less clear apropos of friends and the media. All political groups mention these two groups quite often. These results demonstrate that (with the exception of conservative students in Great Britain, Republicans in the United States, and students on the right or from the center in Austria) most students—whatever their politics or country of origin—mention much more frequently their friends (students and peers) and various ideologists (writers, political leaders, and the media) as having played an important role in their political evolution.

It would seem, then, that the role of the family as an agent of political socialization is seen as much less important, at least by leftist students, than certain studies and widespread opinions lead one to believe. On the other hand, the growing influ-ence of peers or the same age class as an agent transmitting social norms and values is here confirmed; the influence of the media is also, however, very important.

An open-ended question allowed students to specify the nature of this ideological influence and to indicate authors and political leaders having influenced them the most. The analysis of these responses was made for France, Great Britain, and the United States, and revealed several differences. In France the influential groups clearly have a more political character than those in the two other countries. There was a predominance of classical leftist political thinkers—Marx, Lenin, Trotsky, Mao, Bakunin, Proudhon, etc. Numerous political leaders like de Gaulle, Mendès-France, and Rocard were also mentioned. Other popular names include Bergson, Sartre, Wilhelm Reich, Marcuse, and Freud. Political influence was sometimes asso-ciated with a specific party, the French Communist party (PCF) in particular. But the groups or persons mentioned by the student do not automatically imply that the student takes them as a model. Negative reference groups are sometimes named, as influences to be avoided. The students sometimes specify the political position of friends who have influenced them.

In contrast, British students mention few political authors and few specific politi-cal parties. Only 2 students out of 611 named political leaders (Harold Wilson and Churchill). Many authors were considered influential for the moderates and for the far left, but the one most frequently cited was George Orwell. British students were more international in their reading than the French, and mentioned French, Ameri-can, or Russian authors as well as British.

American students mention least often classical political thinkers and specific po-litical parties. Students for a Democratic Society (SDS) was mentioned by only one student! More than the British, American students referred to political leaders; Ken-nedy was the one most often mentioned. Finally, the authors who have most influ-enced American students are those who write science fiction or otherwise write about the future and the fantastic and imaginative, such as Vonnegut, Tolkien, Rand, Barth, Orwell, and Aldous Huxley.

This supplementary question is interesting as revealing the preoccupations and literary tastes of the students. The results confirm what many had already observed: the classical political culture of French students, and of French protesters in par-ticular, still exists when compared with the British tradition, and expecially with the American experience. American students rely much less on Marxism to organize their protest and are more likely to "reinvent" their political theses and directives.

THE 1977 SURVEY

The results (Table 3.7—page 42) show that in France the proportion of friends, teachers, and authors considered as sources of influence has not changed much; a slight increase in family influence can be noted (34 percent as compared to 27 per-cent in 1979). In the United States, on the contrary, there is a striking change. The perception of friends as a source of political influence has diminished from 51 per-cent in 1970 to 25 percent in 1977, whereas the perception of family influence has in-creased from 29 percent in 1970 to 40 percent in 1977. As will become apparent in other sections of the study, an overall increase of family influence was apparent in 1977 as compared with the main study.

TABLE 3.7. Perceived Sources of Political Orientation, 1977 (Percent).

	FRANCE (90)	UNITED STATES (104)
Friends	66	25
Family	34	40
Professors	14	14
Ideologists	58	39
No one	2	1

Social and Environmental Correlates of Political Tendencies

Earlier we tried to present a résumé of the principal explanations regarding possible sociopsychological factors which intervene in the determination of the political orientation of students, in particular of radicals. As we have seen most research on activists has been done in the United States.

From the major data collected, Gezi and Kruschke (1970) have drawn a general portrait of American student activists:

> Middle or upper-middle class origins; parents who were relatively permissive, liberal, and democratic; intellectual orientation and above-average academic achievement; curiosity, impulsiveness, unconventionality; and humanitarianism. Such students tend also to be "altruistic," to some extent "alienated," and to some extent "anxious"; to be relatively non-authoritarian and antonomous; to be disproportionately from Jewish backgrounds or to be irreligious; to be "romantic," "egalitarian," "anti-institutional," and "anti-dogmatic"; to be urban in residential origin; and to be present on the campuses of the "better" American colleges and universities [p. 72].

We tried not only to see if we would find among leftist in contrast to rightist students in our American sample some of these same characteristics but also to determine whether these characteristics would be found in all the countries studied.

A path analysis[12] was undertaken in order to explore the relative influences of familial, environmental, and personal characteristics on the students' political orientations. The analysis required a grouping of the different political categories into two major orientations:[13]

A) *Political positions*
   1. The *right side* (conservative orientation) of the political spectrum, including all the categories from the far right to the center, plus the apolitical
   2. The *left side* (moderate to far left) of the political spectrum, including all the categories from the left to the far left

[12]The method followed was developed by Lindsey (1972). It is a method of path analysis for which the hypotheses of normality and linearity are not required, hence qualitative variables may be used. The parameter estimates for dependence of the political orientations on the sociological variables are calculated by a mathematical model similar to the model type used in the analysis of variance. For the tests of significance of the various effects, the standard F-tests used in the analysis of variance were replaced by estimations of the relative likelihood function. A chi-square test of significance was then derived.

[13]This regrouping was made in all the countries studied except Yugoslavia, where we distinguished the *socialist* orientation (including the ideologists, realists, and humanitarians) from the *oppositionists* (including the elitists and individualists), made up of students unfavorable to their society.

B) *Familial background variables*
   1. and 2. Level of education of the father and the mother (primary, high school, university);
   3. Religious background (Catholic, Jew, Protestant, others, no religion)
   4. Social and professional status of the father (professional and high-ranking executive, businessman, shopkeeper and farm owner, middle-rank executive, white collar, blue collar, others)
   5. Working status of the mother (working or non-working)

C) *The environmental variables*
   1. Living situation (with family, campus, others)
   2. Place of study (type of university and/or location)
   3. Major option (humanities, social science, science, medicine, law and economics, business and engineering)
   4. Perceived sources of ideological influences (peer group, parents, professors, ideologists and political leaders)

D) *Personal characteristics*
   1. Sex
   2. Religious beliefs (believer, nonbeliever)

The results are presented in Table 3.8 (page 44). Only the main effect parameters which are significant at the .05 level are reported.

The results indicate that the political orientation of the student seems to be related essentially to three factors: *religious beliefs, perceived ideological influences*, and the nature of the *major options*.[14] The first two factors emerge in all of the countries studied: a leftist political outlook appears to be associated with atheism and with sources of influence outside the family—cultural agents and/or the peer group. Conversely, a rightist political outlook is usually associated with a religious belief and the adoption of one's family's political views. The third factor—*major options*—intervenes differently in each country.

In Australia, France, Great Britain, and the United States students in the social sciences and the humanities tend to be on the left side of the political spectrum.

In Great Britain, in contrast with the other countries studied, law students tend also to be on the left. In Japan only one option, sciences, appears to be significantly related to a leftist orientation.

In Australia, France, Great Britain, the United States, and Japan engineering and business are related to a conservative political orientation. In France, the United States, and Japan law is also related to a rightist orientation. In Australia, Great Britain, and the United States medical students are likely to have a rightist orientation.

Finally, in Yugoslavia a *socialist* orientation is related only to humanities as a major option, whereas an *oppositionist* orientation does not appear significantly related to a particular option.

In the other countries studied (Austria, Italy, Nigeria and Spain) the major option did not appear to intervene directly in the political orientation of the students.

The other variables which appear to play a significant role in determining the political orientation of students are *family social status* in Australia and in France; in both countries lower social status is associated with a leftist orientation, and higher social status with a rightist orientation. The *mother's working status* plays a role in

[14]*Options* refers to college or university discipline in which the student is concentrating.

TABLE 3.8. Social and Environmental Correlates of Political Tendencies.

VARIABLES ASSOCIATED WITH POLITICAL TENDENCIES*	LEFT	RIGHT
Australia		
1. Religious beliefs	. Nonbelievers	. Believers
2. Socioprofessional status of the father	. Lower status	
3. Major options	. Social sciences and humanities	. Business, engineering, medicine
4. Source of political influence	. Peers and ideologists	. Parents
Austria		
1. Sex	. Men	. Women
2. Source of political influence	. Peers	. Parents
France		
1. Religious beliefs	. Nonbelievers	. Believers
2. Major options	. Social sciences and humanities	. Sciences, business, and law
3. Mother's working status	. Mother works	. Mother does not work
4. Source of political influence	. Peers and ideologists	. Parents
5. Socioprofessional status of the father	. From relatively modest families	. From privileged families
Great Britain		
1. Religious beliefs	. Nonbelievers	. Believers
2. Place of study	. England as opposed to Wales and Scotland	
3. Major option	. Law, social sciences, and humanities	. Business, engineering, and medicine
4. Sex	. Men	. Women
5. Source of political influence	. Friends and ideologists	. Parents
6. Mother's working status	. Mother works	
Italy		
1. Religious beliefs	. Nonbelievers	. Believers
2. Source of political influence	. Friends and ideologists	. Parents
3. Mother's working status	. Mother works	. Mother does not work
4. Sex	. Men	. Women
Japan		
1. Living situation	. Live on campus	. Live by themselves or within the family
2. Major option	. Sciences	. Law, engineering
Nigeria		
1. Working status	. Mother works	. Mother does not work
2. Religious beliefs	. Nonbelievers	. Believers
3. Father's educational level	. No formal education	. Some formal education
Spain		
1. Source of political influence	. Friends and ideologists	. Parents
USA		
1. Major options	. Social sciences and humanities	. Law, medicine, sciences, and engineering or business
2. Mother's working status	. Mother works	. Mother does not work
3. Place of study	. Ivy league and private universities	. State universities
Yugoslavia		
1. Nationality (Slovenians versus other nationalities)	. Slovenians	. Non-Slovenians
2. Religious background of the parents	. Nonbelievers	. Believers
3. Membership of the father in the Communist League	. Was or is in the Communist League	. Has never been a member of the Communist League
4. Major options	. Humanities	

*Level of significance at .05.

France, Great Britain, Italy, Nigeria, and the United States: students situated on the left are more likely to have a mother who works, in contrast to those on the right.

In Nigeria the *father's level of education* was also found to be significantly related to political attitudes, a leftist orientation being associated with a father without formal education and rightist orientation with a father having at least some formal education.

Sex plays a significant role only in Austria, Great Britain, and Italy where men are more likely to appear on the left side on the political spectrum and women on the right.

In Great Britain and the United States the *place of study* is also significantly related to the political orientation of the respondents. In Great Britain students attending universities located in London or in other parts of England tend to be found proportionally more on the left than those in Welsh or Scottish universities. In the United States those attending Ivy League or private universities tend to be found proportionally more often on the left than those in state universities.

Finally, in Japan the students' *living situation* also appears to play a role. Students who are living on campus tend to adhere to leftist positions, whereas those living on their own or with their parents are more likely to identify themselves with the right.

In Yugoslavia, where two variables were added: the *nationality* of the student and the *parent's membership* in the Communist League, it was found that Slovenian students and those with a father who was or is a member of the Communist League are more likely to have a socialist orientation.

The other variables included in the analysis do not appear to play a significant role in the student's political position.

In conclusion it may be noted that the results obtained concerning religious beliefs, major options, source of political influence, and the sex of the students as well as the place of study tend so far to corroborate data provided by Lipset (1968) and Flacks (1967). However, it must be noted that in Great Britain students in law and in Japan students in sciences are more likely to adhere to a leftist position. In Australia, France, and Nigeria, a leftist position is associated with lower socioeconomic background and a rightist position with a relatively high background.

Political Attitudes and Political Self-Definition

We now present a comparison of students' attitudes on some specific political issues. This will allow us to determine variations in particular aspects of ideological content among groups which are apparently located on the same position of the political spectrum in different countries.

ATTITUDES TOWARD DEMOCRACY

The first question concerns some basic tenets of democracy. On the right and on the left, in the East and in the West, governments consider themselves as true representatives of democracy. We therefore looked at student opinions with regard to universal suffrage, considered by many as one of the basic elements of democracy but denounced by others as a masquerade of democracy. The question asked was whether the student agreed with the statement "Popular elections should be abolished because the majority of people cannot be trusted to decide what is good for society."

In all the countries studied only a minority of respondents agree with this statement (Table 3.9), but the differences are quite striking: 20 percent or less of students in Australia, Austria, Italy, Great Britain, Japan, the United States, and Yugoslavia, as compared with 40 percent in Tunisia, 30 percent in France, 28 percent in Nigeria, and 24 percent in Spain, agree that popular elections should be abolished.

When we look at the results by political tendency, we find that the desire to abolish universal suffrage is not characteristic of only one political segment in the countries studied. Thus, compared to other tendencies, this desire is most apparent in the case of the far left in Tunisia (65 percent), Nigeria (43 percent), and Italy (39 percent) and in that of anarchists in France (48 percent). Conversely, this attitude is found on the right and among the apoliticals in Spain (34 percent and 32 percent), the far right (35 percent) in Italy, and the right (46 percent) in France (Table 3.9a).[15]

In Yugoslavia more elitists (32 percent) and individualists (44 percent) hold this attitude than those who are attached to some form of socialism or who hope for a humanitarian society (approximately 20 percent).

In the other countries there are few differences between the various political groups.

THE 1977 SURVEY

The results (Table 3.10, see p. 48) show in both France and the United States a slight decrease in antidemocratic attitudes—in the United States 4 percent versus 9 percent in 1970 and in France 18 percent versus 30 percent in 1970. The small size of the samples precludes a systematic analysis by political tendencies.

ELIMINATING CAPITALISM

There are important cross-cultural differences in the percentages of respondents agreeing with the statement "Capitalism should be eliminated" (Table 3.9).

Among those who agree, first come the Spanish students (81 percent) and the Italians (72 percent), followed by the French (65 percent), the Tunisians (61 percent), and the Nigerians (59 percent). At least half of the students in Great Britain (50 percent), Austria (52 percent), and Japan (50 percent) hold this view. Only in Australia (40 percent) and in the United States (30 percent) are students who have this opinion in the minority.

In Yugoslavia the statement "Capitalism should be eliminated" is certainly ambiguous, as it is not clear whether the question should be applied to countries where this system exists, or to some idea of a possible resurgence of the system in Yugoslavia, or to all the outgrowths of capitalism which exist in disguised form. Whatever the reason, it is surprising to note the spirit of conciliation of Yugoslav students, as only 42 percent are in favor of eliminating capitalism.

The results by political tendency (Table 3.9a), as we would expect, show a very large consensus on this question among students who are on the far left or the left.

[15]This table is on pages 56–60.

TABLE 3.9. Political Attitudes by Country (Percent).

	AUSTRAL.	AUSTRIA	FRANCE	G.B.	ITALY	JAPAN	NIGERIA	SPAIN	TUNISIA	USA	YUG.
Popular elections should be abolished because the majority of people cannot be trusted to decide what is good for society.*	(751) 17	(480) 15	(644) 30	(581) 16	(766) 21	(397) 11	(230) 28	(693) 24	(129) 40	(641) 9	(957) 21
Capitalism should be eliminated.*	(708) 40	(481) 52	(651) 65	(547) 50	(790) 72	(349) 50	(221) 59	(685) 81	(124) 61	(609) 30	(956) 42
I am in favor of destroying the present political system, even without knowing what will replace it.**[1]	(752) 11	(481) 15	(688) 22	(577) 14	(739) 37	(398) 27	(206) 28	(664) 31		(646) 7	(961) 5
A revolution in this country now would destroy the progress currently being made toward improving society.*[1]	(669) 60	(478) 65	(591) 37	(529) 65	(675) 49	(323) 38	(216) 36	(665) 41		(578) 57	(951) 57
A revolution succeeding in overthrowing the present government would sooner or later lead to a new repressive regime.*[1]	(653) 86	(481) 82	(645) 67	(515) 79	(595) 68	(379) 89	(195) 60	(608) 58		(517) 81	(945) 63
In order to build a new society, the freedom and happiness of the present generation must be sacrificed to that of future generations.*	(719) 17	(479) 28	(661) 29	(571) 28	(687) 43	(405) 9	(227) 49	(693) 46	(133) 54	(616) 18	(958) 20

* p < .01
** p < .05

1. Question did not appear on the Tunisian questionnaire.

TABLE 3.10.   Political Attitudes in France and the United States, 1977 Survey (Percent).

	FRANCE	UNITED STATES
Popular elections should be abolished because the majority of people cannot be trusted to decide what is good for society.**	(92) 18	(79) 4
Capitalism should be eliminated.*	1 66	10
I am in favor of destroying the present political system even without knowing what will replace it.**	(91) 26	(106) 8
A revolution in this country now would destroy the progress currently being made toward improving society.	(90) 29	33
A revolution succeeding in overthrowing the present government would sooner or later lead to a new repressive regime.**	48	(105) 62
In order to build a new society, the freedom and happiness of the present generation must be sacrificed to that of future generations.	(91) 22	(79) 16

*p <.01
**p <.05
1. When the number is the same as in the preceding item, it is not repeated.

Thus almost all students on the far left (approximately 90 percent) in Spain, Italy, Austria, France, Australia, Tunisia, and Great Britain desire the elimination of capitalism, as do 75 percent in Japan and Nigeria. In the United States the percentage of far left students opposed to capitalism is only 65 percent.

Students on the noncommunist left are also numerous in hoping to change the system, but their unanimity is less striking than that of the far left. Spanish leftists are the most anticapitalist (90 percent), followed by the Italians and the French (75 percent), the Austrians (73 percent), the Nigerians (72 percent), and the Tunisians (69 percent). Opinions on the left are clearly more divided in Great Britain (66 percent) and in Japan (62 percent), but especially in the United States (59 percent) and in Australia (57 percent). The left in Anglo-Saxon countries and in Japan appears to be most ambivalent about the elimination of capitalism, in comparison with the other countries, where the attitudes of the left (noncommunist) are close to those of the far left on this issue.

It is interesting to note the relatively high percentage of students on the right in Spain (52 percent) and on the extreme right in Italy (40 percent) who favor the elimination of capitalism.

THE 1977 SURVEY

The findings (Table 3.10) indicate no change in attitudes toward the elimination of capitalism in France (66 percent as compared with 65 percent in 1970). In the United States there is a substantial decrease in the percentage of students who agree (10 percent as compared with 30 percent in 1970).

RADICAL DESTRUCTION OF THE POLITICAL SYSTEM[16]

Although we find half or more of the students in the countries studied (except in Australia and in the United States) in favor of the elimination of capitalism, only a

[16]The question on this point could not be asked in Tunisia.

minority agree with the idea "destroying the present political system even without knowing what will replace it."

Differences of opinion do exist, however, in each country (Table 3.9). Thus very few students in Yugoslavia (5 percent), the United States (7 percent), Australia (11 percent), Great Britain (14 percent), and Austria (15 percent) agree with this statement, whereas those who agree represent a substantial minority in Japan (27 percent), Nigeria (28 percent), Spain (31 percent), and especially in Italy (37 percent). In France the proportion falls in between (22 percent).

The findings by political tendency (Table 3.9a) show that even on the far left this idea is not totally endorsed. A majority of Australian (57 percent) and Spanish and Italian students (56 percent) of the far left agree with this idea, whereas in the other countries those who agree represent about 45 percent of the total sample. It should be noted that in France it is the anarchist students who are most favorable (68 percent), and in Italy the communists (57 percent) as compared to those in France (33 percent). The leftist students are, in general, not favorable to this blind destruction (less than 20 percent), yet 41 percent of the left in Spain and about 30 percent in Italy and Nigeria are in favor.

The dissatisfaction within the present system underlying this attitude can be found even among some rightist, centrist, and apolitical students. Thus 18 percent of centrists and 17 percent of apoliticals in Spain are favorable to such a blind radical change, as well as 20 percent of apoliticals and 27 percent of rightists in Nigeria; and in Italy 23 percent of rightists and centrists as well as 45 percent of apoliticals and 62 percent of students of the far right agree with this idea.

THE 1977 SURVEY

The results in 1977 are about identical to those obtained in the 1970 study (in France 26 percent versus 22 percent in 1970, and in the United States 8 percent versus 7 percent in 1970).

ATTITUDES TOWARD THE CONSEQUENCES OF A REVOLUTION

We have seen that students, while rather favorable to the elimination of capitalism, do not usually favor destruction of the present system without knowing what will replace it. Two questions specified the possible consequences of a revolution—"A revolution in this country now would destroy the progress currently being made toward improving society" and "A revolution succeeding in overthrowing the present government would sooner or later lead to a new repressive regime."[17]

The great majority of students (Table 3.9) in the Anglo-Saxon countries (86 percent in Australia, 81 percent in the United States, and 79 percent in Great Britain), in Austria (82 percent), and in Japan (83 percent) agree with the idea that a revolution would lead to a new repressive regime. This opinion is also shared by many Italian (68 percent) and French (67 percent) students. Yugoslav (63 percent), Nigerian (60 percent), and Spanish (58 percent) students are, in general, less likely to believe that a revolution in their country would lead to a new repressive regime.

With regard to the negative consequences of a revolution on the socioeconomic progress which is currently being made toward improving society, students in gen-

[17]These two questions could not be asked in Tunisia.

eral are less in agreement (Table 3.9). However, those who believe there would be negative consequences represent a majority in Austria (65 percent), Great Britain (65 percent), Australia (60 percent), and the United States and Yugoslavia (57 percent). This is a minority opinion in Spain (41 percent), Japan (38 percent), France (37 percent), and Nigeria (36 percent). The proportion in Italy (49 percent) falls in between.

It is interesting to note the Japanese and Yugoslav positions toward the consequences of a revolution. The Japanese are the most numerous in doubting the liberating effect of a revolution and, at the same time, in having no fears of a possible socioeconomic regression. The opposite is true for the Yugoslav students. They foresee a political amelioration and an economic setback. One possible interpretation is that the Japanese are favorable to revolution less out of a desire for political liberalization than for a revision of the socioeconomic objectives of their country. In contrast, Yugoslav students, familiar with the experience of change in government, have less fear of the political repercussions than of the danger to economic and social progress involved in a new revolution.

There are differences by political tendencies in the various countries studied (Table 3.9a), except in Nigeria. Only a minority of far left students fear that a revolution in their country would destroy progress currently being made in the society. This minority is larger in Australia (27 percent), Great Britain (26 percent), and Japan (20 percent) than in the other countries, where it represents less than 15 percent (14 percent in Austria, 13 percent in France, 10 percent in Italy, 9 percent in Spain and in the United States).

Moderate left students are more likely to agree with the statement that a revolution would destroy progress. However, crosscultural differences are marked; in Great Britain (59 percent), Austria (59 percent), and Italy (56 percent) a majority agree. In the other countries, this is the case for a minority of moderate left students (Australia, 41 percent; France, 37 percent; Japan, Nigeria, Spain, and the United States, approximately 30 percent).

The conservative or rightist tendency is not always in agreement with the idea that a revolution necessarily means economic regression. In Spain, only 55 percent of the center, in Japan, 52 percent of the center, in France, 49 percent of the far right, and in Italy, 55 percent of the far right believe that a revolution would annihilate progress already being made. These findings could be interpreted as a sign of social and political dissatisfaction, which is not limited to the left but which appears in all groups, even the most conservative, in every country studied.

In Nigeria about one out of three students, whatever his political identification, agrees with this idea. Thus this question does not appear to discriminate students by political identification.

There is, even among students of the far left, greater fear concerning the political consequences of a revolution than of the future effect on their country's progress. Especially in Australia (75 percent) and Japan (82 percent) the far left fears that a revolution will only result in a regime as regressive as the present one. A minority of the Spanish (26 percent), Italian and French (36 percent), and Austrian (42 percent) far left students express such fear, while the British and Nigerian (52 percent and 53 percent) and American (60 percent) far left students are between these two extremes.

A large majority (70 percent or more) of students on the left in all the countries, except in Nigeria (51 percent) and Spain (49 percent), agree with this idea. On the right also a large majority (more than 70 percent) of students, except in Nigeria (66 percent), agree.

The attitudes of Nigerian students toward the political and the socioeconomic consequences of a revolution appear extremely similar. As the results show, whether conservative, moderate, or radical, only one out of three students believes "a revolution would destroy the progress currently being made" and one out of two believes it would "lead to a new repressive regime."

In Yugoslavia, the various groups respond similarly to the idea of revolution and what will follow. Few students (5 percent) desire a revolution, whatever the results, while 63 percent think that such a revolution would result in a new repressive regime. Differences among the students appear in terms of their relation to the Communist League. Those who refuse to join are more pessimistic (67 percent) about the consequences of a revolution than are members of the League or those who wish to become members (49 percent and 59 percent respectively). The fourth statement, which treats of possible socioeconomic regression following a revolution, is accepted by the majority of all political groups, but especially by the elitists (69 percent).

SACRIFICE

In most countries students are relatively favorable to the elimination of capitalism, although aware that a revolution may present dangers. Are students ready to accept certain sacrifices in order to build a new society? The statement proposed was the following: "In order to build a new society, the freedom and happiness of the present generation must be sacrificed to that of future generations."

The findings (Table 3.9) show that the students are divided into two large groups, according to the economic level of their country. The first group includes relatively poor countries which are in full economic development—Tunisia, Nigeria, and Spain. The second is composed of wealthier countries, industrially more developed. Yugoslavia is in a category by itself. About half of Tunisian (54 percent), Nigerian (49 percent), and Spanish (46 percent) students agree with this idea. It is accepted by only a minority in the other countries. Students ready to accept sacrifices are still relatively numerous in Italy (43 percent) and France, Austria, and Great Britain (about 30 percent) but relatively rare in Australia (17 percent) and in the United States (18 percent).[18] In Japan this feeling is practically nonexistent (9 percent). Yugoslavia, treated separately because of its socialist regime, is not greatly tempted by the idea of sacrifice (20 percent).

These results tend to show that, although hostile to capitalism, students in the majority of countries refuse to sacrifice thier own generation in order to satisfy the needs of the future. This is especially true in the rich Western countries. The notion of sacrifice—which is part of Christian doctrine—is attacked on one side by the liberal, technocratic, bourgeois ideology, which seeks progress, comfort, profit, and general well-being, and on the other by the counterculture, which seeks "the total man," refuses the principle of a society based on the distribution of constraints, and reacts strongly against any deprivations, even when these are shared with others on equal terms. Yugoslav students, little inclined to sacrifice, may be making the same argument.

The data were analyzed in order to see to what extent the idea of personal sacri-

---

[18]The results of the 1977 survey indicate that there are no significant differences in the percentages obtained in France and in the United States on this statement (Table 3.10).

fice is welcomed by the different political groups. It is more frequently accepted on the left than on the right, except in Tunisia, Nigeria, and Spain. In these three countries there is a movement, both on the left and the far left in Spain (50 percent), Nigeria (respectively 47 percent and 62 percent), and Tunisia (65 percent) and on the right (45 percent or more in the three countries), favoring the idea of personal sacrifice necessitated by history. In the other countries the students on the left and especially on the far left, although they accept the idea more readily than do other groups, still manifest a certain reserve with regard to this principle. Those who approve represent about 40 percent of the far left in Italy, Austria, Great Britain, and France, about 20 percent in Australia and the United States, and only 11 percent in Japan. The attitude of the Italian communists is quite distinct from that of the far left, since 57 percent are favorable to the notion of sacrifice versus 44 percent on the far left. In France, no difference emerges between the communists (39 percent) and the far left (38 percent). We should note the clear lack of enthusiasm of the French anarchists (19 percent) in this regard. These results demonstrate, at least in the wealthier countries, that many students on the extreme left do not accept the traditional socialist doctrine which includes collective sacrifice as a revolutionary virtue.

A rapid examination of the attitudes and questions treated up to this point allows us to point out some similarities between the students of those countries included in this present study. First, we remark that in many countries revolution is not regarded as the only means to effect liberation and progress. If we consider the two opinions on which the students most agree and disagree, we can group the countries into two categories. The first includes countries doubting the value of revolution and encouraging democracy; the second includes those where democratic principles such as universal suffrage are upheld but where the elimination of capitalism is desired, without total approval of revolution.

The first group is comprised of students from the three Anglo-Saxon countries, plus the Austrians and the Yugoslavs. For students in these countries revolution would lead to socioeconomic regression. They do not wish to see a revolution based on adventurism, and reject the idea of the abolition of universal suffrage. The second group includes Spain, Italy, France, and Nigeria. Their students judge a possible revolution as nonliberating and would not take part in it without knowing what would replace the existing regime. Acccording to them, elections by universal suffrage are one of the fundamental principles of society. What is important to this group, however, and distinguishes it from the first is its desire to eliminate capitalism.

The desire to eliminate capitalism grows as we move toward the far left students, who most favor this item. This opinion appears, however, as the only one on which most of the far left students agree. Some far left students, in the United States, Australia, and Japan, accord a similar importance to the idea that revolution is not the liberating solution, and might result in a repressive regime. Certain groups on the far left, in Italy, Nigeria, and France, reject the notion that revolution would result in regression. Other results reported in Table 3.9a which should be underlined are the following. In Britain, only a small minority of all political groups believe in the abolition of popular elections. The same is true in Australia, Austria, Japan, and the United States. Both Australian and Japanese students are opposed to sacrificing one's own generation in order to build a hypothetical future. This form of self-sacrifice is, in contrast, seen very favorably by Nigerian and Tunisian students,[19] whether from the left or the right.

The political tendency helps us understand more precisely the findings from all the samples. It underlines the attachment of the majority of the far left (except in Italy, Nigeria, and France) to the principle of universal suffrage and the sceptical attitude of students of the far left in America, Australia, and Japan regarding the merit of revolution and what one may expect after it.

Numerous authors have tried to show that the political orientation of the student is determined in large part by the political institutions in existence and to demonstrate that the degree of political conscience of the students is a function of the degree of tension existing on the national level. We believe that the strong opposition to the status quo which we find in particular among the students in Spain, Italy, and France is due in part to the long revolutionary tradition and to the existence of truly politicized workers' unions, even if, as in Spain, they could not express themselves freely at the time this study was conducted.

In Nigeria, the politicized attitude of many students may be explained by their knowledge of the role they may have to play in the social and political life of their country. They form a privileged class; they are aware of the different systems in the world and can even compare their own system to others. Because of its recent independence, the newness of the country, the lack of political traditions found elsewhere, the future is seen not in terms of continuity or, for the left, of reorganization, but rather in terms of construction and of the organization of society. All these factors result in students' being called upon more quickly than in "old" societies to come to grips with the problems of their country, including that of socialism.

Indeed, a great many of the developing countries, after independence, chose a form of socialism more or less adapted to their particular needs as the most rapid means of transforming their economy and their social system. By contrast, in Anglo-Saxon countries, where the existing political structures leave little room for true opposition, the students are less ready to become involved in politics. Parsons (1962) believes that "the absence of generalized ideological commitment among American students reflects the general political characteristics of the society, which has been a relatively stable system with a strong pluralistic character" (p. 113).

Throughout this study the dominant orientations of the students in each country will become more and more clear as we describe the positions taken on fundamental political questions touching the social system, nationalism, liberty, and peace.

---

[19]Some of these questions could not be asked in Tunisia. We do know that these students are for the elimination of capitalism (especially when they are on the far left), for self-sacrifice, and for the abolition of universal suffrage.

TABLE 3.1a.   Parents' Membership in the Communist League, Yugoslavia (Percent).

PARENTS' MEMBERSHIP IN THE COMMUNIST LEAGUE	STUDENT'S MEMBERSHIP IN THE COMMUNIST LEAGUE			
	Member	*Desire to*	*Refuse to*	*Total sample*
Father	(119)	(173)	(783)	(1,075)
Permanent member*	70	50	25	34
Former member	12	12	11	11
Nonmember*	15	32	59	50
Other	3	6	5	5
Mother	(119)	(174)	(785)	(1,079)
Permanent member*	42	25	14	19
Former member	11	11	6	7
Nonmember*	47	60	78	72
Other	—	4	3	3

*p <.01

TABLE 3.1b.   Parents' Participation in the Struggle for National Liberation, Yugoslavia (Percent).

PARENTS' PARTICIPATION	STUDENT'S MEMBERSHIP IN THE COMMUNIST LEAGUE			
	Member	*Desire to*	*Refuse to*	*Total Sample*
Father	(119)	(174)	(781)	(1,074)
In the armed forces*	61	56	34	40
In clandestine resistance	22	22	27	26
No participation**	12	18	31	27
Other	5	4	9	7
Mother	(119)	(174)	(785)	(1,078)
In the armed forces	13	12	7	8
In clandestine resistance	52	48	42	44
No participation	52	48	42	44
Other	4	4	7	6

*p <.01
**p <.05

TABLE 3.1c.   Reasons Why Yugoslav Students Refused to Join the Communist League (Percent).

	STUDENTS WHO REFUSED TO JOIN THE LEAGUE
	(600)*
1. Results are meager in relation to the time expended in meetings.	32
2. I don't like the opportunism manifested by so many in the Communist League.	29
3. Interpersonal relationships in the League are not satisfactory.	20
4. I do not agree with its program or its philosophy.	18
5. One cannot freely and honestly explain his views in the League.	17
6. I don't like the cliques and what results from them.	16
7. The Communist League is out of date.	15
8. I don't have the time. If I did, I would like to become a member of the Communist League.	15

*More than one response was permitted.

TABLE 3.6a.   Perceived Sources of Political Orientation by Political Tendency (Percent).

The Student Was Influenced By	Austral.	Austria	France	GB	Italy	Japan	Spain	Tunisia	USA	Nigeria
Family										
Right	(39) 26	(78) 39	(42) 37	(88) 44	(58) 33	–	(60) 40	(14) 7	(79) 46	(43) 7
Center	(267) 27	(147) 35	(133) 35	(90) 17	(137) 31	(167) 11	(116) 17	(16) 25*	(129) 29	–
Apoliticals	(184) 17	(42) 41	(150) 23	(148) 18	(190) 21	(44) 5	(170) 22	(33) 30	(90) 28	(54) 14
Left	(228) 13	(132) 23	(203) 33	(199) 37	(196) 23	(124) 7	(264) 15	(50) 14	(138) 28	(45) 9
Far left	(35) 9	(67) 13	(98) 15	(72) 18	(94) 7	(100) 6	(79) 9	(25) 4	(26) 15	(21) 5
Far right	–	–	–	–	(28) 23	–	–	–	–	–
Liberals	–	–	–	–	–	–	–	–	(192) 25	–
Communists	–	–	(49) 35	–	(59) 11	–	–	–	–	–
Friends										
Right	33	21	56	34	27	–	52	57	40	30
Center	30	27	58	53	30	35	64	50*	52	–
Apoliticals	34	10	54	48	39	37	55	58	45	35
Left	43	42	59	43	51	36	61	58	52	29
Far left	37	46	71	49	51	47	51	64	46	48
Far right	–	–	–	–	22	–	–	–	–	–
Liberals	–	–	–	–	–	–	–	–	55	–
Communists	–	–	43	–	55	–	–	–	–	–
Ideologists										
Right	26	35	51	42	48	34	22	71	38	67
Center	32	28	46	53	42	38	29	56*	42	–
Apoliticals	28	50	47	50	30	41	24	76	45	46
Left	31	32	46	53	35	42	32	66	50	69
Far left	40	33	45	52	50	42	47	64	62	48
Far right	–	–	–	–	47	–	–	–	–	–
Liberals	–	–	–	–	–	–	–	–	35	–
Communists	–	–	59	–	44	–	–	–	–	–

*Bourguibist.

TABLE 3.9a. Political Attitudes by Political Self-Definition (Percent).

Australia	RIGHT	CENTER	LEFT	FAR LEFT	APOL.
Popular elections should be abolished because the majority of people cannot be trusted to decide what is good for society.	(40) 15	(268) 15	(229) 17	(32) 22	(182) 21
Capitalism should be eliminated.*	(37) 27	(225) 26	(217) 57	(36) 89	(163) 31
I am in favor of destroying the present political system even without knowing what will replace it.*	(38) 3	(269) 6	(228) 14	(35) 57	(182) 8
A revolution in this country now would destroy the progress currently being made toward improving society.*	(36) 83	(247) 72	(197) 41	(33) 27	(156) 68
A revolution succeeding in overthrowing the present government would sooner or later lead to a new repressive regime.**	(34) 88	(240) 90	(196) 76	(28) 75	(145) 93
In order to build a new society, the freedom and happiness of the present generation must be sacrificed to that of future generations.	(38) 21	(260) 12	(214) 20	(33) 24	(174) 20

Austria	RIGHT	CENTER	LEFT	FAR LEFT	APOL.
Popular elections should be abolished because the majority of people cannot be trusted to decide what is good for society.**	(82) 22	(151) 18	(134) 7	(68) 9	(45) 29
Capitalism should be eliminated.*	¹ 29	28	(135) 73	97	40
I am in favor of destroying the present political system even without knowing what will replace it.*	6	5	(137) 16	(66) 47	11
A revolution in this country now would destroy the progress currently being made toward improving society.*	88	80	(135) 59	(67) 14	(44) 71
A revolution succeeding in overthrowing the present government would sooner or later lead to a new repressive regime.*	87	(152) 91	(136) 81	(66) 42	(45) 96
In order to build a new society, the freedom and happiness of the present generation must be sacrificed to that of future generations.	(81) 17	(151) 29	(135) 28	(68) 40	(44) 30

France	RIGHT	CENT.	LEFT	COMM.	FAR L.	ANAR.	APOL.
Popular elections should be abolished because the majority of people cannot be trusted to decide what is good for society.*	(39) 46	(128) 25	(190) 26	(42) 17	(87) 26	(29) 48	(139) 38
Capitalism should be eliminated.*	(40) 15	(122) 28	(188) 76	(47) 98	(98) 94	(32) 100	(124) 57
I am in favor of destroying the present political system even without knowing what will replace it.*	(43) 0	(132) 5	(191) 20	(43) 33	(96) 48	(31) 68	(144) 17
A revolution in this country now would destroy the progress currently being made toward improving society.*	(37) 49	(104) 60	(168) 37	(43) 19	(90) 13	(30) 17	(118) 43

A revolution succeeding in overthrowing the present government would sooner or later lead to a new repressive regime.*	(39) 92	(121) 88	(188) 67	(45) 7	(93) 36	(29) 52	(130) 85
In order to build a new society, the freedom and happiness of the present generation must be sacrificed to that of future generations.*	(41) 29	(128) 17	(190) 35	(41) 39	(89) 38	(31) 19	(141) 25

Great Britain	RIGHT	CENTER	LEFT	FAR LEFT	APOL.
Popular elections should be abolished because the majority of people cannot be trusted to decide what is good for society.	(88) 15	(90) 14	(191) 12	(68) 12	(144) 24
Capitalism should be eliminated.*	(85) 12	(83) 35	(179) 66	(71) 87	(129) 40
I am in favor of destroying the present political system even without knowing what will replace it.*	(86) 5	(89) 8	(193) 16	(67) 36	(142) 12
A revolution in this country now would destroy the progress currently being made toward improving society.*	(84) 87	(81) 80	(178) 59	(65) 26	(121) 70
A revolution succeeding in overthrowing the present government would sooner or later lead to a new repressive regime.*	(79) 84	(82) 93	(171) 76	52	(118) 85
In order to build a new society, the freedom and happiness of the present generation must be sacrificed to that of future generations.*	(84) 25	(86) 27	(195) 33	(64) 42	(142) 18

Italy	FAR R.	RIGHT	CENT.	LEFT	COMM.	FAR L.	APOL.
Popular elections should be abolished because the majority of people cannot be trusted to decide what is good for society.**	(29) 35	(64) 27	(144) 13	(218) 15	(91) 29	(64) 39	(155) 21
Capitalism should be eliminated.*	(30) 40	30	(141) 57	(205) 76	(113) 100	(70) 100	(157) 70
I am in favor of destroying the present political system even without knowing what will replace it.*	(21) 62	23	(140) 22	(201) 29	(92) 57	(64) 56	45
A revolution in this country now would destroy the progress currently being made toward improving society.*	(20) 55	(58) 72	(122) 74	(175) 56	(97) 7	(63) 10	(140) 56
A revolution succeeding in overthrowing the present government would sooner or later lead to a new repressive regime.*	(23) 83	(48) 79	(105) 71	(156) 76	(85) 52	(58) 36	(120) 73
In order to build a new society, the freedom and happiness of the present generation must be sacrificed to that of future generations.**	(27) 37	(53) 34	(127) 45	(188) 40	(84) 57	(55) 44	(153) 42

(cont.)

TABLE 3.9a.   Continued

Japan	CENTER	LEFT	FAR LEFT	APOL.
Popular elections should be abolished because the majority of people cannot be trusted to decide what is good for society.**	(147) 10	(40) 3	(108) 15	(102) 14
Capitalism should be eliminated.*	(121) 28	(39) 62	(104) 75	(85) 44
I am in favor of destroying the present political system even without knowing what will replace it.*	(146) 16	(40) 13	(114) 48	(98) 26
A revolution in this country now would destroy the progress currently being made toward improving society.*	(110) 52	(31) 32	(101) 20	(81) 44
A revolution succeeding in overthrowing the present government would sooner or later lead to a new repressive regime.*	(138) 93	(38) 84	(106) 82	(97) 94
In order to build a new society, the freedom and happiness of the present generation must be sacrificed to that of future generations.	(148) 9	(41) 12	(116) 11	(100) 4

Nigeria	RIGHT	CRITIC.	LEFT	FAR LEFT	DESCR.	APOL.
Popular elections should be abolished because the majority of people cannot be trusted to decide what is good for society.*	(41) 21	(36) 31	(42) 36	(21) 43	(27) 30	(57) 19
Capitalism should be eliminated.*	34	(35) 66	72	(20) 75	(25) 60	(53) 60
I am in favor of destroying the present political system even without knowing what will replace it.**	27	(30) 33	(40) 30	45	(24) 22	(45) 20
A revolution in this country now would destroy the progress currently being made toward improving society.	(37) 43	(33) 33	30	(21) 33	(26) 38	(54) 35
A revolution succeeding in overthrowing the present government would sooner or later lead to a new repressive regime.*	(35) 66	(34) 68	(39) 51	(15) 53	(20) 75	(47) 51
In order to build a new society, the freedom and happiness of the present generation must be sacrificed to that of future generations.**	(41) 46	56	(44) 48	(21) 62	(26) 54	(53) 42

Spain	RIGHT	CENTER	LEFT	FAR LEFT	APOL.
Popular elections should be abolished because the majority of people cannot be trusted to decide what is good for society.*	(61) 34	(116) 30	(268) 16	(79) 16	(169) 32
Capitalism should be eliminated.*	(58) 52	(108) 74	(272) 90	(83) 100	(164) 71
I am in favor of destroying the present political system even without knowing what will replace it.*	(57) 12	18	(262) 41	(77) 56	(160) 17
A revolution in this country now would destroy the progress currently being made toward improving society.*	(55) 75	(109) 55	(261) 28	(79) 9	(161) 58
A revolution succeeding in overthrowing the present government would sooner or later lead to a new repressive regime.*	(51) 76	(98) 67	(235) 49	(78) 26	(146) 75

In order to build a new society, the freedom and happiness of the present generation must be sacrificed to that of future generations.*	(58) 45	(117) 45	(269) 50	(75) 52	(174) 37

Tunisia²	RIGHT	BOURGUIB.	LEFT	FAR LEFT	APOL.
Popular elections should be abolished because the majority of people cannot be trusted to decide what is good for society.*	(15) 33	(15) 33	(43) 30	(23) 65	(29) 41
Capitalism should be eliminated.*	(11) 18	(11) 55	(49) 69	(24) 92	(25) 48
In order to build a new society, the freedom and happiness of the present generation must be sacrificed to that of future generations.	(13) 46	(16) 44	(47) 65	(23) 65	(30) 40

United States	RIGHT	CENTER	LIB.	LEFT	FAR L.	APOL.
Popular elections should be abolished because the majority of people cannot be trusted to decide what is good for society.	(79) 11	(126) 8	(191) 7	(133) 10	(23) 4	(89) 14
Capitalism should be eliminated.*	(77) 5	(117) 14	(185) 25	(125) 59	65	(82) 29
I am in favor of destroying the present political system even without knowing what will replace it.*	(80) 1	(128) 3	(193) 4	(133) 9	(25) 44	(87) 7
A revolution in this country now would destroy the progress currently being made toward improving society.*	(75) 85	(112) 73	(174) 60	(121) 32	(22) 9	(74) 55
A revolution succeeding in overthrowing the present government would sooner or later lead to a new repressive regime.*	(78) 93	(94) 80	(149) 82	(112) 72	(20) 60	88
In order to build a new society, the freedom and happiness of the present generation must be sacrificed to that of future generations.*	(75) 12	(122) 16	(180) 19	(127) 19	(26) 19	(86) 21

Yugoslavia, by political self-definition	IDEAL.	REAL.	HUMAN.	ELIT.	INDIV.
Popular elections should be abolished because the majority of people cannot be trusted to decide what is good for society.*	(240) 21	(489) 19	(162) 22	(25) 32	(41) 44
Capitalism should be eliminated.*	61	(488) 37	(161) 32	(26) 39	32
I am in favor of destroying the present political system even without knowing what will replace it.**	5	(492) 4	(162) 4	12	12
A revolution in this country now would destroy the progress currently being made toward improving society.	(236) 58	(488) 57	(160) 52	69	54
A revolution succeeding in overthrowing the present government would sooner or later lead to a new repressive regime.	(240) 59	(490) 63	(161) 67	(25) 64	(39) 69
In order to build a new society, the freedom and happiness of the present generation must be sacrificed to that of future generations.	(238) 26	(491) 93	(162) 14	(26) 27	(41) 12

(cont.)

TABLE 3.9a.   Continued

Yugoslavia, by membership in the Communist League	MEMBER	DESIRE TO	REFUSE TO
Popular elections should be abolished because the majority of people cannot be trusted to decide what is good for society.	(118) 14	(173) 19	(784) 25
Capitalism should be eliminated.	(119) 56	(174) 54	(781) 38
I am in favor of destroying the present political system even without knowing what will replace it.	5	(175) 5	(785) 5
A revolution in this country now would destroy the progress currently being made toward improving society.	(110) 56	61	(780) 56
A revolution succeeding in overthrowing the present government would sooner or later lead to a new repressive regime.	(115) 49	(174) 59	(782) 67
In order to build a new society, the freedom and happiness of the present generation must be sacrificed to that of future generations.	(118) 18	(173) 27	(783) 19

*p <.01
**p <.05
1. When the number is the same as in the preceding item, it is not repeated.
2. In Tunisia only these three statements appeared on the questionnaire.

Chapter 4

Sociopolitical Attitudes

The student protest movement had as targets not only the university but also the values and the sociopolitical practices of society in general. The criticisms and the questioning of society cannot, however, be detached from the specific national contexts. This should be kept in mind when we look at the students' judgments of their society as a global entity.

Evaluation of the Good and Bad Aspects of Society

The general attitudes to political and cultural issues, including the role of the university, were determined in the first place by means of questions relating to global judgments of the situation in the students' own country.

Three questions touched on student attitudes toward society as a whole, toward the university, and toward the student movement: "Every society has its good and bad features. In this society would you say the *balance* is on the good or the bad side?" The other two questions were similar, the word "society" being replaced by "university" or "student movement."[1] The respondents could check one of the alternatives—"good" or "bad."[2] In addition, they were asked to note what they considered the two best and the two worst aspects of their society.

SOCIETY: PREDOMINANCE OF GOOD OR BAD ASPECTS

Does one really live so well in Anglo-Saxon countries, or are these students truly optimistic in comparison with those from the other countries of the study? The results of the judgment of society (Table 4.1—page 62) show that 78 percent of the students in Great Britain, 73 percent in the United States, and 70 percent in Australia believe that the good aspects outweigh the bad; only about a third of the French and Italians (37 percent), 34 percent of the Spanish students, and 33 percent of the Nigerians agree. The number of satisfied students is still smaller in Tunisia (25 percent) and in Japan (24 percent).[3]

[1]We treat here the opinions about society. Those concerning the university and the student movement will be considered later—the university in Chapter 5 and the protest movement in Chapter 7.

[2]In all but two countries there were only these two alternatives. In Austria and Yugoslavia the questionnaire included another response: "as many good as bad aspects."

[3]Germans (60 percent) and English-speaking Canadians (75 percent) judged their society rather favorably in comparison to French-speaking Canadians (35 percent).

TABLE 4.1.   Predominance of the Good or the Bad Aspects of Society According to the Students—Total Sample, Right, Left, and Far Left (Percent).[1]

	AUSTRAL.	AUS.	FR.	GB	IT.	JAP.	NIG.	SP.	TUN.	USA	YUG.
Total sample	(740)	(444)	(657)	(585)	(670)	(419)	(225)	(698)	(138)	(640)	(1,076)
Predominance of the—											
Good aspects*	70	33	37	78	37	24	33	34	25	73	36
Bad aspects*	30	26	61	22	60	74	66	62	73	26	16
Right[2]	(40)	(77)	(38)	(88)	(60)	(147)	(38)	(60)	(14)[3]	(79)	
Predominance of the—											
Good aspects*	88	56	76	85	47	28	32	63	7	89	
Bad aspects*	13	14	21	15	50	68	68	30	93	11	
Left	(227)	(125)	(189)	(192)	(210)	(43)	(43)	(265)	(48)	(135)[4]	
Predominance of the—											
Good aspects*	59	30	30	80	41	12	33	20	13	59	
Bad aspects*	41	33	68	20	57	88	67	77	88	41	
Far left	(33)	(63)	(91)	(70)	(63)	(121)	(21)	(82)	(23)	(26)	
Predominance of the—											
Good aspects*	30	13	6	59	11	17	19	6	17	46	
Bad aspects*	70	65	93	41	89	83	81	92	83	50	

1. Percentages total less than 100, since some students replied that the society has as many good as bad aspects.
2. In Japan, since the grouping *right* did not exist, we have quoted the center results.
3. Progovernment: 63 percent good, 38 percent bad.
4. Liberals: 77 percent good, 23 percent bad.
*p < .01

The results obtained in Austria and Yugoslavia are difficult to compare with others because of the third alternative the question had, "There are as many good as bad aspects in society." Forty percent of the Austrians and 48 percent of the Yugoslavs preferred this ambivalent answer to a completely positive (33 percent in Austria, 36 percent in Yugoslavia) or completely negative (26 percent in Austria, 16 percent in Yugoslavia) response.

Political orientation is clearly related to one's judgment of society (Table 4.1). We are not surprised to find that the closer the student is to the majority tendency in his country, the more favorable is his opinion of his society, and vice versa. The national context has an important role in this regard, however, and it is striking to note for each political group the divergent points of view between Anglo-Saxon students and those from other countries—a divergence which is more evident in the case of the left and the far left than among the moderates or those on the right.

Students who define their own position as on the right are in most countries more satisfied with their society. The rightists most numerous with this opinion are the Anglo-Saxons (85 percent or more) and the French (76 percent), followed by the Spanish (63 percent), and the Austrians (56 percent). In contrast, these students are in the minority in Italy (47 percent) and especially in Nigeria (32 percent), Japan (28 percent),[4] and Tunisia (7 percent).[5]

On the left we find a clear difference between the Anglo-Saxon countries and the other countries studied. Only 20 percent of the students on the left in Great Britain and 41 percent in the United States and in Australia judge their society negatively, while the percentage in the case of Tunisians and Japanese rises to 88 percent. The satisfaction of a large majority of leftist students in Great Britain and in Australia may be explained by the alternation of conservative and labor governments. The left in these two countries certainly does not have the same characteristics as elsewhere where the left has so far not been in power.

The number of dissatisfied students grows as we proceed toward the far left. The proportions are higher than 80 percent in all the countries studied except Great Britain (41 percent) and the United States (50 percent). The far left in Australia, however, differs from the other Anglo-Saxon countries in that 70 percent criticize their society. Unlike many other countries, Great Britain has not undergone many violent student manifestations, yet the same is true of Australia, where students on the far left are much more likely to condemn their society.

In the United States the relative lack of criticism of many students who call themselves leftists poses again the question of the definition of the left and the far left in different countries. According to Keniston (1967), the protester rarely demonstrates because his own interests are jeopardized, but rather because he perceives injustices being done to others less fortunate than himself. It is possible, therefore, that a difference exists between protesting students in the United States and those of all other countries, with the former more idealistic and more accustomed to material abundance.

In Austria, a majority of rightist students judge their society positively (56 percent) as compared to only a minority of leftists (30 percent) and even fewer of the ex-

---

[4]No category on the right existed for this country. The percentage represents, therefore, students classified as center.

[5]We must note, however, that students who identified themselves as Bourguibists judged their society favorably (63 percent) in comparison.

treme left (13 percent). In Yugoslavia, student members of the Communist League or those desiring to become members (47 percent and 49 percent respectively, Table 4.1a, page 92) are more favorable to their society than those who refuse to join this organization (31 percent). Idealists (46 percent), egalitarians (35 percent), and humanitarians (32 percent) more often judge their society to be good than do elitists (23 percent) or individualists (24 percent).

The findings confirm the conclusion reached in the previous chapter that protest had a different character in each country, in terms of both the impact it had on society and the demands made. Student movements had greater repercussions in France, Italy, Japan, and the United States[6] than in Great Britain and, especially, Nigeria and Australia. There are also marked national and regional variations in the nature of protest. Students from Latin countries in Europe, for example, are strongly politicized, and often speak in terms of revolution and of the elimination of capitalism. Students in other countries, the Anglo-Saxons in particular, are looking for different solutions. They show great distrust of revolution and other positions taken by the traditional leftist movements. Indeed, in the United States and Great Britain the students on the far left appear relatively satisfied with their society and on the whole judge it positively, which is rare in the other countries. These data throw doubt on the notion of the universality of the student movement. The long-term goal, the methods, and the types of activity may be similar, but the underlying ideology is different.

THE 1977 SURVEY

In 1977 the proportion of American students who evaluate their country positively is still higher (Table 4.2)—84 percent as compared to 73 percent in 1970—whereas in France it has diminished—29 percent in 1977 as compared to 37 percent in 1970. When we compare the results by political orientation, we see that in both countries the right is more favorable—in the United States 100 percent as compared to 89 percent, in France 83 percent as compared to 76 percent. The difference can be seen when we compare liberal students in the United States (96 percent as compared with 77 percent in 1970) and those of the moderate left in France (14 percent as compared with 30 percent in 1970).

SPECIFIC ISSUES

Open-ended questions asking students to give in detail what they regarded as the good and the bad aspects of their society allow us to clarify the very diversified preoccupations of the students.

THE TWO BEST ASPECTS OF SOCIETY

In every country the first answer most often given to the question "What are, in your opinion, the two best features of your society?" was "freedom." This concept included the notions of freedom of expression, of thought, of action, of the press,

---

[6]In this country protest seems less directed toward the political system and more toward social and moral institutions, as we shall see later.

etc., all based on a nonrepressive society where tolerance of others and respect for their rights exist:

Great Britain

No vicious security police system.

Not a police state.

TABLE 4.2.   Predominance of the Good or the Bad Aspects of Society According to Students, 1977 Survey (Percent).

	FRANCE	UNITED STATES
Total sample	(85)	(104)
Predominance of the—		
Good aspects*	29	84
Bad aspects*	65	16
Right	(6)	(25)
Predominance of the—		
Good aspects	83	100
Bad aspects	17	0
Center	(9)	(28)
Predominance of the—		
Good aspects	78	86
Bad aspects	11	14
Left	(35)	(23) Liberal
Predominance of the—		
Good aspects*	14	96
Bad aspects*	80	4
Far left	(15)	(4)
Predominance of the—		
Good aspects	0	(1)[a]
Bad aspects	100	(3)
Apolitical	(18)	(16)
Predominance of the—		
Good aspects**	44	63
Bad aspects	44	38

*p < .01
**p < .05
[a]When absolute numbers are small, no percentages are given.

United States

Freedom to go wherever you like and do whatever you like to do.

Room for individual differences.

A person's ability to express himself, to put his convictions into both words and action, and the possibility of others to decide for themselves when confronted with such convictions.

France

The Bohemian life is possible.

Many students qualify their reply, describing freedom as "relative," or speak of "a certain degree of freedom," or make comparisons with the freedom possible in describing other countries:

France

A certain margin of freedom.

Freedom—it's far from what I'd like it to be, but it's better than that in other countries.

Freedom, in comparison to certain totalitarian countries.

Nigeria

Relative freedom, even under a military regime.

Freedom in contrast with what exists in other African countries.

United States

Freedom is not as limited as most people think, compared to the majority of other countries.

Fundamental freedoms exist, which is not true for other societies.

We should note that "freedom," as "the best aspect of society," is often mentioned in countries like the United States or Great Britain but much less frequently in Tunisia.

Economic progress is also frequently noted as one of the best aspects of society in all countries, although less often in Nigeria. Students believe that their country has achieved a better standard of living or a higher quality of life, comfort, prosperity and wealth:

United States

Most people have enough to eat.

France

Buying power.

The lessening of poverty.

A worker can buy an automobile.

Students in Tunisia, Great Britain, Italy, France, and Nigeria are particularly favorable to developments in the scientific domain—e.g., medicine, research, social sciences:

United States

Research, which will better the human condition, by studying man and his behavior.

France

The progress of science.

The development of the social sciences, which will decrease, if not destroy, all the prejudices of man.

Into this category, which we might entitle "progress for mankind," enters the notion of access to culture and to education:

United States

We are more in contact with culture and the arts.

France

Culture is little by little becoming more available to all.

Great Britain

More education is available to all.

Nigerian and Tunisian students speak of "the campaign against illiteracy." In Great Britain several students mentioned the attempt in their country to organize social services, which include the right to education, good health care, unemployment allotments, and social security.

The growing awareness of social and political problems and the resulting involvement appear as positive traits, important to society, in Italy, France, Tunisia, and Nigeria:

France

Awareness of young people.

Desire to change.

The awareness of the social, economic, and cultural mechanisms of repression.

In the two countries of the Third World in this study, this awakening is translated into an awareness of the ties which unite their country to certain others. This feeling of "fraternity" and of "unity" (implicit or official) is based on the "similarity" between countries. This similarity may center on common problems of development, geography, or ethnic, racial, or religious community, for instance:

Nigeria

African brotherhood.

Tunisia

Arab unity.

These are perceived as positive factors leading to national unification and the end of regional factionalism in Tunisia or tribal conflict in Nigeria.

The movement away from certain traditional values may also be perceived as a form of social progress. French students, for instance, mention sexual freedom among the positive aspects of society. In contrast, certain traditional structures like the "extended family system" are mentioned by some Nigerian students as among the best aspects of their society.

In the United States and Great Britain, the democratic nature of their society is frequently cited by students as a positive trait:

United States

In our society we can vote for the person who best represents our ideas.

Great Britain

The balance of power.

Dialogue between the people and the government.

Americans, British, and Australians mention the idea of equal opportunity and that of social mobility:

United States

You are not assigned to a function in life; you choose your own occupation.

Equal opportunity, regardless of race, creed or religion.

The most frequently mentioned responses in Nigeria and in Spain concern interpersonal relationships and human qualities:

Nigeria

Personal generosity.

Hospitality.

Respect for elders.

Finally, in most countries students do recognize one or two good aspects of their society, whatever their general judgment may be. In Tunisia and Spain, however, compared to the others, judgments are much more unfavorable, and many students declare that their countries have no characteristics which they could support.

The analysis by political tendency shows that students in different countries, even when they identify themselves similarly, still differ in their appreciation of society. Thus in Tunisia, Great Britain, Spain, Italy, and Austria rightist students tend to underline progress in the scientific—as well as the cultural and economic—domain and, occasionally, freedom. The leftists speak more in terms of a growing awareness, of the development of political consciousness, etc. Rightist students in Italy mention traditional values—the family, religion, and so forth.

There seems to exist a fundamental divergence between the right and the left in what they consider the best aspects of society: for the right, results count; for the left, the development of a critical faculty and the change in man from a passive to an active role are given greater importance.

THE TWO WORST ASPECTS OF SOCIETY

The replies to the question "What are the two worst aspects of society?" are very diverse and cover a variety of topics.

The feeling that there exist in every society certain specific negative traits which endanger that society appeared in every country included in the study (although to a lesser degree in Australia and in Nigeria). The students criticize, for example, hypocrisy, egoism, and irresponsibility:

United States

We don't think enough about our neighbors; we are too preoccupied with ourselves.

Freedom to forget about other people.

Inconsistency between what we say and what we stand for.

France

Distance between what we say and what we do.

Egoism of French nationalism.

The negation of responsibility.

The hypocrisy of most of us in conducting our personal affairs.

People think too much about their personal happiness.

Great Britain

An egoistic, egocentric attitude.

The problem of racism is frequently mentioned in Australia, Great Britain, and the United States. The students speak of discrimination by color and the repression of certain radical groups. Certain Italian respondents feel a general moral degradation in their country:

Absence of morality.
Moral decadence.

Students criticize the low level of human behavior and the loss of values but also, in relation to the present social and political situation, the government and the political system. The latter is seen as a vast bureaucracy. Some students speak of the difficulty in introducing reforms into this world:

United States

No communication between bureaucracies.

Its innate ability to form a bureaucracy rather than to act.

The seeming inability of the political machine to make any progress.

The government is too big to be efficient.

The government's ability to ignore the people's will.

France

Impotent government.

Too many political parties.

Great Britain

A democracy so complex that it's disintegrating into a complete muddle.

The total confusion of democracy; its slowness to act.

People's lack of control in government.

The government is not responsive to issues ranging from war to the draft to drugs.

This inefficiency is mentioned especially in Nigeria, but frequently also in Italy and in Austria.

The topics of inequality, social injustice, and exploitation appear often in the replies of students in Spain, Italy, Australia, Great Britain, and the United States, but particularly in France:

France

Exploitation of the majority by a powerful minority.

Continuation of misery.

Exploitation pure and simple by people who are not even aware of what they are doing.

Flagrant inequality.

Great Britain

The tendency of the so-called legal system to discriminate between the rich and the poor.

The fact that some people still must live in disgusting slums.

Bad living conditions and few prospects for the lowest classes.

The feeling that society has become more and more depersonalized characterizes the responses of the Americans, French, British, and Japanese. According to them, human values are overpowered by materialism and the goods of the consuming society. The individual can no longer exist in such an industrialized society, whose goal is no longer to serve man, but to utilize him:

United States

Society prohibits people from being individuals.

Depersonalization by bureaucracy, technology; lack of spontaneity.

Insensitivity to the individual.

France

The alienation of the personality.

Dehumanization of man.

The loss of individuality.

The impression of alienation is especially felt by Americans. It is one of the most frequent criticisms they level against society.

Students also evoke the factors which lead to these conditions and which reinforce them. Mass communication and the media, as well as materialism, are perceived as "brutalizing":

United States

Conditioning by advertising media deprives people of real freedom.

France

Brutalizing of people by the media.

People no longer can think for themselves. They are conditioned in their ideas, their actions.

Great Britain

Preoccupation with materialistic values, with money.

Everything is based on money.

Student protest movements may themselves appear as one of the worst aspects of society. This criticism, frequent in the United States, is rather rare in other countries:

United States

Society's willingness to tolerate those who wish to destroy it.

The violence that has overtaken our ability to settle differences.

Elements in our society that tend to tear down the system.

Preoccupation with violence.

Some Japanese students are preoccupied by ecology and pollution. Some Spanish students and, surprisingly, some Australians complain of a lack of freedom in their societies.

In Nigeria and Tunisia the situation of the developing country and the accompanying problems are often seen as dangers:

Nigeria

General backwardness due to the lack of technological advancement.

Tunisia

Economic problems of an underdeveloped country.

In addition, there are problems posed by Western civilization: it has had an influence on every country in the Third World, but is not usually assimilated into the country's own traditions. It has sometimes been taken as a model, which devalues the specificity of the indigenous culture:

Nigeria

Tendency to always ape the white neocolonial mentality.

Lack of pride in the African personality.

Tunisia

Little assimilation of imported value systems.

Nigerian students speak of two problems in particular which are (1) tribalism

Tribalism is rampant. This endangers the integrity and even the existence of our nation.

Ethnic strife.

Unjustified hatred between tribes.

and (2) corruption:

Corruption pervades every aspect of society.

Leaders steal money by the millions while the people live in misery.

Tendency to view bribery and corruption as one's own share of the national pie.

Everybody who becomes a leader starts to grab wealth for himself.

A student explains this tragic situation by stating:

The majority of young people, intellectually bright but coming from poor homes, have no opportunities for advancement, except through bribery.

The reproaches against society vary as a function of the national context but also of political opinions. In general, students on the left criticize capitalism and social injustice, except for Australia, where the leftists also condemn depersonalization and a society of consumption. In France and in Spain the students on the right criticize specific individual, negative traits; in Austria, the inefficiency of the government; in Italy and Tunisia, the protest movements; in Great Britain, violence; and finally, in Australia, the failings of the government, and protest movements. These students reproach the government for not knowing how to suppress the "leftist" movements. Respect for "the right to disagree"—a fundamental, democratic principle of freedom—does not usually count for these groups. It is perceived by them as a weakness and as an abandonment of power.

The Yugoslav questionnaire did not include the open-ended questions. However, several forced-choice questions provide a picture of how Yugoslav students evaluate some central features of their society and political systems.

The results indicate that 64 percent agree with the following statement: "The official policy of today is characterized by hypocrisy; that is, there is a wide gap between what is said and what is done." Eighty-two percent agree that "the old revolutionary parties have become bourgeois or bureaucratic and no longer represent a revolutionary force. They must, therefore, whether they like it or not, yield their role to the revolutionary students" (Table 4.1b[7]).

A series of questions dealt with Yugoslavia's present foreign policy and present national internal policy (Table 4.1c). At least two-thirds of the students think that the population has every reason to be satisfied with the foreign policy of their country. The students are less clearly in favor of their country's internal policies. According to about half of the students, Yugoslavs should appreciate, first of all, "the process of democratization" (57 percent), then the reorganization of the Communist League (47 percent), the development of workers' self-management (45 percent), and a system of rotation of high government officials at the level of the republics and of the Federation (45 percent). Only one-third (36 percent) judge satisfactory the efforts of the government to raise the standard of living. Economic performance is the most contested point: in fact, only 7 percent of the students think that the people should be satisfied with it.

Other questions approach social problems such as individualism, the search for profits, the social success of workers' children, and the motivations of politicians. Seventy-nine percent agree that "most of our people seek only personal profit and have no understanding of their fellow men." In addition, 63 percent believe that "children of workers and peasants have little chance to succeed in our society" and that "most politicians seek power rather than clinging to principles and ideals" (Table 4.1b).

An additional question specific to the Yugoslav study dealt with the desire to live abroad. Students were asked whether they ever thought of living and working abroad, permanently or temporarily, and, if so, to indicate the countries of their preference. Twenty percent of the students would like to work at least temporarily outside of their country (Table 4.1d). Yugoslav students—and this finding is interesting—are more attracted to Western countries (and more precisely, to Anglo-Saxon countries) than to socialist countries. Nearly 50 percent of them would like to work and live in Canada or the United States. Then comes Great Britain (39 percent), followed by the Scandinavian countries (33 percent), France (29 percent), Switzerland (27 percent), and West Germany (24 percent). Few are attracted to the Soviet Union or to any other socialist country (7 percent).

Above all else, these students seek from their sojourn abroad an improvement in their professional status (65 percent). Some are attracted by the hope of a higher salary (35 percent). Others (23 percent) hope to discover a more exciting and colorful way of living, and to flee the monotony which seems to be part of their system. Very few indicate they would leave for political reasons (1 percent).

In conclusion, we may identify two categories of responses: those which concern the present Yugoslav system directly and those which are more general in nature.

[7]Tables 4.1b through 4.1d are on pages 93–94.

The students show a rather critical attitude toward their country's internal policies, mainly those relating to the economy. They also appear rather disillusioned by politics, their leaders, and their political parties. Some students wish to travel or even to stay in Western countries; they are not attracted by other socialist republics. They hope to find in these other countries better working conditions, means of improving professional skills, and, some of them, a more exciting life style. Progress, money, and exciting life style—such is the image of the West.

Freedom of Expression

One of the major themes of the student protest movement, whatever the country, was the issue of freedom of expression and the condemnation of all forms of repression, whether direct or insidious.

Three questions deal with what the students think of freedom in their country. The first one poses the problem of freedom in the immediate environment of the student: "To what extent do you feel free to express your political point of view within your university?" The respondents are asked to agree with the following statement: "Freedom of expression and freedom of the press represent true achievements of our political system." The third deals with censorship: "Do you agree or not that all censorship should be abolished?"

FREEDOM OF EXPRESSION AT THE UNIVERSITY

Except for students in Spain and in Tunisia, most of the respondents stated that they can express relatively freely their political point of view in the university (Table 4.3, see p. 81). In the United States, Great Britain, and Australia the percentage was at least 85 percent, in Yugoslavia 80 percent, and in Austria 72 percent. The majority of students in Nigeria (66 percent), Italy (65 percent), France (63 percent), and Japan (62 percent) have this same feeling of freedom of expression. In contrast, such students are relatively rare in Tunisia (26 percent) and in Spain (21 percent). In Tunisia (53 percent) and especially in Spain (70 percent) the majority felt not at all free to express their political opinions within their university. This feeling of constraint is shared by only one out of five students in France, Italy, Japan, Nigeria, and Yugoslavia, and by less than 15 percent in Australia, Austria, Great Britain, and the United States.

In Yugoslavia, students who did not feel free explained in general[8] that they preferred to remain silent (25 percent) or did not feel the need to share their opinions with others (21 percent). Some, however, mentioned fear of reprisals (24 percent), either because they had already been victims (16 percent) or because they were afraid (8 percent), or thought that this might make them unpopular or seem ridiculous (9 percent and 6 percent respectively). Students in the Communist League mentioned more often than the others this fear of becoming unpopular or ridiculous, while nonmembers indicated that they preferred to remain silent and keep their opinions to themselves.

[8]In the Yugoslav questionnaire, the students could note why they did not feel free at the university by means of a multiple-choice question.

In the other countries, we attempted to see how the perception of freedom of expression at the university was modified by political orientation (Table 4.3a). In general, politicized students of the right or the left feel less free to express their political opinions than moderate or apolitical students. Political orientation and its role in the perception of freedom may be demonstrated by the students' comments. We look first at students who *feel free* to express their political opinions at the university. This freedom is often seen as a result of the political system of their country:

United States

One of the great aspects about our system of government and our university system is that we are free to express our ideas. Especially at school. There is an open atmosphere of give and take permeated by a genuine interest and concern on the part of the students. [student on right]

In Tunisia, few students feel there is freedom at the university, and only one named freedom as one of the qualities of the system:

Freedom of expression exists because we are in a democratic regime. [Bourguibist]

Other students feel free to express themselves because they feel they are in the majority:

United States

I am not in the minority. [leftist]

France

I have the same opinions as most of my friends. [moderate]

Tunisia

The majority of students have the same opinions as me. [moderate]

Most students, especially in "liberal" countries, refer to the moderation of their own opinions, which could not be perceived as dangerous by those in power:

France

I don't really upset the applecart. [left]

United States

They could not care less how much rhetoric I use as long as what I say doesn't appear to be taken seriously. [left]

"This is the kind of place where most people are receptive to all kinds of ideas and opinions and among individuals the worst result of expressing an opinion would be a heated argument, nothing drastic. Most people here live and let live. [moderate]

and which allow for a certain amount of opportunism:

United States

"In this university we have a wide spectrum of political orientations. Everyone here on both extremes of the political spectrum in particular is quite vociferous in his ideologies. Me, with my middle-of-the-road politics, I can adjust myself to any kind of political discussion. [liberal]

Some students explain the existence of freedom of expression by the indifference of the student body and by the university apparatus itself:

Great Britain

No one listens; no one pays attention. [apolitical]

No one takes notice; people care so little or are so unsure of their feelings that they will listen to any argument without any strong reaction. Also, college authorities are fairly flexible. [left]

Because the students and the staff here walk around with their heads in the sand and are not interested. [far left]

France

People are indifferent. [moderate]

Some students say they feel free at the university but then add some qualifications which show that, in fact, they are referring more to their interactions with their friends than to an atmosphere of freedom at the university:

Tunisia

Freedom of expression is possible as long as one is in a more or less homogeneous milieu. [moderate]

France

I only talk with my friends. [moderate]

United States

My circle of friends tends to support my own convictions. [liberal]

Some students evoke the notion of freedom of expression, not as an element of the political situation, but rather as a fundamental general value, which implies respect for others:

Great Britain

If one is genuine in one's belief, others respect your point of view. [right]

United States

I respect others and I would hope they do the same. [apolitical]

For others, when one has political ideas to convey, what is important is not to worry about other people's reactions, but to have courage:

Tunisia

If I want to say something, I don't care if others agree with me or not. It is a question of courage and of personality. [leftist]

Finally, some students explain that they feel no external restraint but are blocked by inhibitions such as timidity, or they may simply not have any opinions on some subjects.

Thus, apart from those who boast of the freedom of expression at their university, students in general believe that they can express their opinions because they are not risking anything. These students may be conservative, moderate, or indifferent, relying on the apathy of others to protect them or expressing themselves only among their friends. On the other hand, students who do not feel free tend to refer to the general situation in their country.

The following remarks from far left Tunisian students demonstrate this sense that absence of freedom goes beyond the university. The reason, according to them, is obvious:

> It's self-evident, isn't it?
>
> 1+2=3.
>
> You will understand without me telling you.
>
> You ought to already know.

Quite often, their feeling of restraint is reinforced by the idea that spies pollute the university:

> Everything is reported.
>
> The presence of numerous spies.
>
> When one says something at the university, there may be informers—the consequences could be serious.
>
> The university is infested by secret agents.
>
> The existence of the police among us.

Some students state that the university is not autonomous and depends directly on the government:

> The university conforms to the government.
>
> The administrators are closely tied in to the government.
>
> The intervention of the government.

According to some Tunisian students, the absence of freedom of expression is directly due to the political regime of their country:

> A country with only one political party is not a country of freedom of expression.
>
> The consequence of only one party which is weak and opportunistic.
>
> Reactionary government.
>
> Repercussions from the government are unlimited.
>
> Unfortunate consequences.
>
> Any criticism is felt like an insult.

Tunisian students who feel free to express themselves are generally favorable to the government: either Bourguibists (50 percent) or conservatives (40 percent). We should note that the reasons given in explanation for this freedom are based more on an acceptance of the political situation and its rules than on a real impression of freedom of expression:

> In any case, when I want to explain my point of view, I respect in certain ways the external restraints relative to my country. [centrist]

In Nigeria, students who believe they have little or no freedom of expression blame the military government and ethnic conflicts:

My country has a military type of government, where even though there are some elements of democracy, people are not completely free to express their political point of view.

You cannot express your opinion as you would like because of the military regime. Even though there is freedom to speak and to criticize, it is somehow suppressed.

Owing to the recent war in Nigeria, people of my ethnic group are merely tolerated and are not really wanted.

On the other hand, in those countries where freedom of expression has in principle been acquired, numerous students on the left, the far left, and the right deny its existence. We may deduce from this that censorship is not inherent in the system, but, at the university, results from the intolerance of various political groups toward others:

United States

The deference required by the authoritarian structure of the university inhibits all forms of freedom of expression. [far leftist]

France

The repressive attitude of the administration and of part of the teaching staff. [communist]

Great Britain

What one might say could influence his future career or result in black marks on his personal record. [far leftist]

In general, moderates and conservatives in particular complain about the intolerance of the extremists:

France

The adverse groups on the far right intervened quickly and acted. [leftist]

We are faced with extremists on the right and the left. [socialist]

The intolerance of the militants on the far left makes all dialogue impossible. [socialist]

Great Britain

I would be lynched by the two extremes. [moderate]

Students also mention the social pressure of the university environment:

United States

It's not chic these days for a college student to be somewhat conservative, or even moderate. You really can become a social outcast. [moderate]

No formal restrictions or threats of administrative action exist, but there is some sense of being ridiculed and harassed by other students. [apolitical]

France

There is a strong psychological pressure to be on the left. [socialist]

In Great Britain and in France some women attribute the absence of freedom of expression to sexism:

Great Britain

When it comes to discussing women, everyone just laughs and says that they are already liberated enough. [socialist]

France

Men don't listen to us when we talk about politics. [leftist]

THE 1977 SURVEY

For the total USA sample the results (Table 4.4) are identical to those obtained in the main study: 87 percent still feel completely free to express their political point of view at their university. In France there is a slight decrease of respondents agreeing that they are completely free (57 percent as compared to 63 percent in 1970).

TABLE 4.4. Freedom of Expression in France and the United States, 1977 Survey (Percent).

	FRANCE	UNITED STATES
I feel free to express my political point of view within my university	(90)	(106)
Free*	57	87
Between the two	18	8
Not free**	26	6
Freedom of expression and of the press represent true achievements of our political system.*	(92) 53	(80) 89
All censorship should be abolished.	(91) 69	(106) 57

*$p < .01$
**$p < .05$

If we consider the results by political tendency (Table 4.4a—page 96), it may be noted that in the U.S. the *apoliticals* (56 percent) feel comparatively less free than those with definite political opinions (more than 90 percent whatever the tendency). In France, it is the *right* (4 out of 6) which feels unpopular at the university, and the moderate left (74 percent) and apoliticals (63 percent) are the groups most at ease in expressing their own opinions.

"FREEDOM OF EXPRESSION AND OF THE PRESS REPRESENT TRUE ACHIEVEMENTS OF OUR POLITICAL SYSTEM."

A large majority of students in Nigeria (83 percent), the United States (81 percent), Austria (79 percent), Great Britain (78 percent), and Italy (75 percent) think that freedom of the press and freedom of expression already exist in their societies, and a smaller majority of Australians (64 percent), Yugoslavs (62 percent), Japanese (55 percent), and French (54 percent) students have the same opinion about their societies. In contrast, Tunisia (36 percent) and Spain (18 percent) are considered by only a minority not to have censorship (Table 4.3).

In each country the closer the student is to the left, the more he is likely to doubt the existence of certain freedoms in his country. This is true for all countries except for Nigeria, where political tendency in no way modifies students' opinions about freedom of expression in their country (Table 4.3a—pages 94–96).

With regard to the university and society in general, students in Anglo-Saxon countries have the almost unanimous feeling of living in tolerant, democratic societies. This impression is shared by a majority of students in other countries, except in Tunisia and especially Spain, where the majority believe that their governments respect neither freedom of expression nor freedom of the press.[9]

"ALL CENSORSHIP SHOULD BE ABOLISHED."

Should this freedom be total or should it be maintained but under some form of censorship? Here enters the concept of collective responsibility: are people capable of choosing for themselves, or should the state intervene?

Taken all together, the majority of the respondents in the countries studied are in favor of abolishing all forms of censorship. However, countries differ to a certain extent in the frequency with which such agreement is expressed. The distribution ranges from 79 percent in Austria to 49 percent in Nigeria (Table 4.3).

The analysis of the results as a function of political tendency shows that the willingness to maintain some censorship is an attitude clearly more common among those who are on the right or progovernment. Students on the far left and communists reject this notion in the majority of cases (Table 4.3a). It is interesting to note in Italy, for example, the profound differences between the right and the left. Approximately half of the students on the right and far right are favorable to censorship, while the overwhelming majority of the communists and of the students on the far left do not agree. We find in nearly all the countries studied this divergence of opinion between the rightist students and those on the left.

THE 1977 SURVEY

The results indicate a noticeable difference in the United States. Students today are less favorable toward the abolition of all censorship (57 percent versus 73 percent in 1970). This shift is induced by the attitudes of apolitical students (44 percent in 1977 versus 73 percent in 1970), and to a lesser degree by those on the right (42 percent in 1977 versus 54 percent in 1970). In France no changes can be observed.

Ethnocentrism and Nationalism

Young people today live in a world where travel, the mass media, and all the other new forms of communication reveal new frontiers to be experienced, offering to many the chance to know cultures different from their own. We attempted to determine in this context whether prejudices and nationalism are widespread among youth.

[9]The 1977 survey in France and the United States yields similar results; 89 percent of the USA sample and 53 percent of the French sample agree with this statement (Table 4.4).

Some questions attempted to establish the attitudes of students toward ethnic discrimination, immigration, and nationalism. The students were to indicate the degree of agreement or disagreement with the following statements:

1. "Any discrimination against a person because of his race, religion, or color should be considered a crime."
2. "Immigration to this country should be unrestricted."
3. "Nationalism should be eliminated."
4. "An effective worldwide government should be established."

DISCRIMINATION

Whatever their country or political tendency, almost all students completely condemn racial segregation or any kind of discrimination. The small minority of students (less than 20 percent) in all the countries who deliberately take a racist position is almost alway scomposed of individuals who place themselves on the right or in the center politically (Tables 4.5—page 81, and 4.5a—pages 96–98).

IMMIGRATION

The problems of immigration vary with the countries studied here. Some, like Tunisia, Spain, Italy, and Yugoslavia, are more preoccupied by emigration. The latter two countries have also experienced the phenomenon of interior migration from the south to the north. None of these four countries has had first-hand experience of large-scale immigration. For this and other reasons, the problem of immigration must be treated in different terms when talking about the United States and Australia and about most European countries.

The United States and Australia have experienced large waves of immigrants. Their policies on this subject are quite precise. European countries until recently have not been confronted with massive immigration. Since World War II, however, the increase in industrialization has required an influx of manual labor, mainly from African or Mediterranean countries. Countries which had been rather closed to foreign immigration have been faced, especially since 1960, with the presence of foreigners. The latter are seen but often ignored; they may be neglected or exploited and frequently remain poorly adapted to their new environment. It is precisely in these countries that numerous problems of relations between ethnic groups have developed. In Europe today immigrant workers might even be considered as comprising the tenth nation of the European Community. In effect, between 1960 and 1970 about 11 million foreign workers have come to live, with their families, in various European countries. It therefore seemed interesting to discover how students from different countries envisaged this problem of immigration, as presented in the form "Immigration to this country should be unrestricted."

The findings demonstrate that there is great disparity in the opinions expressed. Four out of five students in Austria and in Japan agree with the statement, while this opinion is shared by only about half of the students in France, Australia, Spain, and the United States, by slightly more than a third of the students in Tunisia, Great Britain, and Italy, and by only 25 percent in Nigeria. Less than half of the students

TABLE 4.3.   Freedom of Expression by Country (Percent).

	AUSTRAL.	AUS.	FR.	GB	IT.	JAP.	NIG.	SP.	TUN.	USA	YUG.
I feel free to express my political point of view within my university.	(764)	(482)	(709)	(595)	(808)	(429)	(231)	(719)	(144)	(653)	(1,032)
Free*	85	72	63	90	65	62	66	21	26	88	80
Between the two[1]	8	14	16	4	14	17	13	9	21	7	–
Not free	7	14	21	6	21	21	21	70	53	5	20
Freedom of expression and of the press represent true achievements of our political system.*	(720)	(481)	(677)	(573)	(806)	(383)	(226)	(663)	(129)	(638)	(1,074)
	64	79	54	78	75	55	83	18	36	81	62
All censorship should be abolished.*	(767)	(482)	(686)	(587)	(803)	(414)	(224)	(723)	(131)	(647)	(1,075)
	73	79	70	68	60	75	49	75	71	73	54

*p < .01
1. This response did not appear in the Yugoslav questionnaire.

TABLE 4.5.   Attitudes toward Discrimination and Nationalism by Country (Percent).

	AUSTRAL.	AUS.	FR.	GB	IT.	JAP.	NIG.	SP.	TUN.	USA	YUG.
Discrimination should be considered a crime.**	(756)	(482)	(698)	(588)	(833)	(408)	(234)	(734)	(140)	(636)	(1,076)
	89	90	93	90	96	91	95	93	91	86	81
Immigration to this country should be unrestricted.*	(769)	(480)	(713)	(602)	(813)	(437)	(236)	(717)	(137)	(657)	(1,080)
	44	80	49	38	31	84	25	51	38	43	45
Nationalism should be eliminated.*	(733)	(481)	(668)	(551)	(781)	(383)	(222)	(685)	(135)	(610)	(1,067)
	56	77	78	54	84	57	20	69	41	53	55
An effective worldwide government should be established.*	(709)	(469)	(539)	(559)	(598)	(391)	(203)	(632)	(111)	(587)	(1,077)
	60	61	56	63	64	79	32	73	46	69	40

*p < .01
**p < .05

interviewed in Ljubljana, Slovenia, agree with the statement. A complementary analysis according to student nationality shows that the Slovenes are not very favorable to the arrival of Yugoslavs from other regions, while the non-Slovenes who study in Slovenia—and thus already are immigrants, at least temporarily—are prepared to encourage immigration. The students most favorable toward unrestricted immigration are those of the far left in Austria (94 percent) and Japan (90 percent), followed by the far leftists in the Anglo-Saxon countries, in France (about 70 percent), and in Spain (64 percent). Only a minority of students of the far left in Tunisia (43 percent), Nigeria (29 percent) and Italy (23 percent) agree with this idea. Students of the right or center are less favorable than those on the left, yet still a majority in Japan, Tunisia, Austria, Italy, and Spain.

The results show a general reluctance of the Tunisians and especially of the Nigerians to accept free immigration into their country. This is probably due in Tunisia to the important fact of mass unemployment. A sudden large immigration could only worsen this situation. Already Libyans in particular often come to look for work in Tunisia. Nigeria—more prosperous than its French-speaking neighbor, Niger—attracts from Niger the Hausa tribes, artificially separated from Nigerian kinsmen by the southern border of Niger and the northern border of Nigeria. In addition, there are important internal migrations between the different regions of the north, the east, and the west. Intertribal rivalries do not facilitate exchange of workers or professionals from one region to another.

In Ibadan, where the Nigerian questionnaires were administered, the students (Yorubas for the most part) complained that those holding diplomas from other regions were taking the jobs that they thought were rightfully theirs. Ethnicity interferes with the diverse attempts being made at unification of the country. It may also be that this hostility in regard to immigration is a form of nationalism, implying a rejection, not of African, but of European immigrants. It may also represent a rejection of neo-colonialist cooperation, which is still regarded as existing in both Nigeria and Tunisia. Whatever the differences in attitudes due to the social and economic situation, it is clear that most students in Nigeria and Tunisia are hostile to uncontrolled immigration.

The 1977 Survey

The results indicate a very slight decrease (around 5 percent) in the percentage of students who favor unrestricted immigration in both the United States and France (Table 4.6). In the United States 38 percent favor unrestricted immigration as compared to 43 percent in the first study, and in France 42 percent do so as compared with 49 percent in the first study. Concerning discrimination students in 1977 are somewhat less in agreement on considering any discrimination a crime—in France 87 percent as compared to 93 percent in 1970, and in the United States 75 percent as compared to 86 percent in 1970 (Table 4.6).

NATIONALISM

The term "nationalism" is vague. It can be understood in a pejorative sense (i.e., as chauvinism), in a strictly political-ideological sense (adopted by certain groups on the right), or as signifying the importance of a national culture. Nationalism, as defined by political science, is a relatively new notion in Europe which dates from the end of the eighteenth century. (Great Britain is an exception.) In France it only appeared in 1798, in Germany about 1818 with Fichte, and in Italy about 1850—Cavour was one of the first to fight for Italian unity.

TABLE 4.6. Attitudes toward Discrimination and Nationalism in France and the United States, 1977 Survey (Percent).

	FRANCE	UNITED STATES
Discrimination should be considered a crime.	(92) 87	(106) 75
Immigration to this country should be unrestricted.	(90) 42	(106) 38
Nationalism should be eliminated.*	(89) 66	(79) 32
An effective worldwide government should be established.**	(88) 27	(105) 48

*p < .01
**p < .05

Over the last fifty years, nationalism has become a universally accepted idea of contemporary history, manifested either under the cover of various ideologies or in the search for cultural and political self-determination. In many parts of Africa, Asia, and South America nationalism has been regarded literally as a matter of life or death. We must also note the resurgence of regionalism, or micronationalism. Regionalist movements at present concern only a small minority of people, yet they may incite a great deal of violence (e.g., the Catholics and Protestants in Northern Ireland, the two linguistic groups in Belgium, the Basques in Spain, the Bretons in France).

Renan described nationalism as the feeling of having done important things together in the past and wishing to continue to do so in the future. This definition needs to be modified somewhat, since the active agent is not specified and might be the population as a whole or a political or ethnic group. It is not surprising, in any case, that the concept of nationalism is different for the students in the eleven countries studied.

Italians (84 percent), followed by the French (78 percent), Austrians (77 percent),[10] and Spanish (69 percent), seem the most favorable to the elimination of nationalism. Still, a majority of students in Japan (57 percent), Australia (56 percent), Yugoslavia (55 percent), Great Britain (54 percent), and the United States (53 percent) also approve this idea. On the other hand, there is a strong national feeling in Tunisia and especially in Nigeria: only 41 percent and 20 percent of students in these two countries, respectively, are in favor of the elimination of nationalism.

As expected, in all of the countries political orientation influences the students' attitudes toward nationalism (Table 4.5a). The more one is on the right, the less one desires the elimination of nationalism; the opposite is true of the students on the left.

[10]The findings of the German questionnaire show that the West Germans and the Austrians have a similar attitude toward nationalism.

The opposition between the two extremes is particularly marked in Australia (38 percent of rightists for elimination versus 81 percent on the far left), France (33 percent versus 96 percent), Great Britain (29 percent versus 83 percent), and the United States (22 percent versus 75 percent). In Austria (60 percent versus 94 percent), Italy (58 percent versus 100 percent), Spain (55 percent versus 77 percent), and Japan (53 percent [of the center] versus 63 percent), a majority of rightist students, though less favorable than those of the far left, agree that nationalism should be eliminated. In Tunisia, students of the right (29 percent), Bourguibists (38 percent), and those of the far left (58 percent) are in comparison the least in favor of elimination. The situation in Nigeria is even more striking; only 10 percent of the far left and 28 percent of the right agree with this idea. In this country alone, the far left is the prime defender of nationalism. Except for Nigeria, moderate or center students seem divided on this issue. The left is quite close to the far left, that is, in favor of the elimination of nationalism.

The differences between the countries should be seen in the light of the different contexts in which nationalism is understood. It is quite understandable that for the Austrians and the West Germans nationalism still has a traumatic ring, recalling the recent unhappy past. On the other hand, the concept of Europe appears to be entering more directly into life in France and Italy. In Great Britain, the research was conducted before that country's entrance into the Common Market, and at a time when it faced many interior problems (e.g., Welsh and Scottish nationalism and the tragic situation in Ulster).

On the whole, students in Japan, the United States, Australia, and Yugoslavia have an ambivalent attitude toward nationalism, although a majority are in favor of its elimination. In Japan this phenomenon may be explained as a result of isolation and of a past filled with nationalistic ideologies, as well as the more recent memory of the war and the consequent "occupation" of the country by Americans. Yugoslavia, a federal, socialist state composed of ten republics, has experienced many internal struggles and one external one involving the anterevisionist campaign led by the Soviet Union, from which Yugoslavia wishes to remain independent. These various factors in the experience of Japan and Yugoslavia may explain the substantial "pronationalist" minority.

In Africa, nationalist movements were the primary factor in decolonization. We can easily understand the continuing strength of the nationalist movements developed in Tunisia and in Nigeria before independence (1956 for Tunisia and 1960 for Nigeria). In Nigeria especially, nationalism responds to a need for ethnic and political unification, as opposed to tribalism (Klineberg and Zavalloni, 1969); it is part of a search for national identity. In that country, which underwent the drama of Biafra, there are strong rivalries among the three largest ethnic groups—the Yorubas in the west, the Hausas in the north, and the Ibos in the east. Nationalism is seen as a needed substitute for these rivalries.

INTERNATIONALISM

It is hardly necessary to point out how many phenomena force us to look beyond national boundaries: accelerated economic expansion, multinational companies, the exchange of workers, pollution, and, especially, the disparity between the rich and the poor countries, which becomes more accentuated every day.

The ideal of a world state or a federation of peoples has the approval of a large number of students. Many students, a majority in some countries, agreed to the statement "An effective worldwide government should be established." There were, however, differences between the national groups. The Japanese (79 percent) and the Spanish students (73 percent) were the most favorable to such a goal, followed by Americans, Austrians, Australians, British, and Italians (between 69 percent and 60 percent). French (56 percent), Tunisians (46 percent), and Yugoslavs (40 percent) were less favorable. Nigerian students were the most negative, with only 32 percent in favor of a worldwide government (Table 4.5).

It is interesting to note the relationship between approval of nationalism and internationalism. The comparisons of results obtained show that in Anglo-Saxon countries and in Japan a majority are in favor of an international order, but a substantial minority disagree with the idea that nationalism should be eliminated. On the continent of Europe, students in Spain and Austria are clearly for a worldwide government, but in France, Italy, and Yugoslavia we find a certain hesitancy about the notion even though French and Italian students are among the most favorable toward the elimination of nationalism.

The reluctance of some to accept a world government may truly indicate opposition to this principle, but it may also be the manifestation of a certain prudence vis-à-vis a question whose orientation and nature were obscure. This same ambiguity appeared whenever the students spoke in general terms about unlimited immigration, the dissolution of national boundaries, internationalism, and/or worldwide government without information as to what kind of world would result. Our questions on these issues should have been more specific.

In conclusion, the findings permit us to speak of three major orientations in the countries studied. The first may be defined as *internationalist*. This orientation combines attitudes favorable to immigration, the elimination of nationalism, and the establishment of a worldwide government. This tendency is typical of Austrian, Japanese, and Spanish students. The second orientation, defined as *nationalist*, is opposed to any limitation of national sovereignty, refuses uncontrolled immigration, and is distrustful of supranational organizations. This tendency characterizes Tunisians and Nigerians. The last orientation, which we might term *social protectionism*, is more complex in that it includes attitudes favorable to the limitation of immigration but also those favorable to the elimination of nationalism. The French, Italians, Yugoslavs, Americans, and Australians compose this group. We must note that among these, only American and Australian students hope in the majority for a supranational government. The British students do not fit into this system of classification; they are in favor of world government, but at least half of them wish to retain nationalism.

THE 1977 SURVEY

The results indicate that both in France and in the United States there are changes in attitudes toward nationalism (Table 4.6). Thus in France, 66 percent of the students as compared with 78 percent in 1970 agree that nationalism should be eliminated, and only 27 percent as compared with 56 percent in 1970 are favorable to the establishment of an effective worldwide government. In the United States, the differences are also very marked concerning nationalism (32 percent as compared with 53 percent in 1970 favor its abolition) and concerning the establishment of a world government (48 percent as compared to 69 percent in 1970 favor it). We have seen that the students are also less favorable toward unrestricted immigration, as well as slightly less inclined to consider racial and/or religious discrimination a crime. French and American students, then, appear—at least on these questions—less liberal in 1977 than in 1970.

The Ideal Society

The issues of peace and of internationalism are among the elements that students relate to what they believe to be an ideal society. One question allowed the students to describe this ideal society in more detail, and in that way to express some of their worries and aspirations: "Try to imagine a society of which you really approve. What are the three most important elements of such a society?"

In all the countries studied, the three most frequent responses were freedom, equality, and fraternity among men. All individual freedoms would be guaranteed and all forms of repression banished from this society. It would be based on equality—in wealth, job opportunities, culture, and education. There would be no discrimination by sex, and all would be equal before the law. This society would inspire love and understanding among people, as well as respect for others and mutual communication. To the motto of the French Revolution ("liberté, égalité, fraternité") sometimes were added other concerns specific to one country or to one political group.

In Japan and to a lesser extent in the United States, students speak of world peace and the development of an international spirit. Humanity would experience an international society, without frontiers, peaceful and open. The Japanese students' mention of this characteristic of the ideal society is interesting in that it confirms the international attitude of these students, who are the most numerous in approving the principle of world government. These students dream of a society which will resolve the problems of ecology, pollution, and the degradation of nature and of the human environment which it has produced.

The ideal society according to Nigerians and Tunisians would give new life to traditional values, which today are disappearing. Religion, order, the family, morality, and respect for the law would become the bases of this new society:

Nigeria

To be honest, hard working, and have a high moral code and a fear of God.

Marriage=monogamy.

Law-abiding.

Public and private morality.

Everyone would receive according to the work he does.

Tunisia

Serious work; morality.

Discipline, devotion.

Absence of moral degradation.

For some students, social disparities should be maintained, and there should be acceptance of and satisfaction with one's life as it is. This kind of response is given almost uniquely by students on the right in the other countries, where to students on the left socialism is the ideal. Many students in these two countries also hope that man will cultivate and develop his moral and intellectual qualities—that he will become more honest, more mature, more aware, more dynamic, and more efficient.

In Nigeria and Tunisia it is clear that many students are not describing an indeterminate ideal society, but more specifically what would be ideal for their own country. They hope to see a national consciousness and a sense of patriotism develop. Economic and technological progress would be basic to this society:

Nigeria

Patriotism.

Nationalism.

A high sense of national identity.

Education geared to national needs.

Tunisia

A balance between the resources of the country and demographic growth.

A developed economy.

It is noteworthy that often, particularly in Nigeria, Tunisia, Japan, and the United States, students raise the same issues when speaking about an ideal society and when speaking about the worst aspects of the society in which they live. The Japanese speak of resolving the problems of ecology; the Americans are concerned with peace; and the Nigerians and the Tunisians underscore values, moral qualities, national identity, and development.

In Spain and in France one quarter of the students envision a society where a new conception of work, of pleasure, and of creativity would exist. People would finally be able to develop fully and to communicate with others:

France

Work should be a pleasure.

Interesting work for everyone.

The full development of everyone.

The counterculture introduces the notion of work as an activity which is not alienating and which is creative. This is part of the philosophy of Marcuse, for whom "work should be play." Students were asked to indicate if they approved or disapproved of the following idea: "In an ideal society work and play would be indistinguishable."

In France and in Tunisia we find the greatest percentages of students (79 percent[11] and 75 percent respectively) who favor redefining the concept of work in this manner, while the least favorable are the Japanese (37 percent) and the Nigerians (39 percent) (Table 4.7—page 88).

[11]In 1977 French students are less likely to consider that work and play should be indistinguishable (64 percent); in the United States, 43 percent as compared with 51 percent in 1970 agree with this statement (Table 4.7).

TABLE 4.7.   Agreement That in an Ideal Society Work and Play Should Be Indistinguishable (Percent).[1]

	AUSTRAL.	AUS.	FR.	GB	IT.	JAP.	NIG.	SP.	TUN.	USA	YUG.
Total sample*	(700) 49	(479) 54	(598) 79[a]	(565) 58	(704) 66	(358) 37	(208) 39	(669) 54	(124) 75	(587) 51[b]	(1,078) 41
By political tendency											
Right*	(32) 34	(81) 47	(38) 66	(85) 51	(61) 64[c]	(132) 36[d]	(40) 38	(57) 45	(14) 86[e]	(71) 47	
Far left*	(35) 77	(66) 73	(83) 74[f]	(70) 76	(57) 79[g]	(103) 44	(19) 37	(71) 65	(20) 85	(23) 65	

	AUSTRAL.	AUS.	FR.	GB	IT.	NIG.	SP.	TUN.	USA
By sex									
Men*	(507) 49	(237) 55	(315) 78	(318) 62	(393) 66	(187) 42	(519) 56	(63) 76	(418) 51
Women*	(193) 50	(241) 53	(289) 81	(245) 55	(340) 64	(21) 14	(150) 47	(58) 73	(170) 51

*p < .01
1. "Strongly" and "slightly agree" combined.
a. In the 1977 survey, 64 percent of the total sample.
b. In the 1977 survey, 43 percent of the total sample.
c. Far right 37 percent.
d. Center instead of right.
e. Bourguibists 67 percent.
f. Communists 79 percent, anarchists 93 percent.
g. Communists 80 percent.

If we exclude Nigeria and Tunisia, where the notion of work is perceived in the same way by the different political categories, we find in the other countries that the more the student is on the left of the political continuum, the more he approves the association of work and play. In France there is a rather large difference between the anarchists and the students on the far left: 93 percent of the former group hope to see work and play indistinguishable, compared with 74 percent of the latter. In Italy only 37 percent of the students on the far right agree with this ideal, compared with 64 percent on the right.

We would expect that a redefinition of work would be more favorably welcomed by men than by women, in particular in the countries of the Third World, where women traditionally have not been involved to the same extent in the labor force. The results (Table 4.7) confirm this hypothesis only in Nigeria: 42 percent of the men, compared with 14 percent of the women, agree that work should be closer to play. In industrialized countries, the attitudes of the two sexes are similar.

After having imagined their ideal society, the students were to indicate if this society could be realized and, if so, how. More than half of the students in every country think that such a society is possible to achieve. The most optimistic were the Nigerians (87 percent) and the Italians (74 percent) (Table 4.8).[12] If we exclude Nigeria and Japan, where political tendency does not affect the students' opinions, the more the student identifies with the left, the more likely he is to be optimistic about the chances of realizing such an ideal society. This enthusiasm is very clear among those students in France who are communists: 90 percent believe that such a society is possible, compared to 71 percent of the students on the far left.

Students on the far left often mention socialism as the ideal society and are the most optimistic about its chances of becoming a reality. Other students, who describe the ideal society in value terms (equality, liberty, and fraternity) and who do not propose an outline of this society, see mankind and its organizations in a more pessimistic light.

We should note that men are generally more optimistic than women, especially in Great Britain. In this country 66 percent of the men versus 43 percent of the women believe that the ideal society can be achieved (Table 4.8).

The students were asked to indicate the means which they thought most likely to change society. The responses from all countries are quite similar. Many mention education as the principal means. Some specifically mention enlargement and improvement of the total educational system, some the ability of education to make people more aware of different ways of thinking:

United States

Education can make a revolution in thinking patterns and allow a restructuring of priorities.

Increased education could perhaps increase tolerance.

Great Britain

By education, by accenting personal fulfillment and not competition and materialism.

By educating young people and the workers.

[12]In 1977, students in France were somewhat more optimistic in their estimation that an ideal society can be realized (66 percent as compared to 58 percent in 1970). In contrast, students in the United States appear slightly less optimistic (58 percent as compared to 64 percent in 1970) (Table 4.8—page 90).

TABLE 4.8.   Belief in Possibility of Realizing the Ideal Society (Percent).

	AUSTRAL.	AUS.	FR.[1]	GB	IT.[2]	JAP.	NIG.	SP.	TUN.	USA
Total sample	(720)	(410)	(657)	(558)	(746)	(365)	(196)	(686)	(134)	(592)
	59	50	58[a]	56	74	52	87	63	64	64[b]
By political tendency										
Right**	(38)	(74)	(37)	(80)	(29)	(139)	(23)	(59)	(15)	(75)
	50	47	51	53	71	57	88	56	47	55
Far left	(35)	(61)	(96)	(69)	(70)	(114)	(19)	(79)	(22)	(127)
	77	66	71	74	86	54	74	87	73	71
By sex[3]										
Men**	(531)	(204)	(350)	(317)	(429)	—	(176)	(525)	(67)	(431)
	61	54	65	66	78	—	87	66	69	63
Women	(189)	(202)	(319)	(235)	(338)	—	(20)	(156)	(63)	(166)
	54	46	50	43	69	—	90	55	59	63

1. Communists 90 percent; anarchists 76 percent.
2. Extreme right 61 percent; communists 89 percent.
3. This analysis was not done for Japan, as the sample included few women.
a. In the 1977 survey, 66 percent of the total sample.
b. In the 1977 survey, 58 percent of the total sample.
**p < .05

France

First by the education of the masses.

By a political policy to transform the whole educational system.

The idea that the ideal society can be realized through political, social, and economic reforms appears frequently. Underlying this desire is the notion of a slow, progressive evolution:

United States

By gradual societal evolution.

France

By a reform of socioeconomic institutions, norms, and objectives of the whole society.

Great Britain

By progress and evolution—a natural change—not by revolution.

By perfecting the existing system.

Many students, however, except in Great Britain and the United States, believe that only revolution can affect a change in society. It will lead to the ideal world, represented by socialism:

Great Britain

By political action.

By revolution. Not necessarily by violence but by the reorganization of education and the removal of the vast reactionary influences of the family unit.

France

By a proletarian revolution.

After the revolution.

Revolution to emancipate the workers.

Some students, mostly French, express the hope that this revolution will lead to a "humanized" socialism, which still remains to be defined:

France

Between the crushing socialism of the East and the inhuman capitalism of the West.

A revolution which will lead to an intermediary form of socialism, between that of Sweden and that of Hungary.

More than others, French students look for a change in the form of a "political" revolution. Americans, British, and Australians speak more in terms of reforms, whether on the national and international level or in small individual groups:

Great Britain

In such a way that every person can turn toward others and find at least ten people to love.

There needs to be international cooperation.

United States

Cooperation between individuals.

Guaranteed minimal level of love for each individual.

In Nigeria, where students often mention corruption as one of the worst aspects of their society, it is interesting to note that many believe that the way to achieve the ideal society is to have incorruptible leaders who will become examples for the people:

By having selfless leaders who place the public interest over that of personal gain.

The leaders will educate the masses.

Political leaders who are God-fearing, honest, and impartial.

As we conclude this chapter concerning sociopolitical options, we note certain similarities and certain differences among the students from the various countries. One striking finding is that when we try to define the judgment of society as a global entity, it is only in English-speaking countries that students on the whole indicate a positive attitude. In other countries this judgment appears rather negative. The most dissatisfied students are the Tunisians and the Japanese. In Yugoslavia and in Austria, where the question included a supplementary possible response ("There are as many good as bad aspects"), the majority of students choose this answer.

The existence of freedom of expression was recognized by the majority of students in all countries except in Spain and in Tunisia. Both in the university and in society in general, students in English-speaking countries feel the most free, while students in Tunisia and Spain complain that they cannot express themselves freely at the university, and that freedom of the press and freedom of speech do not exist in their countries.

We have also seen that in all countries the majority of students condemn discrimination.

Students' opinions about nationalism and a supranational government differ according to the country. Three major groups can be differentiated. The first group, which we have characterized as *nationalist*, includes Nigeria and Tunisia: the students are nationalists, opposed to unlimited immigration and to the establishment of a worldwide government. Nigerians and Tunisians wish to preserve and develop national identity, and favor the notion of national sovereignty based on military power. The second group, defined as *internationalist*, includes Austria, Japan, and Spain. In these countries the students are in favor of the elimination of nationalism and accept unlimited immigration and a worldwide government. In this group there is a definite tendency toward pacifism and internationalism. In the last group, which may be called *protectionist*, are France, Italy, Yugoslavia, the United States, and Australia. Their students manifest a favorable attitude toward the limitation and strict control of immigration. This social protectionism is, however, often accompanied by a desire to eliminate nationalism and, in the United States and Australia, to see the establihsment of a worldwide government. The French, Italian, and Yugoslav students are less favorable to a worldwide government than those in the United States.

Political tendency has a profound effect on attitudes. The closer the student is to the left, the more negative is his judgment of society, the more he judges its freedom to be only an illusion, and the more he supports the pacifist and internationalist position. The opposite is true for students on the right. These orientations are affected, however, by the social and political situation in each country. English-speaking students, for example, even those on the far left, are much less critical of their society than are students from the other countries.

The last question concerning the ideal society allowed us to conclude that whatever national or political differences appear among the students, their ideal can be defined in three words: equality, freedom, and fraternity. This formula, which seems like a cliché since the French Revolution, has an almost magic power in the eyes of the students, more than half of whom believe that this ideal can be realized and is not utopian. The most optimistic are the Italians (74 percent) and the Nigerians (87 percent); the least optimistic are the Austrians (50 percent) and the Japanese (52 percent).

TABLE 4.1a.   Predominance of the Good or the Bad Aspects of Society According to Yugoslav Students (Percent).

Self-Definition:	IDEAL. (241)	REAL. (488)	HUMAN. (161)	ELIT. (26)	INDIV. (42)
Predominance of the—					
Good aspects	46	35	32	23	24
Bad aspects	12	17	14	31	26
Good = bad	43	49	54	46	50

Member of Communist League:	YES (118)	NO, BUT DESIRE TO (173)	NO, REFUSE TO (785)
Predominance of the—			
Good aspects	47	49	31
Bad aspects	16	8	18
Good = bad	37	44	51

TABLE 4.1b. Attitudes of Yugoslav Students on Diverse Issues Concerning Society (Percent).

	AGREED (1,130)
"The official policy of today is characterized by hypocrisy; that is, there is a wide gap between what is said and what is done."	64
"The old revolutionary parties have become bourgeois or bureaucratic and no longer represent a revolutionary force. They must, therefore, whether they like it or not, yield their role to the revolutionary students."	82
"Most of our people seek only personal profit and have no understanding for their fellow men."	79
"Children of workers and peasants have little chance to succeed in our society."	63
"Most politicians seek power rather than clinging to principles and ideals."	62

TABLE 4.1c. Aspects of National Political Life Which Yugoslavs Ought to Appreciate, According to Students.

	PERCENTAGE	(N)
Foreign policy in regard to		
The Soviet Union and other socialist countries	87	(1,044)
The United States	75	(1,009)
European countries	87	(1,039)
The Middle East	77	(1,019)
Nonaligned countries of Africa, Asia, and Latin America	80	(1,050)
Aspects of internal policy		
Implementation of economic reform	7	(1,054)
Attempts to better the standard of living	36	(1,045)
The process of democratizing public life	57	(992)
Development of workers' self-management	45	(1,020)
The system of rotation of high government officials in the republics and the Federation	45	(935)
The reorganization and modification of the role of the Communist League	47	(778)

TABLE 4.1d Living Abroad—Where? Why?—According to Yugoslav Students (Percent).

Having finished your studies, would you like to live and work abroad?	(1,130)	
Yes, permanently	1	20
Yes, temporarily	19	
I don't know, I have never asked myself	42	
No, neither permanently nor temporarily	36	
No reply	2	

(cont.)

TABLE 4.1d.   Continued

If yes, in which country? (three choices possible)	(243)[1]
The Soviet Union or another socialist country	7
The United States or Canada	47
A South American country	10
An African country	19
An Asian country	10
Great Britain	39
Scandinavia (Sweden, Denmark, Norway, or Finland)	33
France	29
Switzerland	27
West Germany	24
Italy	9
The Netherlands	7
Austria	5
Belgium	2
Others	5
Why? (two choices possible)	(243)[1]
Improved professional status	65
Higher salary	35
A more exciting life style	23
Professional experience	16
Higher cultural level	9
I don't think I'll find a job here	8
I have friends or parents abroad	8
I disagree with the sociopolitical system	1

1. The total of the percentages is more than 100 percent, as students could give several responses.

TABLE 4.3a.   Freedom of Expression, by Political Tendency (Percent).[1]

Australia	RIGHT	CENT.	LEFT	FAR L.	APOL.
I feel free to express my political point of view within my university.**	(40) 78	(271) 86	(232) 89	(36) 69	(185) 84
Freedom of expression and of the press represent true achievements of our political system.*	(38) 86	(255) 81	(217) 57	(34) 35	(176) 68
All censorship should be abolished.*	(39) 67	(279) 69	(232) 83	(36) 97	(188) 67

Austria	RIGHT	CENT.	LEFT	FAR L.	APOL.
I feel free to express my political point of view within my university.*	(81) 94	(152) 79	(137) 58	(69) 42	(43) 95
Freedom of expression and of the press represent true achievements of our political system.*	(82) 94	(151) 89	(135) 77	(68) 46	(45) 78
All censorship should be abolished.*	(82) 62	(151) 79	(136) 88	(68) 88	(45) 69

France	RIGHT	CENT.	LEFT	COMM.	FAR L.	ANAR.	APOL.
I feel free to express my political point of view within my university.**	(42) 57	(134) 74	(205) 63	(49) 51	(97) 54	(33) 55	(149) 64
Freedom of expression and of the press represent true achievements of our political system.*	(40) 93	(133) 79	(192) 46	(43) 42	(93) 30	(31) 25	(144) 54
All censorship should be abolished.*	(42) 43	(132) 56	(197) 77	(42) 71	(90) 80	(33) 91	(150) 68

Great Britain		RIGHT	CENT.	LEFT	FAR L.	APOL.
I feel free to express my political point of view within my university.**		(89) 93	(91) 93	(197) 89	(72) 76	(146) 92
Freedom of expression and of the press represent true achievements of our political system.**		(84) 85	(88) 88	(191) 77	(69) 64	(141) 76
All censorship should be abolished.*		(88) 57	(91) 62	(193) 78	(73) 86	(142) 54

Italy	FAR R.	RIGHT	CENT.	LEFT	COMM.	FAR L.	APOL.
I feel free to express my political point of view within my university.*	(32) 63	(67) 70	(148) 74	(221) 70	(110) 48	(71) 55	(159) 64
Freedom of expression and of the press represent true achievements of our political system.*	(31) 78	(65) 83	(152) 90	(222) 80	(98) 43	(66) 43	(172) 82
All censorship should be abolished.*	(32) 50	(66) 44	(148) 39	(219) 67	(106) 89	(67) 79	(166) 51

Japan		CENT.	LEFT	FAR L.	APOL.
I feel free to express my political point of view within my university.*		(155) 65	(44) 80	(126) 53	(104) 63
Freedom of expression and of the press represent true achievements of our political system.*		(133) 62	(38) 66	(115) 42	(97) 59
All censorship should be abolished.*		(147) 69	(44) 75	(119) 85	(104) 71

Nigeria	RIGHT	CRITIC.	LEFT	FAR L.	DESCR.	APOL.
I feel free to express my political point of view within my university.*	(43) 70	(37) 54	(44) 73	(21) 48	(28) 75	(52) 67
Freedom of expression and of the press represent true achievements of our political system.	(42) 83	(36) 81	(42) 86	(19) 84	(27) 88	(54) 85
All censorship should be abolished.*	(41) 51	(35) 37	(42) 45	(19) 69	(27) 44	(54) 54

Spain	RIGHT	CENT.	LEFT	FAR L.	APOL.
I feel free to express my political point of view within my university.*	(62) 37	(123) 24	(279) 16	(84) 11	(171) 26
Freedom of expression and of the press represent true achievements of our political system.*	(53) 32	(109) 25	(261) 10	(80) 11	(160) 28
All censorship should be abolished.*	(60) 55	(120) 73	(280) 84	(82) 89	(181) 64

Tunisia	RIGHT	BOURGUIB.	LEFT	FAR L.	APOL.
I feel free to express my political point of view within my university.*	(15) 40	(16) 50	(49) 14	(25) 20	(35) 29
Freedom of expression and of the press represent true achievements of our political system.*	(14) 21	(16) 44	(43) 35	(22) 23	(32) 50
All censorship should be abolished.*	(14) 64	(13) 54	(46) 80	(21) 67	(33) 70

United States	RIGHT	CENT.	LIB.	LEFT	FAR L.	APOL.
I feel free to express my political point of view within my university.	(78) 80	(128) 86	(192) 90	(137) 94	(26) 85	(92) 85

(cont.)

TABLE 4.3a.   Continued

United States	RIGHT	CENT.	LIB.	LEFT	FAR L.	APOL.
Freedom of expression and of the press represent true achievements of our political system.*	(80) 91	(126) 91	(190) 79	(131) 76	(25) 56	(86) 76
All censorship should be abolished.*	(79) 54	(126) 62	(192) 75	(134) 90	(25) 100	(91) 73

1. Completely and relatively free combined.
*p < .01
**p < .05

TABLE 4.4a.   Freedom of Expression in France and the United States by Political Tendency, 1977 Survey (Percent).

France	RIGHT	CENT.	LEFT	COMM.	FAR L.	APOL.
I feel free to express my political point of view within my university.	(6)	(10)	(35)	(3)	(17)	(19)
Free	(1)	40	74	(1)	41	63
Between the two	(1)	30	11	(1)	18	21
Not free	(4)	30	9	(1)	41	16
Freedom of expression and of the press represent true achievements of our political system.**	(6) 100	(10) 60	(35) 46	(4) (1)	(17) 24	(20) 80
All censorship should be abolished.	(6) 100	(10) 60	(35) 46	(4) (1)	(17) 24	(20) 80

United States	RIGHT	CENT.	LIB.	LEFT	FAR L.	APOL.
I feel free to express my political point of view within my university.	(26)	(28)	(24)	(8)	(4)	(16)
Free*	92	93	92	100	(3)	56
Between the two	4	7	8	0	0	19
Not free	4	0	0	0	(1)	25
Freedom of expression and of the press represent true achievements of our political system.	(20) 95	(21) 95	(18) 94	(5) (4)	(3) (2)	(13) 70
All censorship should be abolished.	(26) 42	(28) 64	(24) 75	(8) (5)	(4) (1)	(16) 44

*p < .01
**p < .05

TABLE 4.5a.   Attitudes toward Discrimination and Nationalism by Political Tendency (Percent).

Australia	RIGHT	CENT.	LEFT	FAR L.	APOL.
Discrimination should be considered a crime.*	(40) 78	(269) 89	(230) 94	(35) 97	(182) 84
Immigration to this country should be unrestricted.*	(40) 43	(271) 38	(234) 55	(36) 70	(188) 32
Nationalism should be eliminated.*	(40) 38	(260) 50	(225) 70	(36) 81	(172) 48
An effective worldwide government should be established.*	(38) 50	(247) 51	(218) 73	(33) 61	(173) 59

Austria	RIGHT	CENT.	LEFT	FAR L.	APOL.
Discrimination should be considered a crime.*	(82) 77	(151) 90	(136) 98	(68) 94	(45) 82
Immigration to this country should be unrestricted.*	(81) 68	(151) 72	(137) 88	(66) 94	(45) 78

Nationalism should be eliminated.*	(82) 60	(151) 74	(136) 90	(67) 94	(45) 51
An effective worldwide government should be established.**	(80) 60	(149) 60	(131) 64	(64) 50	(45) 67

France	RIGHT	CENT.	LEFT	COMM.	FAR L.	ANAR.	APOL.
Discrimination should be considered a crime.**	(39) 82	(127) 87	(204) 96	(48) 100	(92) 99	(33) 100	(155) 89
Immigration to this country should be unrestricted.*	(42) 19	(137) 31	(205) 52	(45) 58	(95) 71	(33) 79	(156) 46
Nationalism should be eliminated.*	(39) 33	(129) 64	(194) 81	(43) 84	(96) 96	(31) 90	(136) 82
An effective worldwide government should be established.**	(34) 35	(113) 52	(148) 56	(28) 61	(71) 63	(29) 55	(116) 58

Great Britain			RIGHT	CENT.	LEFT	FAR L.	APOL.
Discrimination should be considered a crime.**			(87) 79	(89) 91	(197) 95	(70) 94	(145) 87
Immigration to this country should be unrestricted.*			(89) 14	(91) 22	(199) 53	(73) 73	(150) 25
Nationalism should be eliminated.*			(82) 29	(87) 54	(177) 64	(66) 83	(139) 43
An effective worldwide government should be established.*			(87) 40	(83) 65	(188) 73	(66) 74	(135) 56

Italy	FAR R.	RIGHT	CENT.	LEFT	COMM.	FAR L.	APOL.
Discrimination should be considered a crime.**	(30) 80	(66) 89	(152) 96	(227) 100	(111) 98	(72) 100	(175) 91
Immigration to this country should be unrestricted.*	(31) 67	(64) 33	(149) 32	(221) 27	(110) 16	(70) 23	(168) 40
Nationalism should be eliminated.*	(31) 36	(62) 58	(146) 79	(212) 90	(103) 96	(67) 100	(160) 84
An effective worldwide government should be established.*	(24) 50	(52) 48	(122) 56	(175) 70	(52) 58	(49) 65	(124) 74

Japan				CENTER	LEFT	FAR L.	APOL.
Discrimination should be considered a crime.				(146) 90	(43) 86	(119) 95	(100) 91
Immigration to this country should be unrestricted.				(157) 78	(44) 84	(125) 90	(111) 86
Nationalism should be eliminated.**				(141) 53	(42) 67	(112) 63	(88) 51
An effective worldwide government should be established.				(146) 82	(41) 83	(11) 72	(93) 83

Nigeria	RIGHT	CRITIC.	LEFT	FAR L.	DESCR.	APOL.
Discrimination should be considered a crime.	(42) 98	(37) 97	(44) 95	(21) 95	(28) 89	(57) 97
Immigration to this country should be unrestricted.	(41) 21	(37) 32	(45) 29	(21) 29	(28) 21	(57) 21
Nationalism should be eliminated.**	(39) 28	(35) 29	(43) 16	(20) 10	(28) 25	(51) 12
An effective worldwide government should be established.**	(36) 20	(31) 36	(37) 38	(20) 20	(25) 32	(48) 42

(cont.)

TABLE 4.5a.   Continued

Spain	RIGHT	CENTER	LEFT	FAR L.	APOL.
Discrimination should be considered a crime.**	(62)	(122)	(281)	(84)	(185)
	87	93	96	77	90
Immigration to this country should be unrestricted.*	(59)	(120)	(279)	(76)	(183)
	51	49	54	64	43
Nationalism should be eliminated.*	(56)	(114)	(267)	(75)	(163)
	55	70	77	77	56
An effective worldwide government should be established.**	(56)	(113)	(251)	(67)	(146)
	60	75	78	67	72

Tunisia	RIGHT	BOURGUIB.	LEFT	FAR L.	APOL.
Discrimination should be considered a crime.	(15)	(14)	(49)	(23)	(35)
	98	100	90	87	94
Immigration to this country should be unrestricted.*	(14)	(16)	(48)	(23)	(32)
	21	69	40	43	25
Nationalism should be eliminated.**	(14)	(16)	(48)	(24)	(29)
	29	38	29	58	48
An effective worldwide government should be established.*	(11)	(13)	(41)	(19)	(25)
	36	69	29	58	60

United States	RIGHT	CENT.	LIB.	LEFT	FAR L.	APOL.
Discrimination should be considered a crime.	(79)	(125)	(190)	(131)	(23)	(88)
	81	83	88	90	83	92
Immigration to this country should be unrestricted.*	(79)	(129)	(196)	(137)	(26)	(90)
	24	38	39	58	73	41
Nationalism should be eliminated.*	(74)	(119)	(186)	(127)	(24)	(80)
	22	40	49	80	75	59
An effective worldwide government should be established.**	(75)	(113)	(173)	(124)	(23)	(79)
	60	65	72	75	61	68

Yugoslavia (self-definition)	IDEAL.	REAL.	HUMAN.	ELIT.	INDIV.
Discrimination should be considered a crime.	(239)	(493)	(161)	(25)	(41)
	82	84	75	74	76
Immigration to this country should be unrestricted.*	(241)	(493)	(162)	(26)	(40)
	35	47	48	54	58
Nationalism should be eliminated.	(238)	(487)	(157)	(26)	(41)
	59	56	54	62	59
An effective worldwide government should be established.	(240)	(491)	(161)	(25)	(40)
	43	42	35	64	30

Yugoslavia (membership in Communist League)	YES	DESIRE TO	REFUSE TO
Discrimination should be considered a crime.	(118)	(171)	(783)
	84	84	79
Immigration to this country should be unrestricted.**	(119)	(175)	(786)
	29	41	49
Nationalism should be eliminated.**	(118)	(172)	(777)
	66	62	52
An effective worldwide government should be established.	(119)	(174)	(784)
	29	38	42

*p <.01
**p <.05

Chapter 5

Career and the University

During the last few years, there has been a considerable challenge to many of the traditional concepts of living—the family; interpersonal relationships; and the notions of profit, work, and career. Students who drop out of the university—or even high school—illustrate the end product of this challenge. Their number seems to be considerably greater in industrialized countries. According to some authors, these dropouts are fleeing responsibility, afraid of entering a system where competition is great.

This phenomenon does not occur to any significant degree in countries like Nigeria and Tunisia, where the students constitute an "elite" in a real sense. The recent development of Western-style universities and the relatively small number of students make for less competition than in the West. These students will frequently have the chance to attain privileged positions and high posts in government. The choice of and preparation for a profession become very important, serving as the key to social position and financial success.

Goals in Life

It appeared to us important to discover how the concept of work and of other activities which are considered important by the society in general have been modified by student protests. We tried to ascertain the professional aspirations of the students in each country by concentrating first on the problem of a career. Just how important is a student's profession in comparison with other aspects of life? What factors play a role in the choice of a particular career? The second part of this chapter reports on students' opinions of the university as an institution leading to a profession. Does the university experience correspond to their aspirations? How do the students judge the university system?

Concerning goals in life and, later in this chapter, professional aspirations, we borrowed from two studies on American students (Gillespie and Allport, 1955; Goldsen et al., 1960). This allowed us to compare our samples with theirs, and to discover which values stayed the same or changed for young people, particularly in the United States.

PRIMARY OBJECTIVES IN LIFE

Primary objectives in life were examined by the use of the following question: "Which are the three activities which you expect will give you the greatest satisfaction in life? Your career; your family life; your leisure or hobby; your participation in political affairs concerning your country; your participation in activities at an international level; your religious beliefs and activities; other." The student could make three choices, the first representing his expected source of greatest satisfaction in life.

COMPARISON OF AMERICAN STUDENTS FROM THE 1950S AND 1960S WITH THOSE OF 1970

In spite of the lapse of twenty years, the stability of the fundamental values of American students is evident. When we compare the findings of Goldsen et al. (1960) and of Gillespie and Allport (1955) with our own, we find few changes in the choice of activities judged important or in the frequency with which they are mentioned. The findings from the 1950s are almost identical to those of today. Family life (90 percent) and career (88 percent) are mentioned as among the three greatest sources of satisfaction by the large majority of students. These astonishing similarities between the two samples are confirmed when we look specifically at the first choice of the students. The most frequently mentioned (Table 5.1) was family life—59 percent in 1970 and 55 percent in 1960 (Goldsen et al., 1960).[1]

TABLE 5.1.   The Three Greatest Sources of Satisfaction of American Students: A Comparison with the Findings Obtained by Goldsen, 1960 (Percent).

	THIS STUDY, 1970 (695)					GOLDSEN, 1960 (2,975)				
	1st choice	2nd choice	3rd choice	Total	No choice	1st choice	2nd choice	3rd choice	Total	No choice
Career	20	47	21	88	12	28	47	14	89	11
Family	59	21	10	90	9	55	27	7	89	11
Leisure pursuits	8	14	41	63	36	5	10	42	57	43
Religion	4	4	5	13	87	4	4	9	17	83
National politics	1	7	9	17	83	1	3	13	17	83
International politics	2	2	5	9	90	1	3	8	12	88

Religion and political activities are practically never mentioned as a primary source of satisfaction in the two studies (less than 5 percent). This continuity leads us to remark that, at least in the United States, the student protest movement has not affected to any major extent the political orientations of American students. The family is still the focal social institution. Student attitudes toward politics, characterized by a certain apathy in the 1950s, remain the same in the 1970s: only 17 percent in each case choose political activities as an important source of satisfaction in life. This finding may be explained by Almond and Verba's (1963) notion of American individualism: personal success supersedes any group or collective activity.

[1]Gillespie and Allport did not distinguish between the three choices.

There were somewhat more marked variations in the frequency of responses for career and leisure activities, which may be due to sampling differences. They may also have been the result of a slight increase in hedonistic values, as compared with the traditional work ethic in the United States, but even in these respects the differences were minor.

The data collected in this study show that the absence of interest in political activities is characteristic of those on the far left as it is of any other category, but, as noted below, not to the same extent. The stability of the fundamental value of American youth throughout the years—"individualism" or "privatism"—is particularly surprising in view of the apparent popularity of the student protest movement and of the counterculture. These appear, however, to represent a minority view. A consensus seems to exist, which we do not find in other countries, which places political activities at the periphery of a person's life. We must emphasize, however, that we studied only those who stayed on at a university.

Eighteen percent of the American students on the left (Table 5.1a[2]) mention political activity as one of the important sources of satisfaction in life, compared with only 13 percent of students on the right. Such a difference is in the expected direction, although not as striking as might be expected. Even among the far left students only a minority are strongly attached to political opinions (35 percent). These results become more interesting when compared to the findings in other countries. In Italy, 71 percent of the students on the far left place politics high on their list of priorities (Table 5.1a). This underlines the importance of the problem of social context. It may be the case, at least in the United States, that considerable continuity in the expression of attitudes may still be compatible with a desire for change in certain specific respects. One may remain attached to the notions of family and society while wishing to modify them, and yet not become a political activist. The relation between American students' attitudes and actions would require a more detailed study.

These findings lead us to believe that the political position of American university students is rather the expression of transitory factors than of a profound involvement, at least in comparison with other countries. The apparent political indifference of American students is compatible with a predisposition to accept changes in the socio-cultural domain. New ideas are easily assimilated. The impact of the counterculture on American youth as well as the resurgence of religious convictions may be considered the symptoms of this orientation.

In Japan the question of the greatest source of satisfaction was explored in a study by Stoetzel (1953). A comparison of his study and our own shows that young people are primarily interested in the family, leisure pursuits, career, and international affairs. We find, however, that family life and leisure pursuits are somewhat less valued today than in 1953. In Stoetzel's study, 60 percent of the students in Kyoto mentioned career and 81 percent family life as among the three most important sources of satisfaction in life. In 1970, the percentages are, respectively, 35 percent and 64 percent. In the 1950s, the fundamental objectives were family life, career, leisure pursuits (57 percent), and international affairs (51 percent). Around 1970, the students mentioned the family only as frequently as leisure activities (64 percent), then came international affairs (44 percent), and finally career (35 percent) (Table 5.2).

When we look only at the Japanese students' first choice, we find that their attitude toward the family has clearly changed: twenty years ago it was the first choice

[2]Tables variously numbered 5.1a through 5.14a are at the end of this chapter, on pages 125–137.

of 36 percent; in 1970 it was the first choice of only 9 percent. These comparisons demonstrate some of the influences of the counterculture: family life and career are now less important than leisure activities and involvement in international affairs. This last point is specific to Japan and does not emerge in the other countries studied.

TABLE 5.2.   The Three Greatest Sources of Satisfaction of Japanese Students: A Comparison with the Findings Obtained by Stoetzel, 1953 (Percent).

	THIS STUDY, 1970 (519)					STOETZEL, 1953 (96 MEN IN KYOTO)				
	1st choice	2nd choice	3rd choice	Total	No choice	1st choice	2nd choice	3rd choice	Total	No choice
Career	18	9	8	35	64	21	22	17	60	40
Family	9	30	25	64	36	36	27	18	81	19
Leisure pursuits	15	22	27	64	36	7	21	29	57	43
Religion	3	1	1	5	96	1	4	5	10	90
National politics	9	11	11	31	68	5	14	8	27	73
International politics	18	15	11	44	55	25	7	19	51	49

The data obtained over many years raise many interesting questions and underline the need for repeated studies on the formation and changes in attitudes over time.

PRINCIPAL GOALS IN LIFE: COMPARISONS BETWEEN COUNTRIES[3]

Family Life

Family life was mentioned by a majority of all students in all countries as one of the principal future sources of satisfaction. In comparative terms, the United States and Great Britain (90 percent for the first, 88 percent for the second) are at the top of the list and Japan, with 64 percent, is at the bottom. These figures refer to the choice of family life as the first, second, or third source of future satisfaction (Tables 5.1, 5.2, 5.3). If we consider only the first choice, family life is cited by the majority in all samples, except in Japan.

TABLE 5.3.   The Three Greatest Sources of Satisfaction in Life by Country, First, Second, and Third Choices (Percent).

	AUSTRAL. (771)	AUS. (485)	FRANCE (730)	GB (603)	ITALY (842)	NIG. (237)	SPAIN (740)	TUN. (145)
Career*	82	59	79	82	73	83	82	79
Family life*	84	83	77	88	84	87	79	77
Leisure*	61	67	56	67	41	31	44	43
Religious activities*	17	10	13	16	22	26	19	12
National politics*	16	24	20	11	30	27	27	23
International politics*	11	31	17	8	17	27	21	28

*p <.01

[3]Comparisons with Yugoslavia were not possible, since the coding was different.

An analysis in relation to political tendency shows that, except for the Nigerian sample, a correlation exists between the students' political attitudes and the three most important activities in life, especially with regard to the family. Conservatives tend to emphasize the role of the family, while the opposite is true for those on the left (Table 5.1a). The greatest distances between the far left and the right appear in Spain (50 percent and 94 percent), in Austria (58 percent and 95 percent), and in Australia (69 percent and 93 percent). These differences are less marked in the other countries and distances are practically nonexistent between the right and the far left in Nigeria (86 percent and 90 percent) and Tunisia (80 percent and 72 percent) and between the center and the far left in Japan (70 percent and 61 percent).

Career

Future career is mentioned almost as frequently as family life as a source of satisfaction in life. In all of the countries studied, the majority choose this option as one of the three most important sources of satisfaction. As the first choice, however, career is in second place, after the family; it is chosen by about 20 percent of all students, and most frequently by the Nigerians (31 percent). The Austrians choose it least often (13 percent).

To the extent that involvement and interest in one's future career reflect an individualistic as opposed to a "social" orientation, we might expect a relationship between political tendency and the value placed on one's personal career. No such relationship was found in the United States, Nigeria, or Tunisia. In contrast, such variations emerge in Italy, where the communists and the far left appear much less oriented toward a career (52 percent and 49 percent respectively) than the right (87 percent) and the other political categories.[4] The distribution of responses is similar in Austria (27 percent and 64 percent) and Spain (54 percent and 94 percent) and a little less marked in Australia (56 percent and 85 percent). The same pattern holds true in France only for the anarchists, who place far less value on their future profession (55 percent) than do those on the right (84 percent). For the far left in general, the Japanese (25 percent) and the Austrians (27 percent) are the least likely to expect that their careers will bring them satisfaction in life, compared with Americans (85 percent), Nigerians (86 percent), Tunisians (80 percent), and even the French (73 percent).

Choice between career and family life as primary source of satisfaction in life, by sex and by political tendency

There is considerable interaction between sex and political orientation on the one hand and the choice of career or family life, respectively, as the primary source of satisfaction in life on the other. We would expect that in general students on the right would value their career and personal success more highly than would other groups, and also that the same would be true of men as compared with women if it is still the case that women hold to a traditional family orientation. This is the case in France, where 36 percent of the men on the right gave career as their primary source of satisfaction in life as compared to 11 percent of the women. For the French sample as a whole, women chose the family more frequently (83 percent) as their primary source of future satisfaction, compared to 40 percent of the men (Table 5.1b). Similar results were found in the United States, Italy, and Great Britain. Politically con-

---

[4]As first, second, and third choices.

servative women are less oriented toward careers in the Anglo-Saxon countries and Austria (less than 10 percent) than in Italy (25 percent) and Tunisia (20 percent).

The profile of responses is completely different for the students on the far left in France—women (20 percent) mention a career as the greatest source of satisfaction more frequently than do men (4 percent)—and in Austria (40 percent and 21 percent). This reversal of attitudes may also, to a lesser extent, be observed among British and Spanish students.

NATIONAL POLITICAL ACTIVITIES

The choice of political activities as one of the three most important sources of future satisfaction differs cross-culturally. This choice is less frequent in the Anglo-Saxon countries (less than 20 percent) than in Nigeria, Spain, Italy, and Japan (about 30 percent). On the far left in Italy, 71 percent expect from their political activities some future satisfaction compared to less than 30 percent of students in other political categories. Japan holds an intermediary position: 46 percent on the left, one-third on the far left and in the center make this choice. In France 61 percent of the communists, 42 percent of the anarchists, and 36 percent of the students on the far left have similar attitudes; in Spain the figures are 63 percent on the far left and 38 percent on the left; in Australia, Nigeria, and Tunisia they are about 39 percent of the far left and in Austria 59 percent. In all of the countries studied, political orientation from the right to the moderate left is associated with only a slight interest in politics.

The significance of these findings is evident: they allow us to clarify the distinction between expressing political opinions and giving them a central position in one's existence. We may conclude that, even in the United States, the political opinions of the individual over the last two decades have shifted slightly to the left, but these changes do not seem to have had an impact on the personal life of the American students, who remain "individualists" or "privatists"—the term introduced by Gillespie and Allport. In contrast, in the other countries having revolutionary opinions implies personal involvement. But everywhere, to be a political moderate or conservative is associated with a relative absence of personal involvement with political ideas, even when these concern the affairs of the nation.

The 1977 survey

The 1977 survey (Table 5.4) reveals some changes in the value orientations of American students. Among the greatest sources of satisfaction, family is the first

TABLE 5.4.   Value Orientations, 1977 (Percent)

	FRANCE (90)	UNITED STATES (106)
Career	76	85
Family life	74	89*
Leisure	58	64
Religious activities	6	21
International activities	9	9

*First choice only 46 percent.

choice of fewer students (46 percent as compared to 59 percent). However, there is little difference between the two surveys if we consider family as one of the first three choices (89 percent versus 90 percent in 1970). An interesting difference is reflected by the increase in the choice of religion as one of the three sources of satisfaction in life (21 percent in 1977 as compared to 13 percent in 1970).

In France the overall frequencies remain the same. However, there is a slight decrease in religiosity. Only 6 percent mention religion among the three principal sources of satisfaction in 1977 as compared to 13 percent in 1970.

PROFESSIONAL ASPIRATIONS

PROFESSIONAL PLANS

The prospect of a career is clearly important to many students. We wondered whether, at this stage in their studies, they already had a precise idea of what they hoped to be doing professionally in the future. We therefore asked the following question: "When you have finished your studies, do you plan to be engaged in a specific occupation?" Except for Yugoslav students, the majority in all countries know what they wish to do in the future (Table 5.5, see p. 112).

Those most definite about the choice of their future profession are the Australians and Italians (93 percent), followed by more than 80 percent of the Austrian, Japanese, Nigerian, American, and Tunisian students. In France, Great Britain, and Spain we find fewer students (about 75 percent) who have definite plans for the future.

In the exceptional case of Yugoslavia, only 39 percent of the students have already made a decision concerning their future profession. The majority (52 percent) cannot answer.

Generally speaking, conservative or moderate students are much more likely than those on the far left to have a specific idea of what they will be doing. On the other hand, political tendency has practically no relation to the professional plans of students in Tunisia, Australia, Japan, and Nigeria, and very little in Italy.

In Spain, although no real difference exists in this respect between conservatives and leftists, the former seem more uncertain about their professional future than do the latter. On the other hand, in France, the United States, and Great Britain we find a significant distance between the far left, in which one-third of the students have no career plans, and the other groups. The students in the center or on the right usually have a specific idea of what they will be doing later.

Certain authors have tried to show that one of the important factors of the student protest movement was anomie. According to Boudon (1970b), this characteristic was often found among radical "students in the Humanities who come from comfortable and wealthy backgrounds" (p. 169). An analysis by university discipline in France, great Britain, and the U.S. shows no significant differences in this respect between students in the humanities and in the sciences (Table 5.6—page 106). In France students studying law and the social sciences, and in Great Britain those studying law and to a lesser degree those in science, were more undecided about their professional future in comparison to the others, particularly those who studied medicine, business, or engineering. But these differences are much less clear than those by political tendency.

The 1977 survey

The results obtained in the second survey indicate change in opposite directions in France and the United States. In France students are somewhat less likely to have precise occupational plans today (66 percent with such plans as compared to 75 percent in the main study). In the United States, on the contrary, 94 percent of the present respondents have such plans, as compared to 84 percent in the main study (Table 5.7).

TABLE 5.6. Professional Plans According to University Discipline in France, Great Britain, and the United States (Percent).

	HUMANITIES	SOCIAL SCIENCES	LAW	SCIENCE	MEDICINE	ENGINEERING, BUSINESS
France	(215)	(112)	(102)	(155)	(79)*	(38)
	76	64	60	71	92	77
Great Britain	(147)	(198)	(53)	(130)	–	(35)
	72	77	66	69	–	86
United States	(126)	(221)	(114)	(119)	–	(92)
	77	82	87	90	–	92

*In France, medicine is not a graduate faculty, students being admitted after high school.

CHANGES IN THE PROFESSIONAL GOALS OF AMERICAN STUDENTS BETWEEN THE 1950s AND THE 1970s

In order to establish the stability or the changes in attitude toward a profession among young people in the United States and to place the replies in a comparative perspective, we proposed to the students a list of goals involving a future profession. These were the same as those used by Goldsen et al. in the 1950s. We asked each student to indicate to which of the following goals the choice of a profession should correspond:

1. Enable me to look forward to a stable, secure future.
2. Give me an opportunity to do something useful for others.
3. Provide me with a chance to earn a good deal of money.
4. Give me a chance to exercise leadership.
5. Give me social status and prestige.
6. Give me a chance to influence the policy of my government.

The following supplementary goals touching on specific current problems were added to the original list:

1. Keep me out of a vast bureaucracy.
2. Avoid any position that contributes to the strengthening of the capitalist system.
3. Allow me to be a free person avoiding long-range commitments.
4. Leave me many free hours to do what I want.

The students were asked to rank these sentences on a Likert scale of five degrees going from "very important" to "very unimportant."

When we compare American students' replies from the 1950s and from 1970, we find that the concept of a professional life and what one expects from it have changed slightly. Motivations such as money and social status have become less important, while altruism has become more important. In the 1950s only 3 percent of the students interviewed judged the possibility of earning a great deal of money as of no importance when it came to deciding on a career. In our study the percentage reaches 35 percent. In the 1950s 43 percent of the students thought it was important to do something useful for others; in our study the figure is 83 percent. In the earlier study only 21 percent denied the importance of obtaining social status and prestige; in the present study this figure reaches 55 percent of the American sample. The importance which students ascribe to power and influence has not changed from one generation to another. One-third of the students in the two studies hope to exercise power and also to influence governmental policies.

TABLE 5.7.   Professional Plans, 1977.

	FRANCE	UNITED STATES
Percent of students knowing what profession they will exercise*	66	94
Percent not knowing	33	6

*p < .01

INTERNATIONAL COMPARISONS OF PROFESSIONAL GOALS

Table 5.8 (see p. 108) shows main findings from eleven countries studied. The large majority of students in Nigeria (86 percent), the United States (83 percent), and Italy (77 percent) believe that altruism is an important professional goal. In the other countries this dimension is not given so high a priority.

Almost all (90 percent) Nigerian students express the desire to have a stable, secure job. Then come the Tunisians (66 percent), followed by the Italians (61 percent) and the Yugoslavs (59 percent). The problem of job security is less important to students in the other countries.

A global view of the responses indicates that the desire to earn a great deal of money and to gain social status and prestige is less important to the students than to be altruistic or to have stability. Nigerians (48 percent) and Tunisians (43 percent) are those who most frequently desire their profession to enable them to gain money—and also prestige for the Nigerians (44 percent)—while the French (20 percent for money and 7 percent for prestige) desire these the least.

The Nigerian students show social ambition and aspire to positions of power. They hope to obtain a position which will allow them to exercise leadership (56 percent) and to have a chance to influence the policies of their government (45 percent). These last two goals, which are almost completely neglected by Yugoslav students (about 8 percent), are judged to be important by a third of the American students.

Another dimension included in this study, designed to test political involvement ("Avoid any position that contributes to the strengthening of the capitalist system") but not included in the Yugoslav questionnaire, shows interesting international variations. In the United States, Australia, and Great Britain students rarely (between 9 percent and 16 percent) choose this statement, while in Spain (47 percent), Tunisia (40 percent), Italy (39 percent), and France (37 percent) those who do constitute a large minority.

A rejection of bureaucracy characterizes many Yugoslav (63 percent) and Austrian and Japanese students (57 percent). Nigerian students appear less concerned by this problem (26 percent). The other countries are situated between these two extremes.

TABLE 5.8. Professional Aspirations by Country (Percent).

	AUSTR.	AUS.	FR.	GB	IT.	JAP.	NIG.	SP.	TUN.	USA	YUG.
To be useful to others*	(713) 59	(470) 46	(697) 52	(495) 57	(759) 77	(389) 35	(217) 86	(646) 78	(133) 60	(582) 83	(1,075) 43
To have a stable, secure future*	(711) 46	(474) 35	(684) 39	(493) 36	(764) 61	53	(207) 90	(647) 50	(131) 66	(580) 47	(1,066) 59
To earn a good deal of money*	(714) 31	(473) 23	(698) 20	(492) 26	(742) 29	(385) 30	(197) 48	(649) 24	(135) 43	(582) 23	(1,078) 28
To have social status and prestige*	(712) 12	(470) 9	(682) 7	(488) 10	(739) 24	24	(195) 44	(646) 19	(132) 24	(580) 13	(1,075) 16
To exercise leadership*	(710) 25	(471) 19	(677) 15	(487) 19	(723) 17	(385) 32	(194) 56	(639) 25	(130) 17	(582) 32	(1,002) 9
To influence the policy of my government*	(709) 19	(469) 18	(665) 21	(485) 12	(726) 31	(388) 26	(202) 45	(638) 35	(131) 35	(581) 32	(1,076) 8
To avoid strengthening the capitalist system*[1]	(710) 11	(471) 25	(668) 37	(488) 16	(716) 39	(387) 24	(198) 30	(640) 47	(130) 40	(575) 9	— —
To avoid the bureaucracy*	(707) 33	(470) 57	(670) 49	(485) 36	(711) 45	(388) 57	(173) 26	(622) 45	(128) 44	(577) 41	(1,074) 63
To avoid long-range commitments*	(711) 37	(473) 68	(668) 60	(491) 39	(744) 74	(385) 25	(197) 35	(642) 69	(131) 66	(580) 34	(1,075) 22
To have many free hours*	(708) 33	49	(692) 56	43	(738) 49	(390) 68	29	(649) 66	48	45	(1,078) 37

*p < .01
1. This item, of course, did not appear in Yugoslavia.

Italian (74 percent) and Spanish, Austrian, Tunisian, and French (between 69 percent and 60 percent) students approve the idea of avoiding long-term professional engagements. Japanese (25 percent) and Nigerian (35 percent) students do not appear to find this issue very important.

An analysis by political tendency (Table 5.8a) shows that the desire for altruism differentiates the far left from the rightists, especially in France (63 percent versus 32 percent) and in Great Britain (64 percent versus 41 percent). The reverse is true in Japan, where only 30 percent of the far left as compared to 45 percent of the center find this issue very important.

Students on the right are more inclined to look for stability, money, and prestige. Job stability is, however, equally important for the students on the left (68 percent) and the far left (56 percent) in Tunisia. In Nigeria, the students on the far left, like those on the right, hope that their profession will assure security (far left 94 percent and right 87 percent) and social status (far left 40 percent and right 44 percent), and that it will become a means of exercising leadership (far left 65 percent and right 46 percent). This desire for power is frequent in Nigeria; in the other countries, it usually coincides with conservative political attitudes, particularly in the United States and, to a lesser degree, in France and in Italy.

Avoiding any position which reinforces capitalism is obviously to be expected among leftists, but this relation is weak in Anglo-Saxon countries where less than 50 percent among students of the far left agree with this item. The desire to stay out of bureaucracy is also more marked among leftists, except in Austria (where even the more moderate students express this wish) and in Nigeria. In the latter country this issue matters little to students whether they are on the right or on the left.

The desire to avoid long-term engagements (rarely expressed in Japan and Nigeria) and to have a lot of free time for oneself is a professional goal of the far left, particularly in Anglo-Saxon countries. The attraction of political power and the desire to influence one's government's policies are more common among students on the far left than among conservatives, especially in Spain, Italy, the United States, and Tunisia.

The relationship between a student's university discipline and his professional aspirations may be summarized as follows: in the United States, students in law value the stability of their future position (59 percent), money (33 percent), power (50 percent), and possible influence on governmental policies (55 percent). Students in the sciences also place great importance on job stability (63 percent). Less concerned with job stability, money, and prestige, students in the social sciences desire above all else to be helpful to others (90 percent).

In Great Britain students most interested in money are those planning to be engineers (57 percent). They also look for job stability (59 percent) and for time for leisure pursuits (42 percent). Students in medicine and in the social sciences (83 percent and 67 percent respectively) hope to help others. The desire to influence governmental policies emerges most frequently among students in law.

In France students in medicine are the first to seek job stability (52 percent), while those in law hope to earn a lot of money (31 percent). Students in the social sciences surpass all others in wishing to influence the policies of their government (31 percent), to avoid any position which will encourage capitalism (61 percent), and to keep out of the bureaucratic system (66 percent).

In Tunisia money is one of the professional goals of students in all disciplines (more than 40 percent), with the exception of those in arts and letters (28 percent), who also value social prestige less than do others (9 percent). Students in the social sciences express more frequently than do others the desire to help others (80 percent), to gain political influence (65 percent), and to avoid capitalism (58 percent) and bureaucracy (60 percent).

The 1977 study

The 1977 study indicates some interesting changes, particularly in the United States. There is a decrease in altruism (68 percent in 1977 as compared to 83 percent in 1970) and in the desire to influence the policy of the government (22 percent as compared to 32 percent), to avoid a bureaucracy (28 percent versus 41 percent), and to avoid long-term commitments (22 percent versus 34 percent). There is an increase in the desires to earn a lot of money (35 percent in 1977 as compared to 23 percent in 1970) and to exercise leadership (41 percent in 1977 as compared to 32 percent in 1970), and there is no clear difference in the desire for security (49 percent versus 47 percent). These results appear to confirm the decrease in idealism of present-day students which has been noted informally by the media and other observers and the increase of privatist concerns (money, career, commitments).

In France, the results are less clear. There is a slight increase in the desire for a secure job (45 percent versus 39 percent) but a decrease in the desire to earn a lot of money (12 percent as compared to 20 percent), to avoid any contribution to capitalism (29 percent versus 37 percent), to avoid a bureaucracy (30 percent as compared to 49 percent), and long-term commitments (54 percent as compared to 60 percent) (Table 5.9).

ESTIMATION OF THE JOB MARKET

The problem of job openings was at the center of the student protest movement in France, not only because it was of obvious interest for the immediate future but also because it called into question the value of a diploma or degree. In the past, students with a degree had access to good jobs. With the expansion of the number of students acquiring diplomas, this is no longer the case to the same extent.

Are the students worried about these problems? We asked the students to evaluate the ease with which they expected to obtain the kind of work they desired after having finished their studies. In some ways, this question shows how the university is perceived as a means of achieving future goals. Rather large differences emerged among the students from the various countries. The majority of students in Tunisia (61 percent), Australia (55 percent), and Austria (63 percent), and 48 percent in Nigeria think it will be easy to find the kind of job they are looking for. In the other countries, only a minority expresses such optimism (less than 40 percent). (Table 5.10, see p. 112.)

The political orientation of the students is closely tied to their optimism or pessimism in this regard. Except for Tunisia, the findings in all countries show that the students on the far left judge their chances of finding suitable employment with pessimism (Table 5.10a).

It is difficult to evaluate the significance of these data in the case of the far left. Do they indicate that (1) the type of work sought is believed to be difficult to find by its very nature? Or (2) are there really fewer openings for those known to be leftist? Differences of opinion among the students on the far left add to the difficulty in interpreting these data. It is not surprising that in Franco Spain in 1970, 58 percent of the students on the far left believed that they would find it very difficult to secure the type of job desired; it is less easy to explain the pessimism of the Japanese (51 percent) and of the Tunisian far left students (16 percent).

TABLE 5.9. Professional Aspirations, 1977 Study (Percent).

	FRANCE	UNITED STATES
To be useful to others	(83)	(100)
	57	68
To have a stable, secure future	(84)	
	45	49
To earn a good deal of	(83)	
money**	12	35
To have social status and		
prestige	7	14
To exercise leadership*	(82)	(99)
	10	41
To influence the policy of my		
government	26	22
To avoid strengthening the	(84)	
capitalist system**	29	7
To avoid the bureaucracy	(79)	(100)
	30	28
To avoid long-range com-	(82)	
mitments*	54	22
To have many free hours	(83)	
	55	43

*p < .01
**p < .05

In Yugoslavia, students grouped in terms of the type of society they hope to realize do not represent a clear consensus concerning the facility or difficulty in finding a suitable position (Table 5.10b).

The 1977 study
The 1977 study does not show any marked change in the evaluation of one's chance to find a desirable job. In France, however, the far left is more pessimistic today (44 percent as compared to 30 percent in the main study) (Table 5.10a).

The Nature of the University

THE UNIVERSITY: PREDOMINANCE OF GOOD AND BAD ASPECTS

As indicated above (see Chapter 4), the respondents were asked to evaluate not only the society in general but also their university.

TABLE 5.5.   Professional Plans.*

	AUSTRAL. (768)	AUS. (885)	FR. (711)	GB (601)	IT. (839)	JAP. (436)	NIG. (236)	SP. (732)	TUN. (140)	USA (638)	YUG. (1,082)
Percent of students knowing what profession they will exercise	93	85	75	74	93	85	84	73	81	84	39
Percent not knowing	7	1	25	25	7	14	6	27	19	16	9

*Percentages do not always reach 100 because of those who said they could not answer.

TABLE 5.10.   Estimates of Job Opportunities by Country (Percent).

Students think they will find the kind of job they seek	AUSTRAL. (769)	AUS. (480)	FR.a (719)	FR. 1977 (92)	GB (596)	IT. (939)	JAP. (435)	NIG. (235)	SP. (733)	TUN. (143)	USA (659)	YUG. (965)
Easily	55	63	38	31	36	30	32	48	16	61	36	28
Without too much difficulty	28	25	41	42	34	41	34	41	46	30	41	44
With difficulty	17	12	21	26	30	29	34	11	38	9	23	28

TABLE 5.11.   Belief in Predominance of Good Aspects at the University (Percent).

Total sample	AUSTRAL. (697)	AUS. (452)	FR.a (640)	FR. 1977 (92)	GB (572)	IT.b (823)	JAP. (378)	NIG. (212)	SP. (695)	TUN. (123)	USA 1977 (626)	USA 1977 (105)
All students*	76	17	35	37	78	25	41	74	22	37	89	83
By political tendency												
Right*	(38) 90	(79) 35	(40) 43	(4) 3	(87) 90	(60)b 28	(139)c 47	(35) 71	(58) 41	(23) 36	(75) 88	(24) 92
Far left*	(33) 49	(61) 7	(93)a 16	(15) 13	(67) 58	(66)b 12	(109) 28	(19) 63	(82) 4	(21) 29	(25) 80	(1) 1

a10 percent of Communists.
b10 percent of Communists; 33 of the far right.
cThe category right was replaced in Japan by center.
*p < .01

The attitude of Anglo-Saxon students vis-à-vis the university is very different from that of the students from other countries. This divergence was noted above when we discussed student opinions concerning society. Almost all (89 percent) of the American students believe that on the whole their university system has more good aspects than bad. This opinion is shared by 78 percent of British and 76 percent of Australian students. In Nigeria, 74 percent of the students judged their university favorably, even though they had a rather negative opinion of their society. As the Nigerian university system is based on the British model, this fact may partially explain the similarity of opinions between the Nigerian and British students (Table 5.11).

In the other countries,[5] students judging the university favorably are, in contrast, relatively few in number. In Spain (22 percent), in Italy (25 percent), and in Austria (17 percent) we find the smallest percentages. France (35 percent), Tunisia (37 percent), and Japan (41 percent) hold intermediary positions on this issue. Thus the university system in Anglo-Saxon countries is clearly more appreciated by the students than the university systems in other countries.[6]

In Austria the students were presented with a third option: "there are as many good as bad aspects of the university." They chose either this moderate (25 percent) or the negative (40 percent) evaluation.[7] These findings indicate that Austrian students are not particularly satisfied with the university system as it now exists.

In non-Anglo-Saxon countries, political tendency (Table 5.11) has some relation to student attitudes toward the university. Opinions are a little more negative for leftists than for those on the right. Even on the right, however, fewer than half of the students are satisfied with the university system. The percentage is 36 percent in Tunisia, 35 percent in Austria, and 28 percent in Italy. In contrast, in Anglo-Saxon countries 90 percent of the students on the right think that the university is in general good. This opinion, which is shared by only 58 percent of students on the far left in Great Britain and by 49 percent in Australia, is the majority opinion among American protesters (80 percent). In Nigeria the difference in opinion between students on the far left (63 percent) and students on the right (71 percent) is minimal.

In Yugoslavia opinions on the university were sought in a different way. Students were asked to choose one of the following answers:

1. It is conservative and out of date and should be radically changed.
2. It is progressive and should remain as it is.
3. I do not know; I have not thought about it.

One-third did not know how to reply, and about half of the students believe that the university is conservative and should be radically changed (Table 5.11a). Fifty-four percent of the students who think that the university is conservative criticize the mediocrity of teaching and 55 percent criticize the attitude of faculty members. Some students go further and question the very structure of the university (21 percent) and even the sociopolitical system of their country (13 percent) (Table 5.11b).

An open-ended question allowed students to express their feelings about the university and to indicate what they considered its best and worst aspects.

[5]In Canada, a majority of English-speaking students have a favorable opinion of the university. The opposite is true for French-speaking students. In West Germany more students think the university system is good (56 percent) than bad (35 percent).

[6]These attitudes have remained remarkably unchanged in the 1977 study. The vast majority of American students (83 percent) evaluate their university positively; only a minority of French students (37 percent) do so (Table 5.11).

[7]The category "in between" was offered in the Austrian questionnaire only.

THE BEST ASPECTS OF THE UNIVERSITY

When asked to identify the two best aspects of the university, students in most of the countries studied mentioned the quality of instruction (good courses, competent professors, adequate facilities, etc.) and the chance to broaden their horizons as well as to increase their knowledge. These students also appreciated the diversity they found in the university.

United States

An atmosphere which allows me to find myself.

Diversity of programs.

Vast resources for all kinds of education.

France

Intellectual satisfaction.

Broadened horizons.

Great Britain

The chance to enrich my spirit through learning.

A wide range of choices and of combinations of courses.

Tunisia

The love of knowledge and of learning.

Nigeria

To be able to acquire mental discipline.

The feeling that there exists at the university an atmosphere of freedom frequently appears in the students' responses. They think they find at the university freedom of thought and of expression (though this type of response is rare in Tunisia) and also that they may choose between various courses with ease:

United States

Freedom to learn anything.

To be free to say and do what I want.

France

There is freedom of expression and of information.

Everybody can do what he wants when he wants to.

Great Britain

Students' independence.

Freedom to work in one's own way.

We may also note that American and British students mention the quality of interpersonal relationships and the advantages of living on campus, which is seen as a community.

Spanish and Italian students think that the development of the critical faculty represents one of the best aspects of the university. This critical spirit may lead to political awareness and possibly to involvement in the student protest movement. Tunisian students often express their satisfaction with the reforms introduced in the university, while British students mention the good rapport between professors and themselves. (Other British students say just the opposite.)

We must note that in Spain and in Tunisia, more than anywhere else, some students refuse to indicate any positive aspect in their university.

THE WORST ASPECTS OF THE UNIVERSITY

In answer to the question "What are the two worst aspects of the university?" students in all countries mentioned the poor quality of teaching. This criticism includes many aspects of university life, especially the quality of the teachers and the teaching methods employed:

United States

The faculty has a tendency to become stagnant.

Old-fashioned teaching methods.

France

A narrow viewpoint and an intellectual sclerosis of the majority of professors, leading to paralysis of the spirit of pedagogical research.

Great Britain

The fact that teaching has only a subsidiary role for the lecturer. He has no teacher training and is mainly interested in research.

Tunisia

A French, medieval type of teaching.

The university is accused of forming robots instead of developing the individual, his mind, and his capacity to think:

United States

The emphasis unfortunately is more on courses and degrees than on knowledge and individual growth.

Tunisia

University = factory.

Students also complain of the abyss between theory and practice

France

The university forms walking dictionaries rather than thinking men.

Gulf between practice and theory.

and, in contrast, of overly specialized teaching:

United States

Too much emphasis on career training.

Students also mention organizational problems, such as the difficulty of choosing courses and planning their own programs:

United States

Inflexible curriculum; no choice of courses.

France

No room.

Overpopulated courses.

Nigeria

Overcrowded programs.

All these factors are regarded as contributing to the poor quality of teaching, to the devaluation of the university degree, and, consequently, to the lack of job openings, especially in France:

Diplomas are only a piece of paper.

No job openings.

The faculty and its hierarchy represent one of the more negative aspects of the university, particularly in Great Britain, France, and Nigeria. A professor is often considered a "Mandarin" who refuses to have any contact with the student, disappearing after having delivered his lecture.

In addition to these criticisms, which deal with the immediate university environment, others concern the political position of the university. According to many leftists, the university system is not democratic and maintains an elitist perspective:

France

The inequality of chances of access.

Great Britain

Lack of equality.

Students, in particular on the far left, judge the university negatively because it supports bourgeois ideology. It is conservative:

France

It avoids Marxist economics.

As they now exist, the courses reinforce bourgeois ideology.

Tunisia

The university impedes an awareness of the political, social, and economic realities of the country.

Thus the educational system is viewed as frustrating. It prevents students from acquiring critical awareness.

Moreover, the education received is expensive—an investment by the individual —yet seems to respond primarily to the needs of the existing society.

Great Britain

More emphasis is placed on the needs of society than on those of the individual.

Large industrial firms attempt to adapt the university to their own needs.

France

Make us good businessmen.

Students also mention the effects of the protest movements. Conservative and moderate students criticize the politicization of the university. It is no longer a sanctuary from political struggles:

United States

Too political.

France

Overwhelming presence of politics.

It provokes dissension among the students, resulting in a climate of intolerance:

France

The lack of freedom of expression among students.

Leftist terrorism.

Great Britain

Growing tendency to allow freedom of expression only to those who agree with you.

According to French students, the introduction of politics into the university and the participation of students in the protest movement have resulted in complete confusion, often the work of "undesirable individuals." This is sometimes the source of violence:

Impossible to do serious work because of the strikes, marches, etc. I should note also the presence of 'undesirable nonstudents' on campus, and I speak from experience.

Times of crisis when the campus becomes a battlefield.

At the same time, students often speak of the apathy and the passivity of the majority of students, notably in Great Britain:

Apathy.

Not enough militants.

Some students, especially in Spain but also in France, dislike repression, whether it comes from the police or from public opinion:

France

Police in civilian clothes at the university; political persecutions; deceitful campaigns by the press before each election.

According to some students, the worst aspect of the university is the lack of cohesion among students on the far left and the resulting internecine struggles which cause them to lose sight of their goals:

France

The large number of political student groups which cannot agree among themselves.

Great Britain

The many, disunited factions.

The only form of action is student protest marches.

Other problems emerge which are specific to particular countries. In Australia, students criticize the excessive specialization they must undergo. In the United States and in France, students feel that they are isolated from the "real world" and live in an ivory tower:

United States

We live in isolation from the outside world.

France

A feeling of being in a ghetto.

American students mention rather frequently personal anonymity, which results from attendance at a large university; each person becomes simply a number. Others speak of lack of rapport between the sexes and of the small proportion of women at the university.

The criticisms made by Nigerian and Tunisian students show once more their preoccupation with social status and the development of their countries. They believe that the education they receive is not adapted to the needs of their country, as the university system is still based on the European model:

Tunisia

Learning is not adapted to our country but tries to imitate developed countries.

Our system follows precisely the French one, even in its worst aspects.

Nigeria

Students copy foreign ideology blindly.

Still too British, not adapted to Nigerian needs.

Nigerians also mention the corruption and the nepotism which exist in government:

Embezzlement of university funds.

Corruption and nepotism at all levels.

Dishonesty on the part of university officials.

RELEVANCE OF UNIVERSITY INSTRUCTION

Many students criticize the futility of acquiring a useless diploma, and many also question the relevance of their course work to their careers. These two criticisms played a fundamental role in student protests, since they were regarded as crucial to their future lives. In most countries students indicate that the university is not well adapted to modern society: its infrastructure is out of date, and its teaching methods have no relation to reality. In addition the students complain about the ineffectiveness of professional instruction. Seeking better to understand these problems, we asked the students, "To what extent is the education that you are now getting relevant to your occupational goals?"

A comparative analysis of the data is difficult, due to the various systems of education in the countries studied (Table 5.12, see p. 121). A rather large percentage of Spanish (58 percent), French (50 percent), and Japanese (40 percent) students believe that their education is only slightly, if at all, relevant to their future profession. This percentage is much lower in the other countries studied. In European countries the university has always had as a primary goal the transmission of scientific knowledge and of classical, humanistic culture. These objectives were only slightly modified by the reforms introduced after the student revolts around 1968. In Japan the results may reflect the division of university courses into two levels. The first one, lasting one to two years, is reserved exclusively for general education. The second, lasting about three years, is designed for specialization. The countries in which the students judge the university training as most relevant are, in order, Nigeria (81 percent), Australia and Yugoslavia (about 72 percent), Great Britain (62 percent), and Tunisia and the United States (about 50 percent). Thus apart from Tunisia, where there is considerable specialized training related to the needs of the country, and Yugoslavia, we find that it is the English-speaking students who are the most satisfied with the relevance of education they are receiving. They participate in a system of education which may be defined as professional and liberal. The cross-cultural differences in evaluating the adequacy of university education for professional training are striking.

In all countries the students on the far left represent the political segment the least satisfied and the most critical of the present system of education. Comparison of the groups on the far left in the various countries shows that Spanish protesters are the most likely to judge their studies irrelevant to their future profession (87 percent), followed by the French (60 percent) and the Japanese (53 percent). In contrast, there are relatively few among the protesters in Great Britain (25 percent), Austria (21 percent), and Nigeria (14 percent) who think that their education is not relevant (Table 5.12a).

The 1977 Study

The 1977 study (Table 5.13—page 120) shows a slight increase in the positive evaluation of university instruction among American students (59 percent versus 47 percent in 1970). In the French sample a change in the direction of a more positive attitude toward the university can be noted: 35 percent today as compared to 21 percent in the main study believe that university instruction is extremely or quite relevant to their future profession, and the proportion of discontented students drops from 50 percent in the main study to 32 percent in 1977.

THE OBJECTIVES OF THE UNIVERSITY

According to the students who do not accept a passive role vis-a-vis the university, what should the university become? Should it offer specialized instruction, or general education whose goal would be the development of the individual? The students were asked two series of questions. The first concerned the content of their education; the second dealt with the university as a means of social mobility. These two issues allow us to ascertain what the students expect from the university on a personal level.

EDUCATIONAL CONTENT

The opposition between specialized and general education is frequently considered to be profound. What should the university "transmit"? Should the university create specialists, "technicians of practical knowledge," to use Sartre's expression, or should it form "men," individuals with broad horizons?

TABLE 5.13.   Relevance of Instruction, 1977 Study (Percent).

	FRANCE (91)	UNITED STATES (106)
Extremely or quite relevant**	35	59
Somewhat relevant	33	33
Slightly or not at all relevant	32	8

**$p < .05$

Except in Japan, Nigeria, and Yugoslavia, students in general do not see any contradiction between these two objectives. The vast majority think that general education should be one of the goals of the university. At the same time, at least 84 percent of the students in English-speaking countries believe that the university should provide specialized training. The percentages are 62 percent in France and about 70 percent in Austria and Spain. In Japan and Yugoslavia 48 percent approve such specialization. In these two countries students think that the university should have as primary objectives stimulation of personal development (respectively 87 percent and 79 percent) and the encouragement of students to pursue their own interests (more than 90 percent). Eclecticism and the broadening of one's own horizons were approved by half only of the Nigerian students (Table 5.14).

Trow (1970) found that 88 percent of American students wished that the university would aid them in their general intellectual development and in their preparation for a career, and also help them to "find themselves" and to develop both professionally and personally rather than merely acquire knowledge.

THE UNIVERSITY AS A MEANS OF SOCIAL MOBILITY

The university frequently represents a means of changing, and more particularly raising, social status. The role of the university as a means to higher income and status is judged to be very important by Tunisians (76 percent) and by Nigerians (68 percent), but also by the Spanish students (63 percent). Only a minority of Japanese and Yugoslavs (20 percent and 27 percent respectively) expect these results from university training. The social ambition of the Tunisian and Nigerian students appears to be typical of students in African countries. In their study of nationalism and tribalism, Klineberg and Zavalonni (1969) indicate that this attitude is found in the six African countries studied, including Nigeria. Nearly everyone, in effect, hopes to obtain a high government post or a good job in diplomacy or in business. Education encourages these hopes, since numerous influential positions remain to be filled. Even though in the countries of the Third World access to the university is in certain respects more closed than in Occidental countries (there are fewer students), it is also more widely open socially, since students from poor families may obtain scholarships.

TABLE 5.12. Relevance of University Instruction for Future Profession (Percent).

	AUSTRAL. (768)	AUS. (477)	FR. (709)	GB (595)	IT. (839)	JAP. (433)	NIG. (235)	SP. (737)	TUN. (143)	USA (659)	YUG. (1,070)
Extremely or quite relevant*	74	63	21	62	34	28	81	5	55	47	71
Somewhat relevant	16	25	29	20	38	32	14	36	21	38	23
Slightly or not at all relevant	10	12	50	18	28	40	5	58	24	15	5

*p < .01

TABLE 5.14. Goals of the University by Country (Percent).

	AUSTRAL.	AUS.	FR.	GB	IT.	JAP.	NIG.	SP.	TUN.	USA	YUG.
To provide a basic general education*	(762) 93	(480) 94	(641) 76	(589) 96	(757) 85	(427) 86	(225) 88	(722) 84	(131) 75	(652) 97	(1,075) 86
To furnish training in highly specialized skills.*	84	(477) 70	(655) 62	(595) 85	(787) 85	(420) 48	(229) 98	(699) 69	(137) 83	(642) 85	(1,074) 47
To stimulate personal development rather than technical competence.*	(745) 89	(480) 81	(631) 83	(573) 92	(769) 80	(418) 87	(218) 50	(705) 73	(130) 83	(622) 91	(1,077) 79
To allow students to pursue personal interests without having to concentrate on one field of study.*	(738) 73	(479) 60	(591) 62	(577) 72	(752) 65	(430) 94	(227) 50	(661) 56		(634) 80	(1,074) 92
To provide the student with means to higher income and status.*	(737) 48	48	(615) 51	(562) 43	(774) 58	(402) 20	(223) 68	(708) 63	(130) 76	(592) 54	(1,073) 27

*p < .01

OBJECTIVES BY POLITICAL TENDENCY

An analysis by political tendency shows that students on the right, center, and even on the left do not desire radical transformations in the teaching system. They insist, however, that this system should emphasize both specialization and general education and allow students (in the case of the conservatives in France, Italy, Tunisia, and Spain) to improve their social status and to earn more money (Table 5.14a).

Students on the far left question the traditional teaching system. According to them, the university should present the opportunity for a general education but should also—and here enters one of the themes of the counterculture—stress the development of the individual and create for him the possibility of pursuing his own interests. In the United States and in Japan students of the far left insist particularly on the need to be able to pursue their own interests (96 percent).

Specialized instruction is usually considered secondary in importance among students on the far left, but differences occur in this respect in the countries studied: practically all Nigerians, 79 percent of the Americans, and more than 60 percent of the British, Tunisians, Australians, and Italians hope that the university will supply this type of education. Half of the Spanish, 41 percent of the French, and only 37 percent of the Austrian and Japanese far left students agree. With the exception of Nigeria and Tunisia, students on the far left do not believe that the university should give rise to a social elite.

Yugoslav students, whatever type of society they desire, hope for the same kind of education as the far leftists in America and in Japan (i.e., more emphasis on the individual, his choices, and his personal development.) There are, however, differences between political tendencies when the notion of social status is raised. Students who envision an elitist or individualist society show more social ambition than those who identify themselves as socialists or humanitarians.

Obviously, the questions posed to the students did not touch upon all the problems of the university system. Yet our analysis does present the students' perceptions of the fundamental values of the university. Conservatives support specialization; student protesters underline the need to develop the whole person; and the traditional left hopes that the university will provide both options at the same time.

It is important to note that student protesters, especially in the United States, Japan, and Yugoslavia, emphasize "the individual." The university, according to them, should provide the opportunity to study many disciplines and to follow one's own interests. The university should cease to be the vehicle for transmitting classical culture or a producer of technicians—that is, an institution representing traditional social values—and become a place where one could learn to be himself. This is also the typical desire expressed in the counterculture.

The 1977 study

The results (Table 5.15) show two opposite tendencies. French students today are less likely to expect from the university a means to higher status and income (36 percent as compared to 51 percent in the main study). American students, on the contrary, are more likely today to expect high status and income from university attendance (67 percent in 1977 as compared to 54 percent in the earlier study).

In conclusion, in this chapter we have discussed various issues pertaining to the professional aspirations of students and to the way the university is perceived as preparing them to realize their desires. Students from the countries included in this study value highly their future family life, especially in the United States, Yugo-slavia, and Great Britain, and their future career. When we compare our sample with that of Stoetzel (1953), we find that in Japan the values associated with careers and family life have decreased, while those associated with leisure activities have increased. In contrast, American students' values have remained remarkably stable, except for the changes noted in the 1977 study.

TABLE 5.15. Goals of the University, 1977 (Percent).

	FRANCE (100)	UNITED STATES (104)
To provide a basic general education	82	97
To furnish training in highly specialized skills*	51	82
To stimulate personal development rather than technical competence	75	82
To allow students to pursue personal interests without having to concentrate on one field of study	57	67
To provide the student with means to higher income and status*	36	67

*$p < .01$

First, there emerged in our study a strong interaction between political orientation, sex, and these two sources of future satisfaction (i.e., family and career). The hypothesis that a student's career would be more valued by conservatives and by men was verified in France, the United States, and Great Britain. In the far left groups in France, Great Britain, and Spain, however, we find that women give greater importance to their future professional success than do men. This may be explained by the influence of the feminist movement, which emphasizes and demands equality between the sexes.

Second, we find that the students have a rather clear idea about their future as professionals. Students on the right are more precise in this regard than those on the left in the United States, France, and Great Britain. Especially among the far left in France, indecision is frequent, since this group refuses to become involved in careerism, but this indecision does not indicate a feeling of anomie or a refusal to face life in the future.

Third, this chapter treats the professional goals of students. For American students a change has occurred: in the 1950s the major motivations were money, social status, and prestige; twenty years later the motivations are different, frequently centering on issues like altruism. Yet the desire to exercise social and political power remains unchanged. In comparison, the analysis by country shows that money, prestige, job stability, power, and political ambition are the key motivations of the students in Nigeria and in Tunisia.

Fourth, an analysis of professional aspirations by university discipline reveals some interesting findings. Students in the humanities usually wish to have a lot of free time and are not particularly interested in money or political power. Those in social sciences prefer to be helpful to others and to stay out of the capitalist system. These students are also relatively uninterested in money, job stability, or power. Students in the natural sciences, however, do generally look for job stability while worrying little about influencing their government's policies or expressing a negative view of the capitalist system. Future doctors, in contrast to what one might have expected, place little value on helping others. Money, power, political activity, and free time count more in their opinion. Finally, business majors or future engineers desire job stability, a good income, and power. To be helpful to others or to become engaged in political activities has little value to them.

There are, however, considerable national variations in all of these tendencies. It is obvious that directly connected to the problem of a student's future profession is job availability. The far left is the most pessimistic group in this regard. According to the country concerned, this issue is perceived in various ways. Students in Nigeria, Tunisia, Australia, and Austria are not afraid of the future in this respect; the opposite is true for Japan, Great Britain, and Spain.

Fifth, students were asked to judge their university in professional and personal terms. The overall evaluation was positive in the Anglo-Saxon countries and in Nigeria, more reserved in Japan, Tunisia, and France. It was negative in Italy and in Spain. It is interesting to note that the far left in the United States and in Nigeria judge the university just as favorably as the right. The same appears to be true in Tunisia.

The positive aspects of the university are the quality of its teaching and the atmosphere of freedom. Americans and Spaniards also mention the good rapport among the students, their *esprit de corps*. In Spain and in Italy the students speak of the development of critical ability and the growing "awareness" of students. Tunisians appreciate the reforms introduced into their university system. A certain number of students, however, particularly in Spain and in Tunisia, deny that their university has *any* positive aspects.

The list of negative traits of the university begins with the poor quality of teaching. This criticism includes inferior quality of the teachers, out-of-date methods, the transformation of the student into a robot unable to think for himself, teaching which is either too theoretical or too specialized, and defects of organization. To these problems must be added that of the lack of job openings. Students also criticize professors who behave as "Mandarins" eager to maintain the university *status quo* and their own superior status. Finally, students criticize the political position of the university. It is seen as an elitist system. Students on the far left believe that the whole university structure tends to reinforce a bourgeois ideology and to respond directly to the needs of society today to the detriment of concern with the individual.

Sixth, attitudes toward the student protest movement itself were examined. Conservative and moderate students think that the movement is one of the negative aspects of the university, as it leads to politicization, dissension among students, and the creation of an atmosphere of disorder and sometimes of violence. The far left complains of the apathy of the students but also of the lack of cohesion among the groups composing the far left. In general, judgments regarding the university differ from country to country. Thus in the United States students complain of anonymity, in Australia of excessive specialization; and in Tunisia and Nigeria preoccupations are mainly related to the development of the country. These latter students criticize a curriculum poorly adapted to the needs of their country and the too obvious influence of European university models.

Finally, this chapter includes the perceptions of students regarding the general function of the university. Should it center its attention on specialized or on general education? How should it respond to demands to allow students to pursue their personal development? Most students desire both specialized and general education, except for the Nigerians, who want specialization, and the Japanese and Yugoslav students, who prefer general education and the chance for personal development.

When we look at these attitudes in relation to political orientation, we find that conservatives favor specialization, the traditional left wishes both specialized and general education, and the far left emphasizes the growth and development of the individual. Yugoslav students, whatever the type of society they desire, share the attitude of the students on the far left in the United States and Japan, particularly with regard to the function of the university. In this respect the Yugoslavs appear to adopt the values of the counterculture.

Most of the results reported in this chapter devoted to the students' professional aspirations and the university show a change in the value systems of young people. Excluding the two African countries, we find a growing importance attached to the notion of the individual and his right to personal growth and development. Abandoning values like money, social prestige, and power, the students, especially those on the left, hope to learn to be themselves and to help others.

TABLE 5.1a.   The Three Greatest Sources of Satisfaction in Life by Political Tendency, First, Second and Third Choices (Percent).

Australia	RIGHT (40)	CENT. (272)	LEFT (234)	FAR L. (36)	APOL. (189)		
Career*	85	86	82	56	83		
Family life*	93	89	78	69	81		
Leisure**	55	58	59	50	66		
Religious activities**	28	23	12	8	13		
National politics*	18	12	25	39	6		
International politics*	3	9	14	31	10		

Austria	RIGHT (82)	CENT. (152)	LEFT (137)	FAR L. (69)	APOL. (45)		
Career	64	72	55	27	69		
Family life	95	89	81	58	87		
Leisure*	74	67	64	48	89		
Religious activities**	21	14	2	7	4		
National politics*	12	19	26	59	4		
International politics*	13	30	34	49	27		

France	RIGHT (43)	CENT. (138)	LEFT (208)	COMM. (49)	FAR L. (99)	ANAR. (33)	APOL. (160)
Career*	84	78	87	80	73	55	77
Family life*	81	79	83	76	63	58	79
Leisure*	60	61	52	31	45	55	69
Religious activities**	12	20	18	–	5	9	12
National politics*	9	9	20	61	36	42	8
International politics	12	13	19	12	23	18	19

(cont.)

TABLE 5.1a. Continued

Great Britain	RIGHT (89)	CENT. (91)	LEFT (200)	FAR L. (73)	APOL. (150)
Career**	89	82	83	68	83
Family life	92	87	89	81	90
Leisure*	69	60	67	55	76
Religious activities	21	14	18	12	13
National politics*	7	11	11	32	1
International politics	6	9	9	14	5

Italy	FAR R. (32)	RIGHT (67)	CENT. (153)	LEFT (228)	COMM. (113)	FAR L. (72)	APOL. (177)
Career*	81	87	79	76	52	49	79
Family life	69	85	86	89	74	71	86
Leisure	38	40	42	42	32	32	47
Religious activities*	19	21	37	23	5	11	23
National politics*	28	24	10	24	65	71	17
International politics**	28	18	10	17	26	28	13

Japan	CENT. (158)	LEFT (44)	FAR L. (126)	APOL. (111)
Career	42	34	25	35
Family life	70	55	61	59
Leisure*	61	52	52	75
Religious activities	6	–	6	4
National politics*	33	46	33	22
International politics	46	34	44	47

Nigeria	RIGHT (43)	CRITIC. (37)	LEFT (45)	FAR L. (21)	DESCR. (28)	APOL. (28)
Career**	84	76	76	86	82	95
Family life	86	86	80	90	93	91
Leisure	26	30	29	10	46	37
Religious activities*	21	32	22	24	21	32
National politics*	23	32	38	38	21	18
International politics*	40	27	24	33	7	28

Spain	RIGHT (62)	CENT. (123)	LEFT (283)	FAR L. (84)	APOL. (188)
Career*	94	91	81	54	87
Family life*	94	87	75	50	88
Leisure**	50	53	37	32	51
Religious activities**	32	16	17	12	25
National politics*	10	11	38	63	10
International politics*	13	21	23	32	17

Tunisia	RIGHT (15)	BOURGUIB. (16)	LEFT (50)	FAR L. (25)	APOL. (35)
Career	73	81	76	80	83
Family life	80	88	76	72	77
Leisure*	60	56	34	32	51

Religious activities	13	13	12	4	17
National politics*	27	6	26	40	14
International politics*	33	19	22	56	20

United States	RIGHT (80)	CENT. (129)	LIB. (196)	LEFT (138)	FAR L. (26)	APOL. (93)
Career**	90	91	86	80	85	74
Family life**	94	89	91	82	77	85
Leisure	65	61	64	61	50	66
Religious activities**	20	14	13	13	4	13
National politics**	13	16	26	18	35	12
International politics	3	9	10	13	8	5

*p < .01
**p < .05

TABLE 5.1b.　Choice between Career and Family Life as First Source of Satisfaction in Life by Sex and Political Tendency (Percent).[1]

		CAREER				FAMILY LIFE			
		RIGHT	CENT.	LEFT	FAR L.	RIGHT	CENT.	LEFT	FAR L.
Australia	Men	17	21	24	33	56	58	64	40**
	Women	–	13	19	20	60	73	69	20
Austria	Men	26	24	26	21**	63	56	38	35
	Women	8	21	29	40	79	62	51	36
France	Men	36**	20	26	4	40*	50	26*	28**
	Women	11	13	13	20	83	61	63	50
Great Britain	Men	30**	32**	16	18	43*	44*	49**	41
	Women	9	6	17	24	87	72	69	35
Italy	Men	55**	19	29	28	15*	46**	48**	22
	Women	25	18	16	11	75	69	70	28
Spain	Men	26	34	22	11	60**	46**	36	11
	Women	13	18	21	15	80	68	46	20
Tunisia	Men	33	–	43	42	83	–	55	56
	Women	20	–	29	25	67	–	72	67
United States	Men	20	20	22	23	59*	60	56	53
	Women	5	20	10	12	90	57	72	49

1. The findings for Japan and Nigeria are not included, as the number of women was very small.
*p < .01
**p < .05

TABLE 5.8a.　Professional Aspirations by Political Tendency (Percent).

Australia	RIGHT	CENT.	LEFT	FAR L.	APOL.
Be useful to others**	(37)	(254)	(216)	(29)	(177)
	51	59	69	59	50
Have a secure future*		(255)	(215)	(28)	
	51	51	37	18	55
Earn a good deal of money*		(256)	(216)	(29)	(176)
	27	33	24	24	39
Have social prestige**		(254)			
	5	16	9	7	13
Exercise leadership**	(36)	(252)	(217)	(28)	(177)
	22	29	21	11	26

(cont.)

TABLE 5.8a.   Continued

Australia	RIGHT	CENT.	LEFT	FAR L.	APOL.
Influence governmental policy*	(37)	(253)	(215)	(29)	(165)
	5	19	28	35	9
Avoid strengthening the capitalist system*		(254)	(216)	(28)	(175)
	11	5	20	47	2
Avoid bureaucracy*		(251)	(214)	(29)	(176)
	16	26	44	62	28
Avoid long-range commitments*		(254)	(215)	(28)	(177)
	22	33	39	61	40
Have many free hours*			(213)		(176)
	11	27	37	57	39

Austria	RIGHT	CENT.	LEFT	FAR L.	APOL.
Be useful to others**	(81)	(148)	(134)	(63)	(44)
	47	42	46	62	39
Have a secure future*	(80)	(149)	(137)		(45)
	50	42	26	10	51
Earn a good deal of money*		(148)	(136)	(65)	(44)
	23	32	18	6	34
Have social prestige**				(63)	(43)
	14	13	6	2	12
Exercise leadership**				(64)	
	18	25	21	8	14
Influence governmental policy*	(79)		(134)	(65)	
	10	11	24	42	
Avoid strengthening the capitalist system*		(147)	(135)	(66)	(44)
	8	8	32	80	5
Avoid bureaucracy**		(149)	(134)	(64)	
	58	55	63	59	41
Avoid long-range commitments**	(80)		(136)	(66)	(42)
	53	69	72	74	72
Have many free hours*				(64)	(44)
	41	48	56	47	50

France	RIGHT	CENT.	LEFT	COMM.	FAR L.	ANAR.	APOL.
Be useful to others**	(41)	(134)	(196)	(43)	(92)	(31)	(150)
	32	49	58	47	63	45	51
Have a secure future*		(131)	(185)	(44)	(94)	(30)	(149)
	68	49	44	25	26	10	33
Earn a good deal of money*		(132)	(194)		(95)	(31)	(151)
	39	24	19	5	7	16	24
Have social prestige**	(40)	(130)	(183)	(45)	(93)	(30)	
	23	9	5	4	3	3	5
Exercise leadership**		(131)	(192)	(44)	(92)	(31)	(147)
	28	14	15	16	12	13	14
Influence governmental policy*	(38)	(133)	(189)	(40)	(91)	(30)	(144)
	11	11	22	35	35	43	14
Avoid strengthening the capitalist system*	(40)	(128)		(44)	(93)	(29)	(145)
	5	14	35	80	71	69	26
Avoid bureaucracy*	(39)	(130)	(192)	(42)	(91)		(147)
	28	40	48	55	63	62	50
Avoid long-range commitments*			(194)	(40)	(89)	(31)	(145)
	59	62	60	40	54	71	66
Have many free hours*	(41)	(133)	(195)	(44)	(92)		(146)
	37	54	55	46	54	61	66

Great Britain	RIGHT	CENT.	LEFT	FAR L.	APOL.
Be useful to others	(73)	(77)	(170)	(59)	(116)
	41	59	60	64	53
Have a secure future*		(76)	(169)		
	50	32	31	14	48
Earn a good deal of money**					(115)
	32	29	24	14	31
Have social prestige**				(57)	(113)
	19	12	5		13
Exercise leadership	(71)	(75)	(168)	(59)	(114)
	27	19	19	17	15
Influence governmental policy**			(167)	(58)	
	1	7	19	24	4
Avoid strengthening the capitalist system*	(72)		(168)		(115)
	1	5	23	40	10
Avoid bureaucracy*	(71)		(167)	(59)	(113)
	17	43	37	64	27
Avoid long-range commitments*	(73)	(76)	(168)	(57)	(117)
	23	41	38	53	41
Have many free hours*			(170)		(115)
	36	32	48	60	37

Italy	FAR R.	RIGHT	CENT.	LEFT	COMM.	FAR L.	APOL.
Be useful to others	(27)	(61)	(141)	(204)	(96)	(64)	(166)
	74	66	77	78	77	77	81
Have a secure future**	(30)	(64)	(145)	(205)		(62)	(162)
	80	75	72	62	33	32	67
Earn a good deal of money*		(59)	(139)	(196)	(94)		
	53	36	29	28	15	16	36
Have social prestige*	(29)	(61)		(199)	(92)	(60)	(159)
	59	36	26	22	10	10	28
Exercise leadership*	(28)	(57)	(135)	(193)		(61)	(157)
	43	28	17	12	11	15	17
Influence governmental policy*		(58)	(136)	(196)	(94)	(59)	(155)
	21	26	16	33	60	56	19
Avoid strengthening the capitalist system*	(27)	(56)	(134)	(192)	(95)	(61)	(151)
	15	14	15	41	78	74	34
Avoid bureaucracy*	(29)	(55)	(136)	(188)	(89)	(60)	(144)
	24	38	35	50	65	70	33
Avoid long-range com-mitments	(31)	(59)	(133)	(201)	(96)	(62)	(162)
	74	68	68	78	77	78	73
Have many free hours**	(28)	(56)	(140)	(199)	(95)	(63)	(157)
	36	46	51	53	53	38	48

Japan	CENTER	LEFT	FAR L.	APOL.
Be useful to others**	(141)	(40)	(108)	(100)
	45	35	30	26
Have a secure future**				
	59	60	40	56
Earn a good deal of money**				
	36	23	19	34
Have social prestige				
	28	33	17	22
Exercise leadership**	(140)	(38)	(107)	
	37	42	29	25

(cont.)

TABLE 5.8a.   Continued

Japan		Center	Left	Far L.	Apol.
Influence governmental policy*		(141) 26	(40) 45	(108) 25	(99) 18
Avoid strengthening the capitalist system**		(140) 18	20	37	19
Avoid bureaucracy**		(141) 52	43	65	60
Avoid long-range commitments**			19	13	33	(96) 28
Have many free hours**		(142) 69	50	71	(100) 70

Nigeria	Right	Critic.	Left	Far L.	Descr.	Apol.
Be useful to others	(39) 85	(35) 91	(37) 89	(20) 85	(27) 78	(54) 83
Have a secure future**	(38) 87	(34) 85	89	(18) 94	(24) 88	(51) 94
Earn a good deal of money*	(36) 47	(32) 31	(31) 52	(19) 47	(21) 43	(53) 57
Have social prestige**	(34) 44	31	(32) 41	(20) 40	(20) 40	(52) 54
Exercise leadership	(33) 46	(34) 59	(37) 62	65	(23) 52	(53) 54
Influence governmental policy*	(35) 34	52	70	(18) 44	(21) 38	32
Avoid strengthening the capitalist system*	(33) 12	24	(34) 47	(19) 32	38	(52) 31
Avoid bureaucracy**	18	(29) 17	(31) 29	(18) 33	14	(46) 35
Avoid long-range commitments**	(35) 26	(31) 36	(32) 47	(19) 37	(22) 41	(53) 34
Have many free hours	29	(35) 21	(34) 32	(18) 33	(20) 40	(52) 25

Spain		Right	Cent.	Left	Far L.	Apol.
Be useful to others		(56) 76	(103) 83	(250) 77	(70) 84	(169) 75
Have a secure future*		(54) 78	(105) 68	(251) 36	(69) 23	(168) 63
Earn a good deal of money*		37	(104) 34	(252) 15	(71) 7	36
Have social prestige*		37	(103) 23	(251) 15	8	(167) 23
Exercise leadership**		(56) 28	(102) 23	(247) 25	(68) 35	(166) 20
Influence governmental policy*		(53) 17	22	47	(70) 80	(166) 12
Avoid strengthening the capitalist system*		(54) 15	(100) 36	(251) 60	(72) 85	(163) 28
Avoid bureaucracy*		(51) 24	(101) 40	(244) 51	(67) 78	(159) 30
Avoid long-range commitments**		(56) 59	(103) 78	(251) 67	(69) 65	(165) 70
Have many free hours**		(54) 61	72	(252) 65	(72) 56	(168) 70

Tunisia	RIGHT	BOURGUIB.	LEFT	FAR L.	APOL.
Be useful to others**	(15) 53	(13) 69	(44) 61	(25) 68	(32) 50
Have a secure future	73	62	(43) 68	56	(31) 65
Earn a good deal of money*	60	(14) 50	(46) 33	28	55
Have social prestige	33	(13) 23	(45) 24	(24) 17	19
Exercise leadership	13	(14) 21	(43) 16	17	19
Influence governmental policy*	33	(13) 23	(42) 38	(25) 56	(32) 22
Avoid strengthening the capitalist system*	40	31	(44) 52	(23) 57	(31) 16
Avoid bureaucracy*	(14) 14	54	(42) 52	(24) 54	32
Avoid long-range commitments*	(15) 80	(14) 50	(43) 65	(23) 57	(32) 69
Have many free hours*	(14) 64	36	(44) 41	52	56

United States	RIGHT	CENT.	LIB.	LEFT	FAR L.	APOL.
Be useful to others	(75) 76	(118) 81	(176) 89	(112) 84	(19) 80	(82) 76
Have a secure future*	(74) 70	60	47	36	5	(81) 36
Earn a good deal of money*	(75) 40	27	24	9	16	(82) 18
Have social prestige**	25	(117) 11	16	5		(81) 12
Exercise leadership*	44	(118) 31	41	19	26	(82) 20
Influence governmental policy*	21	(117) 27	32	42	58	26
Avoid strengthening the capitalist system*	4	(114) 3	(175) 4	(111) 19	42	(81) 9
Avoid bureaucracy*	32	25	47	(112) 47	53	(82) 48
Avoid long-range commitments*	23	(117) 26	(176) 35	37	74	(81) 40
Have many free hours*	47	35	48	(113) 41	74	(80) 53

Yugoslavia (self-definition)	IDEAL.	REAL.	HUMAN.	ELIT.	INDIV.
Be useful to others	(237) 48	(493) 42	(162) 33	(24) 32	(39) 44
Have a secure future	(240) 58	(494) 61	61	(25) 56	(41) 71
Earn a good deal of money**	(238) 24	(493) 27	(161) 34	(26) 39	42
Have social prestige	(237) 15	(432) 16	(162) 13	(22) 8	(35) 13
Exercise leadership	(238) 7	(491) 9	(160) 9	(26) 8	(40) 15

(cont.)

TABLE 5.8a. Continued

Yugoslavia (self-definition)	IDEAL.	REAL.	HUMAN.	ELIT.	INDIV.
Influence governmental policy		(494)	(162)		(39)
	11	7	6	8	8
Avoid bureaucracy	(236)	(492)		(22)	(37)
	61	65	67	50	60
Avoid long-range commitments	(237)	(493)		(26)	(38)
	17	22	26	23	31
Have many free hours*	(239)	(494)	(161)		(40)
	33	34	44	42	53

*$p < .01$
**$p < .05$

TABLE 5.10a.   Estimates of Job Opportunities by Students of the Far Left (Percent).

Students think they will find the kind of job they seek	AUSTRAL. (36)	AUS. (66)	FR. (93)	FR. 1977 (16)	GB (73)	IT. (72)	JAP. (123)
Easily	25	24	25	13	27	24	20
Without too much difficulty	30	44	45	44	35	30	29
With difficulty	45	32	30	44	38	46	51

Students think they will find the kind of job they seek	NIG. (21)	SP. (83)	TUN. (25)	USA (26)	USA 1977 (4)
Easily	33	8	64	31	(1)
Without too much difficulty	38	34	20	23	(1)
With difficulty	29	58	16	46	(2)

TABLE 5.10b.   Estimates of Job Opportunities by Political Self-Definition, Yugoslavia (Percent).

Students think they will find the kind of job they seek	IDEAL. (228)	REAL. (468)	HUMAN. (155)	ELIT. (24)	INDIV. (38)
Easily	32	27	26	29	37
Without too much difficulty	45	46	39	46	26
With difficulty	23	27	36	25	37

TABLE 5.11a.   Yugoslav Students Judge Their University (Percent).

	ALL STUDENTS (959)	IDEAL. (241)	REAL. (489)	HUMAN. (161)	ELIT. (26)	INDIV. (42)
The University is conservative and out of date and should be radically changed.	46	38	49	47	54	36
It is progressive and should remain as it is.	19	22	18	18	19	19
I do not know, have not thought about it.	35	40	33	35	27	45

TABLE 5.11b. Yugoslav Students Who Agree that the University Is Conservative (Percent).

	ALL STUDENTS (483)	IDEAL. (92)	REAL. (241)	HUMAN. (76)	ELIT. (14) (N)	INDIV. (15) (N)
This situation is due to						
the sociopolitical structure of the country	13	15	14	12	–	(1)
the structure of the University	21	17	10	10	(1)	(2)
the mediocrity of teaching	54	46	60	43	(10)	(8)
the attitude of professors	55	43	62	43	(11)	(9)
the lack of equipment	15	11	17	13	(3)	(1)
the attitude of the students	14	10	15	17	(1)	(1)

TABLE 5.12a. Relevance of University Instruction for Future Profession by Political Tendency (Percent).

Australia			RIGHT (40)	CENT. (271)	LEFT (233)	FAR L. (35)	APOL. (189)
Extremely or quite relevant**			83	78	74	37	73
Somewhat relevant			10	14	17	26	19
Slightly or not at all relevant			7	8	9	37	9

Austria			RIGHT (82)	CENT. (150)	LEFT (137)	FAR L. (66)	APOL. (44)
Extremely or quite relevant**			67	65	62	47	77
Somewhat relevant			20	27	26	38	16
Slightly or not at all relevant			13	7	12	21	11

France	RIGHT (43)	CENT. (130)	LEFT (203)	COMM. (49)	FAR L. (92)	ANAR. (32)	APOL. (154)
Extremely or quite relevant	35	28	19	8	14	19	23
Somewhat relevant	37	35	29	16	26	19	29
Slightly or not at all relevant	28	36	52	76	60	63	48

Great Britain			RIGHT (89)	CENT. (91)	LEFT (193)	FAR L. (73)	APOL. (149)
Extremely or quite relevant			71	56	63	55	61
Somewhat relevant			14	24	21	21	20
Slightly or not at all relevant			16	20	16	25	19

Italy	FAR R. (32)	RIGHT (67)	CENT. (153)	LEFT (226)	COMM. (112)	FAR L. (72)	APOL. (177)
Extremely or quite relevant**	38	49	40	30	16	18	45
Somewhat relevant	31	28	44	41	38	40	33
Slightly or not at all relevant	31	22	16	29	46	42	21

(cont.)

TABLE 5.12a.   Continued

Japan			CENT. (156)	LEFT (44)	FAR L. (123)	APOL. (110)
Extremely or quite relevant**			34	39	17	29
Somewhat relevant			31	32	30	30
Slightly or not at all relevant			32	53	53	41

Nigeria	RIGHT (48)	CRITIC. (36)	LEFT (45)	FAR L. (21)	DESCR. (28)	APOL. (57)
Extremely or quite relevant	83	83	87	67	79	81
Somewhat relevant	17	11	11	19	11	14
Slightly or not at all relevant	–	6	2	14	11	5

Spain	RIGHT (62)	CENT. (122)	LEFT (282)	FAR L. (84)		APOL. (87)
Extremely or quite relevant**	10	9	2	2		5
Somewhat relevant	42	45	32	11		47
Slightly or not at all relevant	48	46	66	87		47

Tunisia	RIGHT (15)	BOURGUIB. (16)	LEFT (50)	FAR L. (25)		APOL. (35)
Extremely or quite relevant	67	63	54	52		52
Somewhat relevant	27	19	20	16		24
Slightly or not at all relevant	7	19	26	32		24

United States	RIGHT (80)	CENT. (129)	LIB. (196)	LEFT (136)	FAR L. (26)	APOL. (92)
Extremely or quite relevant**	63	59	53	49	39	47
Somewhat relevant	29	30	35	40	27	38
Slightly or not at all relevant**	9	12	13	11	35	15

Yugoslavia (self-definition)	IDEAL. (236)	REAL. (489)	HUMAN. (161)	ELIT. (25)	INDIV. (42)
Extremely or quite relevant	74	70	73	64	72
Somewhat relevant	23	25	22	28	21
Slightly or not at all relevant	3	5	5	8	7

**p < .05

TABLE 5.14a.   Goals of the University by Political Tendency (Percent).

Australia	RIGHT	CENT.	LEFT	FAR L.	APOL.
Basic general education	(39) 90	(269) 93	(231) 95	(36) 100	(187) 91
Training in specialized skills*	(40) 85	(271) 82	(234) 79	61	(186) 90
Personal development	(38) 79	(268) 87	(228) 93	92	(185) 88
Pursuit of personal interests*	55	(257) 66	(227) 78	89	(180) 75
Means to higher income and status*	(39) 59	(264) 53	(220) 38	(35) 20	(179) 57

Austria	RIGHT	CENT.	LEFT	FAR L.	APOL.
Basic general education	(82) 88	(150) 97	(135) 93	(68) 97	(45) 98

	RIGHT	CENT.	LEFT	COMM.	FAR L.	ANAR.	APOL.
Training in specialized skills*			(80) 84	79	(134) 64	38	82
Personal development*			(82) 68	83	(135) 79	97	73
Pursuit of personal interests*			46	(149) 57	62	78	56
Means to higher income and status*			(81) 64	(150) 57	36	16	73

France	RIGHT	CENT.	LEFT	COMM.	FAR L.	ANAR.	APOL.
Basic general education**	(39) 85	(128) 81	(183) 73	(43) 63	(89) 64	(27) 74	(132) 83
Training in specialized skills*	(38) 87	(126) 73	(190) 65	(46) 59	(88) 41	(28) 29	(139) 63
Personal development*	(33) 73	(116) 77	(182) 86	(37) 81	(93) 88	(30) 100	(140) 79
Pursuit of personal interests*	(30) 40	(120) 55	(170) 63	54	(85) 64	(27) 85	(122) 68
Means to higher income and status*	(36) 94	(115) 68	(183) 50	(42) 21	(84) 22	(28) 18	(127) 63

Great Britain	RIGHT	CENT.	LEFT	FAR L.	APOL.
Basic general education	(88) 92	(90) 96	(192) 98	(72) 94	(147) 99
Training in specialized skills*	(87) 91	(89) 88	(198) 86	(71) 69	(150) 85
Personal development	(85) 87	(85) 95	(195) 93	(69) 93	(139) 90
Pursuit of personal interests*	(86) 56	(84) 67	(193) 80	(70) 84	(144) 67
Means to higher income and status*	(85) 80	(82) 50	(185) 28	(69) 14	(141) 52

Italy	FAR R.	RIGHT	CENT.	LEFT	COMM.	FAR L.	APOL.
Basic general education*	(29) 86	(64) 70	(142) 84	(211) 86	(93) 83	(67) 84	(151) 93
Training in specialized skills*	(32) 100	(67) 96	(147) 95	(216) 87	(100) 62	64	(158) 91
Personal development**	(30) 70	(58) 67	(143) 79	(213) 84	(102) 80	(63) 83	(160) 79
Pursuit of personal interests*	(31) 52	(62) 47	(131) 63	(201) 69	(103) 76	(68) 72	(156) 63
Means to higher income and status*	84	85	(140) 69	(211) 54	(100) 37	(69) 29	(161) 66

Japan	CENT.	LEFT	FAR L.	APOL.
Basic general education	(156) 89	(43) 84	(120) 88	(108) 82
Training in specialized skills*	(153) 50	(41) 61	(117) 37	(109) 51
Personal development	(150) 86	(43) 84	86	88
Pursuit of personal interests	(156) 94	84	(124) 96	(107) 98

(cont.)

TABLE 5.14a.   Continued

Japan			CENT.	LEFT	FAR L.	APOL.
Means to higher income and status			(138)	(42)	(120)	(102)
			20	29	13	25

Nigeria	RIGHT	CRITIC.	LEFT	FAR L.	DESCR.	APOL.
Basic general education	(41)	(36)	(41)	(21)	(26)	(54)
	85	92	83	91	92	89
Training in specialized skills	(42)				(28)	(56)
	95	97	98	100	100	98
Personal development*	(40)	(35)	(37)	(20)	(29)	(53)
	65	54	51	35	48	40
Pursuit of personal interests	(42)	(36)	(39)	(21)	(27)	(56)
	48	47	56	48	48	52
Means to higher income and status*	(40)	(35)	(40)	(20)	(27)	(55)
	63	57	68	65	63	82

Spain		RIGHT	CENT.	LEFT	FAR L.	APOL.
Basic general education*		(60)	(122)	(279)	(80)	(181)
		95	87	81	69	91
Training in specialized skills*		(56)	(119)	(271)	(76)	(177)
		71	82	63	54	75
Personal development		(58)	(121)	(271)	(80)	(175)
		79	76	74	65	70
Pursuit of personal interests**		(55)	(113)	(261)	(79)	(153)
		42	54	59	57	60
Means to higher income and status*		(59)	(119)	(272)	(81)	(177)
		76	76	58	38	71

Tunisia		RIGHT	BOURGUIB.	LEFT	FAR L.	APOL.
Basic general education			(15)	(16)	(41)	(22)	(33)
			73	75	73	77	76
Training in specialized skills			(14)		(46)	(24)	
			86	81	85	71	85
Personal development*				(14)	(43)		(31)
			64	64	70	88	81
Means to higher income and status*			(15)	(14)	(44)	(23)	(31)
			93	72	68	78	77

United States		RIGHT	CENT.	LIB.	LEFT	FAR L.	APOL.
Basic general education		(79)	(125)	(195)	(136)	(26)	(91)
		95	98	99	96	92	98
Training in specialized skills		(80)	(124)	(189)	(134)	(24)	
		84	91	84	80	79	81
Personal development		(75)	(120)	(186)	(131)	(23)	(87)
		84	87	95	95	87	91
Pursuit of personal interests*		(79)	(123)	(189)	(133)	(24)	(88)
		66	75	80	89	96	82
Means to higher income and status*		(72)	(117)	(180)	(123)	(22)	(78)
		78	68	53	34	41	51

Yugoslavia (by membership in the Communist League)				YES	DESIRE TO	REFUSE TO
Basic general education				(119)	(174)	(782)
				90	86	86
Training in specialized skills						(781)
				44	46	48

Personal development		(174)	(784)
	77	84	78
Pursuit of personal interests		(172)	(783)
	94	92	92
Means to higher income and status		(173)	(781)
	19	21	29

*p < .01
**p < .05

Chapter 6

Social and Moral Issues

The analysis of the political opinions and the personal aspirations of students has indicated that a rather significant protest movement has emerged. A large number of students in all countries have taken political positions, frequently against the status quo. Even in Anglo-Saxon countries, where students are in general rather optimistic and not too dissatisfied with their university system or with society in general, there still appears among those on the left a considerable degree of rejection. This rejection includes the university—as an alleged purveyor of bourgeois ideology—and condemns the social necessity of becoming integrated into a system judged as alienating.

How is this questioning of a certain social system translated into attitudes toward culture and the mores of society? In this section of our study, we will deal specifically with various cultural and social values, and the relation between generations. We shall attempt to see how this protest movement, involving politics, the university, and one's own career, corresponds to different life styles and to the attitude toward parents.

The conflict between generations has been one of the most frequently suggested explanations in the literature concerning the student protest movement. Feuer (1968) goes as far as to consider the conflict between generations as more important in history than the conflict between classes. While the conflict of classes is based on socioeconomic considerations, that between generations is more often viewed in a psychoanalytic perspective, seen as a question of personality. As we noted in Chapter 1, it is only one small step from this perspective to an emphasis on the pathological characteristics of the student protesters.

If the generation conflict is worldwide, we must ask why it leads young people to revolt at some times and not at others. Davis (1940) suggests that generation conflict explodes into real social conflict as a function of the interplay between several variables: he mentions

> the interaction of certain universal laws between parents and their children and other dimensions inherent in modern culture. The universal laws are: 1) the fundamental age or the differential birth cycle between parents and off-spring; 2) the slowing down of the socialization process with maturation; 3) intrinsic differences between the young and the old on the psychological and physiological levels as well as on the sociological one. While these factors tend to produce conflicts between parents and children, their interaction depends on four other variables: 1) the rate of social change; 2) the degree of complexity of the social structure; 3) the degree of integration into the culture; and 4) the rapidity of movement (e.g., vertical mobility) within the structure and its relationship to cultural values [in Coser, ed., 1964, pp. 470–471].

In the countries included in our study, we find these four complex variables to be operative in various degrees. Social change and upward mobility are certainly very important in developing countries like Tunisia and Nigeria, and somewhat less so in other countries where the social structure and level of integration are more complex and industrially developed. We shall attempt to see what cultural and attitudinal differences emerge between these two groups of countries as we examine the student replies. We have already noted that Tunisia and Nigeria are among the countries in which criticism of society is most common.

We have already pointed out that one fundamental question remains unanswered: why do some young people and not others from the same society rebel? Psychoanalysis intervenes here, attempting to explain the protest attitude on the basis of unconscious psychological mechanisms. Those who are considered "marginal" may reject their society for economic reasons but also (according to psychoanalytic theory) because of severe personal problems, frequently due to their inability to transcend the Oedipal stage of development.

Who are those who, according to Mendel (1969), "refuse their heritage," who constitute "recalcitrant descendants"? Numerous findings, accumulated especially in the United States, do not indicate that there are more psychopathic personalities among the protesters than among the conformists. Indeed, the opposite seems true. These same studies also reveal, not a revolt against the father, but rather an attempt to revivify values learned at the family table which have become blunted with time.

Too often authors have focused their attention uniquely on the protesters. But why (if Oedipus is responsible!) do not other young people—apoliticals, conservatives, or moderates—also rebel? Do they feel the same way about the generation gap? Do they differ from the protesters in their daily life and aspirations? Are they also looking for another life style and new values? Do they think that the gulf between their generation and the preceding one is greater than in the past? If these differences exist, do they directly affect the relationships between parents and their children? Our questionnaire was designed to clarify and to determine more precisely the reality of the generation conflict among students in our samples who have divergent political views and live in different socioeconomic contexts.

The Generation Conflict

CONFLICT ON THE GLOBAL LEVEL

The media and popular culture, especially in Western countries, tend to emphasize the differences between age groups as constituting a serious social problem. It is therefore not surprising to find that in all the countries studied at least 75 percent of the students think that "in our society today, the conflict of generations is acutely felt." The Tunisians (92 percent) and the Spaniards (91 percent) are the most numerous to perceive this conflict of generations; the Yugoslavs (76 percent) and the Japanese (75 percent) are least so. The other countries occupy a position in between[1] (Table 6.1, see p. 142).

---

[1]In West Germany the percentage is 84 percent, which is quite similar to that in Austria, 86 percent.

Differences among countries emerge more clearly when the students are asked their opinion of the following: "The present differences between social and moral values of youth and the older generation are far greater than in the past." In the two African countries we find the largest number of students (about 90 percent) who are certain that this situation exists. In the Anglo-Saxon countries and in Yugoslavia this feeling is less widely shared (United States, Australia, and Yugoslavia 68 percent; Great Britain 61 percent). Most European countries and Japan are in between these two groups[2] (Table 6.1a). We also find in the United States divergent views: 83 percent of the students on the far left versus 57 percent of the Republicans and 69 percent of the Democrats agree that the gap between the generations is greater today than in the past (Table 6.1a). (Tables 6.1a–6.9a appear on pages 174–191.)

Finally, it is interesting to note the attitude of French communists, since they are quite apart from other political groups on these two questions: about half of the communists do not believe that a generation or value conflict exists between them and the preceding generation as compared to more or less 70 percent for the other political groups in this country.

The perception of a generation conflict and of a change in values is, therefore, found in varying degrees in all the countries studied. It is more accentuated among African and European than among Anglo-Saxon students.

THE 1977 STUDY

In the United States, the 1977 study indicates a striking decrease of respondents who perceive an intergenerational conflict in their society. Only 46 percent of the respondents agree that the differences in social and moral values of youth and the older generation are far greater now than in the past, as compared to 68 percent in 1970. Correspondingly, only 57 percent in 1977 as compared to 88 percent in 1970 agree that in their society today the conflict of generations is acutely felt (Table 6.2).

In France a similar decrease in the perception of existing intergenerational conflicts can be seen: 54 percent versus 73 percent in 1970 consider that the differences between generations are greater today than in the past, and 67 percent as compared to 79 percent feel that the conflict of generations is acutely felt.

CONFLICT AT THE LEVEL OF THE FAMILY

When we compare value systems not between generations but within families, we find that the generation conflict is much less visible on the individual than on the global level. The question (except in Yugoslavia) reads, "Can you indicate how close you feel to your parents in emotional terms, in moral values, and in political outlook?"

The findings show that in general students feel rather close to their parents in *emotional terms*, less close in *moral values*, and clearly less close in *political outlook*. Yet rather distinct differences appear among countries (Table 6.3, see p. 142).

On the whole, except in Austria and to a lesser degree in Japan, few students (less than 20 percent) think they are in *emotional conflict* with their parents. In Japan the percentage rises to 26 percent, while in Austria one out of three students mentions

[2]In West Germany 73 percent and in Austria 78 percent hold this view.

the existence of such an emotional conflict. The large majority of Nigerian and Tunisian students (more than 90 percent) deny the existence of conflict with their parents in this respect. The Spanish and the French (86 percent) students seem to get along somewhat better with their parents than do Italian students (79 percent). Finally, few differences exist among Anglo-Saxon countries (between 80 percent and 85 percent).[3]

TABLE 6.2.   Conflict between Generations, 1977 (Percent).

	FRANCE	UNITED STATES
Differences between social and moral values of youth and the older generation are far greater than in the past.	(91) 54	(101) 46
In our society today, the conflict of generations is acutely felt.	67	(104) 57
The family is a universally oppressive institution.	29	13

The analysis by political tendency shows that moderate students and those on the right are, in general, in much closer agreement with their parents in all three domains than are the students on the left and especially those on the far left. Fewer than one-fifth of students on the right in all countries (except in Austria, where the proportion was about one-third) mention an emotional conflict with their parents. In contrast, about one-quarter of the students on the far left in Australia and Great Britain and about one-third of such students in Spain, Italy, Japan, and the United States speak of such conflict. In France, Tunisia, and Nigeria, however, even the far left—like the right—does not experience such an emotional conflict (about 10 percent). This conflict seems most important in Austria, since it is mentioned by half of the students on the far left and 41 percent of the students on the left (Table 6.3a).

The gulf between students on the right and on the left in relation to their parents is greater when we examine *moral values* (Table 6.3a). Excluding Nigeria, where no differences emerged, the students on the right feel much closer to the moral values of their parents than those on the far left. Moral conflicts appear relatively unimportant in the United States, where 75 percent of the students on the right feel close to their parents on moral issues, compared to 54 percent of students on the far left; similar differences are found in Japan (center, 57 percent; far left, 39 percent) and in Australia (right, 65 percent; far left, 38 percent). In Tunisia, 87 percent of the Bourguibists endorse the moral value system of their parents, compared to 63 percent of the students on the far left. The distance between the conservatives and the protesters with regard to their families on moral issues is more accentuated in France (77 percent and 44 percent respectively), in Great Britain (68 percent and 32 percent), and in Austria (49 percent and 9 percent). The difference is greatest in Spain (72 percent and 23 percent) and in Italy (94 percent and 39 percent respectively).

Political opinions give rise to even greater variations between parents and their children, especially if the latter adhere to the ideologies of the far left. This is clear, for example, in Italy, where only 23 percent of the students on the far left share the political opinions of their parents, compared to 78 percent of the students on the right. The corresponding figures for Austria are 17 percent and 70 percent, for Spain 18 percent and 60 percent, for France 33 percent and 79 percent, for the United States 35 percent and 79 percent, for Australia 35 percent and 80 percent, and for

[3]In the 1977 study (Table 6.4) this percentage remains the same, both for the French and the US sample.

TABLE 6.1. Conflict between Generations by Country (Percent).

	AUSTRAL.	AUS.	FR.	GB	ITALY	JAPAN	NIGERIA	SPAIN	TUNISIA	USA	YUG.
Differences between social and moral values of youth and the older generation are far greater than in the past.*	(732) 68	(480) 78	(681) 73	(580) 61	(787) 79	(411) 78	(230) 90	(699) 78	(137) 92	(639) 68	(1,077) 69
In our society today, the conflict of generations is acutely felt.**	(762) 82	86	(678) 79	(598) 80	(811) 89	(409) 75	(214) 83	(722) 91	(133) 92	(655) 88	76
The family is a universally oppressive institution.*	(750) 20	(479) 32	(693) 31	(582) 18	(803) 32	(394) 34	23	(718) 40	(128) 53	(630) 14	(1,072) 37

*p < .01
**p < .05

TABLE 6.3. Emotional, Moral, and Political Proximity between Students and Their Parents by Country (Percent).

Student feels close	AUSTRAL.	AUS.	FR.	GB	ITALY	JAPAN	NIGERIA	SPAIN	TUNISIA	USA
Emotionally*	(753) 80	(479) 65	(721) 87	(580) 84	(776) 79	(399) 74	(230) 92	(728) 86	(143) 91	(652) 85
Morally*	(757) 57	31	(712) 59	(587) 56	(825) 70	(417) 48	(228) 89	(723) 54	(139) 68	(654) 62
Politically*	(722) 56	(481) 39	(706) 50	(553) 56	(769) 50	(403) 28	(200) 50	(688) 40	(136) 40	(627) 57

*p < .01

Great Britain 34 percent and 81 percent. The distance between the right and the far left is smaller in Nigeria (29 percent and 57 percent), Tunisia (29 percent and 54 percent), and Japan (20 percent and 38 percent).

In reviewing the data collected from the students concerning the three domains mentioned above, it seemed to us particularly interesting to see how the relationship with the family among students on the right differed from that for students on the far left, the protesters. Various studies completed in the United States (Keniston, 1967; Flacks, 1967) suggest that students who were most favorable to the protest movement tended to be in agreement with their parents politically and shared their liberal value system. This continuity between generations is not confirmed by our findings, especially in regard to politics. Only one-third or fewer of the students on the far left in all of the countries studied agree with their parents politically. In contrast, we find that a majority of students on the right in all of the countries studied except Japan say that their political opinions are close to those of their parents. This percentage is slightly lower in the two African countries (55 percent), Spain (60 percent), and Austria (70 percent) than in the other countries (about 80 percent). In Japan, only 38 percent of the centrist students feel that they agree with their parents regarding politics.

These findings show that there exists a definite difference of opinion between student protesters on the far left and their parents. This difference is most apparent in the continental European and to a lesser degree in the Anglo-Saxon countries than in the two African countries and Japan. Studies conducted in the United States found similar results. For example, Braungart (1971), when comparing conservative students (Young Americans for Freedom, YAF) to leftists (Students for a Democratic Society, SDS), discovered that a rather large proportion of students on the left believe that their parents do not approve of their political position. According to his data, more YAF than SDS members felt a close relationship with one or both parents. The generation conflict in politics exists more acutely among the students on the far left than among those on the right.

The hypothesis of Feuer (1968) and of others who derive student activism from an "animus" against the fathers, representing a protest which hides a much more personal rebellion on the emotional level, is not confirmed in our findings for the majority of the students. On the other hand, we cannot deny that the rapidity with which society changes and the process of modernization itself may disrupt modes of thinking and living conditions. All this introduces between generations, as K. Davis wrote, "a different social content, so that they possess conflicting norms. There is a loss of mutual identification and the parents will not 'catch up' with the child's point of view . . ." (in Coser, ed., 1964, pp. 465–466).

If our findings do not confirm the notion of an Oedipal conflict, they do demonstrate that awareness of new political realities and changes in ways of life may more and more become the real sources of conflict among family members. The conflict seems more intense concerning politics than morals, particularly in the two African countries. We must underline the very special case of Austria, however, which is clearly different in this respect from the other countries studied. In Austria a profound generation conflict appears to exist. Not only are the students generally in disagreement with their parents concerning moral values (and to a lesser degree politics), but there is also, for approximately half of the students, an emotional conflict as well.

In Yugoslavia, the three questions discussed above did not appear on the questionnaire. They were replaced by two others which are relatively similar. First, "How would you describe your relationship with your mother? With your father?" In general, the students feel closer to their mother (88 percent) than to their father (71 percent). Ideological orientation and membership in the Communist League are not accompanied by any difference in the relationship with the father. They do slightly modify the relationship with the mother: the humanitarians feel very close to her (91 percent), the elitists less so (72 percent) (Tables 6.3b and 6.3c).

The second question concerned politics: "Do you agree or disagree with your parents about politics?" Overall, 70 percent of the students report that they have the same political opinions as their parents. Idealists, realists, and humanitarians are slightly more frequently in agreement with their parents than are elitists and individualists (64 percent). We also find that membership in the Communist League is accompanied by more ideological agreement with parents (80 percent) than nonmembership in the League (67 percent).

THE 1977 STUDY

The results of the 1977 (Table 6.4) study indicate few changes among French students. There is only a slight increase in moral closeness (67 percent) as compared to the main survey (59 percent). Among American students, moral closeness with the parents is more marked: 82 percent as compared to 62 percent in the main study. There is also somewhat greater agreement on political matters (67 percent as compared to 57 percent).

We turn now to a discussion of those areas in which differences between generations seem most marked.

TABLE 6.4. Proximity between Students and Parents, 1977 (Percent).

Student feels close	FRANCE	UNITED STATES
Emotionally	(92)	(104)
	88	84
Morally	(91)	(105)
	67	82
Politically	51	67

SPECIFIC DIFFERENCES

The counterculture challenges in particular the middle-class values that dominate Western society. Traditional values like money and success are rejected; one of the principal characteristics of the counterculture is the accent placed on the present, on immediate gratification. In addition, this movement is oriented toward nature, the environment, and personal sensual experiences, especially through drugs and sexual liberation. The principal values proposed are creativity, imagination, and mastery of one's own destiny. In the present study these issues were approached by asking the respondents to state if there were any differences between them and their parents concerning the following life experiences: leisure, religion, achievement, individualism, creative pursuits, importance of the present moment, sexual experiences, money, communion with nature, the arts, drugs, and "other." The students could specify the nature of and the reasons for the differences or the similarities. We shall quote examples of the responses from questionnaires completed in France, the United States, Great Britain, Nigeria, and Tunisia.

SEXUAL EXPERIENCES

Apart from Japan, where this question was not used, our findings indicate that in all countries except Austria the majority of students believe they have had sexual experiences quite different from those of their parents (Table 6.5—page 146). Age, of course, plays a part here, since some students have so far had little experience:

> They have had more experience. [United States]

The reason most often given for difference is an evolution in sexual mores:

> My parents are Puritans; I'm more liberal. [United States]
>
> The principle of sexual freedom. [France]

Also, parents are perceived as strongly attached to conventions:

> I assume my parents were virgin when they got married. [United States]
>
> They see marriage as an ideal and can't conceive of any other alternative. They are intolerant of any sexual deviation. [France]
>
> I am for sexual experience before marriage. They are against this. [Tunisia]

Young people do not feel as guilty about sexual experiences as they perceive their parents to be:

> They don't feel sex to be natural. [United States]
>
> My parents are really hung up on the dirtiness of sex. [United States]
>
> To parents, sex is an unpleasant duty; to me, a pleasure to be enjoyed. [Great Britain]

The differences of opinion surrounding the topic are particularly felt by Tunisian (88 percent) and Spanish (82 percent) students, less so (about 66 percent) by students in Anglo-Saxon countries, France, Italy, and Nigeria. Only 39 percent of Austrian students judge this subject to be a source of conflict with their parents.

Conservative students are rarely in conflict with their parents concerning sexual matters, which is not true for students on the left and the far left. In Tunisia, Spain, the United States, and Australia about 90 percent of the students on the far left report an attitude to sex different from that of their parents. This percentage, which is about 75 percent in Nigeria, Italy, Great Britain, and France, drops to 46 percent in Austria (Table 6.5a).

SUCCESS

The notion of success appears to be a focal point in the conflict between generations. It involves the concept of the nature of the individual as a psychological entity and also as a member of a society whose norms derive from the past.

TABLE 6.5.   Specific Points of Divergence between Students and Their Parents by Country (Percent).

	AUSTR.	AUS.	FR.	GB	IT.	JAP.	NIG.	SP.	TUN.	USA	YUG.[1]
Sexual experiences*[2]	(691) 67	(471) 39	(617) 69	(535) 75	(748) 64	– –	(197) 64	(683) 82	(124) 88	(588) 68	– –
Success*	(740) 52	(473) 32	(621) 54	(573) 54	(807) 62	(372) 51	(211) 72	(702) 74	(128) 62	(642) 43	(1,069) 59
Money*	(751) 51	(472) 31	(681) 55	(585) 49	(804) 49	(238) 24	(213) 58	(718) 66	(131) 51	– 47	(1,072) 66
Leisure*	(745) 55	– 24	(692) 74	– 59	(822) 77	(390) 46	(216) 62	(716) 80	(143) 86	(643) 43	54
Present moment*	(719) 42	(461) 35	(631) 57	(540) 38	(798) 58	(345) 42	(197) 54	(688) 64	(121) 74	(630) 41	– –
Art*	(738) 52	(470) 36	(658) 63	(581) 53	(797) 47	(364) 52	(191) 60	(708) 61	(119) 76	(635) 37	(1,069) 37
Creative pursuits*	(745) 45	(471) 19	(648) 54	(569) 45	(716) 57	(358) 35	(212) 58	(700) 65	(109) 69	(633) 35	– –
Communion with nature*	(712) 32	(469) 13	(615) 34	(490) 24	(806) 27	(361) 24	(182) 51	(655) 45	(110) 64	(612) 29	– –
Individualism*	(741) 46	(471) 38	(630) 52	(570) 42	(765) 55	(374) 50	(206) 47	(682) 65	(120) 63	(639) 35	– –
Religion*	(753) 52	(476) 22	(704) 48	(584) 53	(817) 44	(396) 33	(227) 36	(728) 61	(139) 45	(648) 57	(1,072) 67
Drugs*[3]	(642) 35	(467) 23	(657) 29	(576) 47	(786) 18	(374) 13	– –	(691) 24	(104) 30	(635) 57	12

*p < .01
1. The blank items did not appear in the Yugoslav questionnaire.
2. This item did not appear in the Japanese questionnaire.
3. In Nigeria, results were unreliable, since a number of students understood "drugs" to mean "medicines."

The concept of success lends itself to many interpretations when the students try to define what differentiates them from their parents. In general, the notion of success when attributed to the parents is associated with money, material security, and social status. Students do not always agree with this definition:

I consider money as secondary. [France]

They are much more worried than I am about making money and having a "good life." [United States]

My parents want socioeconomic success in life for me. They do not agree nor understand my communitarian ideas. [Great Britain]

My parents want immediate success for me. [Tunisia]

To the student, success frequently means realization of inner happiness, of "feeling good," and, sometimes, of being able to communicate with the world:

It is not related to social success for me. I want my life to be a success. [Tunisia]

It is interesting to note that students who describe themselves as coming from the middle and upper classes refuse the traditional definition of success, preferring "to make their life a success than to be successful in life." Students from the lower classes explain their parental conflicts differently. Indeed, these students think in terms of social mobility and are aware they have more chance to succeed in this regard than did their parents precisely because of their education:

My parents did not have the opportunity to pursue advanced studies. [France]

My parents are peasants. [Nigeria]

Sometimes these students are more ambitious than their parents:

I want to achieve, my father wants me to marry. [United States]

I want much more out of life than my parents ever did. They were content to sit on their little farm. [United States]

They are happy with what they have. Not me. [Tunisia]

The comparison among the countries included in the study shows several major differences. Spanish and Nigerian students (about 75 percent) most often mention a difference in attitude concerning success between themselves and their parents, followed by about 60 percent of the students in Tunisia, Yugoslavia, and Italy and about 55 percent of the students in Australia, France, Great Britain, and Japan. Students in the United States (43 percent) and in Austria (32 percent) report less frequently a feeling of being in conflict with their parents over this issue (Table 6.5).

Differences of opinion as to the definition of success characterize especially those on the far left, except in Tunisia, where few differences emerge by political tendency. Attitude toward success is the source of conflict especially for students on the far left in Spain (90 percent), in Australia (79 percent), in Tunisia (77 percent), and in France (73 percent), for two-thirds of such students in Nigeria, Italy, the United States and Great Britain, 56 percent in Japan, and only 49 percent in Austria (Table 6.5a).

MONEY

The attitude of students toward money is quite similar to that concerning success. The differences which exist between students and their parents in regard to money arise, according to some students, from the fact that they are dependent on their parents:

> They earn it, I spend it. [France]

> I depend almost entirely on them. [France]

This situation of dependence is often frustrating. Some parents reproach their children for spending too much and for not respecting money:

> My father thinks I don't know the value of money. [Tunisia]

> They think I spend too much. [Tunisia]

Some of the divergence in attitude is due to the definition the students and parents give to money. For the former it is in many cases not a goal per se, but a means to an end; the students reject the materialism of their parents:

> I use money; it uses them. [United States]

> They save; I spend. [Great Britain]

> They believe it is the greater part of happiness; I don't. [Great Britain]

We find some students who are more ambitious in this regard than their parents—eager to achieve more—and who are careful to economize:

> Having money in the bank is very important for me. [United States]

> I want more than my father has. [Great Britain]

This attitude is related to the socioeconomic background of the student. Those who have led fairly easy lives question the real purposes of money, while those from more humble backgrounds are more likely to refuse the poverty and the hard life of their parents.

Our findings in these respects are in agreement with the results of a poll by Yankelovitch (1969) in the United States. He found that a student who considers his studies as a means to social success and material gain believes that there is no real gulf between himself and his parents. In contrast, those students who see their studies as a means to acquire culture and to induce social change are more apt to believe that their parents are much more concerned about money than they are.

The differences of opinion between students and their parents regarding money are mentioned more frequently in Spain and Yugoslavia (66 percent) and France and Nigeria (about 55 percent) than in Austria (31 percent) and Japan (24 percent). In the other countries about half of the students define money differently than do their parents.

The more the student is to the left, the more his opinions about money are likely to differ from those of his parents. This is particularly true for the students on the far left. In descending order the percentages of differences between students on the far left and their parents are Spain and Australia (about 70 percent); France, Great Britain, and Italy (about 60 percent); Nigeria and Tunisia (52 percent); the United States (48 percent); Austria (41 percent); and finally Japan (30 percent) (Table 6.5a).

LEISURE ACTIVITIES

It is not surprising to find that leisure activities, like money and success, are a point of conflict between students and parents. There are a number of factors responsible, the first and most radical being that some parents have no leisure activities at all. This situation is especially true in Nigeria and Tunisia for parents described by students as having very low social and professional status:

> They don't have leisure as such. [Nigeria]

We also find differences arising from varying tastes, due in part to moral considerations and education,

> They are obsessed by the Protestant ethic. [United States]
>
> My parents are intoxicated by television. [France]
>
> My parents are not well educated. [Tunisia]

in part to age difference and cultural milieu:

> My parents let me do what I want, but my leisure activities are not theirs. [Tunisia]
>
> We are not the same generation; we don't have the same types of leisure activities. [Tunisia]

These differences appear sometimes in the form of a real conflict, a confrontation between parents and students:

> According to my parents, I must earn my free time by working. [United States]
>
> I find my leisure activities are indispensable. According to my parents, this is a form of laziness. [Great Britain]
>
> My parents think that my leisure activities are forbidden by our religion. [Tunisia]

The majority of students in Tunisia (86 percent), Spain (80 percent), Italy (77 percent), and France (74 percent) believe that their concept of leisure differs from that of their parents. The same is true, to a lesser degree, in Nigeria (62 percent), Australia (55 percent), Great Britain (59 percent), and Yugoslavia (54 percent). Students holding this opinion are in the minority in Japan (46 percent), the United States (43 percent), and Austria (24 percent).

THE IMMEDIATE PRESENT

The importance which many young people appear to attach to the immediate present, without worrying about the future, led us to introduce this notion as one of the possible sources of conflict between generations. The students' comments demonstrate that their orientation to the present is often at variance with the social aspirations of their parents:

> My parents are more willing to sacrifice the present for assured happiness in the future than I am. [United States]
>
> They only live to retire. [France]
>
> My father tends to look to the future for security and so becomes closed, blinded to the pleasures of the present. [Great Britain]

We also find the reverse phenomenon. Students look toward the future and reproach their parents for living from day to day:

> I think more of the future; they think of the past and the present. [United States]
>
> As strange as this may seem, my parents live for the present, while I worry about the future. [Nigeria]

Many students did not comment on this question, so that our data are limited, but we still find that Tunisian (74 percent) and Spanish (64 percent) students most frequently regard themselves as different from their parents in this respect. The same is true for about half of the students in Italy, France, and Nigeria and, to a lesser degree, in Australia, Japan, and the United States (about 42 percent). The Austrians and the British are the least likely to express such feelings (about 36 percent) (Table 6.5).

As in the case of other issues, we find greater continuity between generations among students on the right than among those on the left, especially on the far left. The "cult of immediacy," as Myerhoff calls it (1969), with its hedonistic attitude which is often at odds with the "fear of tomorrow" of the parents, characterizes especially students on the far left in Spain (83 percent) and in Tunisia (77 percent), followed by those in Italy (72 percent) and France (68 percent) and about half of the students on the far left in the other countries. The Austrians (46 percent) are again those who feel least different from their parents with regard to this issue (Table 6.5a).

ART

Art often constitutes another important point of divergence between students and parents. Three factors seem to intervene: education, time, and taste. Students are interested in art, which may remain a closed domain to their less well-educated parents. Also, students have the time to appreciate art, to attend concerts, to read, etc., which their parents frequently do not have:

I'm more interested in art because I have more time and another kind of education. [France]

Art appreciation is learned; they never had the chance. [France]

My parents had little formal education. [Tunisia]

When we find in the family itself a certain appreciation of art, the differences arise from questions of taste: the parents have in general classical, conventional artistic preferences, while the students are attracted to modern styles, new modes of expression, and artistic innovations:

Different tastes and interests. [France]

My parents are conservative and don't like modern art. [United States]

Their concept of art is very restricted; they classify a lot as pornography. [Great Britain]

Art for them means folklore and traditional songs. [Tunisia]

The majority of students in Tunisia (76 percent), France (63 percent), and Nigeria and Spain (60 percent), followed by about half of the students in Australia, Great Britain, and Japan, mention differences in opinion about art between themselves and their parents. The percentages are lower in Italy (47 percent) and the United States, Austria, and Yugoslavia (about 37 percent) (Table 6.5).

Students on the far left differ most from the attitudes of their parents. More than 70 percent of these students in Tunisia, Spain, and France believe their definitions of art are very different from those of their parents. This is also true for more than half of the far left students in the other countries, except in the United States (38 percent) (Table 6.5a).

CREATIVE PURSUITS

Creative pursuits represent a point of divergence which varies from country to country. The explanation may lie in the fact that many students believe themselves less ossified by habits, social norms, and prejudices. They think they are more active and imaginative than their elders:

My parents act like spectators; I think everyone should participate. [United States]

Their imagination is sterilized. [France]

They are against all innovations. [Tunisia]

Some parents are believed to associate creative pursuits with leisure activities, considering both a waste of time:

My parents think I'm wasting time. [United States]

But this is also a question of formal education, as the students indicate:

The creative capacity of my parents has been frustrated by circumstances. I read and write poetry. [Great Britain]

My parents simply don't understand. [Tunisia]

Two-thirds of the students in Tunisia and Spain state they have attitudes toward creative pursuits very different from those of their parents. This percentage is a little more than half in Italy, France, and Nigeria, and somewhat less in Australia and Great Britain (45 percent). It drops to 35 percent in Japan and the United States and to 19 percent in Austria (Table 6.5).

On the far left large variations appear. Eighty percent of the Spanish students experience differences of opinion with their parents, and the percentages are about 60 percent in Tunisia, Australia, Italy, Nigeria, and France. They are less than half in Japan (46 percent), Great Britain (39 percent), the United States (30 percent), and Austria (26 percent) (Table 6.5a).

COMMUNION WITH NATURE

With the exception of those from Nigeria and Tunisia, students do not feel very different from their parents with regard to nature. Forty-five percent of the students in Spain, about one-third of those in France and Australia, about 28 percent of Americans and Italians, 24 percent of the Japanese, and only 13 percent of Austrian students express an attitude different from that of their parents in this regard. This similarity comes from the fact that they all either appreciate nature (excursions, picnics, etc.) or do not think about it at all.

In Tunisia and Nigeria, where more than half of the students (64 percent and 51 percent respectively) indicate that they differ in their opinions about nature from their parents, this might be explained by the fact that these countries have developed from an agrarian culture into one in which leisure activities are possible, and also from rural into urban societies, at least in part. For many parents, nature represents a way of life and a call to work. For the students, nature is either "foreign" and distant or represents a harmony of rediscovered values—those of poetry, literature, philosophy, etc., acquired by the newly defined culture:

They've never heard of it. [United States]

At my age I enjoy dreaming; and I have the time. [France]

Because I am more educated than they are. [Tunisia]

My parents are materialists; I feel more. [Tunisia]

When students are not interested in nature or seem less so than their parents, this may be due to a reaction to a social or religious context

They are really believers, therefore pagans. I am farther away from nature than they are. [Tunisia]

For them, nature is God; for me, I substitute society for this concept. [Tunisia]

or to the fact that the students do not have enough time:

My parents are at the contemplative age; right now, I'm too busy. [Great Britain]

Sometimes it is a question of taste which separates the students from their families:

They are closer to nature than I am. [France]

I am less sensitive about it than they are. [France]

I feel more in harmony with nature. [United States]

In each country we find that the relation between political tendency and family rapport regarding nature is less marked than for the other issues. The few differences which do exist tend to show that conservatives are quite similar to their parents, while students on the far left are the most distant. For these students the divergences are striking. The majority of far left Tunisian students (77 percent) and Spanish and Nigerian students (about 62 percent) feel quite differently about nature than do their families. These percentages are lower in the other countries: about 33 percent in France, Australia, and Italy, 29 percent in the United States, 25 percent in Japan and Great Britain, and 18 percent in Austria (Table 6.5a).

INDIVIDUALISM

When students feel differently than their parents do about individualism, the usual interpretations of this word either are in terms of interpersonal relations or suggest the issue of conformism to the social norms of the group. Many students explain that their parents are attached to the unity of their family and to its self-interest, while they themselves are more open to the community and to the different influences which change life. As a consequence, the individualism of the student becomes egoism in the eyes of the parent, opposed to the spirit of solidarity:

My parents are very attached to the perpetual unity of the members of the family. [France]

They are against all outside friendships. [Tunisia]

The reference group in question may be the family, society in general, or the state. Individualism is often seen as a defense of the freedom of the individual as he confronts the power exercised by the government and the social environment. Parents are seen as living in a state of dependence:

They are very caring and don't know how to live for themselves. [France]

I want to do what I enjoy. They want me to do what is socially acceptable. [Great Britain]

My parents are strongly influenced by local conditions. [Nigeria]

The idea of the extended family dominates their thinking. [Nigeria]

Sometimes this notion of individual liberty corresponds to a need to express originality. Parents who conform to social norms and to the rules of appearance are seen as afraid of those who are "different." Young people, by their nonconformism, are searching for, and wish to emphasize, their own unique qualities:

They are cultural puppets who cannot forget the social norms. [United States]

I like to stand out from the mass. [France]

They are embarrassed by my desire to be unique, to be different, especially by my clothes. [Great Britain]

For some students, individualism consists in looking for their own personal identity and thus removing themselves to some extent from their families. The parents are seen as dominating the child, and the latter must break these ties of dependence, become autonomous, and find other models of identification:

I don't want to become a prolongation of my parents. [United States]

My parents want to impose their own volition on me. [Nigeria]

Two-thirds of the Spanish and Tunisian students and a little more than half of the Italian, French, and Japanese students believe that their concept of individualism is different from that of their parents. This proportion is lower in the other countries—Nigeria and Australia 47 percent, Great Britain and Austria about 40 percent, and the United States 35 percent. A student's position on the political left or far left accentuates the distance between him and his family. On the far left, four-fifths of students in Spain, 71 percent of the Tunisians, about 60 percent of the Australians, French, Italians, and Japanese, half the Austrians and the British, and 44 percent of the Americans have a notion of individualism different from that of their parents. Nigeria is the only country in which students on the far left do not express a great deal of difference from their parents on this issue. In Nigeria, in fact, only one-third of these students, compared to half of the students who define themselves as on the right or progovernment, mention a divergence of opinion on this subject.

RELIGION

Differences of opinion concerning religion emerge either because the students do not share the opinions of their parents or because they themselves are athiests

As I chose a scientific profession, I do not have any faith. My parents have it and I envy them a little. [Great Britain]

or because they are less traditional and more tolerant than their parents:

They practice classical, ritual Catholicism. I believe in God but not in the Church. [France]

They call themselves Christians but don't think or act as such. I have found satisfaction in a personal religious concept of Karma. [Great Britain]

They are fanatics; I'm not. [Tunisia]

The student often criticizes the superficial character and conformist nature of the faith found in his family:

I have chosen my religion. My parents were born with theirs. [United States]

Religious experience is a personal act, something mystical, which brings peace. [Great Britain]

To my parents religion is the social act of going to church. [Great Britain]

In a few cases the parents and the children have different religions, especially in Nigeria:

My parents are Protestants; I am Roman Catholic. [Nigeria]

My parents are still strongly influenced by traditional religions, that is, tribal religions. [Nigeria]

The proportion of students who differ from their parents in their religious attitudes is rather high in Yugoslavia (67 percent) and Spain (61 percent), a little less so in the Anglo-Saxon countries (about 55 percent) and France (48 percent), a little less again in Tunisia and Italy (about 45 percent), and relatively low in Nigeria (36 percent), Japan (33 percent), and Austria (22 percent) (Table 6.5).

Differences in attitude concerning religion are strongest between the students on the far left and their parents. This is particularly true in countries where the Catholic Church has a strong influence, notably in Spain and in Italy. In fact, the students on the far left in Spain (81 percent) and in Italy (66 percent) differ most frequently with their parents on this issue. The proportion is about two-thirds for the same political group in Australia and Tunisia, and somewhat lower in the United States, Great Britain, and France (about 60 percent). It drops in Austria (42 percent) and especially in Japan and Nigeria (35 percent) (Table 6.5a).

DRUGS

The problem of drugs is usually regarded as an important source of conflict between students and their parents, especially in the United States and Great Britain. Although 57 percent of the American students and 47 percent of the British students do not agree with their parents on this subject, in the other countries only one-third or less mention opposition with their parents on this issue. These percentages are very small in Japan (13 percent) and in Yugoslavia (12 percent) (Table 6.5). (The results from the questionnaire used in Nigeria were not applicable, as many students understood "drugs" as medicine. This was the only country in which such a misunderstanding arose.)

In general, the absence of a divergence of opinion about drugs means that the students, like their parents, reject them completely:

I hate it. [France]
I have the same hostility as my parents. [France]
The worst human downfall. [France]

When there is a difference in attitudes, this is often due, in the opinion of the student, to the fact that parents have an attitude based on general principles, rejecting *a priori* and totally a form of behavior about which they may know very little. The student, in contrast, even without having tried drugs personally, tries to understand and to be tolerant:

They condemn; I understand. [France]

My parents take an attitude that reveals a lack of familiarity with the problem. [United States]

I am against the total unacceptance of my parents, which is based on nothing except ignorance. [Great Britain]

Or the student distinguishes between "hard" drugs and others which he does not condemn:

I accept the use of hashish and marijuana. [France]

They don't discriminate between marijuana and heroin. [United States]

My parents condemn all drugs blindly. I believe that we should take into account research data concerning the psychological effects of drugs to find out if they are dangerous or not. [United States]

According to other students, it is simply a question of personal liberty:

I believe that each individual has the right to choose any kind of drug he desires. [United States]

Others remind their parents that they too use "drugs" sanctioned by society, like tobacco, coffee, and alcohol:

My parents see drugs as a refuge for the unstable, but that doesn't stop them from drinking. [United States]

They cannot admit that alcohol and tobacco are drugs, which they consume, and yet they condemn marijuana. [Great Britain]

Throughout the commentaries of the students only a minority—almost exclusively American—report having tried drugs "out of curiosity," which, in general, means marijuana:

I've smoked grass and hash.

My parents are afraid of all drugs. I avoid some and take others in moderation.

Again, the greatest conflict between generations occurs between students on the far left and their parents, particularly in Anglo-Saxon countries (70 percent or more). This percentage is lower in Austria and France (about 50 percent) and in Tunisia and Spain (about 44 percent). In Italy (33 percent) and in Japan (21 percent) this divergence of attitudes characterizes fewer students on the far left.

In conclusion, we may say that in general students who feel most distant from their parents are those who live in continental Europe and in developing countries. Lipset (1968), in speaking of the latter countries, notes:

Movements concerned with value change are more prevalent and stronger in the underdeveloped countries than in the developed ones. Talcott Parsons and S. N. Eisenstadt have suggested the need to look at the magnitude of the differences between the values of the adult and youth generations in varying types of societies. They indicate that generational conflict is caused, at least in part, by sharp value differences among generations, and that such cleavages—particularly between the better educated (younger on the average) and the uneducated (older)—are great in modernizing societies, but relatively minor in the developed societies [p. 9].

The students who mention the fewest points of divergence with their family are the Japanese, the Americans, the Yugoslavs, and, especially, the Austrians.[4] The latter rarely feel in conflict with their parents. At the same time, this same group appears most distant from their parents on the political, the moral, and especially the emotional level, compared to the other countries. These findings, seemingly contradictory, may perhaps be explained by the fact that those Austrian students who believe themselves to be distant from their families keep discussions with their parents to a minimum in order to avoid conflict.

The intracountry comparison shows that being on the left or the far left increases the sources of conflict, notably in the domain of culture, of morals (drugs, sexual practices, and religion), and of society (money, success, leisure pursuits). Issues related to creativity, art, and one's attitude toward nature show fewer differences of opinion. We find in Spain the strongest opposition between parents and students on the far left on both social and cultural matters. Only the attitude to drugs is similar for both groups in Spain. (Drugs constituted a problem only in Anglo-Saxon families at the time of our study.)

As has been noted above, political orientation plays an important role in relationships with parents, but other factors, such as sex, introduce few differences, except in Tunisia. In that country there was a rather clear difference between men and women. Men more frequently report conflict with their parents than women in connection with drugs (26 percent of the women compared to 40 percent of the men), creativity (58 percent and 78 percent), and success (50 percent and 72 percent).

The poll by Yankelovich (1969) mentioned above shows that generally young Americans have the feeling of "being more open to the world," "more tolerant of others' opinions," "more altruistic," and "more concerned with national events." They reproach their parents for being ready "to compromise," "to respect established authority," "to accept things as they are," and to fear "material insecurity." These findings are similar to those of our own study. When it is a question of individualism, art, or drugs, students show an awareness and a desire to understand which, according to them, are rarely found in their parents. Students also criticize the conformism and the materialism of their parents, who prefer "to succeed in life" rather than "to lead successful lives."

Few empirical studies have been conducted concerning the conflict of generations outside of the United States and Great Britain. It is interesting to note, however, that studies in these two countries several years ago showed that the values of young people were quite similar to those of the preceding generation despite differences in age and social status. In Great Britain studies conducted on the cultural values of young people (Hancock and Wakeford, 1965; Niles, 1968), especially concerning music and clothing, rarely reveal conflict between the basic sociomoral values of parents and those of their children. Studies concerning politics, also in Great Britain, found no political and social characteristics peculiar to young people. Abrams and Little (1965) also showed that young people follow the patterns established by their elders. Riley and Moore (1961) noted that by the time of adolescence young people have already internalized the ideals and the values of their surrounding environment and, in most cases, do not participate in any antiadult culture. Previous American studies, like those of Gillespie and Allport (1955) and Goldsen et al. (1960), also found a marked degree of continuity between generations.

The findings of these earlier studies differ from the present one, however, con-

---

[4]In Yugoslavia, several questions were not included in the questionnaire; these related to sexual experience, the immediate present, nature, and creative activities.

cerning similarity of opinions of students on the far left with those of their parents. We observed in this group a reaction against the competitive nature of industrialized society, regarded as typical of the parental generation. Myerhoff (1969) noted with regard to the United States that there is a desire for a new style of interpersonal relationships. According to Howard (1969), again speaking of the United States, "The reign of petit-bourgeois success which dominated the parental generation is now considered by the young as ended: 'to have a nice home, a swimming pool, a television . . . but then what?'" The orientation to the nonutilitarian and to the immediate present found expression in the counterculture, which developed first in the Anglo-Saxon countries and then found its way to Europe and Africa, especially among students on the far left.

THE 1977 STUDY

The 1977 survey indicates that in the United States there is a decrease in the frequency of perceived differences between students and parents on the following points: *success* (29 percent state there is a difference as compared to 43 percent in 1970); *money* (37 percent as compared to 47 percent in 1970); *importance of the present* (26 percent versus 41 percent); *individualism* (30 percent as compared to 35 percent); *religion* (49 percent as compared to 57 percent); and *drugs* (46 percent as compared to 57 percent). These differences concern many of the values considered to be important in the counterculture, the impact of which is apparently declining among the general student population. There is a somewhat increased difference as regards *leisure,* and no difference in the case of the remaining alternatives (Table 6.6 —page 158).

In France there is not such a clear-cut pattern. A slight decrease in reports of difference can be noted in relation to all the alternatives with two exceptions. Concerning *sexual experiences* (78 percent in 1977 as compared to 69 percent in 1970) and *drugs* (34 percent in 1977 as compared to 29 percent in 1970), the differences between students and their parents have increased.

Interpersonal Relations and Value Systems

We have seen in the opinions of many students the outline of an antiestablishment movement which is in direct conflict with traditional social roles and "the system." This movement negates, in part, the values and ideals of the previous generation. It seemed it would be interesting to discover whether this questioning by the students of the status quo leads to a desire to create a new reality more in accord with the students' own needs and experience.

In this section we present the choices of the students regarding general value systems (e.g., morals, religion, drugs) and a number of more personal choices (e.g., interpersonal relationships between men and women, life styles, equality between the sexes, and birth control).

MORALS, RELIGION, AND DRUGS

The present social order, sustained mainly by religion and traditional morality, is questioned by a large segment of students in all the countries of this study. More than half of the students in the majority of these countries—particularly in Europe and Japan—believe that the influence of *religion* has been too great. The desire to see the role of religion diminish is expressed by about 40 percent of the students in Nigeria and the Anglo-Saxon countries and reaches its greatest frequency in Japan (61 percent) and Spain (71 percent). The other countries are situated between these two extremes (Table 6.7, see p. 164).

TABLE 6.6. Specific Points of Divergence between Students and their Parents, 1977 (Percent).

	FRANCE	UNITED STATES
Sexual experiences	(100)	(101)
	78	68
Success*		(104)
	47	29
Money		(100)
	49	37
Leisure	(90)	(104)
	69	50
Present moment*	(100)	(94)
	53	26
Art	(89)	(102)
	52	38
Creative pursuits	(100)	(104)
	54	40
Communion with nature	(86)	(98)
	22	29
Individualism	(100)	(106)
	41	30
Religion	(90)	(104)
	39	49
Drugs	(89)	(102)
	34	46

*p <.05

Middle-class morality is perceived as oppressive by the majority of students in all of the countries studied, and is considered a hindrance to individual development. It appears to be most frustrating to students in Spain (79 percent). In other countries this percentage is 67 percent or above, except in Japan (59 percent) and in Nigeria (50 percent).

As we might expect, in all of the countries (except Nigeria) opposition to middle-class morality is somewhat stronger among the students on the far left than among those on the right. In Japan we find the greatest difference between the moderates (48 percent) and the far left (74 percent). In Nigeria political tendency does not show any relation to attitudes to morality (53 percent on the right and 50 percent on the far left) (Table 6.7a). It should be noted that the responses to this question show even on the right a certain opposition to traditional values.

The attitude concerning the role of religion shows greater intercountry variations between the right and the far left. In the United States (19 percent), France (23 percent), and Great Britain (27 percent) the right seems less opposed to religion than the right in Spain (47 percent) or in Japan (58 percent). In the other countries about two-thirds agree that the role of religion should diminish. On the far left more than half of the students in most countries are opposed to religion. This rejection is greater in a number of European countries (Spain, 95 percent; Italy, 77 percent; France, 71 percent; and Austria, 84 percent) than in most other countries (about 63 percent), and is least frequent on the far left in Tunisia (55 percent) and Nigeria (48 percent). The results also underline the strong opposition to religion on the part of the Italian (85 percent) and French (87 percent) communists (Table 6.7a).

Although Yugoslav students could not be differentiated by their own self-definitions with regard to attitudes to bourgeois morality, they are clearly divided by the question of religion. Students affiliated with the Communist League are much more clearly against religion (79 percent) than those who refuse to join this organization (47 percent). Students who have an egalitarian concept of society (idealists, 63 percent; realists, 57 percent) hope to see the role of religion diminish more than do elitists (39 percent).

More than morality, the question of religion shows great divergence between opinions of conservatives and those on the far left. The former on the whole remain attached to religion, while the latter reject it.

Drugs, particularly in the counterculture, are often considered a means of escaping conventional morality. Two questions centered on the use of drugs, distinguishing between marijuana and LSD: "Restrictive measures should be taken against the use of marijuana and hashish" and "Restrictive measures should be taken against the use of LSD."

It is striking to note that the position of the Anglo-Saxons, especially Americans, is definitely more "liberal" than that of students in the other countries, in particular concerning marijuana and hashish. Forty-nine percent of the Australians, 42 percent of the British, and only 27 percent of the Americans favor legal restrictions of these two "soft" drugs, while the figures reach two-thirds in France, about 75 percent in Austria and Spain, and 85 percent or more in the other countries in this study. There are smaller differences of opinion concerning LSD. In fact, more than 75 percent of the students from all the countries studied hope to see its use limited. The Anglo-Saxon countries (as well as France, Austria, and Spain) are, as was the case for marijuana and hashish, somewhat less severe than other countries, notably Italy (92 percent) and Yugoslavia (90 percent) (Table 6.7).

The right and the far left in the two African countries as well as in Italy and Japan share the same negative attitude toward drug usage. In most of the other countries almost all of the students on the right condemn all uses of drugs without making any distinction between them (except in Anglo-Saxon countries, where LSD is condemned but where about 40 percent accept the use of marijuana and hashish). Students on the far left not only distinguish between the drugs but also are much more favorable to their use. Thus about half of the students on the far left in Europe (Spain, 46 percent; Austria, 56 percent; France, 58 percent) and more than 80 percent of the Anglo-Saxon far left oppose restrictions on the use of hashish and marijuana. In France fewer communists oppose restrictions (41 percent) than far left students (58 percent) and, particularly, anarchists (73 percent).

Free use of LSD was opposed by students in all countries, even by those on the far left. This was especially the case in Austria (74 percent), Spain (64 percent), Great Britain (62 percent), and France (59 percent). About half of the Australian students and 36 percent of the American students on the far left approved restrictions on LSD.

Unlike students elsewhere, those in the Anglo-Saxon countries frequently disagree with their parents on the subject of drugs. There is no doubt that especially in the United States and in Great Britain, many young people have tried one or more drugs at least once (cf. Gallup, 1970). By contrast, in the other countries students appear to distrust drugs, even if their use does grow daily, particularly in Europe. (At the time of this study the use of drugs was marginal; it has clearly increased during the past few years).

THE 1977 STUDY

The 1977 study indicates a slight increase in the United States of students who are in favor of restrictive measures against marijuana and hashish (34 percent in 1977 versus 27 percent in 1970). There is on the contrary almost no change in the percentage of students agreeing that the role of religion in society should diminish (29 percent versus 34 percent in 1970).

In France the data indicate an opposite trend concerning drugs. There is a decrease in the percentage of students favoring restrictive measures against marijuana (52 percent in favor of such measures as compared to 65 percent in 1970) and against LSD (69 percent as compared to 78 percent in 1970). These results indicate, however, that French students remain less tolerant of the use of marijuana than are American students (Table 6.8).

TABLE 6.8.   Moral and Cultural Values by Country, 1977 (Percent).

	FRANCE	UNITED STATES
The role of religion in society should diminish.*	(90)	(79)
	56	29
Middle-class morality destroys the spontaneity of individual experience.**	(92)	(106)
	62	42
Restrictive measures should be taken against the use of marijuana.**	(92)	(80)
	52	34
Restrictive measures should be taken against the use of LSD.	(92)	(80)
	69	80

*p < .01
**p < .05

LIFE STYLE

Urbanization and industrialization, as Goode (1963) among others suggests, have altered the traditional family structures, allowing new types of conjugal living to appear. In particular the "extended" family has already undergone profound changes, due in part to greater job mobility and urban residence.

THE FAMILY

The first question asked of the students in this connection concerned the very principle of the family as a social institution. They indicated on a Likert scale the extent of their agreement or disagreement with the statement that "the family is a universally oppressive institution." Students who judge the family unit as oppressive are a minority in all countries except Tunisia (53 percent), but they are a substantial minority in several countries—40 percent in Spain, 37 percent in Yugoslavia, 31 percent in France, 34 percent in Japan, and 32 percent in Austria and Italy. In Nigeria (23 percent) and in the Anglo-Saxon countries, especially in the United States (14 percent),[5] the percentages are lowest. The difference between the right and the far left is very marked, except in Nigeria, Great Britain, and the United States (Table 6.1).

About 10 percent of the students on the right in the Anglo-Saxon countries, France, and Austria judge the family as an oppressive institution; the figure is about 20 percent for those on the right in Nigeria, Italy, and Spain. The largest proportions of rightists and moderates who make the same judgment are in Japan (27 percent of the centrists) and especially in Tunisia (43 percent of those on the right, 36 percent of the Bourguibists).

On the other hand, if we exclude Nigeria (11 percent on the far left and 29 percent of those who oppose their government[6]), and the United States (28 percent), a substantial number of the students on the far left consider the family as an oppressive institution. The most critical are the Tunisians (82 percent), the Spaniards (78 percent), the Italians (64 percent), and the Austrians (66 percent), followed by the Australians (50 percent), the French (48 percent), the Japanese (43 percent) and the British (41 percent) (Table 6.1a).

It is interesting to note that it is in those countries where moral and official religious values are the most rigid, Tunisia and Spain, that the family is most often perceived as oppressive. It is difficult to know, however, whether students who judge the family as oppressive are referring to it as an institution or are thinking of personal experiences in their own family (e.g., parental authority). This distinction is important, since the first position implies a radical questioning of society. From society's point of view, the family is the transmitter of social values. Fromm writes (1936):

> In spite of individual differences that exist in different families (of the same society), the family represents primarily the content of the society; the most important social function of the family is to transmit this content, not only through formation of opinions and point of view but through the creation of a socially desirable attitudinal structure [p. 87].

The function of the family is thus primary, even if its role of socialization is today rivaled in part by the educational system (including the peer group) and the mass media. As the first agency which socializes the child, the family also inculcates in him social restraints, as Cooper (1971) notes: "We don't teach the child how to survive in society, but how to surrender to it" (p. 28).

The family is thus at the same time the guarantor of the social order and one of the principal institutions of social integration. It is interesting to note that a substantial number of students, particularly those on the far left (except in the United States and Nigeria) consider this institution as oppressive.

LIFE STYLE IN THE FUTURE

We wondered how students envisioned life and the family in their society in the year 2000. Also, what kind of life style would they themselves prefer and what kind

[5]In the 1977 survey, 13 percent of the students agree with the statement in the United States, and 29 percent in France. The opinions on the family have remained remarkably stable in these two countries (Table 6.2).

[6]These are students who criticize the system and the government but do not define themselves politically.

did they think actually possible? The students could choose among the five following replies:

The present form of marriage will persist.

Marriage will persist but will be accompanied by even greater liberty regarding extramarital sex, for both men and women.

Legal marriage will be replaced by free union.

Marriage will persist, but families will live together communally with other families.

Other.

In analyzing the responses from the various countries studied, we find that, on the whole, students do not foresee major life style changes in the future. Most of them think that in the year 2000 marriage will still exist, but many think it will be accompanied by more freedom for extramarital sex. This is the opinion of about 50 percent of the students in Australia, Great Britain, Nigeria, Tunisia, and Japan and of approximately 40 percent of the students in the other countries, except in Austria (28 percent) and Yugoslavia (26 percent). The second most frequent choice was that marriage will persist in its traditional form (a little less than one-third of the students in all countries, except in Austria, 46 percent). Only 15 percent or less of the students envision really radical changes in sexual relationships, such as living together informally or in communal association (Table 6.9, see p. 164).

Students show themselves also relatively conformist in their aspirations, hoping in a large number of cases to marry traditionally. The two African countries (Tunisia, 61 percent, and Nigeria, 49 percent), the Anglo-Saxon countries (about 50 percent), Yugoslavia (59 percent), and Italy (46 percent) seem the most conventional in their preferences, followed by Austria (38 percent), France (37 percent), and Spain (36 percent). The Japanese choose in not very different proportions marriage in its present form (32 percent), greater sexual freedom (28 percent), and free union (27 percent).

It is curious to note that even though most of the students foresee a more liberal style of marriage in the future, very few want this type of relationship for themselves (about 15 percent), except in Japan (28 percent). On the other hand, some students, particularly in Japan, France, Austria, Spain, Nigeria, and Australia (about one-quarter), would like to live in a free union. Only 10 percent hope to live in communes or express a preference for any other style of living. It should be noted, however, that 19 percent of the Austrian students would like to have a communal life with other families after marriage, and that 20 percent of the Italian students are in favor of communal living without marriage, thus breaking away from the traditional norms.

It seems that aspirations and expectations are more or less the same in most countries. The students who plan to marry traditionally constitute 81 percent in Tunisia, two-thirds in the Anglo-Saxon countries, and somewhat less elsewhere (between 50 percent and 63 percent). This drops, however, to 39 percent in Austria.

The great majority of students foresee for themselves traditional marriage, with greater sexual freedom for both partners. However, when asked not what they would do but what they would prefer to do, the number selecting a "free union" increased. The Japanese in particular (40 percent) desire a more liberalized form of marriage, followed by about 25 percent of the Austrians and Australians.

These findings show that the majority of students remain rather conformist and expect only moderate modifications in the relationships between the sexes and in the family unit. The attachment to a traditional life style seems greater in the Anglo-Saxon countries, in the two African countries, and also in Yugoslavia and Italy than elsewhere in Europe (France, Spain, and especially Austria) and in Japan. We have already seen that the Anglo-Saxon students are not very critical of the family as an institution.

Once again political orientation is accompanied by marked differences in the opinions and the attitudes of the students (Table 6.9a). Traditional marriage as a preferred and expected life style corresponds to a political orientation on the right (more than 60 percent express a preference and at least 75 percent an expectation in that direction, except in Japan, where the figures are 41 percent and 56 percent respectively). In contrast, communal life is chosen by the left and especially the far left in the majority of countries (about 50 percent or more in all countries except France, Spain and the United States, about 37 percent, and Japan 15 percent). Except for those on the far left in Austria, more than 50 percent of whom think it truly possible to live either in a commune or in another nonconventional style, less than one-third of far left students hope to realize this ideal. Many students on the far left, whether French (49 percent), British (42 percent), Japanese (40 percent), or Italian (32 percent), expect a very traditional form of marriage, at most accompanied by great sexual freedom. Thirty-nine percent of the Spanish students think it possible to live in a free union. A majority of Americans on the far left either think they will marry traditionally (36 percent) or think they will live in free union (32 percent). The Australians believe that they will marry traditionally, without extramarital sexual freedom (26 percent), that they will marry and have extramarital freedom (29 percent), or even that they will live in free union (25 percent).

In Nigeria[7] and in Tunisia,[8] one out of two students on the far left chooses to marry traditionally. The only other choice made with any frequency (about 30 percent) was for free union. Twenty-nine percent of the Nigerian students and 15 percent of the Tunisian students foresee this kind of life.

The future of the family as a patriarchal institution and its legal consecration by marriage are not questioned by moderate students or those on the right in the countries studied. Their aspirations correspond to their expectations, and they do not foresee major changes in the relations between men and women or in the family structure. The family's role as intermediary between the individual and society is also not questioned by the majority of these moderate students. Those on the far left, even if a minority of them anticipate for themselves life styles other than the family unit, often reveal on the level of their preferences that there exists a new movement which seeks to establish a different family structure. This phenomenon is important, for these new communal life styles abolish the limits of the family unit and the hierarchy of interpersonal relationships. These students refuse to accept the present social order and its authoritarian structures. As Reich (1969) indicates, "The family is part and parcel and, at the same time, prerequisite of the authoritarian state and of authoritarian society" (p. 71).

In addition, these new life styles represent a real revolutionary potential, as Cooper (1971) notes: they are the proof that viable relationships different from those

---

[7]In Nigeria polygamy is still practiced. Thus the choice of responses presented to monogamous societies could only lead to confusion.

[8]At independence, reforms were adopted in the Koranic laws in Tunisia forbidding polygamy. Marriage, which for ages had been arranged by families, became a contract between two individuals, whose consent is required by law. Ambiguity arises, however, as it is not clear what kind of marriage the student has in mind when he chooses traditional marriage.

TABLE 6.7.   Moral and Cultural Values by Countries (Percent).

	AUSTRAL.	AUS.	FR.	GB	IT.	JAP.	NIG.	SP.	TUN.	USA	YUG.
The role of religion in society should diminish.*	(720) 43	(479) 59	(613) 54	(515) 42	(766) 52	(341) 61	(225) 42	(718) 71	(129) 51	(586) 34	(1,080) 55
Middle-class morality[1] destroys the spontaneity of individual experience.*	(703) 66	(473) 71	(651) 72	(558) 68	67	(343) 59	(166) 50	(705) 79	–	(611) 74	82
Restrictive measures should be taken against the use of marijuana and hashish.*	(734) 49	(480) 74	(662) 65	(580) 42	(798) 89	(399) 86	(219) 86	(701) 78	(126) 87	(637) 27	(1,079) 85
Restrictive measures should be taken against the use of LSD.*	84	(479) 85	(666) 78	(574) 76	(786) 92	(390) 87	(192) 88	(702) 85	(98) 86	(630) 79	90

*p<.01
1. This item was not included in the Tunisian questionnaire.

TABLE 6.9.   Life Style for the year 2000, Foreseen for the Society and Preferred and Expected by the Student (Percent).

Society's way of life	AUSTRAL. (763)	AUS. (403)	FR. (814)	GB (576)	IT. (814)	JAP. (421)	NIG. (220)	SP. (729)	TUN. (131)	USA (631)	YUG. (964)
Present form of marriage**	31	46	34	30	29	32	22	24	31	27	46
Marriage with greater extramarital freedom**	48	28	40	50	43	56	49	36	50	42	26
Free union	7	9	12	5	7	6	16	16	12	10	9
Marriage but families living communally	5	–	6	6	8	1	7	9	5	10	4
In communities without marriage	3	–	4	4	11	2	5	7	2	4	2
Other	6	–	4	5	2	3	1	8	–	7	2
Don't know	–	17	–	–	–	–	–	–	–	–	11

Preferred way of life	AUSTRAL. (758)	AUS. (477)	FR. (775)	GB (567)	IT. (775)	JAP. (425)	NIG. (204)	SP. (709)	TUN. (117)	USA (584)	YUG. (853)
Present form of marriage*	47	38	37	46	46	32	49	50	81	69	63
Marriage with greater extramarital freedom**	13	14	14	17	9	28	10	18	10	13	19
Free union**	21	24	26	12	10	27	23	16	6	7	3
Marriage but families living communally	8	19	10	12	13	4	11	6	2	6	1
In communities without marriage	7	4	11	8	20	9	3	4	–	2	1
Other	5	1	2	5	2	–	3	6	1	3	2
Don't know	–	–	–	–	–	–	–	–	–	–	11

Expected way of life	AUSTRAL. (755)	AUS. (465)	FR. (748)	GB (544)	IT. (748)	JAP. (423)	NIG. (184)	SP. (729)	TUN. (128)	USA (612)	YUG. (934)
Present form of marriage*	66	39	62	65	52	50	55	36	61	51	59
Marriage with greater extramarital freedom**	22	23	16	20	27	40	10	14	13	13	14
Free union**	5	18	11	4	5	5	16	24	16	16	10
Marriage but families living communally	3	15	4	4	6	1	11	8	4	10	2
In communities without marriage	1	2	3	3	9	2	5	11	5	8	2
Other	3	2	4	4	1	2	3	7	1	2	2
Don't know	–	–	–	–	–	–	–	–	–	–	11

*p < .01
**p < .05

assumed by traditional bourgeois morality can exist. Cooper takes up the notion of a parallel society, important to Marcuse: it would allow another kind of behavior to function in order to show the majority that a different life style is possible.

Finally, the present era sometimes is considered to be the end of women's enslavement, described in rather extreme terms by Engels (1931): "The modern individual family is founded on the open or concealed slavery of the wife. . . . Within the family *he* is the bourgeois and his wife represents the proletariat" (p. 79).

THE 1977 STUDY

The results indicate that in the United States more students (44 percent) expect the continuation of the traditional form of marriage in the year 2000 than expected this at the time of the main study (27 percent). This seems an indication of decreased popularity of the counterculture. In France there is no big change (39 percent) as compared to 34 percent in 1970). Concerning the preferred way of life, in the United States there is a slight increase in the acceptance of a traditional life style; 57 percent of the students versus 51 percent in 1970 select marriage in its traditional form. In France, on the contrary, there is a clear-cut diminution in the proportion which favors marriage. Only 20 percent (compared to 37 percent in the main study) consider marriage as a desirable life style. Concerning real-life expectations, there is no change in the two studies. The majority of United States students expect to marry in the traditional manner (about 70 percent in both studies). In France no significant changes appear (62 percent in 1970 and 54 percent in 1977). These results indicate some marked cross-cultural differences between the United States and France (Table 6.10).

TABLE 6.10. Life Style for the Year 2000, Foreseen for the Society and Preferred and Expected by the Student, 1977 Survey (Percent).

France	FORESEEN (89)	PREFERRED (87)	EXPECTED (84)
Present form of marriage	39	20*	54
Marriage with greater extramarital freedom	21	10	14
Free union	18	35*	19
Marriage but families living communally	8	13	1
Communities without marriage	3	14	5
Other	10	9	7
United States	(104)	(102)	(103)
Present form of marriage	44	57*	70
Marriage with greater extramarital freedom	34	11	14
Free union	6	11*	4
Marriage but families living communally	3	2	0
Communities without marriage	4	7	2
Other	10	13	11

*p < .01, significant differences between French and American students in 1977.

Women in Society

For several years, first in the United States and then throughout Western Europe, a feminist movement has been developing which not only demands equality but also questions the present social order, the institution of the family, sexual norms, and occupational discrimination. Underlying this movement is the vision of global changes in society, according to Limpus (1970):

> Since the problems that face women are related to the structure of the whole society, ultimately our study of our particular situation as women will lead us to the realization that we must attempt to change this whole society [p. 74].

It is only since the beginning of the industrial revolution of the last century that one may truly speak of a collective, feminist awakening, which created the feminist movement in Great Britain, then in the United States and in France. This movement in Europe was often based on socialist ideas; in the United States it tended to be rather conservative and often indifferent to the special conditions of working women. This movement in its contrasting European and American forms was active through the 1930s and then endured a long eclipse. In the United States, during the 1940s and 1950s women returned to the home and lived the social phenomenon which Betty Friedan (1963) termed "the feminine mystique." In Europe, a similar situation could be observed.

Psychoanalysis played an important role in the United States in providing support for the traditional role of women in society. Popular medical writers such as Dr. Spock glorified maternity and "the mystical relationship between the mother and the child." The mass media picked up this interpretation and celebrated "the return of women to the home," the "real" place for their self-development.

The protest of women in its present form began in the 1960s. Before then there were obviously many women who fought against their own inferior situation, but these were rather isolated cases involved in personal rebellion.

At the time of this study, in the United States only 11 percent of all Ph.D. holders were women, compared with 15 percent forty years earlier (Burn, 1972). In 1971 J. Egginton noted:

> Only 9% of all professional people in America are women; only 7% of the doctors and only 3% of the lawyers. There is not a single woman in the Federal Cabinet; no woman is a State Governor or mayor of any large city. . . . And while 90% of the nation's elementary school teachers are women, 80% of the school principals are men [p. 7].

It is against this background that the feminist movement in its present form has emerged. It does not limit its goals to an amelioration of women's social and economic status or of job equality. It calls for a more profound change in value systems:

> What all new feminists have in common is a vehement impatience with the continuance of second class citizenship and economic handicaps for women, a determination to bring our legal and value systems into line with current sexual mores, an awareness of the psychological damage to women of their subordinate position, and a conviction that changes must embrace not only laws and institutions, but also the minds, emotions, and sexual habits of men and women [Lerner, 1970, p. 24].

While capitalism is usually accused by Marxists of being the origin of the oppression of women, most women who have written on this subject believe that men, rather than any specific economic system, are responsible. Marxists tend to forget the role of men in the exploitation of women and make capitalism, as Alzon (1973) notes, "the great, and almost the only, oppressor responsible for the 'misery of women'" (p. 9).

Socialism clearly does not lead automatically to women's liberation. In fact, in all socialist countries the apparent victory of the working class does not seem to be accompanied by a profound change in the situation of women. As elsewhere, they are viewed first as mothers and housekeepers. Even when there is a more expanded job market for professional women, they must perform two jobs, one inside and one outside the home. This is not considered by feminists as liberation. This complex situation made it important to discover whether an awareness of this issue would appear in the different countries studied.

THE RIGHTS OF WOMEN

Opinions regarding the position of women—their role and their place in society—were approached by means of the following four items in the questionnaire:

In our society, women as a group are oppressed.

Men and women should have equal access to positions of highest political responsibility.

The same standards should be used concerning the sex life of men and women.

Women can improve their position only by organizing protest movements.

In this research (see Table 6.11) it was necessary to distinguish between responses from men and responses from women. Our findings, though, show that if we do not consider political orientation, the analysis by sex does not show any marked differences between the two sexes, except in Tunisia. In that country, where the patriarchal tradition and religion are still very strong, the male reaction to the sexual and economic emancipation of the woman is clearly more negative than that of the women, who manifest a desire to be liberated. The fact that three out of four Tunisian women consider women an oppressed group, in comparison to 42 percent of the men, is significant. In Muslim countries in general, the emancipation of women has proceeded very slowly. Generally considered inferior, women are excluded from a large part of social life and have few opportunities in the professions. According to Islam, in fact, the rights of women are limited with regard to inheritance (a woman has the right to only one-half of what the man receives), in access to education (few women pursue advanced studies), in work opportunities (discrimination by sex is more frequent than in the West), and in religion (women may only enter certain places in a mosque—the basic rule is that women must be isolated and hidden). Within-country comparisons indicate that in Tunisia, there is a striking difference between males and females concerning the statement "in our society, women as a group are oppressed": only 42 percent of men agree as compared to 75 percent of women. In the remaining countries, men/women differences on this item are smaller and vary from 7 percent (Austria) to 13 percent (Australia) and 12 percent (Spain).

Between-country differences on this issue are more marked than within-country comparisons. In France, Italy, and Tunisia, less than 50 percent of the men recognize

TABLE 6.11. Women in Society, Responses by Sex (Percent).

		AUSTRAL.	AUSTRIA	FRANCE	GB	ITALY	SPAIN	TUNISIA	USA
There should be equal access for men and women to high political positions.	Men	(541) 86	(235) 92	(346) 95	(344) 92	(456) 91	(555) 93	(67) 64	(429) 89
	Women	(197) 94	(241) 98	(343) 95	(251) 94	(388) 98	(170) 99	(66)* 99	(190) 97
Same standards should be used concerning the sex life of men and women	Men	(541) 86	(222) 84	(350) 80	(325) 91	(431) 79	(542) 87	(68) 77	(430) 89
	Women	(199) 92	(241) 84	(308) 77	(242) 88	(368) 81	(161) 91	(64) 89	(176) 92
In our society, women as a group are oppressed.	Men	(558) 56	(235) 72	(348) 48	(338) 57	(453) 47	(541) 75	(66) 42	(430) 69
	Women	(201) 69	(240) 73	(324) 55	(250) 66	(384) 54	(168) 87	(65)* 74	(187) 79
Women can improve their position only by organizing protest movements.	Men	(537) 32	(235) 50	(346) 45	(325) 42	(402) 40	(515) 40	(66) 50	(428) 40
	Women	(200) 23	(240) 40	(298) 40	(244) 34	(364) 32	(163) 31	(61)** 77	(181) 35

*p < .01
**p < .05

that women as a group are oppressed; more do so in Australia (56 percent) and Great Britain (57 percent), while in Austria (73 percent), Spain (75 percent), and the United States (69 percent) a substantial majority of men agree with this view. Between-country comparisons of women responses indicate a rank order in the percentages similar to the one obtained from men. However, the female percentages are higher than the ones of their male counterparts. Italian (54 percent) and French (55 percent) women are least likely to feel that women as a group are oppressed. Spanish women (87 percent) are most likely to feel oppressed, the remaining countries falling in between.[9]

In Tunisia the very favorable attitude of women students toward the liberation movement may in part be explained by the fact that Bourguiba in general supported the emancipation of women and numerous groups have emerged which favor the improvement of the feminine condition. This attitude may also be explained by the education women respondents have received, which puts them in a privileged position. S. Klineberg (1974), in a study of modernism in Tunisia, showed that, on the whole, women participate little in social change and are, for the most part, confined to their homes. Parents in general maintain the distinction traditionally made between men and women. In a study of a group of adolescent girls, this same author showed the importance of formal education in relation to the "modern" attitude. The more formal education a girl had received, the more were her attitudes in opposition to the traditional values of her patriarchal family.

In general, it should be noted that, although sex introduces a difference of opinion, political orientation plays a much more important role in the development of attitudes about the rights of women. Thus we note that the more a man or woman perceives himself or herself as on the left, the greater the likelihood of approval of the principles of equality, recognition of the inferior status of women, and acceptance of a liberation movement. The influence of political position is clearer for issues dealing with oppression and protest than for those dealing with sex and equal access to high political position. The general principles of equality appear to be recognized in most countries today, even if these notions are not always put into practice. The recognition of a state of oppression implies action, however, and this action goes counter to the patriarchal system, which has influenced all the societies in this study. A radical position is thus very difficult for conservative men and women, who have already integrated the norms and values of "masculine" society.

Rather than a war between the sexes, there seems to exist a war of ideologies. As proof, at least in this present study, we may point to the small proportion of women compared to men who accept the feminine liberation movement. The situation in Tunisia, however, has special characteristics. There the women are more conscious of their oppression and more willing to fight against it than are women in other countries. In this Third World country, where the woman in general holds a very inferior position, there does seem to exist an open conflict between traditional and modern views of women's role.

THE 1977 STUDY

The results indicate some interesting changes. In France men are slightly less likely to favor sexual equality in professional life (86 percent as compared to 95 percent in 1970) and women about equally likely to demand it (98 percent as compared to 95

---

[9]The number of women in Japan, Nigeria, and Yugoslavia was too small to make such comparisons.

percent). Men are also less likely today to favor equality in sexual standards (67 percent as compared to 80 percent in 1970). There is an insignificant decrease in the percentage of women who advocate it (72 percent as compared to 77 percent). However, there are more students of both sexes who consider women as an oppressed group (men 59 percent as compared to 48 percent in 1970, and women 70 percent as compared to 55 percent). This increase in the awareness of female oppression by both sexes is not accompanied by a corresponding increase of acceptance by men of feminist movements. Men are less likely to accept them today than in 1970 (33 percent versus 45 percent) (Table 6.12). The decrease in the popularity of feminist movements is not found among women (43 percent versus 40 percent).

TABLE 6.12. Women in Society, Responses by Sex, 1977 Survey (Percent).

	FRANCE*		UNITED STATES	
There should be equal access for men and women to high political positions.	Men	(55) 86	Men	(35) 91
	Women	(96) 98	Women	(47) 98
Same standards should be used concerning the sex life of men and women.	Men	(59) 67	Men	(54) 89
	Women	(46) 72	Women	(55) 95
In our society, women as a group are oppressed.	Men	(56) 59	Men	(54) 66
	Women	(46) 70	Women	(55) 87
Women can improve their position only by organizing protest movements	Men	(54) 33	Men	(54) 30
	Women	(46) 43	Women	(55) 40

*n.s.

In the United States there is no change concerning the views on professional and sexual equality between men and women. There is an increase of women who feel oppressed (87 percent versus 79 percent in 1970) and, very slightly, who favor feminist movements (40 percent as compared to 35 percent in 1970). As in France, men on the contrary are less likely to agree with feminist views (30 percent as compared to 40 percent in 1970). These results do not support the opinion currently spread by the media that feminism is dying. Such views seem more to reflect masculine wishes than female attitudes (Table 6.12).

BIRTH CONTROL

The redefinition of sexuality in terms of equality is an important step in the liberation of women, but liberation also involves the control of procreation.

Although the Roman Catholic Church has for so long declared that procreation is the only goal of the sex act, the right to sexual pleasure is now expressed more and more openly nearly everywhere. This right implies the refusal of an unwanted birth. Feminist movements have greatly contributed to the awareness of this problem and have demanded the right of the woman to decide if, and when, she will have a child.

At the same time the Church's position still weighs heavily in predominantly Catholic countries. In contrast, Protestant countries were among the first to liberalize the use of contraceptives and to institute sexual education. In 1966 birth control devices were available everywhere in the United States. Some states have authorized free abortions. Great Britain did so in 1967. In France, the liberalization of contraception was initiated during these years (with many restrictions and no publicity), and abortion became legal only in 1975. In Yugoslavia, free abortion has been available since 1955, and contraceptive devices have been available for a long time. In Third World countries like Nigeria and Tunisia, governments, aided by international organizations, favor the diffusion of all types of contraceptives in order to check the spiral of overpopulation. Some countries even facilitate abortions.

The problem of birth control in terms both of contraceptives and of the availability of abortion was approached by asking students whether they agreed or disagreed with the following statements:

Contraceptive devices should be made available to all.

Abortion should be an individual choice without legal restrictions.

In general, the students in all the countries studied react more favorably to the notion of contraceptives than to the liberalization of abortion.

More than 80 percent of the students in France, Tunisia, Japan, Austria, and the Anglo-Saxon countries believe that contraceptive devices should be available to everyone. This figure drops in Spain (70 percent), Italy (69 percent), and Nigeria (68 percent). Yugoslavia (78 percent) is in between (Table 6.13). More differences appear concerning abortion. Most American students (90 percent) believe that abortion should be an individual choice, followed by about three out of four students in France (77 percent), Australia (75 percent), Austria and Great Britain (73 percent), and Tunisia (71 percent). The least favorable are the Spanish and Italian students (52 percent), and also the Japanese and Yugoslavian (63 percent).[10] We see that the majority of French students are in favor of liberalizing abortion, while those in Spain and in Italy, where the Roman Catholic Church is very strong, are significantly less so.

On the whole, there are few differences in attitudes between men and women in regard to birth control, except in Italy and Tunisia. In Italy men have a more favorable attitude to contraception than do women (78 percent as compared to 59 percent). In Tunisia the liberalization of abortion is more favored by women (87 percent) than by men (64 percent) (Table 6.13).

The attitude of the student to birth control—a problem which involves cultural, social, and political issues—is almost always related to the student's political and ideological orientation, except in Tunisia, where sex differences in this respect are marked. As expected, the more the student is on the left, the more he is favorable to birth control. In general, our findings indicate that birth control is widely accepted by students, even if the specific problem of abortion remains relatively controversial.

THE 1977 SURVEY

The 1977 study indicates no significant changes in attitudes toward contraception in France (87 percent favoring it as compared to 81 percent in 1970) and in the United

---

[10]This item was not included in the Nigerian questionnaire.

TABLE 6.13. Birth Control Responses by Sex and by Country (Percent).

	AUSTRAL.	AUSTRIA	FRANCE	GB	ITALY	SPAIN	TUNISIA	USA
Contraceptive devices available to all								
Men	(544)	(237)	(346)	(343)	(453)	(536)	(65)	(429)
	85	94	83	94	78	72**	80	97
Women	(200)	(241)	(344)	(248)	(377)	(163)	(62)	(188)
	83	90	79	88	59	64	89	96
Total sample[1]	(708)	(399)	(653)	(545)	(755)	(704)	(129)	(617)
	84	92	81	91	69	70	83	96
Abortion an individual choice without legal restrictions								
Men	(552)	(237)	(342)	(342)	(455)	(535)	(67)	(425)
	75	72	76	77	55	54	64**	89
Women	(201)	(242)	(331)	(247)	(382)	(162)	(63)	(163)
	75	77	78	68	49	50	87	91
Total sample[2]	(707)	(398)	(652)	(539)	(750)	(701)	(123)	(588)
	75	73	77	73	52	52	71	90

**p < .05
1. Japan (398) 90 percent; Nigeria (232) 68 percent; Yugoslavia (968) 78 percent.
2. Japan (404) 63 percent; Yugoslavia (963) 63 percent.

States (96 percent favoring it in 1977 and 1970). On the issue of abortion there is a slight diminution of approval in the United States only (77 percent as compared to 90 percent in 1970). No significant differences exist between men and women in either country (Table 6.14).

TABLE 6.14. Birth Control Responses in France and the United States, 1977 Survey (Percent).

	FRANCE	UNITED STATES
Contraceptive devices available to all		
Men	(54)	(36)
	85	97
Women	(48)	(47)
	89	96
Total sample	(92)	(83)
	87	96
Abortion an individual choice without legal restrictions		
Men	(54)	(54)
	72	78
Women	(47)	(55)
	83	76
Total sample	(101)	(109)
	77	77

Concluding Note

This chapter, which has focused on relations between generations and between the sexes on a number of social and moral issues, once again reveals differences both between nations and between groups of different political orientation within each nation. In general we have found considerable adherence to traditional norms and values with, however, a marked tendency among students on the far left in favor of changes that counter the ideas and aspirations of their parents.

TABLE 6.1a.   Conflict between Generations by Political Tendency (Percent).

Australia		Right	Cent.	Left	Far L.	Apol.
Differences between social and moral values of youth and the older generation are far greater than in the past.		(39) 67	(261) 69	(221) 69	(35) 74	(176) 64
In our society today, the conflict of generations is acutely felt.**		(40) 70	(270) 75	(231) 88	(36) 95	(185) 85
The family is a universally oppressive institution.*		(39) 13	14	(226) 25	(34) 50	(181) 19

Austria		Right	Cent.	Left	Far L.	Apol.
Differences between social and moral values of youth and the older generation are far greater than in the past.		(82) 78	(152) 75	(136) 81	(66) 79	(44) 75
In our society today, the conflict of generations is acutely felt.		78	85	(135) 93	86	(45) 87
The family is a universally oppressive institution.*		11	(151) 18	(136) 47	(65) 66	18

France	Right	Cent.	Left	Comm.	Far L.	Anar.	Apol.
Differences between social and moral values of youth and the older generation are far greater than in the past.*	(42) 71	(134) 66	(195) 79	(40) 60	(93) 81	(32) 78	(145) 70
In our society today, the conflict of generations is acutely felt.*	(40) 83	(133) 69	(199) 86	55	(88) 84	(30) 87	(148) 80
The family is a universally oppressive institution.*	(42) 10	15	30	(43) 44	(93) 48	(32) 72	(151) 30

Great Britain		Right	Cent.	Left	Far L.	Apol.
Differences between social and moral values of youth and the older generation are far greater than in the past.		(87) 51	(86) 56	(192) 63	(70) 64	(145) 65
In our society today, the conflict of generations is acutely felt.*		77	(90) 76	(199) 79	(73) 85	(149) 84
The family is a universally oppressive institution.*		(89) 11	(88) 13	(193) 18	(68) 41	(144) 14

Italy	Far R.	Right	Cent.	Left	Comm.	Far L.	Apol.
Differences between social and moral values of youth and the older generation are far greater than in the past.**	(30) 87	(65) 72	(147) 73	(210) 87	(104) 78	(64) 81	(167) 77
In our society today, the conflict of generations is acutely felt.	(29) 93	(64) 86	(150) 89	(223) 90	(106) 92	(69) 84	(170) 87
The family is a universally oppressive institution.*	(30) 23	(65) 23	(149) 15	(205) 30	65	(70) 64	(168) 20

Japan	CENT.	LEFT	FAR L.	APOL.
Differences between social and moral values of youth and the older generation are far greater than in the past.	(148) 74	(44) 77	(113) 80	(106) 81
In our society today, the conflict of generations is acutely felt.**	(147) 67	(40) 83	(119) 80	(103) 77
The family is a universally oppressive institution.*	(144) 27	43	(120) 43	(100) 31

Nigeria	RIGHT	CRITIC.	LEFT	FAR L.	DESCR.	APOL.
Differences between social and moral values of youth and the older generation are far greater than in the past.	(42) 93	(36) 95	(45) 93	(19) 84	(28) 89	(54) 87
In our society today, the conflict of generations is acutely felt.	(39) 85	89	(39) 82	(20) 75	(25) 80	(50) 86
The family is a universally oppressive institution.**	(42) 17	(34) 29	(44) 25	(18) 11	(27) 30	(53) 23

Spain	RIGHT	CENTER	LEFT	FAR L.	APOL.
Differences between social and moral values of youth and the older generation are far greater than in the past.**	(60) 72	(116) 83	(272) 80	(79) 86	(172) 71
In our society today, the conflict of generations is acutely felt.	(62) 87	(120) 91	(277) 95	85	(182) 88
The family is a universally oppressive institution.*	(60) 23	23	(278) 48	(78) 78	28

Tunisia	RIGHT	BOURGUIB.	LEFT	FAR L.	APOL.
Differences between social and moral values of youth and the older generation are far greater than in the past.**	(14) 100	(16) 81	(47) 94	(25) 88	(31) 94
In our society today, the conflict of generations is acutely felt.	93	88	(46) 94	(24) 96	(29) 86
The family is a universally oppressive institution.*	43	(14) 36	48	(22) 82	(28) 46

United States	RIGHT	CENT.	LIB.	LEFT	FAR L.	APOL.
Differences between social and moral values of youth and older generation are far greater than in the past.*	(79) 57	(124) 69	(191) 67	(136) 84	(24) 83	(85) 64
In our society today, the conflict of generations is acutely felt.**	(80) 79	(127) 91	(195) 85	(137) 92	(26) 100	(90) 93
The family is a universally oppressive institution.*	(77) 8	(122) 11	(190) 13	(132) 17	(25) 28	(84) 17

Yugoslavia	IDEAL.	REAL	HUMAN.	ELIT.	INDIV.
Differences between social and moral values of youth and the older generation are far greater than in the past.	(238) 70	(493) 66	(162) 67	(26) 84	(40) 76
In our society today, the conflict of generations is acutely felt.	(240) 74	(490) 75	75	88	(39) 74
The family is a universally oppressive institution.	(241) 34	(487) 36	42	(25) 40	(40) 43

*p < .01
**p < .05

TABLE 6.3a.   Emotional, Moral, and Political Proximity between Students and Their Parents by Political Tendency (Percent).

Australia	RIGHT	CENT.	LEFT	FAR L.	APOL.
Student feels close					
Emotionally	(40) 83	(268) 70	(227) 80	(34) 77	(184) 80
Morally*	65	(270) 64	(228) 53	38	(185) 58
Politically*	80	(262) 66	(221) 47	35	(155) 50

Austria	RIGHT	CENT.	LEFT	FAR L.	APOL.
Student feels close					
Emotionally*	(79) 67	(150) 75	(137) 59	(69) 49	(44) 68
Morally*	(81) 49	(148) 37	21	9	36
Politically*	70	(150) 41	32	17	27

France	RIGHT	CENT.	LEFT	COMM.	FAR L.	ANAR.	APOL.
Student feels close							
Emotionally*	(43) 91	(136) 93	(207) 90	(47) 75	(97) 88	(32) 66	(159) 86
Morally*	77	(134) 75	(205) 56	(46) 52	(96) 44	(31) 26	(157) 61
Politically*	(42) 79	(132) 70	(206) 47	52	(97) 33	(33) 30	(150) 44

France 1977	RIGHT	CENT.	LEFT	COMM.	FAR L.	ANAR.	APOL.
Student feels close							
Emotionally*	(6)	(10) 90	(35) 89	(4)	(16) 82	–	(20) 85
Morally*	(6)	100	(34) 65	(4)	91	–	65
Politically*	(4)	100	46	(2)	31	–	55

Great Britain	RIGHT	CENT.	LEFT	FAR L.	APOL.
Student feels close					
Emotionally	(87) 87	(88) 84	(191) 85	(71) 78	(143) 85
Morally*	(88) 68	(89) 65	(190) 53	(72) 32	(148) 59
Politically*	(85) 81	(85) 59	(188) 52	(71) 34	(124) 56

Italy	FAR R.	RIGHT	CENT.	LEFT	COMM.	FAR L.	APOL.
Student feels close							
Emotionally	(31) 78	(61) 82	(141) 80	(206) 81	(104) 71	(67) 69	(166) 83
Morally*	74	(65) 94	(152) 84	(223) 75	(111) 36	(72) 39	(171) 75
Politically*	(30) 53	(64) 78	(142) 71	(213) 48	28	(71) 23	(138) 51

Japan		CENT.	LEFT	FAR L.	APOL.
Student feels close					
Emotionally**		(147) 80	(40) 78	(117) 72	(95) 65
Morally**		(153) 57	(42) 38	(122) 39	(100) 49
Politically		(144) 38	24	(120) 20	(97) 24

Nigeria	RIGHT	CRITIC.	LEFT	FAR L.	DESCR.	APOL.
Student feels close						
Emotionally	(40) 88	(34) 88	(44) 89	(21) 95	(28) 93	(57) 97
Morally	(41) 88	88	(43) 88	90	89	(55) 89
Politically*	(36) 57	(29) 38	(38) 45	(18) 29	(26) 46	(47) 66

Spain		RIGHT	CENT.	LEFT	FAR L.	APOL.
Student feels close						
Emotionally*		(62) 95	(120) 87	(280) 86	(82) 68	(184) 91
Morally*		(61) 72	66	(278) 43	23	(182) 70
Politically*		(62) 60	(110) 46	(274) 31	(83) 18	(159) 56

Tunisia		RIGHT	BOURGUIB.	LEFT	FAR L.	APOL.
Student feels close						
Emotionally		(15) 87	(15) 93	(49) 90	(25) 88	(35) 94
Morally*		60	87	(47) 68	(24) 63	(34) 68
Politically*		(13) 54	47	36	29	(33) 42

United States	RIGHT	CENT.	LIB.	LEFT	FAR L.	APOL.
Student feels close						
Emotionally*	(80) 89	(125) 90	(194) 87	(136) 85	(26) 73	(91) 78
Morally**	75	(126) 69	(193) 63	(137) 50	54	(92) 61
Politically*	(75) 79	(119) 66	(184) 57	(136) 43	35	(87) 51

United States 1977	RIGHT	CENT.	LIB.	LEFT	FAR L.	APOL.
Student feels close						
Emotionally*	(26) 92	(27) 70	(23) 91	(8) (7)	(4) (4)	(16) 75
Morally**	96	(28) 71	78	(8)	(3)	69
Politically*	73	68	79	(3)	(2)	69

*p < .01
**p < .05
1. Completely and relatively free combine.

(cont.)

TABLE 6.3b.   Proximity to Parents, Yugoslavia, by Self-Definition (Percent).

	IDEALISTS	REAL.	HUMAN.	ELIT.	INDIV.
Relationship with father	(213)	(434)	(137)	(23)	(35)
Close	72	72	68	70	69
Distant	28	28	32	30	32
Relationship with mother	(236)	(478)	(158)	(25)	(40)
Close	89	88	91	72	85
Distant	11	12	10	28	15
Agreement with political opinions of					
the parents	(235)	(482)	(159)	(26)	(42)
Agree	74	72	70	65	64
Disagree	22	23	25	31	29
Don't know	4	5	6	4	7

TABLE 6.3c.   Proximity to Parents, Yugoslavia, by Membership in the Communist League (Percent).

	MEMBERS OF THE COMMUNIST LEAGUE	NONMEMBERS OF THE COMMUNIST LEAGUE	
		Wish to join	*Refuse to join*
Relationship with father	(106)	(150)	(688)
Close	78	74	68
Distant	22	26	32
Relationship with mother	(116)	(172)	(764)
Close	89	90	88
Distant	11	10	12
Agreement with political opinions of			
the parents	(116)	(173)	(771)
Agree	80	75	67
Disagree	18	19	26
Don't know	2	6	7

TABLE 6.5a.   Specific Points of Divergence between Students and Their Parents by Political Tendency (Percent).

Australia	RIGHT	CENT.	LEFT	FAR L.	APOL.
Sexual experiences*	(37)	(238)	(214)	(30)	(172)
	57	66	69	87	65
Success*	(39)	(259)	(227)	(34)	(181)
	46	45	53	79	59
Money*		(264)	(229)	(35)	(184)
	41	49	52	69	50
Leisure**	(38)	(266)	(225)	(34)	
	55	53	59	71	51
Present moment	(37)	(252)	(215)	(35)	(180)
	32	38	50	49	39
Art	(35)	(262)	(226)	(34)	(181)
	46	50	56	53	51
Creative pursuits*	(36)	(266)	(225)	(35)	(183)
	47	42	48	63	40
Communion with nature	(33)	(255)	(214)		(175)
	18	28	35	34	37
Individualism**	(39)	(261)	(226)		(180)
	39	41	52	57	46

	RIGHT	CENT.	LEFT	FAR L.	APOL.
Religion*	(38) 42	(265) 43	(230) 61	(35) 66	(185) 52
Drugs*	21	(262) 26	(225) 46	69	(182) 32

Austria	RIGHT	CENT.	LEFT	FAR L.	APOL.
Sexual experiences**	(82) 29	(145) 37	(132) 46	(67) 46	(45) 36
Success*	(81) 20	(147) 27	(133) 35	49	29
Money	(82) 27	25	(128) 35	(66) 41	33
Leisure	(79) 20	(148) 18	(133) 29	(67) 31	27
Present moment**	(80) 28	(145) 35	(126) 35	(65) 46	38
Art**	(82) 29	(147) 29	(131) 42	51	33
Creative pursuits	(81) 12	16	(132) 22	(66) 26	20
Communion with nature	16	8	(129) 15	(67) 18	13
Individualism**	33	(148) 30	(131) 48	49	(44) 30
Religion*	(82) 10	16	(134) 31	42	9
Drugs*	(81) 7	(146) 15	(129) 28	(66) 49	24

France	RIGHT	CENT.	LEFT	COMM.	FAR L.	ANAR.	APOL.
Sexual experiences**	(35) 57	(117) 62	(180) 72	(38) 71	(83) 75	(27) 78	(137) 69
Success*	(37) 32	(126) 53	(181) 53	61	(85) 73	(28) 61	(136) 49
Money	(40) 50	(129) 52	(195) 53	(44) 57	(95) 60	(31) 65	(147) 57
Leisure**	68	(131) 73	(198) 74	(46) 67	(96) 78	(32) 84	(149) 73
Present moment*	(38) 42	(119) 50	(184) 58	(36) 42	(83) 68	(31) 74	(140) 59
Art*	(40) 58	(125) 57	(189) 66	(41) 68	(91) 75	(30) 87	(142) 53
Creative pursuits*	(31) 36	(106) 52	(163) 54	(25) 44	(74) 58	(28) 75	(121) 53
Communion with nature*	(35) 31	(120) 35	(181) 35	(35) 26	(82) 33	(26) 58	(136) 32
Individualism*	51	(124) 44	(185) 54	(36) 47	(86) 55	(28) 71	53
Religion**	(42) 41	(136) 40	(203) 47	(47) 53	(95) 60	(31) 61	(150) 48
Drugs*	(40) 15	(126) 14	(191) 25	(42) 29	(85) 54	(30) 60	(143) 30

(cont.)

TABLE 6.5a. Continued

Great Britain	RIGHT	CENT.	LEFT	FAR L.	APOL.
Sexual experiences	(79) 73	(81) 68	(182) 80	(68) 77	(125) 73
Success*	(81) 32	(87) 54	(193) 65	(66) 65	(146) 48
Money	(87) 48	(88) 51	(195) 48	(70) 59	(145) 45
Leisure	(85) 50	(87) 59	(193) 62	(72) 65	(147) 56
Present moment	(79) 30	(84) 43	(177) 36	(62) 47	(136) 40
Art	(87) 46	(87) 46	(192) 60	(71) 59	(144) 48
Creative pursuits	(85) 39	(85) 38	(185) 50	(70) 39	47
Communion with nature	(78) 15	(65) 17	(165) 28	(63) 25	(119) 27
Individualism	(85) 31	(84) 44	(189) 41	(68) 50	(144) 44
Religion*	(86) 37	(89) 52	(193) 62	(72) 57	51
Drugs*	(88) 28	(87) 38	(185) 57	(70) 74	(146) 38

Italy	FAR R.	RIGHT	CENT.	LEFT	COMM.	FAR L.	APOL.
Sexual experiences*	(27) 63	(58) 53	(138) 49	(206) 70	(101) 76	(63) 71	(155) 62
Success*	(30) 50	(64) 42	(147). 52	(217) 68	(108) 73	(71) 68	(170) 62
Money	(29) 45	(66) 46	(149) 46	(218) 46	(106) 57	(69) 57	(169) 50
Leisure**	(31) 87	(65) 68	77	(224) 74	(108) 76	(71) 79	(174) 82
Present moment*	(26) 46	(63) 50	(147) 44	(216) 63	(104) 60	72	(171) 60
Art*	(29) 48	(64) 42	39	(219) 47	(103) 49	(69) 55	(166) 52
Creative pursuits*	(30) 40	(61) 48	(127) 54	(190) 55	(89) 62	(62) 66	(157) 62
Communion with nature	33	(66) 18	(149) 19	(215) 29	(103) 22	(71) 32	(172) 33
Individualism	50	(64) 52	(136) 51	(205) 51	(102) 65	(65) 57	(163) 58
Religion*	(31) 36	(65) 26	(150) 27	(220) 46	(110) 74	(71) 66	(170) 36
Drugs*	(27) 7	(62) 10	(145) 5	(215) 17	(103) 37	(69) 33	(165) 20

Japan[1]	CENT.	LEFT	FAR L.	APOL.
Success	(138) 49	(36) 50	(113) 56	(85) 47
Money*	(86) 24	(24) 13	(77) 30	(51) 22

Leisure	(149) 42	(37) 43	(115) 50	(89) 49
Present moment**	(131) 37	32	(104) 51	(73) 45
Art*	(138) 59	(36) 44	(112) 51	(78) 45
Creative pursuits**	(130) 28	(37) 30	(110) 46	(81) 36
Communion with nature	(135) 27	(39) 15	(111) 26	(76) 20
Individualism	(137) 45	(37) 54	(115) 54	(85) 48
Religion**	(148) 27	(39) 28	(118) 34	(91) 45
Drugs*	(140) 8	(41) 5	(106) 21	(87) 15

Nigeria[2]	RIGHT	CRITIC.	LEFT	FAR L.	DESCR.	APOL.
Sexual experiences**	(34) 62	(34) 65	(38) 58	(13) 77	(25) 60	(48) 65
Success	(40) 73	(33) 67	74	(18) 67	(24) 67	(52) 75
Money*	(37) 60	(34) 62	(39) 67	(19) 53	(26) 58	50
Leisure*	65	(35) 49	(41) 66	53	62	(53) 66
Present moment	(35) 60	(31) 55	(37) 51	53	(23) 48	(46) 61
Art*	(34) 65	(32) 66	(31) 39	(16) 56	(24) 67	(48) 67
Creative pursuits	(37) 62	59	(40) 63	(20) 55	(25) 60	(52) 50
Communion with nature*	(33) 49	(29) 52	(29) 45	(16) 63	(22) 59	(47) 47
Individualism*	(36) 42	(33) 58	(36) 39	(19) 32	(26) 58	(50) 46
Religion*	(40) 40	(35) 37	(44) 43	(20) 35	(27) 26	(55) 31

Spain	RIGHT	CENT.	LEFT	FAR L.	APOL.
Sexual experiences**	(53) 77	(111) 75	(273) 86	(77) 90	(169) 76
Success*	(61) 61	(118) 80	(269) 78	(81) 88	(173) 62
Money	(60) 62	(120) 66	(279) 67	(79) 70	(180) 64
Leisure	(61) 80	(118) 81	(274) 80	(81) 89	(182) 76
Present moment*	(57) 61	(117) 62	(270) 67	(78) 83	(166) 52
Art**	(58) 53	(118) 59	(275) 66	72	(179) 54
Creative pursuits*	(60) 65	(114) 61	(272) 70	(79) 80	(175) 54

(cont.)

TABLE 6.5a. Continued

Spain		RIGHT	CENT.	LEFT	FAR L.	APOL.
Communion with nature*		(57)	(112)	(254)	(68)	(164)
		35	42	48	62	37
Individualism		(58)	(117)	(262)	(75)	(170)
		64	60	69	77	59
Religion*		(62)	(120)	(277)	(82)	(187)
		45	56	69	81	49
Drugs*		(59)	(113)	(262)	(78)	(179)
		12	16	30	44	16

Tunisia		RIGHT	BOURGUIB.	LEFT	FAR L.	APOL.
Sexual experiences*		(13)	(14)	(41)	(25)	(27)
		100	71	85	92	89
Success*			(15)	(43)	(22)	(31)
		77	67	54	77	61
Money**		(14)	(14)	(45)	(23)	
		43	64	51	52	45
Leisure		(15)	(16)	(49)	(24)	(35)
		86	81	86	92	89
Present moment**		(12)	(14)	(43)	(22)	(26)
		67	86	74	77	73
Art		(13)		(39)	(20)	(29)
		77	71	72	80	83
Creative pursuits*		(11)	(13)	(38)	(22)	(22)
		64	53	68	68	77
Communion with nature*		(13)	(14)	(35)	(17)	(28)
		62	43	60	77	79
Individualism**			(15)	(42)	(21)	(25)
		62	53	62	71	72
Religion*		(14)	(16)	(47)	(24)	(34)
		57	25	34	67	50
Drugs*		(10)	(12)	(37)	(16)	(26)
		10	25	35	44	27

United States	RIGHT	CENT.	LIB.	LEFT	FAR L.	APOL.
Sexual experiences*	(74)	(111)	(178)	(126)	(24)	(75)
	53	66	69	71	88	72
Success*	(78)	(123)	(193)	(134)	(25)	(89)
	30	30	44	52	68	54
Money*	(79)	(124)	(192)	(136)		(86)
	30	43	44	57	48	56
Leisure			(194)	(135)	(24)	(87)
	46	36	43	46	50	41
Present moment*	(78)	(121)	(190)	(132)	(25)	(84)
	24	26	45	44	56	60
Art*	(80)			(134)	(24)	(86)
	36	27	36	43	38	43
Creative pursuits**	(78)			(135)	(23)	(87)
	33	30	32	39	30	48
Communion with nature*	(74)	(115)	(186)	(132)	(24)	(81)
	22	22	25	36	29	46
Individualism	(77)	(124)	(192)	(135)	(25)	(86)
	26	32	31	42	44	43

Religion	(80)		(196)	(136)	(24)	(88)
	50	52	54	63	58	66
Drugs*	(79)	(122)	(187)		(25)	(86)
	30	45	56	72	80	66

*p < .01
**p < .05

1. The item "sexual experiences" did not appear in the Japanese questionnaire.
2. It was not possible to utilize the results of the item concerning drugs, since numerous students understood "drugs" as medicine.

TABLE 6.7a.   Moral and Cultural Values by Political Tendency (Percent).

Australia	Right	Cent.	Left	Far L.	Apol.
The role of religion in society should diminish.*	(38) 37	(256) 31	(219) 54	(33) 73	(174) 43
Middle-class morality destroys the spontaneity of individual experience.*	50	(248) 55	(221) 77	94	(163) 67
Restrictive measures should be taken against the use of marijuana and hashish.*	(37) 59	(266) 62	(223) 36	(34) 18	(174) 51
Restrictive measures should be taken against the use of LSD.*	(40) 88	88	(220) 79	(33) 52	(175) 88

Austria	Right	Cent.	Left	Far L.	Apol.
The role of religion in society should diminish.*	(82) 33	(148) 49	(136) 76	(68) 84	(45) 49
Middle-class morality destroys the spontaneity of individual experience.*	(80) 51	(150) 67	(134) 83	(66) 86	(43) 63
Restrictive measures should be taken against the use of marijuana and hashish.*	(81) 88	(151) 82	(135) 67	(68) 44	(45) 80
Restrictive measures should be taken against the use of LSD.	(82) 90	(149) 89	84	74	84

France	Right	Cent.	Left	Comm.	Far L.	Anar.	Apol.
The role of religion in society should diminish.*	(35) 23	(122) 36	(176) 53	(47) 87	(82) 71	(30) 80	(121) 53
Middle-class morality destroys the spontaneity of individual experience.*	(39) 44	(123) 46	(189) 76	(40) 95	(89) 96	(32) 91	(139) 71
Restrictive measures should be taken against the use of marijuana and hashish.*	(40) 88	(130) 85	(188) 70	(44) 59	(85) 42	(30) 27	(145) 57
Restrictive measures should be taken against the use of LSD.*	93	(132) 92	(191) 82	(45) 80	(86) 59	(31) 42	(141) 77

Great Britain	Right	Cent.	Left	Far L.	Apol.
The role of religion in society should diminish.*	(78) 27	(79) 37	(173) 49	(62) 65	(123) 35
Middle-class morality destroys the spontaneity of individual experience.*	(84) 44	(86) 69	(190) 75	(64) 89	(134) 64
Restrictive measures should be taken against the use of marijuana and hashish.*	(88) 60	(87) 55	(196) 33	(71) 16	(140) 51
Restrictive measures should be taken against the use of LSD.*	(83)	92	(191) 70	(68) 62	(142) 76

(cont.)

TABLE 6.7a.   Continued

Italy	FAR R.	RIGHT	CENT.	LEFT	COMM.	FAR L.	APOL.
The role of religion in society should diminish.	(31) 48	(65) 38	(143) 31	(204) 55	(100) 85	(64) 77	(159) 41
Middle-class morality destroys the spontaneity of individual experience.*	(22) 32	(63) 44	(146) 59	(213) 72	(101) 90	(63) 89	(158) 60
Restrictive measures should be taken against the use of marijuana and hashish.*	(32) 97	(66) 95	(151) 97	(218) 88	(97) 70	(60) 83	(174) 93
Restrictive measures should be taken against the use of LSD.*	97	(65) 97	(147) 97	(213) 91	(102) 77	(59) 93	(168) 95

Japan			CENT.	LEFT	FAR L.	APOL.
The role of religion in society should diminish.			(122) 58	(34) 65	(96) 62	(189) 63
Middle-class morality destroys the spontaneity of individual experience.*			124) 48	(35) 63	(101) 74	(83) 56
Restrictive measures should be taken against the use of marijuana and hashish.**			(146) 91	(43) 93	(108) 75	(102) 86
Restrictive measures should be taken against the use of LSD.			(142) 93	(42) 91	(105) 82	(101) 84

Nigeria	RIGHT	CRITIC.	LEFT	FAR L.	DESCR.	APOL.
The role of religion in society should diminish.	(41) 37	(36) 36	(42) 62	(21) 48	(26) 31	(53) 36
Middle-class morality destroys the spontaneity of individual experience.*	(32) 53	(25) 44	(27) 67	(10) 50	(20) 55	(47) 36
Restrictive measures should be taken against the use of marijuana and hashish.	(38) 87	(32) 84	(42) 88	(19) 79	(28) 82	(54) 89
Restrictive measures should be taken against the use of LSD.	(35) 89	(26) 92	(36) 83	(16) 81	(23) 83	(50) 92

Spain		RIGHT	CENT.	LEFT	FAR L.	APOL.
The role of religion in society should diminish.*		(60) 47	(121) 65	(274) 79	(82) 95	(181) 58
Middle-class morality destroys the spontaneity of individual experience.*		50	(114) 79	91	94	(175) 65
Restrictive measures should be taken against the use of marijuana and hashish.*		97	(120) 85	(266) 74	(78) 54	(177) 83
Restrictive measures should be taken against the use of LSD.*		93	(122) 91	(264) 83	64	(178) 89

Tunisia[1]		RIGHT	BOURGUIB.	LEFT	FAR L.	APOL.
The role of religion in society should diminish.*		(12) 33	(16) 31	(46) 54	(22) 55	(29) 54
Restrictive measures should be taken against the use of marijuana and hashish.		(14) 93	(14) 86	80	(20) 85	(28) 96
Restrictive measures should be taken against the use of LSD.*		(13) 92	(9) 67	(34) 88	(15) 73	(24) 96

United States	RIGHT	CENT.	LIB.	LEFT	FAR L.	APOL.
The role of religion in society should diminish.*	(73) 19	(116) 28	(171) 33	(122) 52	(21) 62	(83) 36
Middle-class morality destroys the spontaneity of individual experience.*	(74) 53	(120) 76	(185) 63	(126) 84	(25) 88	(81) 80
Restrictive measures should be taken against the use of marijuana and hashish.*	(73) 56	(125) 36	(191) 21	(136) 10	8	(87) 25
Restrictive measures should be taken against the use of LSD.*	(78) 94	(126) 87	(189) 82	(128) 69	36	(84) 79
Yugoslavia (self-definition)	IDEAL.	REAL.	HUMAN.	ELIT.	INDIV.
---	---	---	---	---	---
The role of religion in society should diminish.*	(240) 63	(494) 57	(162) 52	(23) 39	(41) 54
Middle-class morality destroys the spontaneity of individual experience.	(236) 80	(491) 85	(163) 77	(25) 84	(39) 74
Restrictive measures should be taken against the use of marijuana and hashish.	(241) 90	(490) 81	(162) 76	84	(42) 81
Restrictive measures should be taken against the use of LSD.	(95)	(491) 90	85	(26) 96	(41) 88

*p < .01
**p < .05
1. The question on middle-class morality did not appear in the Tunisian questionnaire.

TABLE 6.9a.   Life Style for the Year 2000 Foreseen, Preferred and Expected by the Student, by Political Tendency (Percent).

Australia

		Present Form of Marriage*	Marriage with Greater Extra Marital Freedom	Free Union**	Marriage but Families Living Communally	In Communities without Marriage*	Other
Right							
Preferred way of life	(38)	55	16	16	–	3	10
Expected way of life	(40)	75	13	2	–	–	10
Left							
Preferred way of life	(232)	36	11	25	13	9	6
Expected way of life	(239)	61	25	7	2	2	3
Far left							
Preferred way of life	(35)	6	9	34	12	34	6
Expected way of life	(35)	26	29	25	9	8	3

Austria

		Present Form of Marriage*	Marriage with Greater Extra Marital Freedom*	Free Union*	Marriage but Families Living Communally*	In Communities without Marriage*	Other
Right							
Preferred way of life	(82)	72	10	6	11	–	1
Expected way of life	(79)	75	16	4	4	–	1
Left							
Preferred way of life	(134)	20	20	38	22	–	–
Expected way of life	(135)	21	31	26	21	–	1
Far left							
Preferred way of life	(65)	2	2	38	33	23	2
Expected way of life	(63)	–	18	29	33	17	3

France		Present Form of Marriage*	Marriage with Greater Extra Marital Freedom	Free Union**	Marriage but Families Living Communally	In Communities without Marriage**	Other
Right							
Preferred way of life	(42)	67	17	14	2	–	–
Expected way of life	(40)	79	12	9	–	–	–
Left							
Preferred way of life	(209)	34	11	28	11	12	4
Expected way of life	(208)	63	14	11	6	2	4
Communists							
Preferred way of life	(49)	14	9	42	5	21	9
Expected way of life	(47)	43	14	29	–	11	3
Far left							
Preferred way of life	(99)	17	15	28	17	21	2
Expected way of life	(98)	49	21	16	4	4	6

Great Britain		Present Form of Marriage*	Marriage with Greater Extra Marital Freedom	Free Union	Marriage but Families Living Communally	In Communities without Marriage**	Other
Right							
Preferred way of life	88	71	11	5	7	2	4
Expected way of life	(83)	83	12	–	2	–	3
Left							
Preferred way of life	(186)	38	18	13	16	10	5
Expected way of life	(182)	63	21	6	4	4	2
Far left							
Preferred way of life	(68)	18	10	18	19	27	8
Expected way of life	(65)	42	22	8	11	11	6

(cont.)

TABLE 6.9a. Continued

Italy		Present Form of Marriage*	Marriage with Greater Extra Marital Freedom	Free Union	Marriage but Families Living Communally	In Communities without Marriage*	Other
Right							
Preferred way of life	(62)	63	8	10	5	13	1
Expected way of life	(61)	56	26	7	5	5	1
Left							
Preferred way of life	(214)	47	12	10	15	13	3
Expected way of life	(211)	56	29	2	6	5	2
Communists							
Preferred way of life	(102)	14	4	19	15	48	–
Expected way of life	(92)	30	27	12	8	21	2
Far left							
Preferred way of life	(68)	13	4	19	19	40	5
Expected way of life	(68)	32	28	10	10	13	7

Japan		Present Form of Marriage**	Marriage with Greater Extra Marital Freedom	Free Union	Marriage but Families Living Communally	In Communities without Marriage	Other
Center							
Preferred way of life	(155)	41	24	22	4	6	3
Expected way of life	(154)	56	37	3	–	4	–
Left							
Preferred way of life	(37)	41	32	18	–	5	4
Expected way of life	(32)	62	32	2	2	–	2
Far left							
Preferred way of life	(119)	19	30	35	2	13	1
Expected way of life	(119)	40	40	11	3	3	3

Nigeria		Present Form of Marriage*	Marriage with Greater Extra Marital Freedom	Free Union	Marriage but Families Living Communally	In Communities without Marriage	Other
Right							
Preferred way of life	(37)	65	3	19	8	2	1
Expected way of life	(35)	60	11	11	11	6	–
Left							
Preferred way of life	(37)	35	16	22	22	5	–
Expected way of life	(32)	53	9	9	16	6	7
Far left							
Preferred way of life	(17)	53	12	29	6	–	–
Expected way of life	(17)	53	6	29	6	6	–

Spain		Present Form of Marriage*	Marriage with Greater Extra Marital Freedom	Free Union*	Marriage but Families Living Communally	In Communities without Marriage*	Other
Right							
Preferred way of life	(62)	65	16	38	5	5	1
Expected way of life	(59)	73	17	7	2	–	1
Left							
Preferred way of life	(279)	23	17	32	11	15	6
Expected way of life	(273)	41	21	20	9	4	5
Far left							
Preferred way of life	(83)	6	7	39	4	34	10
Expected way of life	(78)	10	18	39	8	15	10

(cont.)

TABLE 6.9a. Continued

Tunisia		Present Form of Marriage	Marriage with Greater Extra Marital Freedom	Free Union**	Marriage but Families Living Communally	In Communities without Marriage	Other
Bourguibists							
Preferred way of life	(30)	60	17	10	10	3	–
Expected way of life	(28)	79	21	–	–	–	–
Left							
Preferred way of life	(40)	63	13	15	–	8	1
Expected way of life	(38)	84	5	5	3	3	–
Far left							
Preferred way of life	(22)	45	14	31	5	5	–
Expected way of life	(20)	75	10	15	–	–	–

United States		Present Form of Marriage*	Marriage with Greater Extra Marital Freedom	Free Union*	Marriage but Families Living Communally	In Communities without Marriage**	Other
Right							
Preferred way of life	(78)	77	13	3	4	2	1
Expected way of life	(76)	78	19	–	3	–	–
Liberal							
Preferred way of life	(119)	51	12	22	6	6	3
Expected way of life	(118)	75	12	8	2	–	3
Left							
Preferred way of life	(180)	63	12	13	5	5	2
Expected way of life	(174)	79	14	1	2	1	3
Far left							
Preferred way of life	(22)	14	23	27	9	27	–
Expected way of life	(22)	36	18	32	5	9	–

Yugoslavia (Self-Definition)		Present Form of Marriage**	Marriage with Greater Extra Marital Freedom*	Free Union	Marriage but Families Living Communally	In Communities without Marriage	Other	Don't Know
Idealists								
Preferred way of life	(234)	65	10	9	3	2	–	11
Expected way of life	(214)	70	13	3	1	–	1	12
Realists								
Preferred way of life	(479)	59	14	11	2	2	3	9
Expected way of life	(436)	63	18	3	1	1	3	11
Humanitarians								
Preferred way of life	(156)	55	17	10	3	2	1	12
Expected way of life	(143)	61	22	1	1	1	1	13
Elitists								
Preferred way of life	(26)	50	17	8	–	8	–	17
Expected way of life	(25)	52	28	–	–	4	–	16
Individualists								
Preferred way of life	(41)	42	20	15	–	10	–	13
Expected way of life	(35)	46	34	3	–	–	–	17

*p < .01
**p < .05

Chapter 7

The University and the Protest Movement

The Role of the University in Society

The important student protest movement, which gained momentum throughout the world in 1968, at first concerned itself mainly with the university but then widened to include political and social criticism. With regard to the university, the movement may be seen either as a call for organizational reforms or as a questioning of the institution itself. This issue was widely expressed in pamphlets reflecting the rhetorical style of the time by asking whether the functioning of the university or its *function* should be changed. This second aspect of the student demands is treated in this chapter. The first part of the analysis deals with the attitudes of students in regard to the relationships between the university and the power structure, the different forms of selection and admission, and the objectives of "pure" research. The second part of the chapter approaches more specifically the often-discussed problem of the politicization of the university, that is, the role the university should play in the political life of the country and the means necessary to change the university in this respect.

THE POLICY OF THE UNIVERSITY

A series of issues frequently raised in connection with the university was presented to the students. These may be grouped under four categories: (1) cooperation between the university and the government, (2) the place of basic research, (3) grades, and (4) selection and admission of students.

COOPERATION BETWEEN THE UNIVERSITY AND THE GOVERNMENT

Two questions allowed us to determine the opinion of the students on the relation between the university and the government. The students were asked to indicate whether they thought the university should be prepared "to fill the manpower needs of business and government" and "to conduct research for government and industry within the university."

Nearly all Nigerian students (98 percent for the first question and 86 percent for the second) approved of this cooperation. According to them, the university prepares people to be of future service to their country. In contrast, the majority of students in Japan rejected this role. Only 20 percent agreed with the first item, 17 percent with the second. In the case of American students, only 42 percent were in favor of the research role described in the second question, but the idea of fulfilling manpower needs of business and government was acceptable to the majority (70 percent) (Table 7.1—page 194).

With the exception of Great Britain, Nigeria, Tunisia, and Japan, we find that the desire for close cooperation between the government and the university is characteristic of students whose political opinions range from the center to the right: at least 70 percent of these students approved both statements. The students in the four countries mentioned above showed no difference of attitudes as between the various political groups (Table 7.1a). (Tables 7.1a through 7.13b are at the end of this chapter, between pages 222 and 244.)

In Yugoslavia, a majority of the elitists approve the notion that the university should conduct research for business and government (52 percent). Those who were least frequently in agreement were the individualists (27 percent) (Table 7.1a).

A comparison of the groups on the far left shows that those most favorable to these two items are the Nigerians (more than 90 percent) and the Tunisians (more than 74 percent). In contrast, the Japanese (9 percent) are rarely in favor of this kind of cooperation. Students on the far left in France, Great Britain, Austria, and Australia are more favorable to these propositions than the Japanese (about 30 percent in each of these four countries). In the other countries studied, the percentages of approval are close to 50 percent.

PURE RESEARCH

The problem of "pure" research appeared as a controversial subject. For many, pure or fundamental or apolitical research does not exist; research cannot be divorced from power and the military-industrial complex, which, as Touraine (1972) remarks, transforms "progress into profit and, more generally, into power" (p. 128). Thus any questioning of society or of the political system may also involve the notion of pure research and its objectives. The issue of "relevance," widely debated in 1968 and in the years that followed, also enters here.

The students were asked if they approved or not of the statement that one of the functions of the university should be "to advance fundamental research regardless of immediate practical applications." A large majority of students in most of the countries studied (77 percent or more) and a smaller one in Yugoslavia and Japan (69 percent and 54 percent respectively) are favorable to this idea. This attitude is particularly marked in Nigeria and Tunisia (more than 92 percent) (Table 7.1).

Concerning this question, few differences emerged by political orientation in the countries studied, although the students on the right seemed a little more favorable to the idea of basic research than those on the left. The difference was greater in Japan (66 percent favorable in the center; 34 percent on the far left) and in Australia (80 percent favorable on the right; 58 percent on the far left). (Table 7.1a). In other countries the percentages of approval on the far left rose to more than two-thirds.

GRADES

In order to tap the students' opinions about grading systems, they were asked whether they were in favor of "eliminating all grading of students by the faculty." Grades and examinations were contested during the student protests as barriers designed to reinforce the admissions process in favor of existing ruling groups. According to Touraine (1968b):

TABLE 7.1.   University Policy (Percent).

	AUSTRAL.	AUS.	FR.	GB	IT.	JAP.	NIG.	SP.	TUN.	USA	YUG.
To fill manpower needs of government and business[1]*	(748) 63	(479) 61	(610) 38	(567) 61	(782) 74	(421) 20	(230) 98	(658) 73	(131) 76	(631) 70	
To conduct research for government and industry within the university*	(745) 70	(477) 63	(643) 48	(564) 60	(738) 60	(414) 17	(229) 86	(699) 69	(127) 83	(607) 42	(1.071) 33
To advance fundamental research*	(759) 80	(478) 87	(647) 77	(583) 86	(786) 89	(418) 54	(232) 100	(701) 82	(139) 92	(640) 81	(1.075) 69
To eliminate all grading of students by faculty*	(707) 34	(479) 36	31	(506) 44	(683) 66	(401) 64	(215) 19	(700) 52	(130) 47	(611) 54	(1.074) 63
The present educational system maintains discrimination[2]*	(756) 84	(481) 68	(701) 79	(592) 83	(821) 73	(410) 74	(227) 79	(718) 84		(648) 82	(1.072) 52
To open the university only to serious students*	(766) 52	62	(710) 61	(597) 52	(827) 67	(434) 59	(219) 56	(729) 53	(141) 55	(653) 47	(1.072) 82
To open the universities to anyone, without selective admission*	(755) 52	63	(681) 59	(582) 34	(809) 75	(423) 70	(228) 15	(721) 68	(137) 74	(632) 33	(1.074) 60

*p < .01
1. This item was not included in the Yugoslav questionnaire.
2. This item was not included in the Tunisian questionnaire.

What is refused is not only a type of testing or a grading system, but also the role of examination which defines the students' situation. . . . Examinations are not criticized because they are poorly organized, but because they represent the time when the relationships of power burst forth. The student is forced to adapt his behavior to certain patterns imposed upon him, which pertain more to his entrance into the system than to his pursuit of knowledge [p. 236].

Touraine (1972) also remarked that "many students in all countries wonder if learning is not a means whose end is the examination, when the examination is supposed to be only a means of controlling and judging knowledge acquired" (p. 192).

Almost two-thirds of the students in Italy, Japan, and Yugoslavia agree with the principle of eliminating grades, followed by about half of the Americans, Spaniards, and Tunisians, about 40 percent of the Austrians and the British, 34 percent of the Australians, 31 percent of the French, and only a few of the Nigerians (19 percent) (Table 7.1).

Conservative students are less in agreement with the elimination of grades than are those on the far left, except in Tunisia and Nigeria, where every political group shows about the same percentages. The students on the far left who most approve this idea are the Italians (83 percent), the Japanese (78 percent), and the Austrians (74 percent). This figure is considerably lower among the Nigerians (28 percent). In the other countries the percentages oscillate between 69 percent and 54 percent.

ADMISSIONS

The idea of restricting admissions (or the selection process) represents one of the most contested points about the university system. During the protests, students demanded a real democratization of the university as an institution and questioned the use of examinations for admission.

References to this issue appeared in our questionnaire: "The present educational system maintains social discrimination." "Opening the university only to students who wish to study seriously." And, "To open all the universities to anyone who wants to attend, without selective admission."

Overall, more than 70 percent of students believe that the present system does encourage social discrimination. In Yugoslavia this proportion is 52 percent. This relatively lower frequency in Yugoslavia may reflect the fact that in 1964 half of the student population was composed of young people from working-class backgrounds. This proportion appears in a report published by UNESCO and the Organization for Economic Cooperation and Development (OECD) in 1967.[1] In this document we also find the proportions of students from working-class backgrounds in Great Britain, Italy, Austria, France and Spain, with a comparison of the percentages in 1960 and 1964 (Table 7.2—page 196). Note that few students in Western countries come from working-class families: the maximum is 25 percent in Great Britain, in 1961, followed by 15 percent in Italy and 8 percent or less in the other countries. Further, the rise in these percentages is very small (3 percent at most) if not inexistent during these four years.

The recognition of a situation which discriminates against certain social groups does not necessarily imply, however, the desire to ensure unlimited access to the university. Only a minority of Nigerian students (15 percent) are favorable to this

---

[1] UNESCO and OECD: *Access to Higher Education*, 4, Vienna, Nov. 1967, p. 28.

alternative. About one-third of American and British students and about half of Australian students share this opinion. Students in the other countries are much more favorable (between 60 percent and 75 percent) to the elimination of all selection procedures (Table 7.1).

TABLE 7.2. Students from Manual-Labor Backgrounds (Percent).

COUNTRY	1960	1964
Yugoslavia	56	53
Great Britain	25 (1961)	–
Italy	13	15
Austria	6	5
France	5	8
Spain	–	4 (1962)

In general, more than half of the students included in this study, particularly the Yugoslavs (82 percent), Italians (67 percent), and Austrians (62 percent) believe that admissions policies should favor students who wish to study seriously.

In each country, students whose opinions place them at the center or on the right are favorable to the traditional university system and to the maintenance of a selection policy, except in Spain, where students on the right (69 percent) are in favor of the elimination of such a policy. The lowest favorable percentages on the right appear in Nigeria (10 percent), the United States (17 percent), Great Britain (16 percent) and France (21 percent). The majority of students on the right hope that serious students will be favored (Table 7.1a).

Students who endorse the opinions of the traditional left emphasize the importance of a liberal university whereas those on the far left rather emphasize their opposition to any form of selection process.

This general outline, applicable to the different political groups in almost all of the countries studied, includes some variations specific to certain nations. In Italy, students in the center or who define themselves as apolitical have opinions similar to those on the traditional left. In Spain and Tunisia students of all political orientations, from the right to the far left, are in a great majority in favor of an open university. In Yugoslavia, no differences appeared among groups as a function of their political outlook.

Although within-country comparisons indicate that students on the far left generally oppose the ideas of the conservatives and the moderates, between-country comparisons indicate that there are differences within the far left concerning the issue of a university open to all without any selection procedures. The Italian (99 percent), Austrian (90 percent), French (85 percent), and Tunisian (79 percent) students of the far left are most in favor of open admission, followed by Australian (71 percent), Spanish (63 percent), British (61 percent), and American students (57 percent). This opinion is shared by only 14 percent of the far left in Nigeria.

In all the countries studied, we may summarize the results by indicating that different political groups tend to choose three types of ideal universities. The first type would be conservative, nationalistic and selective (far right, right, center, apolitical); the second, liberalized and selective (left); and the third, one which basically contests the traditional role of the university (far left and, in Italy, the communists).

For those on the far left, we find that the Nigerians do, however, support the traditional university system. According to them, the university serves the state, with

regard both to research and to fulfilling the manpower needs of the country (91 percent and 100 percent respectively). In this perspective, the university provides an
elite by maintaining a grading system and a selective admissions policy. In contrast,
the students on the far left in Japan question the very nature of the university. Few of
them want it to serve the state (approximately 10 percent), and most of them refuse
the ideas of a grading system (78 percent) and of a selective admissions policy (81
percent).

The 1977 survey (Table 7.3)

The results indicate that in the United States the arguments advanced by the radicals have lost ground to a significant degree. Thus 63 percent are in favor of research
for government and industry in the university as compared to 42 percent in the main
study. Only 26 percent as compared to 54 percent in 1970 favor the elimination of
grades, and 24 percent as compared to 33 percent are in favor of opening the university to everyone, without selective admission. There is little or no change concerning
the other alternatives.

**TABLE 7.3. University Policy in France and the
United States in 1977 (Percent).**

	FRANCE	UNITED STATES
To fill manpower needs of government and business	(88) 31	(105) 74
To conduct research for government and industry within the university	(89) 44	(106) 63
To advance fundamental research	44	(105) 79
The present educational system maintains discrimination	(91) 84	(106) 76
To eliminate all grading of students by faculty	(89) 35	(104) 26
To open the university only to serious students	49	(105) 46
To open the universities to anyone, without selective admission	(91) 61	(106) 24

In France the only important difference is in the decrease in the proportion of students who see as one of the roles of the university the advancement of fundamental
research (44 percent versus 77 percent in 1970). There is also a slight decrease in the
notion that the university should be open only to serious students (49 percent versus
61 percent).

POLITICS AT THE UNIVERSITY

Although political issues have always been to some extent present at the university, they became more important during the years which preceded this study. One
widespread opinion holds that politics should be absolutely separate from the university and insists that this separation is possible; the university should be outside of

politics. The opposite opinion endorses the notion of a university as a political arena where political movements may be organized. In this perspective, the university becomes a frontier in the class struggle through the very fact that knowledge has become an essential element of economic production. The third opinion is intermediary and liberal. It underlines the need of the students to join together in order to become informed and to discuss whatever issues arise. Thus the university should encourage the development of a critical attitude toward all institutions.

Most of the questionnaire items in this area concerned the politicization of the university: "To provide a place of learning and investigation as free as possible of political involvement"; "A forum for the critical analysis of the national life": "To be a base for radical political action"; and its avant-garde role: "To act as a vanguard for changing society." The students were also asked to indicate their degree of approval of the following two statements: "The university as a bourgeois institution should be destroyed and replaced by a proletarian culture." and "Effective change in the university could only be achieved by a political revolution."

The politicization of the university is a concept which particularly interests the students on the far left. Numerous student publications in May 1968 and a number of different investigations showed that many young people criticized what they saw as the false neutrality of the university system, especially in France. The following is an extract from a report of one student committee (Comité étudiant pour les libertés universitaires, 1969):

> This "neutralism" which the State hopes to impose on the university implies a concept of learning which is out of touch with the realities of the mind, unless it represents a profound contempt for our diversified cultures and for all progress on the spiritual level [p. 61].

In the samples as a whole, the results indicate that 80 percent of the students are for the separation of the university from the political arena, except in Spain and Tunisia, where these percentages are about 65 percent, and in Yugoslavia, where the percentage is 48 percent (Table 7.4). Even on the level of the far left, however, significant differences appear. Far left students are the most favorable to the nonpoliticization of this institution in Austria (79 percent) and in Nigeria (76 percent) and the least favorable in Spain (41 percent), Tunisia (38 percent), and France (29 percent). The percentages for the other countries are between 64 percent and 70 percent (Table 7.4a).

The majority of all students (more than 70 percent) think that the university should act as an avant-garde in order to change society; this is particularly true in Nigeria and Austria (92 percent) (Table 7.4). There are contrasts in attitudes, however, in France, Great Britain, and the United States, where the right accepts this role less often (46 percent, 62 percent, and 64 percent respectively) than does the far left (90 percent, 93 percent, and 92 percent respectively).

Reactions to the notion of the university as an avant-garde institution allow us to discover in what countries the students on the far left support traditional political revolutionary strategies. For example, the view may be held that the revolution should occur from the bottom to the top of the social order, or on the other hand students on the far left may see themselves as intellectual leaders carrying the message of the revolution to the masses. At the same time, the student may think of himself as "only" an intellectual who occupies a marginal position and not as a true leader. In this case, in an attempt to rationalize the social movement and a desire to

TABLE 7.4. Role of Politics in the University by Country (Percent).

	AUSTRAL.	AUS.	FR.	GB	IT.	JAP.	NIG.	SP.	TUN.	USA	YUG.
Place of learning and investigation as free as possible of political involvement*	(759) 83	(478) 93	(674) 76	(585) 89	(804) 92	(413) 82	(229) 79	(712) 65	(138) 63	(638) 78	(1,073) 48
To act as a vanguard for changing society*	(736) 88	(475) 92	(656) 72	(556) 84	(782) 87	(407) 73	(226) 92	(693) 81	88	(623) 83	(1,071) 81
A forum for the critical analysis of national life*	(756) 95	(478) 91	(645) 73	(576) 91	(767) 73	(411) 87	(228) 89	(674) 75	88	(643) 96	51
A base for radical political action*1	(743) 28	25	(593) 38	(553) 29	(745) 66	(402) 22	(223) 34	(654) 52		(598) 18	(1,058) 38
The university as a bourgeois institution should be destroyed and replaced by a proletarian culture*1	(671) 20	(473) 23	(603) 47	(524) 25	(742) 47	(349) 41	(207) 46	(668) 64		(585) 12	(1,074) 22
Effective change in the university could only be achieved by a political revolution*1	(738) 19	(481) 31	(689) 57	(561) 20	(778) 52	(397) 35	(212) 40	(694) 61		(630) 14	(1,079) 19

* p < .01
1. This item did not appear on the Tunisian questionnaire.

become reintegrated into it, the student sometimes considers himself as a worker, and thus identifies with the bottom of the social order.

The majority of students, again more than 70 percent, also support the idea that the university should be a place for the development of a critical spirit. In Yugoslavia, the figure is 51 percent. It is only in France that we find a divergence of opinion between the right and the left. Conservatives who favor the transformation of the university into a forum for social criticism are in the minority (47 percent), compared to a large majority of students on the far left (94 percent).

These findings show that a strong majority of students in most countries included in this study, plus those on the left in France, appear convinced of the relative isolation of the university from society. This confirms the analysis of Touraine (1968b), who, speaking of the student movement, wrote:

> The university it [the student movement] combats no longer serves either the old or the new bourgeoisie. But the university fails in its scientific and social function as critic. Its "abstraction" and its "disinterest" irritate its administrators but provoke even more the rebellion of those who legitimately expect that the university will fulfill its role, which is to analyze the specific nature and the limits of all forms of social and cultural life [p. 76].

The following ideas, which suggest the transformation of the university into a center for leftist activities or its replacement by a proletarian culture, interest only the students on the far left. The university as a center for radical action is approved by the far left in Italy (91 percent), France (78 percent), Austria, Australia and Great Britain (about 72 percent), Nigeria (67 percent), Spain (64 percent) but less frequently in the United States (48 percent) and in Japan (43 percent).

The idea of destroying the university as a bourgeois institution and replacing it by a proletarian culture attracts, in descending order, the far left in Spain (89 percent), France and Italy (80 percent), Austria (72 percent), Nigeria (65 percent), Australia and Japan (about 56 percent), Great Britain (49 percent) and, finally, the United States (36 percent).

The belief that the university can only be changed by a political revolution is approved particularly by students on the far left in Spain, France and Italy (about 90 percent), followed by Austria (77 percent), Australia (71 percent), Nigeria (58 percent), Great Britain (54 percent), half of the students in Japan, and least often in the United States (44 percent)

We are thus able to distinguish those countries which refuse the politicization of the university. The Anglo-Saxon countries, Yugoslavia, Japan and Austria wish in general to establish a university independent of politics, which will neither be overthrown by a revolution nor replaced by proletarian culture. In addition, students in Austria and Australia desire that the university produce an elite, capable of playing an avant-garde role in social change.

THE 1977 SURVEY

In the United States there is very little change in the responses obtained concerning the role of politics at the university (Table 7.5).

In France the differences are more marked on several alternatives and in opposite directions. There is less agreement concerning the statement that the university should be a place of learning as free as possible of political involvement (58 percent versus 76 percent in the main study) but also a decrease in the belief that the university should act as a vanguard for changing society (54 percent versus 72 percent in 1970) and that the university as a bourgeois institution should be destroyed and replaced by a proletarian culture (36 percent versus 47 percent in 1970).

TABLE 7.5. Role of Politics in the University in 1977 (Percent).

	FRANCE	USA
Place of learning and investigation as free as possible of political involvement	(91) 58	(106) 82
To act as a vanguard for changing society	(88) 54	(105) 77
A forum for the critical analysis of national life	65	(106) 88
A base for radical political action	(87) 35	(104) 16
The university as a bourgeois institution should be destroyed and replaced by a proletarian culture	36	(106) 9
Effective change in the university could only be achieved by a political revolution	(92) 52	10

The Student Movement

In this section we examine more specifically the attitudes of the students with regard to the student movement in each of their countries. What do the students think about the movement in general? Has it accomplished anything? Did it result in modifications in the institutions in question? What were the goals of the movement in terms of the university, society and politics?

CAUSES OF THE STUDENT MOVEMENT

After 1964 student rebellion became remarkably widespread. What at its beginning was only a vague discontent changed into a powerful student protest movement. The literature on the causes of this movement is abundant, with marked differences of interpretation. What do the students themselves think?

In six countries (France, Great Britain, the United States, Italy, Japan, and Yugoslavia) the following ten possible causes of the student movement were proposed:

Poor university system
Authoritarianism of teachers
Lack of employment possibilities for college (or university) graduates
Political discontent
Socioeconomic discontent
Crisis of civilization

Foreign conspiracy
Conflict between generations
Inspired by agitators
Other

CAUSES OF THE STUDENT MOVEMENT IN FRANCE

Almost all French students (91 percent) believe that the poor organization of the university and the lack of available jobs played an important role at the beginning of the student movement. Political malaise and the socioeconomic crisis also contributed as sources of discontent (more than 70 percent). Somewhat less frequently came authoritarianism of teachers (58 percent), the role of agitators (45 percent), and the crisis of civilization (54 percent) (Table 7.6).

TABLE 7.6. Students' Views on Causes of the Student Movement in France, Great Britain, Italy, Japan, and the United States (Percent).

	FRANCE	GB	ITALY	JAPAN	USA
Political discontent**	(853)	(625)	(998)	(518)	(690)
	77	79	94	99	99
Socioeconomic discontent**			(999)	(517)	(691)
	73	67	91	81	86
Poor university system*		(624)	(998)	(516)	(692)
	91	37	99	83	47
Conflict between generations*1	(851)			(517)	(688)
	57	68		71	91
Authoritarianism of teachers*	(852)	(625)	(997)	(518)	(689)
	58	44	92	87	43
Agitators*	(851)		(998)	(515)	(691)
	45	67	68	33	72
Crisis of civilization*	(850)	(624)	(995)	(516)	(692)
	54	35	62	39	80
Lack of employment possibilities*	(852)		(997)	(512)	(688)
	91	47	88	7	31
Foreign conspiracy*	(849)	(623)	(989)	(514)	(687)
	33	15	40	16	15

*$p < .01$
**$p < .05$
1. This item did not appear on the Italian questionnaire.

Differences tied to political tendencies appear with regard to the suggestion that the origin of the protest movement was to be found in political malaise, the generation conflict, foreign conspiracy, or agitators. Students on the right were the most likely to believe that the movement was fomented by agitators (88 percent; but this was believed also by as many as 49 percent of those on the far left) or could be explained by the generation conflict (67 percent compared to 40 percent) or by foreign conspiracy (54 percent compared to 33 percent). Students on the far left most often mention political discontent (90 percent compared to 67 percent on the right) (Table 7.6a).

CAUSES OF THE STUDENT MOVEMENT IN THE UNITED STATES

American students attribute the student protest movement to political malaise (99 percent), the generation conflict (91 percent), a socioeconomic crisis (86 percent), and a crisis of civilization (80 percent). Seventy-two percent also mention the role of agitators. Factors pertaining to the university, such as its poor organization (47 percent), the authoritarianism of the teachers (43 percent), or the lack of job opportunities (31 percent) seem less important. The student rebellion in the United States occurred, according to the students, as a reaction to a political and cultural system—not because of conditions at the university, as was the case in France (Table 7.6).

Differences of opinion emerged as a function of political orientation when the role of agitators, the poor organization of the university, and the crisis of civilization were evoked. Students on the right believe that the role of agitators was very important in the beginning of the protest movement (90 percent), compared to poor university organization (37 percent) or a crisis of civilization (64 percent). Students on the far left think, in contrast, that the role of agitators was minor (33 percent) in comparison to problems pertaining to the university (71 percent) or to a crisis in civilization (94 percent) (Table 7.6a).

CAUSES OF THE STUDENT MOVEMENT IN GREAT BRITAIN

British students are far from unanimous in their evaluation of the roles played by these different factors in the protest movement. Many cite political malaise (79 percent), socioeconomic discontent (67 percent), the generation conflict (68 percent), and the role of agitators (67 percent). Factors specifically related to the university, such as the lack of job opportunities (47 percent), the authoritarianism of the teachers (44 percent), and the poor organization of the university itself (37 percent), did not play a preponderant role in the opinion of these students (Table 7.6). The absence of a clear pattern in these responses is perhaps due to the sporadic character of the protest movement in this country and to the absence of a repressive government; the government did not create, as sometimes happened elsewhere, an atmosphere of rebellion throughout the country.

In general, students on the far left have the most clear-cut opinions about the causes of the student movement in Great Britain. According to them, the principal cause was political discontent (94 percent). A majority of these students also cite the authoritarianism of teachers (67 percent), the crisis of civilization (53 percent), and the poor organization of the university (52 percent). Students on the right tend rather to believe that agitators played a major role in the birth of the student movement (90 percent), compared to 42 percent on the far left. While students on the right also mention political malaise (75 percent), they only rarely (about 20 percent) speak of the other factors (Table 7.6a).

CAUSES OF THE STUDENT MOVEMENT IN ITALY

Almost all students in Italy think that the poor organization of the university (99 percent) contributed significantly to the beginning of the protest movement. Other factors also cited include political malaise (94 percent), the socioeconomic crisis, the authoritarianism of teachers (91 percent each), the lack of job opportunities (88 percent), the role of agitators (68 percent), and a crisis in civilizátion (62 percent) (Table 7.6). (The response "conflict between generations" did not appear on the questionnaire in Italy.) Thus the student revolt began in opposition both to an outdated university system and to the political situation.

Students on the right and on the far left differ in their opinions about the roles of authoritarianism of teachers, the crisis of civilization, and the role of agitators at the beginning of the student movement. Those on the right think that agitators were very influential (79 percent versus 15 percent of the students on the far left), followed by the authoritarianism of the teachers (66 percent) and the crisis in civilization (38 percent) as secondary causes. Students on the far left think that the protesters rebelled primarily against the authoritarianism of teachers (90 percent) (Table 7.6a).

CAUSES OF THE STUDENT MOVEMENT IN JAPAN

Almost all Japanese students (99 percent) believe that the student movement began because of political discontent. Other causes emphasized were the authoritarianism of teachers, the poor organization of the university, and the socioeconomic crisis (more than 80 percent each). Also cited was the generation conflict (71 percent) (Table 7.6).

As in other countries, students of the center are more inclined to consider the protest as the result of actions by agitators than are students on the far left (Table 7.6a).

CAUSES OF THE STUDENT MOVEMENT IN YUGOSLAVIA

Yugoslav students could choose among eleven possible responses to indicate what they believed to be the sources of the student protest movement in their country. The list included the following:

Imitation of protest movements in other countries
Social inequality
Students' financial conditions and lack of jobs
Unemployment
Conflict between generations
Broken promises and governmental hypocrisy
Students' indecision about what they want
Bureaucracy and anti-democratic attitudes
Lack of autonomy
Students' abuse of democracy due to society's tolerance
Extremists' agitation but not a movement

In fact, only a few of these factors were mentioned by the students. According to them, the students' financial conditions and lack of jobs (27 percent), broken promises and governmental hypocrisy (19 percent), unemployment (14 percent), and finally, bureaucracy and anti-democratic attitudes (10 percent) were the principal causes of the protest movement in Yugoslavia (Table 7.6b). As can be seen from these percentages, there was very little consensus.

We did not find any major differences among the students who defined themselves politically by the type of society to which they aspire. The only exceptions were the elitists, who believed that the student movement started because contemporary society was too indulgent and too tolerant (13 percent).

The analysis of our findings allows us to point out those areas which, according to the students, truly contributed to the beginning of the student protest movement. In France and Italy the student movement is perceived mainly as a response to the poor functioning of the university. In Japan, the movement began both as a result of university problems and political malaise. In the United States and Great Britain, these movements corresponded to a reaction to more general problems and to a worldwide, political and cultural protest. Finally, in Yugoslavia the sources of the movement were seen as due to the social situation of the students, who lacked money, and to the political situation of their country—i.e., hypocrisy of the government and the bureaucratic system.

Significant differences were also found between students on the right and on the far left. In all the countries studied, students on the right show a tendency to accuse agitators of having largely contributed to the emergence of the student movements. In France and Italy some students mention the influence of foreign agents—professional agitators who are part of a vast international conspiracy. Unlike conservative students, those on the far left mention political and social issues frequently, together with other factors like the crisis in civilization (especially in the United States, Great Britain, and Italy). These students try to explain the student protest movement, not in terms of manipulation or of foreign intervention, but in theoretical and philosophical terms.

GOOD AND BAD ASPECTS OF THE STUDENT MOVEMENT

As we have seen, students endorse different explanations of the student protest movement and the factors which led to it. Touraine (1972), in comparing the student movements in the United States and France, distinguished those factors which pertained specifically to the movements' origins and those which remained at the center of the students' demands:

> The American movement is full of cultural content and combats a modern adversary, as the universities participate actively in forming a technocratic society. . . . The French movement, in contrast, attacks an outdated university, overwhelmed by its own growth, which does not play a major role in the recruitment of elite groups or of techno-bureaucratic middle-level staff, which is assured by the independent schools of the university. The French movement turns toward the workers' movement. . . . [p. 205].

The fact that students in different countries have both similar and different demands, at least in terms of their priority, and that students have called in nonstudents in some countries but not in others, renders a detailed comparison difficult.

We asked the students to indicate what they thought of the movement and, as they had previously done for society and the university, to choose its two best and two worst aspects. This question required a general judgment on the student movement in each country studied. But it is clear that the attitudes expressed may be compared with those elsewhere only if we understand the specific student situation in each country.

As a matter of fact, this study includes countries where the student protest movement was very active during the 1960s—the United States, Japan, France, and Italy —but also countries in which the movement was less influential—like Great Britain, Yugoslavia, Australia, Austria, Nigeria, Tunisia, and Spain. We must also mention that the term "student movement" does not have the same meaning everywhere. In Nigeria and Tunisia the students understand the words to mean politically organized associations in agreement with the state; the organizations may be either national or local. In other countries, the student movement is marginal in relationship to officially recognized student organizations, which frequently take the form of trade unions; thus the student movement tends to have a leftist character accompanied by a questioning of the university, of society, and of traditional cultural and social values.

We shall begin by comparing the attitudes of the students from the first group of countries, where the movement was particularly active. In France and in Italy the students are somewhat divided concerning the movement: about 40 percent judge it positively *a posteriori*, about 60 percent negatively. The differences are more extreme in the United States, where the majority judge the movement positively (70 percent), and in Japan, where the students are clearly more negative than positive (79 percent negative and 20 percent positive)[2] (Table 7.7).

In the second group of countries, we find that more than two thirds of the Nigerian and British students and 61 percent in Australia judged the movement positively. In Spain and Tunisia, students favorable to the movement represent about 45 percent of the two samples.[3]

In Austria, the question included an additional possible response: "The movement has as many good as bad aspects." Most students selected this choice (45 percent), while 34 percent gave a negative and 21 percent a positive reply.

Political tendency greatly influenced the opinion of the students toward the student movement, particularly in those countries where the movement was especially strong. The more the student placed himself on the left, the more likely he was to be favorable to the protest movement (Table 7.7).

As we see, the divergences between the students on the right and the far left are particularly evident in Italy (75 percent of the students on the far left judged the movement positively, 9 percent of those on the right), in the United States (90 percent compared to 42 percent), and in France (60 percent compared to 19 percent). In Spain and in Tunisia the corresponding percentages were about 65 percent and 30 percent. In contrast, in Japan the students on the far left appear, even if their opinion is more positive than that of the moderates, to be critical of the protest movement. In the other countries there is not much distance between political groups. It is true that in Great Britain, Australia, Nigeria, and Austria the student protest movement was rather limited and usually took the form of demands related to the university.

The negativism which seems to exist in some students on the far left does not necessarily imply a rejection of the movement. It may also be explained by their disillusionment concerning its efficacy and the means it adopted, which were often judged as "too violent and too spontaneous" (dogmatism, lack of unity and coordination, useless violence, etc.)

[2]In West Germany, 58 percent of the students were favorable to the movement.

[3]In Canada we found no difference in this regard between the English-speaking and the French-speaking students: about half of each group was favorable to the movement.

TABLE 7.7. Students' Evaluation of the Student Movement[1] (Percent).

	AUSTRAL.	AUS.	FR.	GB	IT.	JAP.	NIG.	SP.	TUN.	USA
Total Sample	(688)	(384)	(604)	(501)	(679)	(385)	(204)	(661)	(124)	(595)
Predominance of good aspects*	61	21	41	67	37	20	69	47	44	70
Predominance of bad aspects	39	34	57	33	60	79	30	50	54	28
By Political Tendency										
Right	(36)	(66)	(37)	(75)	(59)	(140)	(33)	(57)	(15)	(72)
Predominance of good aspects*	47	29	19	60	9	14	64	32	20	42
Predominance of bad aspects	53	21	78	39	90	85	36	68	60	58
Left	(212)	(111)	(175)	(174)	(187)	(41)	(42)	(262)	(43)	(130)
Predominance of good aspects*	72	17	49	72	33	20	69	56	42	83
Predominance of bad aspects	28	41	50	27	64	81	31	43	56	15
Far left	(34)	(48)	(84)	(60)	(56)	(107)	(19)	(81)	(22)	(21)
Predominance of good aspects*	56	25	60	63	75	34	79	67	64	90
Predominance of bad aspects	44	66	39	37	25	65	16	32	36	10

*p <.01
1. Alternatives such as "don't know" and "good and bad aspects" are not included in the table.

In Yugoslavia, the question about the good or bad aspects of the student movement did not appear on the questionnaire. In its place, the students were asked whether what one might call a student movement existed in their country. Although 29 percent of the students evidently did not know how to reply to this question, 40 percent affirmed the existence of such a movement versus 31 percent who denied it (Table 7.8).

TABLE 7.8.   Opinions of Yugoslav Students on the Expression "Student Movement" (Percent).

Different countries in the world have experienced the phenomenon of student protest, which is termed the "student movement." Do you think such a movement exists in Yugoslavia?	TOTAL
The term is inappropriate. There is no student movement because the revolutionary students have no political program of their own. It is at best a student revolt.	31
The student movement exists, and the term is appropriate. The absence of a clearly formulated program is a sign that the old revolutionary parties are facing a crisis, or, in other words, the movement reflects the troubles of our turbulent age.	40
I do not know, having given it no thought.	29

The 1977 Study

The results indicate that the students in the United States are less likely to evaluate the student movement positively (49 percent as compared to 70 percent in the main study). This does not indicate an increase of negative evaluation, but a lack of opinion on this issue (27 percent).

In France, the percentage of positive evaluation remains essentially unchanged (43 percent versus 41 percent), and there is a decrease of negative evaluation (44 percent versus 54 percent) (Table 7.9).

TABLE 7.9.   Evaluation of the Student Movement, 1977 Survey (Percent).

	FRANCE (90)	USA (104)
Predominance of good aspects	43	49
Predominance of bad aspects	44	24
No opinion	13	27

THE TWO BEST ASPECTS OF THE STUDENT MOVEMENT

As in the case of similar questions concerning society and the university, the students were asked to comment on what they believed to be the two most positive and the two most negative aspects of the student movement in their country.

In all of the countries studied, the students emphasized the general spirit at the beginning of the movement. They spoke of the good intentions which inspired them, such as generosity, sincerity, idealism, and involvement, and also of the satisfaction at having actively done something together:

Strong sense of involvement. [United States]

Keeps inertia from taking over in the system. [United States]

We are not all sitting back on our asses by our pools complaining. We're trying to do something about things we don't like. [Great Britain]

Activity: absence of passivity. [Tunisia]

Expressions like "awakening" or "awareness" appear frequently in the description of the student movement. The feeling of unity which is implied by working with others for common goals is also often cited as a positive trait:

Involves large numbers of students in the political process. [United States]

Develops a feeling of unity among the students. [United States]

Fraternity. [France]

Group solidarity. [Nigeria]

In addition, many students feel that the movement has truly resulted in something important and has had real influence on the university by creating forums where the students can express their needs and by establishing a liaison between the students and the administration. The action of the movement has also been felt outside of the university in political and social areas:

Tends to accelerate sociopolitical progress. [United States]

Initiates meaningful dialogue that leads to immediate beneficial changes. [United States]

Has awakened the country from a certain kind of conformism. [France]

Develops an awareness among those in power. [Tunisia]

Stands on civil rights, pollution, Vietnam. [United States]

In general, the responses as to the good aspects of the movement are similar in each country. British students, however, underline more frequently than others the importance of the nonviolent and moderate nature of the movement:

Absence of excessive violence.

Militant students are still in the minority.

In Austria, France, and Italy, there is more emphasis on the fact that the movement has been responsible for effective change within the university.

THE TWO WORST ASPECTS OF THE STUDENT MOVEMENT

The question of the two worst aspects of the student movement elicited very different responses from one country to another. Some of these responses, however, seem quite common to all countries except Australia and Japan, where they appeared relatively less frequently. Thus the students often evoke the lack of realism and the ineffectiveness of the movement. They use words or phrases such as "too idealistic," "naive," "romantic," and "out of touch with reality" to express the major negative aspects of the movement:

They are judging a world from which they have been sheltered all their short lives. [United States]

They know little of reality. [France]

The movement is frequently regarded as unrealistic and romantic both at the level of ideas and in the methods used to realize its goals:

Failure to consider what is rational and practical at the present moment. [United States]

Inept methods. [United States]

Lack of real thorough tactical thinking. [Great Britain]

Lack of ability to see objectives clearly and to plan well. [Nigeria]

In this category of criticisms there is frequent mention of the ineffectiveness and powerlessness of the student movement:

Too many words, too little action. [France]

A false sense of true effectiveness. [Great Britain]

There is no power. [Tunisia]

In Spain, Austria, Italy, and the United States some students allude to the vague and confusing ideology of the movement, which in this perspective seems more a result of adolescence than of maturity:

It is neither morally nor sociopolitically consistent. [United States]

One aspect of the student movement that is most often criticized is the tendency toward violence. This type of response is, however, less frequent in Spain, Austria, Australia, and Tunisia than in the other countries. Many students judge the violence to be totally irresponsible and gratuitous:

Violence for violence's sake. [France]

No aims except to disrupt. [Great Britain]

They prefer violence to negotiation. [Nigeria]

It is interesting to note that students often believe that violence corresponds to a feeling of powerlessness. It is the proof of failure:

Students often feel that violence is necessary as other ways have failed. [United States]

Tendency toward violence in the face of frustration. [United States]

They want to change what they fear they are incapable of changing. [Great Britain]

According to some students, violent methods only result in negative outcomes, such as discrediting the movement in the eyes of the public or inciting repression:

The violence of some demonstrations alienates too many people. [United States]

The militants are giving us a bad name. [Great Britain]

Acts of violence result in immediate repression. [France]

In France, Spain, and Japan, there is frequent mention of lack of unity and cohesion:

The student movement is divided. [France]

Internal struggles. [France]

Absence of dialogue among different tendencies. [France]

In Tunisia and Nigeria, the absence of unity is also mentioned, more as a result of ethnic or regional factions than because of politics. In Tunisia the students speak of "regionalism"; in Nigeria they speak of "tribalism" and the "clan."

In Japan, Austria, the United States, and France, the student movement is often condemned for its dogmatism and intolerance. Thus French students say:

It is intransigent.

It lacks tolerance.

Fascism on the left and on the right.

American students remark:

It is incapable of admitting its errors.

Too sure of itself.

Wild dogmatism.

A certain degree of intolerance directed at those who do not form part of the movement.

Students in Australia and Tunisia often denounce the demagoguery of the leaders of the student movement. In addition, in Australia students are worried by the fact that the movement has a tendency to alienate the workers and to intensify conflicts between the two groups. Thus the movement is more destructive than constructive, they say. This kind of criticism is rare in the other countries.

A rather large number of students in Great Britain and in Italy believe that the movement is too politicized and often falls into the hands of militants. In their opinion the movement should have occupied itself solely with problems within the university. In Austria and Great Britain in particular, the members of the movement are often perceived as dilettantes who participate in the movement only because it is fashionable.

As we noted above, the expression "student movement" has special meanings in some of the countries included in this study. This is especially true of Tunisia and Nigeria. In fact, many Tunisians emphasize that the student movement in their country is not independent, but is rather an extension of the government:

Movement conditioned by the government.

Too much submission to the government.

It defends the government more than the students.

When we asked Tunisian students if they were members of a student organization, almost all students who replied affirmatively cited the General Union of Tunisian Students. This is an official association which offers the students certain administrative facilities and organizes leisure activities and excursions. Thus when asked about the good and bad aspects of the student movement, the majority mention "the poor utilization of our dues" and "the organization of leisure activities" which indicates that these students are referring, not to the protest movement, but to the official student association at the university.

In Nigeria, one of the most frequently mentioned problems relates to the fact that the "student movement," which in reality is the Union of Nigerian Students, has control over the money it receives for organizing university activities. This situation results, according to the students, in "corruption," "the absence of morality," and "the misuse and appropriation of funds."

In a number of countries, judgment as to the bad aspects of the student movement varies with political tendency. Thus in Italy, France, Great Britain, Spain, and Nigeria, there are marked differences between the responses of the students on the right and the responses of those on the left. Conservatives tend to criticize the student movement as violent, militant, and too politicized, while the students on the far left contest its efficacy and its unity.

EVALUATION, CONTRIBUTIONS, AND GOALS OF THE STUDENT MOVEMENT[4]

EVALUATION OF THE STUDENT MOVEMENT

Students in general are favorable to the student movement. We note that a rather large group of students in certain countries, including those who do not identify with the far left, feels sympathetic toward the protest movement and believes that, in spite of everything, it has made positive contributions to society.

Four items on the questionnaire allowed the students to evaluate the student movement:

The student movement usually reflects a considerable degree of immaturity.

The militant students are only a small minority.

The student movement is essentially democratic in regard to its goals.

The student movement is essentially democratic in regard to its means.

The majority of students (more than 80 percent), including those on the far left, recognize that militant students comprise only a minority of the student population. We find, on the other hand, rather significant differences of opinion concerning the maturity of the movement. Those who believe that it lacks maturity are the Japanese (83 percent) and the Italians (77 percent), followed by the Austrians and the British (62 percent each), the Australians (58 percent), the Spaniards, Americans, and French (about 50 percent each), the Nigerians and the Tunisians (35 percent), and finally the Yugoslavs (15 percent) (Table 7.10).

Although the students on the far left might be expected to deny the immaturity of the student movement, many do, on the contrary, accept this criticism. Seventy-two percent of the far left students in Japan share this opinion, followed by about half of those in the other countries (Table 7.10a). It is interesting to note the situation of the communists and anarchists in France. The communists are much more critical in regard to the immaturity of the movement (67 percent) than is the left (41 percent); this negative view is expressed by only one out of four anarchists in France (Table 7.10b).

On the right, the most critical are the Italians (94 percent) and the Japanese (87 percent), followed by the British, Australians, Austrians, and Americans (about 72 percent), and the French (65 percent) (Table 7.10b). Only one student out of two on the right in Tunisia and in Nigeria criticizes the lack of maturity of the movement. This unexpected attitude, especially on the right, may be explained by the fact that a

[4]Not all the questions concerning the student movement were asked in the 1977 survey.

TABLE 7.10. Evaluation, Contributions, and Goals of the Student Movement by Country (Percent).

	AUSTRAL.	AUS.	FR.	GB	IT.	JAP.	NIG.	SP.	TUN.	USA	YUG.
The militant students are only a small minority.**	(750) 95	(478) 89	(700) 92	(587) 91	(763) 82	(416) 87	(228) 83	(667) 83	(132) 80	(638) 90	(1,074) 87
The student movement usually reflects a considerable degree of immaturity*	(749) 58	62	(688) 53	(577) 62	(791) 77	(354) 83	(213) 35	(716) 50	(133) 35	(641) 52	(1,077) 15
The student movement is essentially democratic in regard to its goals.*	(702) 54	(469) 76	(628) 61	(530) 51	(737) 52	(388) 58	(222) 77	(667) 61	(122) 78	(588) 52	(1,073) 87
The student movement is essentially democratic in regard to its means.*1	(669) 36	(472) 63	(613) 25	(495) 43		25	(208) 67	(667) 41		(592) 29	
The student movement has revealed truths new to the older generation.*	(721) 68	(480) 66	(668) 82	(562) 67	(786) 76	(402) 82	(219) 84	(694) 83	(134) 89	(630) 66	56
The student protest has led to the improvement of the university.*	(712) 68	(481) 75	(666) 50	(548) 79	75	(397) 63	(228) 84	(692) 63	80	(615) 77	(1,080) 57
One of the goals of the student movement should be to establish a common front among students and workers.*2	(709) 47	(478) 41	(647) 51	(543) 55	(771) 63	(353) 62	(223) 81	(671) 64		(550) 61	(1,072) 67
Students throughout the world should coordinate their efforts toward a revolutionary goal.*2	(729) 32	(474) 40	(617) 50	(561) 32	(725) 44	(359) 42	(222) 72	(675) 51		(642) 32	(1,075) 76
Students should leave the university for the factory in order to help the workers in their struggle.*3	(733) 8	26	(663) 14	(563) 11	(775) 26	(371) 11	(220) 35	(700) 24		(614) 5	
One of the goals of the student movement should be the destruction of the present form of government.*2	(742) 22	(480) 33	(662) 45	(570) 28	(733) 72	(393) 73	(225) 33	(666) 60		(635) 16	(1,078) 18

*p < .01
**p < .05
1. This item did not appear in the Italian, Tunisian, or Yugoslav questionnaire.
2. This item did not appear in the Tunisian questionnaire.
3. This item did not appear on the Tunisian or Yugoslav questionnaire.

marginal protest movement characterized by a leftist tendency did not really exist in these two countries. The movement to which these students refer is the national unions of students in their countries. As indicated above, these are associations to which any student may belong, which aspire to be nonpolitical, but which in reality are closely supervised by the government.

We also find differences of opinion among the countries as to whether the student movement is democratic in its goals. Students in Yugoslavia (87 percent) and Tunisia, Nigeria, and Austria (77 percent) accept this view more often than do students elsewhere (between 52 percent and 61 percent). This opinion is widely supported by the extreme left (70 percent or more).

Students on the right in Nigeria and Tunisia (more than 70 percent) judge their student movement democratic in its goals, but they are referring to their national student association. There is usually considerably less enthusiasm in the other countries, where "student movement" signifies for the right and the moderates a movement led by the far left. In Austria, however, 63 percent of the students on the right judge the goals of the movement democratic, followed by half of the Spaniards and Japanese, about 40 percent of the British and the Australians, 35 percent of the Americans, 22 percent of the French, and only 13 percent of Italians.

In Yugoslavia there are differences in the attitudes of the students as they define themselves in terms of the society they would prefer. Those who seek absolute equality among individuals agree almost unanimously (90 percent) that the movement is democratic in its goals. This percentage drops to 73 percent of the individualists, according to whom society should be organized so that each person can do what he wishes (Table 7.10b). Differences according to membership or nonmembership in the Communist League were minor.

Students, while in general approving the goals of the student movement, are more negative in regard to the means utilized. Are these means democratic? Two out of three students reply affirmatively in Nigeria and Austria, compared to fewer than 40 percent of the students in the other countries. Those on the far left, who are in general the most ardent defenders of the movement, are themselves frequently critical in some countries in judging the methods used by the protest movement. Only one-third of such students sampled in the United States believed that the means employed were democratic. The same proportion is found in France and Japan, compared to half of the students on the far left in Australia and Great Britain, about 70 percent of the Nigerians and Spaniards, and 82 percent of the Austrians. (This question did not appear on the questionnaires in Italy, in Yugoslavia, and Tunisia.)

These findings confirm what has been noted above concerning evaluation of the good and the bad aspects of the movement. Students, including those on the far left, showed a concern with the effectiveness of actions and of the means to be used.

The student movement thus appears to the majority of the respondents as composed of a small number of militants and as having idealistic and democratic goals, but is frequentls judged to lack maturity. The means which it employs are often seen as debatable. However, whether the movement is judged favorably or not, what has been its impact? Has it, according to the students, brought about an improvement in the university? More generally, has it changed the collective consciousness of society?

With regard to these issues, the students were asked to indicate their degree of agreement on the following two items included in the questionnaire:

The student movement has revealed truths that the older generation had previously not recognized.

The student protest in general has led to the improvement of the university.

More than two-thirds of the students in almost all of the countries studied believed that the student movement had produced an awareness of certain truths which the preceding generation had not recognized. In Yugoslavia this percentage is 56 percent. The same pattern appears concerning the contribution of the student movement to university reform, except in France, where the percentage is 50 percent (Table 7.10).

The students on the far left are much more likely than other political groups to agree that the student movement has made significant contributions (Table 7.10a). Although in general students on the far left believe that the contributions of the student movement are about equal as regards the university and the "awakening" of society in general, some of these students, especially in the United States, place much more emphasis on the former (92 percent compared to 64 percent). In Spain and in France the latter is emphasized more frequently (Spain, 85 percent versus 58 percent; France, 93 percent versus 47 percent). Thus for the students on the far left in Europe and in Japan, the fundamental success of the student movement is to have revealed truths new to the older generation, even though the movement was launched from the university. In the United States, on the other hand, where according to the students the movement began as a social and cultural protest, its essential contribution has been at the university level. What the students recognized as the contributions of the movement, it seems, were not the outcomes expected at the beginning of the movement.

GOALS OF THE STUDENT MOVEMENT

The image that we have in general of the student movement, especially in Europe, is that it centered on university problems, stimulated an awareness among students, and served as a catalyst for a general protest against the present form of government or society outside the university domain. This image on the whole describes what the students in our samples believe. They were also asked how they saw the future of this movement and its political objectives. In May 1968, among the popular slogans there were references to the idea of an international student movement and of a struggle common to students and workers alike. A series of statements in our questionnaire attempted to identify the opinions of the students concerning these ideas.[5]

An International Student Movement

The simultaneous emergence of movements of student protest in different countries suggested to many militants, as well as to those who only sympathized with the idea, the need to coordinate efforts and activities. There was even talk of an international "conspiracy," but it seems more likely that the almost simultaneous occurrence of student movements was due to the influence of the mass media rather than to the "conspiracy" that many conservatives, some students, and a portion of public opinion regarded as responsible. Protesters in various countries reached the same

[5]These statements did not appear on the questionnaire in Tunisia.

conclusion about industrialized society at approximately the same time, and also realized not only the force they represented in their own country but also, in many cases, the force they could have if they united and formed an international student movement. We attempted to study the attitudes of students concerning such an international organization, particularly at a time when many people were talking more and more about federation, internationalism, and the abolition of borders between countries.

The students were asked whether they agreed or disagreed with the following:

Students throughout the world should coordinate their efforts toward a revolutionary goal.

Although the notion of an international student movement attracts many Nigerians (72 percent) and Yugoslavs (76 percent), it does not appear nearly so frequently in the other countries of the study. Fifty percent of Spanish and French students approve of this idea, 40 percent to 44 percent of Italians, Japanese, and Austrians, and 32 percent of Australians, Americans, and British (Table 7.10).

Students on the far left are the most favorable to such an international movement. The majority of them (more than 80 percent) adhere to this idea, although less frequently in Great Britain (72 percent) and in Japan (65 percent) (Table 7.10a).

Unity with the Workers

In some countries, such as France, Italy, and Germany, activists attempted to join forces with workers. According to Touraine (1972), the "events" of May 1968 in France illustrate the following phenomenon:

the student movement always plays a role which is at the same time central and marginal, of which it is perfectly aware, since one of the most constant traits of the student protest is that it calls in the intervention of others and never defines its action in purely university terms [p. 196].

One of the themes which occurs over and over again in the slogans of the students is the need to destroy their social isolation, which they feel is maintained by the state. In "Nous sommes en marche" (1968) we read, "*Workers-students*, we are the revolutionary class, we represent the true, dominant ideology, for our wish is to abolish ourselves as a class. . . . We only want to be young workers."

Should unity with the workers be an objective of the student movement? Two statements were included in the questionnaire in order to determine the opinions of the students:

One of the goals of the student movement should be to establish a common front among workers and students.

Students should leave the university for the factory in order to help the workers in their struggle.

(The second statement did not appear on the questionnaire in Yugoslavia).

Students, whatever their political orientation, are much more likely to support the creation of a common front with the workers than they are to accept the idea of leaving the university for the factory.

Among the students on the far left in each country, we note that a large majority approve the common front with workers: in Italy (93 percent) and Spain (92 percent), more than 80 percent in Nigeria, Austria, France and Great Britain, and more than 70 percent in Australia, Japan, and the United States (Table 7.9a). In Yugo-slavia, the percentages are as follows: those who seek absolute equality, 78 percent; the elitists, 77 percent; those who seek equal opportunities, 68 percent; the humani-tarians, 64 percent; and finally, the individualists, 56 percent (Table 7.9b).

Fewer students on the far left endorse the idea of leaving the university for the factory, except in Austria and Nigeria, where two thirds of these students agree with this objective. About half of the students on the far left in Italy and Spain also ap-prove, followed by one third of the British and the Australians, 26 percent of the French, 18 percent of the Japanese, and only 9 percent of the Americans. These find-ings show that in the most industrialized countries there is the greatest resistance on the part of the far left to the kind of involvement which would require their active participation and the abandonment of their studies.

Destruction of the Present Regime

In order to discover the attitudes of the students, especially on the far left, con-cerning a possible objective of the student movement, namely, the destruction of the present form of government, the following statement was included in the question-naire:

One of the goals of the student movement should be the destruction of the present form of government.

While relatively few Nigerians on the far left adhere to this objective (38 percent), many of those in other countries do support this idea: 96 percent in Spain; 87 per-cent in Italy; about 82 percent in Japan, France, and Austria; 71 percent in Great Britain; and 58 percent in the United States (Table 7.10a).

The attitudes of the Nigerian students may be explained by the fact that their country had just undergone a change of government, a civil war, and a new military government. The students apparently hoped that this new regime would be capable of solving some of the social, ethnic, economic, and political problems of the coun-try. Another explanation for their responses, as has been mentioned above, may be the fact that they interpret "student movement" to mean the student association to which most students belong. They may therefore believe that the destruction of the present regime is not a suitable objective for their organization.

A rather important disparity exists between the responses of the students on the far left in the different countries concerning this question. Difficulties in interpre-tation arise, as the attitudes of students depend on the political regime of their coun-try. Spain under Franco, for example, would certainly lead students on the far left to hope for a change. Other elements, such as the attitude toward violence, also may intervene.

MEANS OF ACTION OF THE MOVEMENT AT THE UNIVERSITY

ATTITUDE TOWARD VIOLENCE

Student protesters hope, in differing degrees, that society and the university will be modified by their actions. Some students (particularly in Spain, France, and Ita-ly) expect that the university will be politicized and changed by a revolution. The idea that a revolution is necessary to transform the political situation and the university appeared with some frequency in the responses, although still remaining a minority opinion.

We turn now to the attitudes of the students in regard to violence, especially violence at the university. The notion of violence as part of the protest movement is particularly important, as it darkened the image of the movement in public opinion and divided the students among themselves. As we noted earlier in this chapter, students supported the movement for its idealism, its altruism, and the awareness it produced, but criticized it for being ineffective, nonrepresentative, intolerant, fragmented, and, in particular, violent.

The attitude of the students toward violence was approached through the following three statements:

Violence as a political technique is in general to be condemned.

Violence is the most effective form of action capable of producing profound social changes.

Violence by students, when used to reach valid goals rapidly, is legitimate.[6]

In most of the countries studied, more than two-thirds of the students condemn violence in general. Eighty percent or more of the students in all countries, except France (64 percent), adopt this position.

The effectiveness of violence for social change is accepted by 45 percent of the students in Spain, 43 percent in France, 44 percent in Nigeria, about 30 percent in Japan, Great Britain, the United States, and Italy, and about 25 percent in Australia, Austria, and Yugoslavia (Table 7.11).

The conditional legitimacy of violence "to reach valid goals" is more frequently acceptable than are the other two statements. The majority of students in Nigeria (70 percent) and Spain and France (about 50 percent) endorse this statement. Only a minority do so in the other countries: 43 percent in Yugoslavia, 36 percent in Italy, about 30 percent in Japan and Austria, and about 20 percent in the Anglo-Saxon countries.

Although in general the far left is the political group most favorable to violence, we find important differences among the various countries. Eighty percent on the far left in Japan condemn the use of violence, followed by about 70 percent of the British and Australians, 64 percent of the Americans, about 50 percent of the Italians, Nigerians, and Tunisians, and 37 percent of the Austrians, but only about 30 percent of the French and Spanish students. Somewhat similar percentages emerge in connection with the principle of the conditional legitimacy of violence. The students on the far left who are the most favorable to the use of violence are the Nigerians, Italians, French, Austrians, and Spaniards. They judge violence as legitimate and effective and condemn its use relatively infrequently.

The analysis of the findings by political tendency allows us to evaluate more clearly the frequent *a priori* judgment that the far left is the only political group which supports the use of violence. In fact, although the right is in general unfavorable to violence—fewer than 30 percent of far rightist students approve—this is not the case in France, Tunisia, and Nigeria. In these three countries at least 40 percent of the conservative students support the notion that violence is effective and legitimate under certain conditions (Table 7.11a).

[6]This item did not appear on the Tunisian questionnaire.

The 1977 Study

Table 7.12 (page 220) indicates that in the United States attitudes toward violence are becoming more negative: 90 percent as compared to 82 percent in the main study agree that violence as a political technique should be condemned; only 10 percent versus 20 percent in 1970 agree that violence is legitimate when used to reach valid goals, and 14 percent as compared to 30 percent in 1970 agree that violence may be the most effective form of action.

TABLE 7.11. Attitudes toward Violence by Country (Percent).

	AUSTRAL.	AUS.	FR.	GB	IT.	JAP.
Violence as a political technique is to be condemned.*	(762) 90	(480) 77	(686) 64	(594) 87	(805) 85	(419) 86
Violence, when used to reach valid goals rapidly, is legitimate.*[1]	(745) 22	(497) 29	(680) 55	(579) 24	(795) 36	(401) 32
Violence is the most effective form of action capable of producing profound social changes.**	(741) 26	(481) 25	(693) 43	(584) 31	(802) 32	(392) 34
	NIG.	SP.	TUN.	USA	YUG.	
Violence as a political technique is to be condemned.*	(227) 67	(712) 77	(140) 71	(642) 82	(1,079) 90	
Violence, when used to reach valid goals rapidly, is legitimate.*[1]	(229) 70	(713) 57		(626) 20	(1,072) 43	
Violence is the most effective form of action capable of producing profound social changes.**	(232) 44	(708) 45	56	(628) 30	(1,079) 25	

*p < .01
**p < .05
1. This item did not appear on the Tunisian questionnaire.

A similar but less marked tendency can be seen among French students: 67 percent as compared to 64 percent condemn violence; 50 percent versus 55 percent consider that violence may be legitimate in order to reach important goals; and 32 percent versus 43 percent consider that violence can be an effective form of action. It is interesting to note the cross-cultural difference in acceptance, at least in principle, of violence. The French seem much more tolerant of it than the Americans.

ACTIONS WHICH CAN BE UNDERTAKEN AT THE UNIVERSITY

During the height of the student protest movements in many countries, students undertook various kinds of actions to convince or, in some cases, "oblige" authorities to satisfy their demands and to introduce transformations in the system. While these actions found considerable support among the students, they also created marked cleavages within the student population.

For public opinion and the government, as well as for the different political parties and the students themselves, there exists a kind of code of morality which limits the range of actions considered as legitimate in order to realize certain goals. Beyond this threshold certain acts are seen as "violent" or as the consequence of "anarchy" or "vandalism" practiced by the far left. The scale of "acceptable" methods varies from country to country. The student movement in Japan is known for having most often used violent action. In the United States, even "sit-ins" are frequently placed in this category.

TABLE 7.12.   Attitudes toward Violence by Country, 1977 (Percent).

	FRANCE	USA
Violence as a political technique is to be condemned.*	(92) 67	(79) 90
Violence, when used to reach valid goals rapidly, is legitimate.*	(91) 50	(100) 10
Violence is the most effective form of action capable of producing profound social changes.**	(92) 32	(79) 14

*p < .01
**p < .05

We attempted to discover the opinions of students concerning different means of action in one specific area, the university. We asked the students to indicate whether they approved or not of the following

Working through the elected student representatives.

Directly petitioning and meeting with administrative officials.

Demonstrations and marches.

Picketing and blocking access to university facilities.

Striking or boycotting classes.

Disrupting classes.

Sit-in and occupation of buildings.

Destroying records and property.

Physical attack on members of the faculty who disagree.

Physical attack on members of the administration.

The choice of actions undertaken within the university depends on the students' attitudes toward violence. The more the individual accepts the principle of violence, the more likely he is to approve of such extremist acts. Moderate students would be expected to favor petitioning and meeting with administrative officials or with elected assemblies; at most these students accept demonstrations and strikes. These choices equally well characterize the right, the moderates, and the traditional leftists as well as the apoliticals (Tables 7.13 and 7.13a).

A comparison by country shows that the great majority of students in most countries studied approved of working through elected student representatives (about 80 percent except in Italy, 62 percent, and Japan, 57 percent), as well as petitioning and meeting with the administration (more than 70 percent except in Nigeria, 56 percent). Also a majority were in favor of demonstrations (more than 50 per-

TABLE 7.13.   Agreement with Certain Kinds of Actions Undertaken at the University by Country (Percent).

	AUSTRAL.	AUS.	FR.	GB	IT.	JAP.	NIG.	SP.	TUN.[1]	USA	YUG.
Working through elected student representatives*	(758) 86	(482) 83	(665) 78	(590) 81	(823) 62	(412) 57	(226) 83	(729) 84	(126) 82	(656) 87	(1,072) 90
Petitioning and meeting with administration*[2]	(762) 89	(481) 88	(688) 84	(596) 84		(428) 73	(225) 56	(697) 77	(129) 85	(658) 93	(1,070) 88
Demonstrations*	(766) 52	(483) 45	(683) 63	(593) 51	(830) 47	(431) 69	(230) 56	(714) 61		(657) 67	(1,069) 79
Picketing and blocking access to university facilities**[3]	(761) 11	(481) 17	(673) 32	(589) 16	(820) 25	(413) 24	(217) 12	(708) 33		(652) 16	
Striking and boycotting classes*	(751) 24	(483) 28	(678) 54	(595) 21	(833) 27	(428) 43	(229) 35	(712) 49		(656) 29	(1,065) 27
Disrupting classes*	(759) 6	17	(678) 41	(591) 9	(827) 22	(426) 14	(211) 12	(720) 39		(655) 4	(1,070) 8
Sit-in and occupation of buildings*	(764) 14	17	(674) 40	(586) 14	(816) 27	(424) 61	(201) 19	(722) 51		(653) 13	(1,065) 26
Destroying property	(761) 3	(482) 6	(690) 6	(594) 5	(826) 4	8	(215) 3	(718) 9		(649) 2	1
Attack on members of the administration[3]	(762) –	(483) 8	(699) 4	(596) 1	(821) 4	(418) 6	(220) 3	(714) 7		(656) 1	–
Attack on members of the faculty who disagree	(765) 1	1	(697) 5	(597) 1	(823) 4	(422) 5	(219) 2	(718) 9		(654) 1	2

*p < .01
**p < .05
1. Only two items appeared in the Tunisian questionnaire.
2. This item was not available in the Italian questionnaire.
3. This item was not included in the Yugoslav questionnaire.

cent except in Italy, 47 percent, and Austria, 45 percent). The other actions were approved only by a minority (30 percent or less) except in France, Italy, and Japan, where at least 40 percent of students approved strikes, boycotts, and the disrupting of classes as well as the sit-in and occupation of buildings. Extremist actions such as the destruction of property and attacks on persons were approved by less than 10 percent of the students in all the countries studied (Table 7.13).

Students who accept extremist actions, as is the case for many on the far left, are nevertheless generally hostile to the destruction of property and to physical attack on members of the faculty or administration. Our findings show that most students on the far left believe in the power of demonstrations (about 90 percent) and accept their use as a means of obtaining certain demands. Only the Austrians and the Spaniards are less respectful of authority and property. For these groups on the far left, protest becomes an open struggle; the destruction of property (Austrians 29 percent and Spaniards 40 percent) and physical attacks on members of the administration (Austrians 37 percent and Spaniards 28 percent) or on members of the faculty who disagree (Austrians 7 percent and Spaniards 38 percent) are approved by a sizable number (Table 7.13a), but still represent a minority position.

A comparison among different countries shows that the students on the far left who are the most violent and the most extreme are found most frequently, in descending order, in Spain, Italy, France, and Austria. The most moderate are the Americans and the Japanese, who prefer meeting with administrators and working through elected assemblies. (The Japanese movement did, however, show considerable violence; perhaps it was a small minority which was responsible.)

TABLE 7.1a.   University Policy (Percent).

Australia	Right	Center	Left	Far L.	Apol.
To fill manpower needs of government and business*	(39)	(267)	(226)	(36)	(180)
	77	70	51	28	71
To conduct research for government and industry within the university*		(269)	(225)	(35)	(177)
	74	78	64	37	72
To advance fundamental research**	(40)	(272)	(227)	(36)	(184)
	80	83	82	58	77
To eliminate all grading of students by faculty*		(248)	(219)	(32)	(168)
	18	30	43	66	28
The present educational system maintains discrimination*	(38)	(269)	(231)	(35)	(183)
	66	81	94	97	79
To open the university only to serious students**	(40)	(272)	(234)	(36)	(184)
	45	60	43	42	54
To open the universities to anyone, without selective admission**	(39)	(266)	(230)	(35)	(185)
	44	45	62	71	48

Austria	Right	Center	Left	Far L.	Apol.
To fill manpower needs of government and business*	(81)	(150)	(135)	(68)	(45)
	74	75	48	31	80
To conduct research for government and industry within the university*		(149)	(134)		
	72	77	56	27	78
To advance fundamental research**	(78)	(150)	(136)		
	95	83	82	71	91
To eliminate all grading of students by faculty*	(82)		(134)		
	13	28	47	74	18
The present educational system maintains discrimination*		(151)	(137)	(66)	
	42	57	91	91	45

To open the university only to serious students*			(149) 77	(135) 46	27	89	
To open the universities to anyone, without selective admission*			(81) 46	(150) 57	73	90	49

France	RIGHT	CENT.	LEFT	COMM.	FAR L.	ANAR.	APOL.
To fill manpower needs of government and business*	(36) 72	(115) 57	(174) 33	(42) 7	(87) 23	(31) 13	(125) 45
To conduct research for government and industry within the university*	(39) 74	(125) 70	(183) 47	(43) 16	29	19	(135) 50
To advance fundamental research*	(41) 88	(128) 88	(187) 79	(44) 68	67	(28) 43	(132) 80
To eliminate all grading of students by faculty*	7	(123) 18	(189) 29	(42) 36	(85) 54	(27) 70	(140) 27
The present educational system maintains discrimination*	39	(132) 58	(200) 88	(48) 100	(96) 99	(33) 94	(151) 76
To open the university only to serious students*	(43) 93	(134) 79	(201) 63	31	38	(32) 31	(156) 62
To open the universities to anyone, without selective admission*	(38) 21	(130) 42	(196) 60	(45) 91	(92) 85	(31) 84	(149) 52

Great Britain	RIGHT	CENTER	LEFT	FAR L.	APOL.
To fill manpower needs of government and business*	(88) 78	(85) 61	(187) 60	(68) 30	(139) 65
To conduct research for government and industry within the university*	(85) 75	(86) 69	(181) 51	31	(144) 72
To advance fundamental research*	(86) 98	(90) 91	(189) 86	(70) 61	(148) 88
To eliminate all grading of students by faculty*	(75) 23	(75) 37	(168) 49	(62) 69	(126) 41
The present educational system maintains discrimination*	(86) 65	(90) 81	(198) 89	(72) 96	(146) 81
To open the university only to serious students*	(87) 68	59	44	35	(150) 56
To open the universities to anyone, without selective admission*	(88) 16	(88) 25	(189) 43	61	(145) 23

Italy	FAR R.	RIGHT	CENT.	LEFT	COMM.	FAR L.	APOL.
To fill manpower needs of government and business*	(32) 100	(63) 94	(145) 91	(218) 76	(99) 31	(61) 39	(164) 84
To conduct research for government and industry within the university*	(27) 63	(59) 81	(137) 72	(205) 58	(102) 35	(65) 45	(143) 69
To advance fundamental research**	(31) 90	(62) 97	(146) 97	(221) 90	(99) 72	(63) 76	(164) 95
To eliminate all grading of students by faculty*	(26) 62	(59) 56	(127) 53	(192) 68	(84) 86	(53) 83	(142) 61
The present educational system maintains discrimination*	(29) 55	(63) 41	(150) 55	(227) 77	(111) 98	(70) 99	(171) 73
To open the university only to serious students*	(32) 81	(67) 85	73	(225) 68	(109) 48	42	(174) 71
To open the universities to anyone, without selective admissions*	(29) 55	(63) 41	(150) 55	(227) 77	(111) 98	(70) 99	(171) 73

(cont.)

TABLE 7.1a Continued

Japan			CENTER	LEFT	FAR L.	APOL.
To fill manpower needs of government and business**			(153) 26	(43) 30	(123) 10	(102) 18
To conduct research for government and industry within the university			(149) 21	(41) 24	(119) 9	(105) 16
To advance fundamental research*			66	(42) 64	(123) 34	(104) 46
To eliminate all grading of students by faculty*			(143) 53	50	(116) 78	(100) 69
The present educational system maintains discrimination*			(44) 61	76	(119) 89	(105) 73
To open the university only to serious students			(156) 64	(44) 66	(124) 57	(110) 51
To open the universities to anyone, without selective admission*			(151) 58	(43) 67	(123) 81	(106) 73

Nigeria	RIGHT	CRITIC.	LEFT	FAR L.	DESCR.	APOL.
To fill manpower needs of government and business	(42) 98	(36) 95	(42) 100	(20) 100	(28) 100	(56) 95
To conduct research for government and industry within the university	81	92	83	(21) 91	(27) 93	(55) 84
To advance fundamental research	100	100	(43) 100	100	100	(57) 98
To eliminate all grading of students by faculty	(38) 13	(34) 24	(39) 23	(18) 28	11	(54) 17
The present educational system maintains discrimination*	(41) 73	(35) 94	(44) 82	(20) 80	(28) 57	(53) 85
To open the university only to serious students	(40) 53	54	(41) 51	55	(25) 64	(52) 58
To open the universities to anyone, without selective admission**	(41) 10	(35)	(44)	(20) 14	(28)	(53)

Spain	RIGHT	CENTER	LEFT	FAR L.	APOL.
To fill manpower needs of government and business*	(56) 84	(113) 85	(257) 70	(72) 46	(160) 78
To conduct research for government and industry within the university*	(60) 78	(119) 83	(274) 66	(78) 44	(168) 73
To advance fundamental research**	(57) 86	(118) 87	(275) 76	(79) 68	(172) 91
To eliminate all grading of students by faculty**	(54) 37	(117) 50	55	62	(175) 51
The present educational system maintains discrimination**	(60) 70	(118) 77	(278) 94	(84) 94	(178) 74
To open the university only to serious students*	(61) 62	(122) 62	(283) 48	(81) 33	(182) 61
To open the universities to anyone, without selective admission	(58) 69	(120) 63	(282) 67	(80) 63	(181) 73

Tunisia	RIGHT	BOURGUIB.	LEFT	FAR L.	APOL.
To fill manpower needs of government and business*	(11) 82	(16) 75	(47) 70	(23) 74	(30) 83
To conduct research for government and industry within the university	(12) 100	(13) 77	75	82	(29) 93
To advance fundamental research	(15) 93	(16) 100	(48) 88	(24) 92	(32) 94

	RIGHT	CENT.	LIB.	LEFT	FAR L.	APOL.
To eliminate all grading of students by faculty**		(13) 46	(14) 43	(46) 48	58	(29) 38
The present educational system maintains discrimination¹						
To open the university only to serious students*		(15) 67	(16) 33	(48) 56	(25) 56	(33) 58
To open the universities to anyone, without selective admission		(13) 85	(14) 79	71	(24) 79	73

United States	RIGHT	CENT.	LIB.	LEFT	FAR L.	APOL.
To fill manpower needs of government and business*	(77) 91	(117) 81	(191) 69	(134) 58	(22) 50	(90) 62
To conduct research for government and industry within the university*	(72) 71	(116) 54	(183) 40	(125) 25	(23) 22	(88) 35
To advance fundamental research**	(79) 95	(124) 88	(190) 79	(134) 74	78	(90) 77
To eliminate all grading of students by faculty*	(73) 36	(120) 48	(186) 60	(127) 66	(22) 68	(83) 42
The present educational system maintains discrimination**	(76) 70	(127) 80	(193) 81	(135) 90	(26) 88	(91) 81
To open the university only to serious students*	(78) 60	(128) 53	(196) 45	(137) 39	(25) 32	(89) 44
To open the universities to anyone, without selective admission*	(79) 17	(126) 25	(192) 36	(130) 45	(23) 57	(85) 28

Yugoslavia	IDEAL.	REAL.	HUMAN.	ELIT.	INDIV.
To fill manpower needs of government and business²					
To conduct research for government and industry within the university**	(238) 34	(490) 31	(160) 37	(25) 52	(41) 27
To advance fundamental research**	(240) 70	(493) 68	(163) 66	88	66
To eliminate all grading of students by faculty**	(239) 67	62	(160) 64	44	63
The present educational system maintains discrimination	(237) 50	(490) 57	(161) 47	(26) 42	46
To open the university only to serious students	(238) 80	(492) 83	(160) 81	(25) 84	76
To open the universities to anyone, without selective admission	(240) 66	(493) 59	56	64	54

*p <.01
**p <.05
1. This item was not included in the Tunisian questionnaire.
2. This item was not included in the Yugoslavian questionnaire.

TABLE 7.4a.   Role of Politics in the University by Political Tendency (Percent).

Australia	RIGHT	CENT.	LEFT	FAR L.	APOL.
Place of learning and investigation as free as possible of political involvement**	(40) 88	(267) 82	(231) 82	(36) 64	(185) 87
To act as a vanguard for changing society**	(35) 86	(261) 80	(227) 95	(35) 97	(178) 87
A forum for the critical analysis of national life	(40) 95	(268) 95	(233) 99	97	(180) 91

(cont.)

TABLE 7.4a   Continued

Australia	RIGHT	CENT.	LEFT	FAR L.	APOL.
A base for radical political action*	20	(269) 19	(223) 41	(36) 72	(175) 17
The university as a bourgeois institution should be destroyed and replaced by a proletarian culture*	(38) 11	(239) 13	(205) 28	(31) 55	(158) 15
Effective change in the university could only be achieved by a political revolution*	8	(260) 11	(224) 24	(34) 71	(172) 17

Austria	RIGHT	CENT.	LEFT	FAR L.	APOL.
Place of learning and investigation as free as possible of political involvement**	(82) 96	(149) 97	(135) 90	(67) 79	(45) 100
To act as a vanguard for changing society	(79) 92	92	93	85	93
A forum for the critical analysis of national life**	(80) 86	(150) 93	93	(68) 96	78
A base for radical political action*	(81) 4	11	35	74	7
The university as a bourgeois institution should be destroyed and replaced by a proletarian culture*	(82) 4	(149) 8	(134) 34	(64) 72	(44) 9
Effective change in the university could only be achieved by a political revolution*	10	(152) 15	(137) 42	(66) 77	21

France	RIGHT	CENT.	LEFT	COMM.	FAR L.	ANAR.	APOL.
Place of learning and investigation as free as possible of political involvement*	(43) 95	(130) 85	(195) 65	(41) 24	(90) 29	(30) 30	(145) 82
To act as a vanguard for changing society*	(37) 46	(122) 56	(191) 79	(42) 60	(95) 90	(32) 84	(137) 73
A forum for the critical analysis of national life*	(36) 47	(119) 55	(185) 77	(46) 87	(92) 94	(30) 90	69
A base for radical political action*	(41) 2	(116) 11	(167) 44	(39) 72	(87) 78	(25) 84	(118) 19
The university as a bourgeois institution should be destroyed and replaced by a proletarian culture*	12	(122) 21	(173) 50	(38) 79	(84) 81	(30) 73	(115) 39
Effective change in the university could only be achieved by a political revolution*	(42) 14	(129) 31	(195) 63	(48) 100	(97) 91	(32) 81	(146) 44

Great Britain	RIGHT	CENT.	LEFT	FAR L.	APOL.
Place of learning and investigation as free as possible of political involvement*	(86) 95	(89) 92	(194) 88	(70) 64	(146) 97
To act as a vanguard for changing society*	(78) 62	(87) 91	(189) 92	(69) 93	(133) 76
A forum for the critical analysis of national life	(85) 85	(89) 90	(195) 93	(71) 97	(136) 91
A base for radical political action*	(86) 7	(85) 14	(180) 40	(64) 72	(138) 18
The university as a bourgeois institution should be destroyed and replaced by a proletarian culture*	(85) 13	(83) 17	(167) 32	(59) 49	(130) 21

Effective change in the university could only be achieved by a political revolution*	(84) 7	(89) 11	(189) 25	(65) 54	(134) 11

Italy	FAR R.	RIGHT	CENT.	LEFT	COMM.	FAR L.	APOL.
Place of learning and investigation as free as possible of political involvement*	(31) 100	(66) 97	(152) 99	(222) 97	(103) 71	(65) 71	(165) 95
To act as a vanguard for changing society*	61	(62) 76	(139) 89	(214) 94	(109) 84	(70) 81	(157) 90
A forum for the critical analysis of national life**	(30) 87	(59) 68	(138) 76	(205) 73	(103) 66	(67) 66	(165) 75
A base for radical political action*	(29) 48	(62) 27	(136) 46	(203) 69	(105) 96	91	(143) 68
The university as a bourgeois institution should be destroyed and replaced by a proletarian culture*	(28) 18	(61) 13	(134) 23	(192) 43	(109) 92	(64) 80	(154) 45
Effective change in the university could only be achieved by a political revolution*	(29) 43	(59) 19	(141) 22	(212) 51	(111) 96	(70) 91	(156) 43

Japan	CENT.	LEFT	FAR L.	APOL.
Place of learning and investigation as free as possible of political involvement**	(153) 86	(44) 91	(121) 71	(105) 85
To act as a vanguard for changing society	(146) 71	(43) 74	(117) 80	(101) 70
A forum for the critical analysis of national life	(150) 87	(44) 84	(115) 90	(102) 84
A base for radical political action*	(149) 11	(42) 21	(113) 43	(98) 13
The university as a bourgeois institution should be destroyed and replaced by a proletarian culture*	(144) 29	(38) 37	(106) 58	(84) 40
Effective change in the university could only be achieved by a political revolution**	27	(40) 38	(112) 50	(101) 30

Nigeria	RIGHT	CRITIC.	LEFT	FAR L.	DESCR.	APOL.
Place of learning and investigation as free as possible of political involvement	(42) 81	(37) 76	(41) 85	(21) 76	(26) 73	(56) 79
To act as a vanguard for changing society	(40) 93	(35) 89	(43) 93	95	(27) 93	(54) 96
A forum for the critical analysis of national life	(41) 90	(33) 94	91	(20) 90	(28) 82	(57) 86
A base for radical political action*	(40) 23	(35) 34	(42) 52	(21) 67	(26) 8	(54) 28
The university as a bourgeois institution should be destroyed and replaced by a proletarian culture*	(35) 34	(28) 65	52	(20) 65	31	(50) 40
Effective change in the university could only be achieved by a political revolution*	(40) 30	(36) 44	(43) 47	(19) 58	(22) 18	(47) 38

Spain	RIGHT	CENT.	LEFT	FAR L.	APOL.
Place of learning and investigation as free as possible of political involvement*	(57) 72	(119) 71	(275) 56	(80) 41	(181) 82

(cont.)

TABLE 7.4a   Continued

Spain	Right	Cent.	Left	Far L.	Apol.
To act as a vanguard for changing society**	(55) 78	(115) 84	(274) 84	(78) 63	(171) 83
A forum for the critical analysis of national life**	(56) 71	(117) 74	(267) 81	69	(156) 72
A base for radical political action*	(58) 33	(108) 46	(265) 61	(70) 64	(146) 39
The university as a bourgeois institution should be destroyed and replaced by a proletarian culture*	(56) 41	(110) 47	(261) 77	(82) 89	(159) 51
Effective change in the university could only be achieved by a political revolution*	(60) 33	(113) 44	(271) 78	(83) 94	(167) 37

Tunisia[1]	Right	Bourguib.	Left	Far L.	Apol.
Place of learning and investigation as free as possible of political involvement	(15) 80	(16) 75	(47) 60	(24) 38	(32) 69
To act as a vanguard for changing society*	(14) 86	(15) 93	(48) 88	(25) 90	(32) 78
A forum for the critical analysis of national life	(15) 87	(16) 94	(47) 89	88	(31) 81

United States	Right	Cent.	Lib.	Left	Far L.	Apol.
Place of learning and investigation as free as possible of political involvement**	(78) 87	(121) 76	(193) 78	(133) 68	(24) 67	(89) 90
To act as a vanguard for changing society*	(75) 64	(113) 77	(191) 87	(131) 95	(26) 92	(87) 77
A forum for the critical analysis of national life	(79) 94	(122) 96	98	(136) 97	100	(89) 91
A base for radical political action*	(78) 1	(119) 6	(181) 22	(118) 32	(23) 48	(78) 17
The university as a bourgeois institution should be destroyed and replaced by a proletarian culture*	(73) 4	(117) 10	(176) 9	(120) 17	(22) 36	(77) 16
Effective change in the university could only be achieved by a political revolution*	(76) 4	(121) 8	(190) 16	(134) 17	(23) 44	(86) 20

Yugoslavia (by membership in the Communist League)	Yes	Desire To	Refuse To
Place of learning and investigation as free as possible of political involvement**	(119) 35	(172) 35	(782) 53
To act as a vanguard for changing society	94	(171) 83	(781) 79
A forum for the critical analysis of national life	56	54	50
A base for radical political action**	(116) 57	(164) 44	(708) 35
The university as a bourgeois institution should be destroyed and replaced by a proletarian culture**	(119) 27	(171) 35	(784) 19
Effective change in the university could only be achieved by a political revolution	22	(173) 16	(787) 19

*p < .01
**p < .05
1. Only the following three items appeared in Tunisia.

TABLE 7.6a. Views of Causes of the Student Movement in France, Great Britain, Italy, Japan, and the United States, Right to Far Left Students (Percent).

	POLITICAL DISCONTENT	SOCIOECON. DISCONTENT	POOR UNIV. SYSTEM	GEN. CONFLICT[1]	AUTHORIT.	AGITATORS	CRISIS OF CIVILIZATION	LACK OF EMPLOYMENT	FOREIGN CONSPIRACY
U.S.A. Right (80)*	99	76	37	91	37	90	64	31	26
Far left (26)*	90	68	71	96	79	33	94	38	14
G.B. Right (85)*	75	55	6	56	28	90	21	53	18
Far left (67)*	94	75	52	70	67	42	53	38	7
Italy Right (32)*	81	72	91		66	79	33	76	42
Far left (113)*	91	81	89		90	15	57	83	25
Japan Center (152)*	99	79	78	72	81	44	33	5	13
Far left (126)*	98	87	82	68	94	21	60	10	8
France Right (43)*	67	63	91	67	51	88	63	91	54
Far left (101)*	90	81	94	40	68	49	65	92	33

*p .01
1. This item was not on the questionnaire in Italy.

TABLE 7.6b.   Causes of the Student Movement According to Yugoslav Students (Percent).

		TOTAL (906)		IDEALISTS (226)		REALISTS (446)		HUMAN. (152)		ELITISTS (24)		INDIV. (38)	
University	Students' financial conditions and lack of jobs	27		29		26		30		29		29	
			28		31		27		30		29		29
	Lack of autonomy	1		2		1		–		–		–	
Society	Broken promises and governmental hypocrisy	19		20		20		16		17		18	
	Unemployment	14		11		14		16		17		18	
	Bureaucracy and anti-democratic attitudes	10	57	9	56	11	59	9	54	8	55	8	52
	Social inequality	7		10		6		6		–		3	
	Society's tolerance	7		6		8		7		13		5	
Values	Conflict between generations	3		33		4		1		8		–	
Criticisms	Imitation of protest movements in other countries	7		6		7		8		–		16	
	Students' indecision about what they want	1	12	–	9	–	11	1	14	–	8	–	19
	Extremists' agitation but not a movement	4		3		4		5		8		3	

TABLE 7.10b.   Student Judgment of the Student Movement by Political Tendency (Percent).

Australia	RIGHT	CENT.	LEFT	FAR L.	APOL.
Evaluation					
The militant students are only a small minority.	(39) 98	(265) 96	(229) 92	(35) 89	(182) 98
The student movement usually reflects a considerable degree of immaturity.*	72	(266) 64	(230) 49	49	(179) 59
The student movement is essentially democratic in regard to its goals.*	(38) 40	(251) 45	(221) 70	(32) 69	(160) 45
The student movement is essentially democratic in regard to its means.*	(32) 19	(241) 30	(211) 46	53	(153) 32
Contributions					
The student movement has revealed truths new to the older generation.**	(38) 58	(256) 64	(222) 76	(33) 79	(172) 65
The student protest has led to the improvement of the university.**	58	(249) 61	(226) 80	(35) 80	(164) 62

TABLE 7.10a. Evaluation, Contributions, and Goals of the Student Movement by Students of the Far Left (Percent).

	AUSTRAL.	AUS.	FR.	GB	IT.	JAP.	NIG.	SP.	TUN.	USA
Evaluation										
The militant students are only a small minority. **	(35) 89	(66) 92	(99) 83	(72) 83	(68) 78	(120) 77	(21) 67	(81) 72	(23) 65	(25) 68
The student movement usually reflects a considerable degree of immaturity. *	49	53	(93) 41	(71) 56	(65) 59	72	43	(82) 44	39	52
The student movement is essentially democratic in regard to its goals. *	(32) 69	89	(91) 80	(59) 71	(64) 80	(105) 66	81	(81) 79	(22) 82	(21) 57
The student movement is essentially democratic in regard to its means.[1]	53	82	(80) 39	(58) 53		(113) 35	68	(77) 72		33
Contributions										
The student movement has revealed truths new to the older generation. *	(33) 79	79	(94) 93	(68) 71	(66) 85	(119) 88	(18) 78	(78) 85	(25) 96	(25) 64
The student protest has led to the improvement of the university. *	(35) 80	76	47	(65) 82	(69) 75	(115) 64	(21) 87	(80) 58	80	(24) 92
Goals										
One of the goals of the student movement should be to establish a common front among students and workers.[2]	(36) 78	88	(95) 83	(69) 80	93	(111) 76	(20) 85	(83) 92		(21) 71
Students throughout the world should coordinate their efforts toward a revolutionary goal.[2]	(36) 84	(65) 89	(89) 92	(68) 72	(64) 92	(104) 65	(21) 86	(80) 88		(23) 83
Students should leave the university for the factory in order to help the workers in their struggle.[2]	(33) 39	(66) 70	(87) 26	(67) 33	(67) 55	(107) 18	62	(81) 46		9
One of the goals of the student movement should be the destruction of the present form of government.[2]	(34) 74	82	(83) 82	(68) 71	87	(115) 84	38	(83) 96		(24) 58

* p < .01
** p < .05
1. This item did not appear in the Italian or Tunisian questionnaire.
2. This item did not appear in the Tunisian questionnaire.

TABLE 7.10b   Continued

Australia	RIGHT	CENT.	LEFT	FAR L.	APOL.
Goals					
One of the goals of the student movement should be to establish a common front among students and workers.*	(39) 26	(244) 37	(219) 60	(36) 78	(171) 43
Students throughout the world should coordinate their efforts toward a revolutionary goal.*	(40) 15	(256) 22	(226) 46	84	23
Students should leave the university for the factory in order to help the workers in their struggle.*	(38) –	(262) 5	(219) 10	(33) 39	(181) 4
One of the goals of the student movement should be the destruction of the present form of government.*	(39) 8	(268) 11	(221) 35	(34) 74	(180) 16

Austria	RIGHT	CENT.	LEFT	FAR L.	APOL.
Evaluation					
The militant students are only a small minority.	(82) 93	(150) 92	(136) 86	(66) 92	(43) 88
The student movement usually reflects a considerable degree of immaturity.**	72	63	56	53	(44) 70
The student movement is essentially democratic in regard to its goals.**	(81) 63	(147) 77	(130) 79	89	(45) 69
The student movement is essentially democratic in regard to its means.*	(80) 61	(150) 58	(131) 66	82	47
Contributions					
The student movement has revealed truths new to the older generation.*	(81) 48	(152) 64	(136) 76	79	48
The student protest has led to the improvement of the university.**	(82) 67	76	(137) 83	76	(44) 57
Goals					
One of the goals of the student movement should be to establish a common front among students and workers.*	(79) 16	22	(137) 57	88	(45) 31
Students throughout the world should coordinate their efforts toward a revolutionary goal.*	(81) 14	(148) 21	60	(65) 89	(44) 21
Students should leave the university for the factory in order to help the workers in their struggle.*	(79) 4	(149) 11	(135) 40	(66) 70	(45) 7
One of the goals of the student movement should be the destruction of the present form of government.*	(81) 15	(152) 19	(137) 37	82	(44) 23

France	RIGHT	CENT.	LEFT	COMM.	FAR L.	ANAR.	APOL.
Evaluation							
The militant students are only a small minority.	(40) 85	(134) 95	(196) 94	(48) 96	(99) 83	(30) 97	(153) 93
The student movement usually reflects a considerable degree of immaturity.*	(43) 65	(132) 60	(195) 49	(45) 67	(93) 41	(31) 26	(149) 57
The student movement is essentially democratic in regard to its goals.*	(36) 22	(120) 38	(183) 73	(43) 77	(91) 80	(27) 74	(128) 53
The student movement is essentially democratic in regard to its means.*	(39) 5	12	(178) 26	(40) 43	(80) 39	(25) 44	(131) 25

Contributions

The student movement has revealed truths new to the older generation.*	(41) 68	(131) 76	(190) 84	(41) 63	(94) 93	(31) 87	(140) 88
The student protest has led to the improvement of the university.*	(39) 51	44	(187) 58	(44) 61	47	(30) 27	(141) 48

Goals

One of the goals of the student movement should be to establish a common front among students and workers.*	(38) 11	(126) 21	(184) 55	98	(95) 83	(31) 81	(129) 42
Students throughout the world should coordinate their efforts toward a revolutionary goal.*	11	15	(169) 53	(38) 90	(89) 92	(30) 90	(127) 42
Students should leave the university for the factory in order to help the workers in their struggle.**	(42) 7	(128) 8	(192) 11	(44) 23	(87) 26	(28) 25	(142) 10
One of the goals of the student movement should be the destruction of the present form of government.*	12	13	(191) 51	(43) 81	(83) 82	(31) 81	(138) 35

Great Britain	RIGHT	CENT.	LEFT	FAR L.	APOL.
Evaluation					
The militant students are only a small minority.	(87) 93	(88) 95	(195) 90	(72) 83	(145) 92
The student movement usually reflects a considerable degree of immaturity.*	(89) 76	(87) 68	(188) 54	(71) 56	(142) 63
The student movement is essentially democratic in regard to its goals.*	(80) 43	(84) 42	(183) 50	(59) 71	(124) 52
The student movement is essentially democratic in regard to its means.**	(67) 30	(77) 34	(173) 46	(58) 53	(120) 48
Contributions					
The student movement has revealed truths new to the older generation.**	(84) 57	(84) 58	(189) 75	(68) 71	(137) 64
The student protest has led to the improvement of the university.**	(82) 61	(82) 83	(185) 84	(65) 82	(134) 78
Goals					
One of the goals of the student movement should be to establish a common front among students and workers.*	(85) 22	(77) 36	68	(69) 80	(127) 57
Students throughout the world should coordinate their efforts toward a revolutionary goal.*	(88) 10	(84) 20	(182) 41	(68) 72	(139) 22
Students should leave the university for the factory in order to help the workers in their struggle.**	(89) 2	(81) 10	(184) 10	(67) 33	(142) 6
One of the goals of the student movement should be the destruction of the present form of government.*	(86) 7	(91) 10	38	(68) 71	(141) 19

(cont.)

TABLE 7.10b   Continued

Italy	Far R.	Right	Cent.	Left	Comm.	Far L.	Apol.
Evaluation							
The militant students are only a small minority.*	(28) 89	(60) 92	(141) 87	(209) 83	(105) 67	(68) 78	(152) 81
The student movement usually reflects a considerable degree of immaturity.*	(30) 90	(64) 94	(144) 85	(218) 78	(106) 56	(65) 59	(164) 78
The student movement is essentially democratic in regard to its goals.*	(27) 15	(62) 13	(132) 37	(205) 50	(99) 83	(64) 80	(148) 59
The student movement is essentially democratic in regard to its means.[1]							
Contributions							
The student movement has revealed truths new to the older generation.*	(31) 58	(63) 44	(141) 70	(216) 79	(107) 87	(66) 85	(162) 82
The student protest has led to the improvement of the university.*	(29) 59	46	(147) 74	(211) 75	(100) 85	(69) 75	(167) 83
Goals							
One of the goals of the student movement should be to establish a common front among students and workers.*	(28) 32	(59) 25	(131) 39	66	(112) 96	93	(161) 60
Students throughout the world should coordinate their efforts toward a revolutionary goal.**	(27) 15	(61) 10	(133) 23	(190) 36	(97) 87	(64) 92	(153) 44
Students should leave the university for the factory in order to help the workers in their struggle.*	(29) 3	(64) 6	(146) 8	(206) 23	(100) 60	(67) 55	(163) 23
One of the goals of the student movement should be the destruction of the present form of government.**	(26) 69	(51) 63	(128) 66	(210) 71	(106) 88	87	(145) 64

Japan	Cent.	Left	Far L.	Apol.
Evaluation				
The militant students are only a small minority.	(150) 91	(42) 91	(120) 77	(104) 92
The student movement usually reflects a considerable degree of immaturity.	87	(43) 88	72	(103) 87
The student movement is essentially democratic in regard to its goals.	(126) 48	(39) 64	(105) 66	(84) 58
The student movement is essentially democratic in regard to its means.	(139) 19	(42) 31	(113) 35	(94) 19
Contributions				
The student movement has revealed truths new to the older generation.	73	(41) 85	(119) 88	(93) 86
The student protest has led to the improvement of the. university.	(144) 63	59	(115) 64	(97) 65
Goals				
One of the goals of the student movement should be to	(124)	(36)	(111)	(82)

establish a common front among students and workers.**	50	69	76	59
Students throughout the world should coordinate their efforts toward a revolutionary goal.*	(127) 31	(38) 42	(104) 65	(90) 32
Students should leave the university for the factory in order to help the workers in their struggle.	(136) 6	(37) 11	(107) 18	(91) 12
One of the goals of the student movement should be the destruction of the present form of government.	(140) 67	(41) 78	(115) 84	(97) 67

Nigeria	RIGHT	CRITIC.	LEFT	FAR L.	DESCR.	APOL.
Evaluation						
The militant students are only a small minority.**	(41) 88	(36) 89	(44) 84	(21) 67	(27) 81	(54) 82
The student movement usually reflects a considerable degree of immaturity.**	(40) 45	39	(40) 35	43	(26) 31	28
The student movement is essentially democratic in regard to its goals.**	(39) 85	(35) 63	73	81	73	(55) 82
The student movement is essentially democratic in regard to its means.**	(37) 59	(31) 61	63	68	(21) 72	76
Contributions						
The student movement has revealed truths new to the older generation.**	(39) 74	(34) 82	(42) 93	(18) 78	(26) 77	(54) 89
The student protest has led to the improvement of the university.	(41) 81	(36) 92	(43) 77	(21) 87	(28) 86	(53) 83
Goals						
One of the goals of the student movement should be to establish a common front among students and workers.	(40) 75	(36) 89	86	(20) 85	(25) 76	81
Students throughout the world should coordinate their efforts toward a revolutionary goal.*	(41) 51	67	(41) 83	(21) 86	(24) 63	(54) 80
Students should leave the university for the factory in order to help the workers in their struggle.*	(37) 27	(34) 53	(43) 37	62	(26) 19	(53) 23
One of the goals of the student movement should be the destruction of the present form of government.**	(42) 24	32	(44) 50	38	(27) 26	(51) 27

Spain	RIGHT	CENT.	LEFT	FAR L.	APOL.
Evaluation					
The militant students are only a small minority.	(60) 87	(108) 85	(268) 83	(81) 72	(150) 87
The student movement usually reflects a considerable degree of immaturity.	(61) 56	(118) 41	(272) 52	(82) 44	(183) 56
The student movement is essentially democratic in regard to its goals.*	(54) 50	(113) 58	(265) 67	(81) 79	(154) 48
The student movement is essentially democratic in regard to its means.*	(55) 27	(109) 40	(267) 45	(77) 72	(159) 27
Contributions					
The student movement has revealed truths new to the older generation.**	(60) 68	(112) 87	(275) 88	(78) 85	(169) 75
The student protest has led to the improvement of the university.**	(61) 56	(113) 63	(265) 72	(80) 58	(173) 54

(cont.)

TABLE 7.10b   Continued

Spain	Right	Cent.	Left	Far L.	Apol.
Goals					
One of the goals of the student movement should be to establish a common front among students and workers.*	(58) 35	(105) 49	(269) 80	(83) 92	(156) 46
Students throughout the world should coordinate their efforts toward a revolutionary goal.*	(59) 29	(108) 31	(263) 70	(80) 88	(165) 25
Students should leave the university for the factory in order to help the workers in their struggle.*	(60) 13	(114) 18	(270) 32	(81) 46	(175) 10
One of the goals of the student movement should be the destruction of the present form of government.*	(53) 30	(111) 43	(267) 73	(83) 96	(152) 39

Tunisia[2]	Right	Bourguib.	Left	Far L.	Apol.
Evaluation					
The militant students are only a small minority.*	(14) 93	(15) 80	(49) 78	(23) 65	(27) 85
The student movement usually reflects a considerable degree of immaturity.*	50	20	(48) 33	39	(31) 36
The student movement is essentially democratic in regard to its goals.**	71	73	(46) 87	(22) 82	(22) 68
Contributions					
The student movement has revealed truths new to the older generation.**	(11) 82	(16) 81	(48) 98	(25) 96	(30) 77
The student protest has led to the improvement of the university.**	(12) 75	(14) 64	88	80	83

United States	Right	Cent.	Lib.	Left	Far L.	Apol.
Evaluation						
The militant students are only a small minority.**	(76) 92	(125) 93	(190) 91	(136) 89	(25) 68	(86) 88
The student movement usually reflects a considerable degree of immaturity.*	(77) 70	(124) 54	(191) 47	(135) 43	52	(89) 55
The student movement is essentially democratic in regard to its goals.*	(69) 35	(116) 51	(186) 54	(124) 65	(21) 57	(72) 42
The student movement is essentially democratic in regard to its means.	22	(118) 28	(185) 30	(125) 30	33	(74) 30
Contributions						
The student movement has revealed truths new to the older generation.	(77) 61	(126) 66	(184) 68	(135) 68	(25) 64	(83) 61
The student protest has led to the improvement of the university.*	(74) 43	(119) 77	(187) 81	(131) 87	(24) 92	(80) 76
Goals						
One of the goals of the student movement should be to establish a common front among students and workers.*	(61) 38	(102) 49	(170) 59	(124) 73	(21) 71	(72) 63
Students throughout the world should coordinate their efforts toward a revolutionary goal.*	(75) 1	(126) 21	(181) 28	(131) 54	(23) 83	(76) 33
Students should leave the university for the factory in order to help the workers in their struggle.	(73) 7	(124) 5	(188) 4	(126) 6	9	(80) 5

One of the goals of the student movement should be the destruction of the present form of government.*	(75) 0	(128) 9	(194) 11	(131) 31	(24) 58	(83) 14

Yugoslavia[3]	IDEAL.	REAL.	HUMAN.	ELIT.	INDIV.
Evaluation					
The militant students are only a small minority.	(238) 80	(491) 88	(161) 87	(26) 85	(40) 83
The student movement usually reflects a considerable degree of immaturity.	(237) 14	(494) 13	17	12	(41) 29
The student movement is essentially democratic in regard to its goals.	(239) 90	(489) 88	85	(25) 76	(40) 73
Contributions					
The student movement has revealed truths new to the older generation.	(241) 62	(487) 54	(160) 49	(26) 62	53
The student protest has led to the improvement of the university.	(239) 62	(495) 55	56	65	(42) 52
Goals					
One of the goals of the student movement should be to establish a common front among students and workers.**	(237) 78	(489) 68	64	77	(40) 56
Students throughout the world should coordinate their efforts toward a revolutionary goal.	(238) 71	(491) 77	(161) 74	(24) 67	(41) 73
One of the goals of the student movement should be the destruction of the present form of government.	(239) 23	(494) 17	12	(25) 12	17

*$p < .01$
**$p < .05$
1. This item did not appear in the Italian questionnaire.
2. Only the following items appeared in the Tunisian questionnaire.
3. Only the following items appeared in the Yugoslavian questionnaire.

TABLE 7.11a. Attitudes toward Violence by Political Tendency (Percent).

Australia	RIGHT	CENT.	LEFT	FAR L.	APOL.
Violence as a political technique is to be condemned.*	(40) 93	(271) 92	(230) 90	(35) 69	(186) 91
Violence, when used to reach valid goals rapidly, is legitimate.*	(39) 13	(264) 17	(225) 28	(34) 47	(183) 20
Violence is the most effective form of action capable of producing profound social changes.*	15	(265) 22	(223) 31	(32) 47	(182) 24

Austria	RIGHT	CENT.	LEFT	FAR L.	APOL.
Violence as a political technique is to be condemned.*	(82) 88	(150) 86	(135) 76	(68) 37	(45) 89
Violence, when used to reach valid goals rapidly, is legitimate.*	18	(151) 13	34	(66) 67	27
Violence is the most effective form of action capable of producing profound social changes.*	18	15	29	(68) 56	13

France	RIGHT	CENT.	LEFT	COMM.	FAR L.	ANAR.	APOL.
Violence as a political technique is to be condemned.*	(42) 71	(133) 83	(194) 66	(42) 38	(97) 31	(33) 33	(145) 78

(cont.)

TABLE 7.11a   Continued

France	RIGHT	CENT.	LEFT	COMM.	FAR L.	ANAR.	APOL.
Violence, when used to reach valid goals rapidly, is legitimate.*	(41) 44	32	(196) 58	(41) 68	(95) 79	(28) 89	(146) 51
Violence is the most effective form of action capable of producing profound social changes.*	(42) 41	28	(199) 46	(44) 48	63	(32) 78	(148) 33

Great Britain		RIGHT	CENT.	LEFT	FAR L.	APOL.
Violence as a political technique is to be condemned.*		(89) 94	(91) 97	(197) 83	(70) 70	(147) 92
Violence, when used to reach valid goals rapidly, is legitimate.*		(88) 6	(87) 18	(190) 29	(71) 55	(143) 17
Violence is the most effective form of action capable of producing profound social changes.*		(89) 25	(90) 37	(189) 29	(68) 56	(148) 23

Italy	FAR R.	RIGHT	CENT.	LEFT	COMM.	FAR L.	APOL.
Violence as a political technique is to be condemned.*	(31) 81	(63) 94	(153) 92	(220) 93	(99) 59	(67) 46	(172) 95
Violence, when used to reach valid goals rapidly, is legitimate.*	(27) 15	(66) 12	(148) 12	(213) 30	(105) 85	(66) 74	(170) 32
Violence is the most effective form of action capable of producing profound social changes.*	(28) 39	(65) 14	12	22	(103) 74	(68) 72	(167) 25

Japan			CENT.	LEFT	FAR L.	APOL.
Violence as a political technique is to be condemned.*			(153) 89	(44) 86	(117) 80	(105) 90
Violence, when used to reach valid goals rapidly, is legitimate.*			(142) 23	(41) 29	(116) 48	(102) 29
Violence is the most effective form of action capable of producing profound social changes.*			(138) 27	(40) 35	(114) 47	(100) 26

Nigeria	RIGHT	CRITIC.	LEFT	FAR L.	DESCR.	APOL.
Violence as a political technique is to be condemned.**	(39) 69	(36) 61	(44) 64	(21) 52	(27) 70	(54) 74
Violence, when used to reach valid goals rapidly, is legitimate.**	(40) 60	75	71	81	(28) 64	(55) 71
Violence is the most effective form of action capable of producing profound social changes.**	(42) 41	56	(45) 53	52	(27) 41	33

Spain	RIGHT	CENT.	LEFT	FAR L.	APOL.
Violence as a political technique is to be condemned.*	(61) 87	(121) 89	(274) 77	(79) 32	(177) 84
Violence, when used to reach valid goals rapidly, is legitimate.*	(62) 32	(120) 56	(272) 69	(82) 95	38
Violence is the most effective form of action capable of producing profound social changes.*	24	(119) 31	(271) 54	(80) 86	(176) 28

Tunisia[1]	RIGHT	BOURGUIB.	LEFT	FAR L.	APOL.
Violence as a political technique is to be condemned.*	(15) 73	(16) 75	(47) 68	(25) 48	(33) 88

Violence is the most effective form of action capable of producing profound social changes.*	(14) 57	(15) 47	(49) 55	84	39

United States	RIGHT	CENT.	LIB.	LEFT	FAR L.	APOL.
Violence as a political technique is to be condemned.**	(78) 83	(197) 84	(192) 86	(131) 78	(25) 64	(89) 80
Violence, when used to reach valid goals rapidly, is legitimate.*	6	(126) 12	(187) 21	(129) 28	(23) 39	(83) 24
Violence is the most effective form of action capable of producing profound social changes.*	(79) 18	(125) 19	(185) 30	40	(24) 54	(88) 35

*p < .01
**p < .05
1. Only these following two items were included in the Tunisian questionnaire.

TABLE 7.13a. Agreement with Certain Kinds of Actions Undertaken at the University by Political Tendency (Percent).

Australia	RIGHT	CENT.	LEFT	FAR L.	APOL.
Working through elected student representatives*	(39) 95	(269) 90	(231) 85	(35) 63	(184) 86
Petitioning and meeting with administration	(40) 93	(268) 89	(233) 92	(36) 78	(185) 87
Demonstrations*	23	(270) 40	74	89	(187) 40
Picketing and blocking access to university facilities*	(39) 3	(268) 4	(232) 18	50	(186) 8
Striking and boycotting classes*	(40) 18	(264) 17	(231) 33	(35) 66	(181) 13
Disrupting classes*	–	(268) 3	10	37	(185) 3
Sit-in and occupation of buildings*	8	(270) 7	19	(36) 47	(187) 11
Destroying property**	–	1	(233) 5	(34) 21	(184) 1
Attack on members of administration	–	(271) –	(232) –	(35) 3	–
Attack on members of the faculty who disagree	–	(270) –	(233) 1	3	(187) –

Austria	RIGHT	CENT.	LEFT	FAR L.	APOL.
Working through elected student representatives*	(82) 90	(151) 88	(137) 83	(67) 61	(45) 82
Petitioning and meeting with administration**	(81) 86	91	93	69	91
Demonstrations*	(82) 23	33	61	(68) 82	18
Picketing and blocking access to university facilities*	2	(150) 8	23	(67) 52	7
Striking and boycotting classes*	15	(151) 15	35	(68) 68	11
Disrupting classes*	7	5	18	57	7
Sit-in and occupation of buildings*	9	4	17	59	9
Destroying property**	–	1	(136) 4	29	2

(cont.)

TABLE 7.13a   Continued

Austria	Right	Cent.	Left	Far L.	Apol.
Attack on members of administration*			(137)		
	–	–	8	37	2
Attack on members of the faculty who disagree	–	–	1	7	2

France	Right	Cent.	Left	Comm.	Far L.	Anar.	Apol.
Working through elected student representatives*	(37)	(131)	(189)	(49)	(92)	(32)	(135)
	84	83	85	78	65	47	76
Petitioning and meeting with administration*	(39)	(133)	(198)	(47)	(94)	(31)	(146)
	100	87	86	81	70	48	90
Demonstrations*			(197)	(46)		(32)	(142)
	26	37	75	86	89	75	50
Picketing and blocking access to university facilities*	(41)	(131)	(194)	(43)	(88)	(30)	(146)
	2	9	39	68	65	67	14
Striking and boycotting classes*	(40)	(132)	(191)	(45)	(93)	(31)	
	10	26	66	89	84	81	43
Disrupting classes*	(41)		(188)			(30)	(148)
	12	21	42	69	75	70	32
Sit-in and occupation of buildings*	(39)	(133)	(190)	(43)	(94)	(31)	(144)
	8	14	43	67	76	81	31
Destroying property**	(41)	(135)	(195)	(47)	(90)		(151)
	5	2	2	4	16	29	5
Attack on members of administration**	(39)	(136)	(202)	(46)	(92)		(153)
	3	2	2	4	8	23	4
Attack on members of the faculty who disagree		(135)	(200)	(47)	(91)		(154)
	3	2	3	9	10	19	4

Great Britain	Right	Cent.	Left	Far L.	Apol.
Working through elected student representatives*	(87)	(88)	(195)	(70)	(150)
	90	90	82	61	80
Petitioning and meeting with administration		(90)	(199)	(71)	(149)
	82	87	85	88	86
Demonstrations*	(88)	(91)	(197)		(146)
	24	39	65	87	41
Picketing and blocking access to university facilities*		(89)	(195)	(70)	(147)
	3	8	21	44	8
Striking and boycotting classes*		(91)	(196)	(71)	(149)
	7	13	26	54	13
Disrupting classes**		(90)	(194)		(148)
	2	2	13	31	3
Sit-in and occupation of buildings**				(70)	(144)
	2	4	19	37	10
Destroying property**		(91)	(197)		(148)
	–	–	6	20	2
Attack on members of administration			(198)		(149)
	–	–	1	4	1
Attack on members of the faculty who disagree			(197)	(71)	(150)
	–	–	2	3	1

Italy	Far R.	Right	Cent.	Left	Comm.	Far L.	Apol.
Working through elected student representatives*	(29)	(65)	(151)	(226)	(111)	(70)	(171)
	48	66	76	72	37	34	68
Petitioning and meeting with administration[1]							

Demonstrations*	(31) 19	(67) 11	24	(225) 52	82	(72) 86	(173) 41
Picketing and blocking access to university facilities*	(30) –	(65) 2	(150) 7	20	70	60	(167) 15
Striking and boycotting classes*	(31) 3	(67) 3	(152) 12	(227) 24	68	67	(173) 15
Disrupting classes*	3	–	7	(225) 16	(109) 65	(71) 58	(172) 10
Sit-in and occupation of buildings	(30) 7	5	(148) 8	(227) 21	(107) 70	(72) 71	(165) 15
Destroying property	(32) 3	–	(152) –	· 1	(109) 14	(70) 11	(169) 2
Attack on members of administration	(31) 7	–	(153) –	(226) 1	(108) 12	(68) 16	(168) 2
Attack on members of the faculty who disagree	3	–	–	(227) 2	(107) 9	(70) 16	2

Japan	CENT.	LEFT	FAR L.	APOL.
Working through elected student representatives	(153) 60	(42) 62	(120) 51	(97) 57
Petitioning and meeting with administration	(154) 68	(44) 68	(124) 81	(106) 72
Demonstrations*	53	75	(125) 86	(108) 56
Picketing and blocking access to university facilities**	(152) 14	(43) 26	(124) 41	(104) 17
Striking and boycotting classes*	(158) 35	42	(122) 65	(105) 31
Disrupting classes**	(153) 8	14	(124) 29	(106) 6
Sit-in and occupation of buildings**	(154) 12	(42) 19	(123) 39	(105) 9
Destroying property	(153) 5	–	18	(106) 3
Attack on members of administration	(149) 3	(44) 7	(121) 13	(104) 3
Attack on members of the faculty who disagree	(151) 1	–	(119) 12	(108) 4

Nigeria	RIGHT	CRITIC.	LEFT	FAR L.	DESCR.	APOL.
Working through elected student representatives	(41) 88	(36) 78	(42) 81	(20) 75	(28) 86	(56) 84
Petitioning and meeting with administration**	56	(35) 57	52	60	(26) 81	(55) 47
Demonstrations	(42) 48	54	62	65	(28) 57	(57) 54
Picketing and blocking access to university facilities	(40) 15	(32) 16	10	(19) 16	(25) 4	(53) 11
Striking and boycotting classes**	(42) 26	(35) 49	(43) 35	(20) 55	(28) 29	(55) 29
Disrupting classes	(40) 13	(34) 18	(40) 5	20	(27) 11	(54) 11
Sit-in and occupation of buildings**	(37) 14	(32) 28	13	(19) 47	(23) 13	(44) 11

(cont.)

TABLE 7.13a   Continued

Nigeria	RIGHT	CRITIC.	LEFT	FAR L.	DESCR.	APOL.
Destroying property	(39)	(34)	(41)		(24)	(52)
	–	3	2	11	–	4
Attack on members of administration	(40)	(35)		(20)	(27)	
	–	6	7	5	–	–
Attack on members of the faculty who disagree		(34)				
	–	3	7	5	–	–

Spain	RIGHT	CENT.	LEFT	FAR L.	APOL.
Working through elected student representatives	(60)	(122)	(281)	(81)	(185)
	83	91	82	69	89
Petitioning and meeting with administration*	(59)	(116)	(270)	(79)	(173)
	76	83	77	49	83
Demonstrations*	(60)	(120)	(271)	(83)	(180)
	28	50	77	88	42
Picketing and blocking access to university facilities*	(61)	(118)	(267)	(81)	(181)
	8	18	45	79	13
Striking and boycotting classes*	(60)	(117)	(272)	(82)	
	22	34	64	92	27
Disrupting classes*	(61)	(120)	(276)	(80)	(183)
	11	32	49	83	19
Sit-in and occupation of buildings*			(277)	(82)	(182)
	20	37	69	92	27
Destroying property*	(60)	(119)	(275)	(80)	(184)
	2	4	9	40	2
Attack on members of administration**	(58)	(122)	(273)	(76)	(185)
	–	7	7	28	1
Attack on members of the faculty who disagree**	(60)	(121)	(275)	(79)	(184)
	2	7	6	38	3

Tunisia²	RIGHT	BOURGUIB.	LEFT	FAR L.	APOL.
Working through elected student representatives*	(15)	(13)	(42)	(22)	(30)
	11	10	91	77	80
Petitioning and meeting with administration		(14)	(47)	(20)	(29)
	93	86	81	75	90

United States	RIGHT	CENT.	LIB.	LEFT	FAR L.	APOL.
Working through elected student representatives**	(80)	(127)	(196)	(135)	(26)	(92)
	93	92	88	85	65	83
Petitioning and meeting with administration	(79)	(129)		(137)		(91)
	91	97	93	94	81	87
Demonstrations*	(80)		(194)			
	40	55	75	84	85	63
Picketing and blocking access to university facilities*		(128)	(193)	(135)		(90)
	3	9	16	28	39	14
Striking and boycotting classes*			(195)	(136)		(91)
	8	14	29	47	62	35
Disrupting classes**		(129)	(194)			(90)
	–	4	–	10	19	4
Sit-in and occupation of buildings**	(79)	(127)	(193)	(137)		(91)
	4	8	13	24	27	11
Destroying property	(80)		(192)	(135)	(25)	(90)
	1	–	1	3	12	2

Attack on members of administration	(129)	(195)	(134)	(26)	(91)
1	–	1	–	4	4
Attack on members of the faculty who disagree	(128)				
–	–	1	–	4	1

	By Political Self-Definition				
Yugoslavia[3]	IDEAL.	REAL.	HUMAN.	ELIT.	INDIV.
Working through elected student representatives	(239) 89	(490) 91	(161) 93	(26) 92	(41) 81
Petitioning and meeting with administration	(236) 89	90	89	77	83
Demonstrations	(237) 80	(491) 82	(160) 81	(25) 85	64
Striking and boycotting classes	(238) 26	(494) 28	(163) 31	(24) 31	(41) 22
Disrupting classes	(237) 9	(491) 7	(160) 9	8	5
Sit-in and occupation of buildings	29	(486) 24	(161) 31	(25) 39	(38) 13
Destroying property	(238) 2	(490) –	1	(24) –	(41) 2
Attack on members of the faculty who disagree	3	(491) –	1	(26) –	(42) 5

	By Member Comm. League		
Yugoslavia[3]	YES	DES. TO	REF. TO
Working through elected student representatives	(117) 92	(174) 91	(781) 89
Petitioning and meeting with administration	(118) 87	(173) 87	(779) 88
Demonstrations	(116) 83	(172) 81	78
Striking and boycotting classes	37	(174) 24	(780) 26
Disrupting classes	9	9	(778) 7
Sit-in and occupation of buildings	35	(173) 24	(774) 26
Destroying property	1	(174) 2	(781) 1
Attack on members of the faculty who disagree	3	1	2

*p < .01
**p < .05
1. This item was not available in Italy.
2. Only the following two items were available in Tunisia.
3. Only the following items were available in Yugoslavia.

TABLE 7.13b. Far Left Students' Agreement with Certain Kinds of Actions Undertaken at the University (Percent).

	AUSTRAL.	AUSTRIA	FRANCE	GB	ITALY	JAPAN	NIG.	SP.	USA
Working through elected student representatives*	(35) 63	(67) 61	(92) 65	(70) 61	(70) 34	(120) 51	(20) 75	(81) 69	(26) 65
Petitioning and meeting with administration	(36) 78	69	(94) 70	(71) 88		(124) 81	60	(79) 49	81
Demonstrations*	89	(68) 82	89	87	(72) 86	(125) 86	65	(83) 88	85
Picketing and blocking access to university facilities*	50	(67) 52	(88) 65	(70) 44	60	(124) 41	(19) 16	(81) 79	39
Striking and boycotting classes*	(35) 66	(68) 68	(93) 84	(71) 54	67	(122) 65	(20) 55	(82) 92	62
Disrupting classes*	37	57	75	31	(71) 58	(124) 29	20	(80) 83	19
Sit-in and occupation of buildings*	(36) 47	59	(94) 76	(70) 37	(72) 71	(123) 39	(19) 47	(82) 92	27
Destroying property*	(34) 21	29	(90) 16	20	(70) 11	18	11	(80) 40	(25) 12
Attack on members of administration*	(35) 3	37	(92) 8	4	(68) 16	(121) 13	(20) 5	(76) 28	(26) 4
Attack on members of the faculty who disagree*	3	7	(91) 10	(71) 3	(70) 16	(119) 12	5	(79) 38	4

*p <.01

Chapter 8

A Political Typology

In this chapter, we present the results of a different statistical approach based on a recent development in factor analysis known as "analysis of correspondences." In one sense this follows, and should be read in connection with, the data treated in Chapter 3. It is, however, somewhat more technical, and the results have been obtained in such a different manner that we regarded it as advisable to present this chapter after the analysis had been completed in terms of cross-tabulation.

We shall try to answer two questions. First, to what degree do the political self-definitions of the students reflect a particular attitudinal reality? In other words, what is the degree of coherence between general attitudes toward society, the social and political decisions one is prepared to make, and one's political self-definition?

The second question refers to the problems of disparities and similarities among political groups. To what extent, for example, do the French students of the right differ from those of the center or the apoliticals in terms of a general attitude? Does a political spectrum going from the right to the extreme left exist in all the countries studied?

We are less interested in specific attitudes than in the general configuration of opinions which distinguishes one political orientation from the others. We shall attempt to determine whether one finds, from one country to another, a particular attitudinal configuration paired with a particular political orientation.

In order to establish the relations between political self-definition and sociopolitical attitudes as well as to determine the common points which may exist between the various political groups, we proceeded to a factor analysis of correspondences.[1]

[1]Generally, factor analysis is one of the methods used to extract the dimensions (called factors or axes) that appear to sustain a given set of attitudes and opinions. These factors may be conceived as hypothetical variables that explain in a simple manner the relations observed between different objects of attitudes. In fact, factor analyses have good descriptive capacities for the distribution of variables in terms of their proximities as well as their associations and oppositions. They thus permit us to go beyond discrete responses by making apparent structural facts which escape direct observation. It is through these structural facts or interrelations of a certain number of attitudes that one may clarify the nature and extract the "factors" or essential dimensions that subtend the set of attitudes and opinions seen in a given population.

Factor analysis of *correspondences* was developed by Benzecri (1973). The method differs mainly from the other systems of factor analysis in that it is based on the principle of distributional equivalence, and defines a distributional distance similar to the distance of the chi square between two laws of frequency. Furthermore, the null hypothesis corresponds to a table in which all lines (or columns) have the same profile, that is, they are *proportional among themselves* and not, as in other analyses, to a table in which the lines (or columns) are equal. Differences in the weights of the elements may thus be eliminated (see for details Appendix 2, section A).

The forty-six questions[2] retained for this analysis represent all the variables included in our study on the social and political system and on the role of the university within the society as well as questions on the student movement's goals and tactics.

The method of analysis permits us also to determine the distribution of variables describing the respondents' political orientation, social class, sex, age, discipline, etc., in relation to that of the attitudinal variables. Thus, in addition to attitudinal variables (active variables) a number of socioenvironmental characteristics of the students and their political self-definition[3] were included as *supplementary* variables. This method has a special advantage where supplementary variables can be used as nonactive variables, i.e., where they do not intervene in the determination of the factorial axes. Nevertheless, their distribution upon each axis may be calculated in order to know exactly their degree of association and proximity with regard to the active variables.[4]

RESULTS

Only the first two factors (or axes) extracted by the respective analyses in each country will be retained in this study, since they are the most important in explaining the total variance of the responses.[5] In order to determine the degree of similarity of these axes between countries, we proceeded besides to an analysis of correlation between axes. Results indicate the existence (except in Tunisia) of a very strong correlation between the first, as well as the second, axes of all countries (Table 8.1, parts a, b, and c).[6]

Identification of the Basic Dimensions of the Sociopolitical Orientation

The results of the analyses of interaxial correlation permit us to state that in all the countries studied except Tunisia, the essential orientations with regard to the principal matters of political and social life are organized around two large dimen-

[2]The forty-six questions represent ninety-four variables. See Appendix 2, section B, for the complete description of the questions listed and the coding of responses.

[3]The identifiers retained are nine in number, representing about forty variables depending on the country studied. See Appendix II, section C, for details of the variables.

[4]We were unable to include in this volume the graphics to which reference is made in the present chapter; the need to reduce their size for purposes of inclusion would have made it impossible for the reader to understand them. The graphics are, however, in our possession and remain at the disposition of those who might wish to examine them.

[5]The total variance of the responses explained by the first two factors ranges from 17 to 20 percent according to the country studied. The first factor represents between 13 and 15 percent of the total percentage of inertia and the second between 5 and 7 percent. Other consecutive factors represent less than 3 percent each of the total variance, thus giving meanings which cannot be easily interpreted. It should be noted that in correspondence analysis of a questionnaire, we have a very secure first factor with a 10 percent ratio.

[6]These tables will be found at the end of the chapter. On the first axis the relatively weakest correlation appears to be between Yugoslavia and France (.80, Table 8.1a), the strongest between the United States and Australia (.95, Table 8.1b).

sions. The first, of an ideological nature, indicates the direction of political orientation, while the second reflects the intensity of political involvement.

TABLE 8.1.   Interaxial Correlation, First and Second Axes.

a	*France*	
	Axis 1	Axis 2
Italy	.89*	.85*
Spain	.87*	.79*
Austria	.91*	.88*
Yugoslavia	.80*	.74*
Great Britain	.88*	.86*
United States	.83*	.83*
Tunisia	.40	.18

b	*United States*	
	Axis 1	Axis 2
Australia	.95*	.91*
Japan	.88*	.74*
Great Britain	.92*	.87*

c	*Great Britain*	
	Axis 1	Axis 2
Nigeria	.83*	.81*

*Highly significant correlation.

The first dimension, or first factorial axis extracted by the analyses, has been characterized as the *ideological axis*, and opposes the "conservative" ideology to the "transformationist" ideology.

The *conservative ideology* is defined by a set of attitudes favorable to the dominant social and political system of the country. In fact, one observes an intercorrelation of attitudes opposed to the elimination of nationalism, elimination of nuclear and biological armaments, and changes in the university system, as well as an opposition to all movements or acts which attempt to question society as it currently exists. On the other hand, there is a desire to maintain neutrality at the university—the view that students should use their energy for study and not attempt social or political action which could only harm their development. In this view, the role of the university in the society is not to innovate, and even less to foment revolution; on the contrary, it should be the privileged conveyor, transmitting the system as it is.

The correlation among the second axes of all countries is equally high, the lowest being between Yugoslavia and France, between the United States and Japan, (.74, Table 8.1a, 8.1b), and the highest being again between the United States and Australia (.91, Table 8.1b).

In Tunisia, on the other hand, the correlation of the first axis with those of the other countries is weak (.40, Table 8.1a) and practically nonexistent on the second axis (.18, Table 8.1a). The peculiarity of the factorial axes in Tunisia is due to the fact that numerous political questions were removed from that country's questionnaire, in particular those concerning revolution, violence, and types of action to be undertaken at the university. Thus a totally different orientation profile appeared.

The results indicate—except for Tunisia—that the sociopolitical orientation is structured by the intercorrelation of a certain number of attitudes that are very similar from one country to another. The basic dimensions (or factorial axes) extracted by the analyses thus will be very similar in all countries studied and can be presented all at once.

The *transformationist ideology* regroups a set of attitudes and opinions which, contrary to the conservative ideology, reflect a desire for change—more or less radical as it appears more or less distant from the origin of the axis. We find there all the great themes expressed by the "socialist" current of thought, with the extreme attitudes relating to revolutionary ideology. There must be a fight against capitalism, for more equality; and to the extremists, all kinds of action, even the most violent, appear as legitimate and effective means to combat the existing institutions.

Contrary to the conservatives, the transformationists are favorable to student movements, accenting the positive changes they have brought about at the university as well as in raising the consciousness of a certain number of people with regard to social, economic, and political problems and the effectiveness of protest. The transformationists consider that one of the important functions of the university is to act as an agent of change, whether by consciousness-raising or by participating in the revolutionary struggle. For the most extreme, the student movement should not remain within the university framework, but should participate in the workers' struggles and act as a liaison between the revolutionary movements of its own and other countries.

If the first axis indicated the direction of political orientation, the second axis extracted by the analyses shows that there is another essential dimension in political orientation: *intensity of political involvement*. The axis of intensity of political involvement seems to be structured by a set of attitudes once again very similar from one country to another (except Tunisia), and opposes extremism to moderation, whether on the conservative or transformationist side.

Extremism is defined on the conservative side as a very strong adherence to the status quo, the society as it exists being judged as very positive. The accent is on nationalism and economic protectionism. A strong army, equipped with the most modern weaponry, is also considered indispensable for guarding national integrity. Naturally this view comprises a strong reaction against any protest movement which attempts to question the existing society. Rapid and dramatic changes could only take the country to the brink of chaos. Thus the right to act, if not the right to speak out, must be limited for certain groups which desire the destruction of a system which is seen as having more positive than negative aspects.

Conversely, extremism on the transformationist side favors the dramatic and radical changes that only a revolution could bring about. There is a refusal to compromise, and violence is judged the only really effective means of attaining profound changes. Whatever a revolution might bring could only be an improvement, the present society being judged very negatively. As on the conservative side, there is great intolerance of the differing opinions of certain groups, whose right to freedom of expression and action is contested. The university should become a privileged base of action in the anticapitalist struggle; the neutrality of the university is denounced as a trap set by the system to maintain and reinforce its power.

It can generally be said that *moderation*, contrary to extremism, is primarily defined by a set of attitudes expressing a certain tolerance with regard to freedom of expression which should exist for all groups, whatever their opinions. It reflects attitudes favorable to more or less radical and rapid changes, according to its placement on the conservative or transformationist side. But these changes should be, as far as possible, realized by means within the framework of legality. In fact, on both sides there is a certain repugnance with regard to violence.

Finally, it is in the moderate orientation that we observe the greatest agreement with the concepts of the elimination of nationalism, reduction of the arms race, the opening of frontiers to allow greater exchanges between peoples, condemnation of racial discrimination as a crime, and the creation of a supranational agency capable of more effectively solving current world problems.

Outside of the general tendencies just described, moderation, like extremism, takes on a somewhat different meaning according to its position in conservative or transformationist ideology. On the conservative side, moderation signifies above all a certain disinterest in politics or a refusal to let politics invade the university. Some positive contributions of the student movement are recognized, especially where university reforms are concerned, but there is a clear refusal to see the university transformed into a political battlefield, and even stronger refusal to see it transformed into the base of revolutionary action in the society. Only debates, discussions, and negotiations respecting the rights of all parties are acceptable; all other types of constraining or violent action are condemned. The orientation is more toward reforms than toward the introduction of profound changes, since society on the whole, like the university, is seen as offering more positive than negative aspects. The attitudes of moderate conservatives may be summarized by the idea, dear to centrists, of "change within continuity."

In contrast, on the transformationist side, the evaluation of society and the university dips to the negative pole, and the final objective remains the changing of existing institutions. But, differing from extremism, moderation shows a concern for legality, revolution and violence being only a last resort. As for the university, it cannot remain enclosed in an ivory tower, but should open itself to the outside world, encouraging the critical analysis of various aspects of national life, and should become a vanguard in the transformation of society.

We have just seen the importance, in describing the structure of political orientations, of taking into account not only the direction of these orientations but also a second essential dimension—the intensity or degree of involvement. The typological approach based on these two dimensions will permit us to specify more clearly the clusters of attitudes shown by the analyses, and to determine their relation—proximity or distance—to the political groups (political identifiers) and the sociological characteristics (sociological identifiers) describing the students in each country.

We have shown the clear relationship existing among elements of attitudinal systems in all countries except Tunisia. However, although between-country comparisons permit to detect a similar attempt at adaptation to society's social and political situation, the ideological content, as we shall see, takes on a different shading according to each country's history and particular situation.

Toward a Typology of Sociopolitical Orientation

The data we present are the result of a classification which takes into account, in a bidimensional system, the two basic dimensions structured by factor analysis. As abscissa (horizontal) there is the first axis (ideological axis: conservatism-transformationism) and as ordinate (vertical) the second axis (intensity of involvement: extremism-moderation).

The intersection of the two axes results in four planes, each of which could be considered to yield an approximate type.

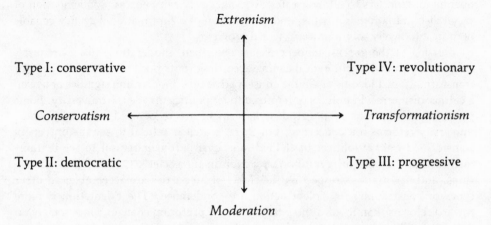

Extremism

Type I: conservative   Type IV: revolutionary

Conservatism ←——————————————→ *Transformationism*

Type II: democratic   Type III: progressive

Moderation

Type I, defined as *conservative*, is situated in the extremism-conservatism quadrant; type II, the *democratic*, in the moderation-conservatism quadrant; type III, the *progressive*, in the moderation-transformationism quadrant; and finally type IV, defined as *revolutionary*, in the extremism-transformation quadrant.[7]

We must note that this system of attitudinal representations refers to ideal types in a Weberian sense and few students fit perfectly into one or the other. It is, then, less a matter of final and exclusive types than of the direction or pole toward which the attitudinal system of the student in question seems to be oriented. Certainly, this classification in terms of two essential dimensions (ideology and intensity) in orientation has a great advantage over a classification in terms of only one dimension, bringing the difference between opinions down to only two poles.

There has been an open debate for quite some time between those attempting to interpret political orientations according to a dualistic principle and those who, on the contrary, go by the principle of a pluralistic classification (multiple dimension). In the first interpretation, the older and more traditional of the two, political tendencies are seen as distributing themselves along a one-dimensional continuum, going from the conservative (or right) pole to the radical (or left) pole. In daily life there is, in fact, a tendency to speak of the right and the left, some people being more to the right, others more to the left, with those between the two at the center. The dualist principle is still commonly adopted in numerous studies in order to facilitate comparisons, and among the public to create a caricature of politicians. But as a consequence of some important studies, in particular those of Eysenck (1954) in Great Britain, this principle appeared as an excessive reduction, not taking into account the diversity of political attitudes and orientations. In fact this author showed, on the basis of results obtained through factor analysis, that the structure of political attitudes cannot be described without reference to two essential dimensions—one dimension which indicates the ideological preferences of the respondents and opposes radicalism to conservatism (factor R), and a second dimension reflecting the personal style in which these preferences are expressed, opposing what Eysenck (following James) calls "tough-mindedness" to "tender-mindedness" (factor T).

The basic dimensions (ideological and intensity axes) that we found are close to those presented by Eysenck, with, of course, many nuances due to the different

[7]In Tunisia we found a different pattern that will be presented later on.

questions used in the two studies. Now we must discover whether, in the typology, we find the same distribution of principal political tendencies along the factors as well.

With Lancelot (1969), we may raise the following question: to how many orientations may the diversity of political attitudes be reduced? Must the traditional distinction between the right and the left be maintained, or may the principle of a pluralistic classification be established? This question is interesting particularly in the international context of this study, which regroups countries with different political systems.

Each country will be taken separately, beginning with the non-Anglophone European countries France, Italy, Spain, and Austria. Then we will take the English-speaking countries—Great Britain, the United States, and Australia—and finally Japan and the two African countries, Nigeria and Tunisia. Yugoslavia is not included. It was found impossible to present a satisfactory account of a typology which emerged from the factor analysis, and the political system in that country was too different from those elsewhere to permit useful comparisons.

One question that may be answered through correspondence analysis is the identification, in general ideological terms, of respondents who refused to define their particular political orientation. Do they tend to cluster in a definite ideological sector or is the no-answer choice unrelated to a specific ideology but reflects instead heterogeneous social views? The results support the "heterogeneous" alternative, since in all countries studied the no-answer choice is located near the origin of the ideological axis (axis 1), and in almost all countries near the origin of the intensity axis (axis 2).

FRANCE (FIGURE 8.1—see page 252)[8]

Type I, Conservative

The conservative type reacts negatively, in general, to the notion of a university as an institution that criticizes all aspects of national life or as an avant-garde agent for changing society. This kind of student is favorable to the idea of conserving a university which is elitist, based on intellectual merit, and regulated by an admissions policy and examinations. He condemns the student movement as antidemocratic both in its means and its goals. He believes that, instead of helping to achieve positive changes at the university or a general awakening of social conscience, the protest movement has only jeopardized the university and public order. In particular, he judges very negatively all types of action undertaken at the university, including assemblies, the use of spokesmen, nonviolent marches, etc. All of these activities manifest, according to him, a lack of maturity. The role of the student is neither to fight together with the workers nor to desert the university for the factories.

Politically speaking, the conservative is a nationalist, supporting the development of atomic and biological armaments. He is against any form of world government. Not agreeing that racial or religious discrimination is a crime, he favors the restriction of immigration.

[8]For each country a figure is provided. The graph, which represents in detail the major attitudinal variables and the political and sociological factors, is not presented here for reasons indicated above. The figure represents only the distribution of the political identifiers on these axes, in order to give a clear picture of the relations between the different political groups.

The conservative reacts against whatever might menace the actual political system and fears an international "plot" organized by forces which seek a revolution to destroy capitalism. He is persuaded that a revolution would not only stop present progress but also end up by being more repressive than the system it would replace.

Figure 8.1.   FRANCE

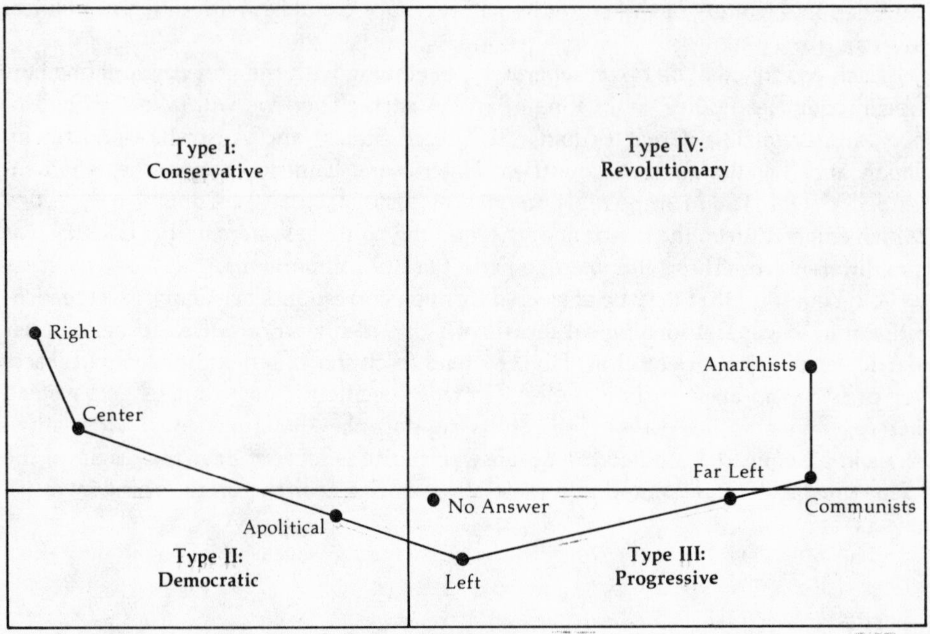

NOTE: It should be noted that in order to make it easy to visualize the similarities or differences of the graphic profiles between countries, we have reproduced exactly, but in a reduced format, the original graphs as printed by the computer. In each of the countries studied, the position and the intersection of the horizontal axis (1) and the vertical axis (2) will vary as functions of the results.

Finally, the conservative rejects the idea of a politicized university. Neither a martyr nor a hero, he is not ready to sacrifice the happiness of the present generation for the potential well-being of future generations. He resembles his parents closely in the three domains we have mentioned—emotional, moral, and political (see Chapter 6).

This type of attitude is common in France to students identifying themselves as right or center. The difference between these two positions is less one of ideology than of intensity of involvement, as the rightists appear to be more extreme than those in the center. The typical conservative student is likely to be studying medicine or law, does not work to support himself, and comes from a family whose educational background is high (i.e., both the father and mother usually have had university training). The majority of these students are Roman Catholic and believers.

TYPE II, DEMOCRATIC

Like the conservative, the democratic type is antirevolutionary and procapitalist, respecting the established order. Yet the democratic type is particularly characterized by his antiviolence attitudes. He condemns violence in general and every kind of radical action undertaken at the university—interruption of courses, occupation of buildings, destruction of goods and records, and the physical abuse of teachers and administrators.

On the other hand, he favors action by means of elected assemblies and by spokesmen. Words—but not acts—by any political group are tolerated. Not really interested in politics, the democratic type hopes that the university will remain as independent as possible from the political arena; he does not agree that the only way to change the university is through revolution.

An optimist about society, which he judges as rather "good" in general, the democratic type does not wish any profound changes and reacts strongly against the idea of revolution. He thinks that one of the strong points of the present system is the freedom of the press and of other kinds of expression. Finally, he is the most favorable to elections by universal suffrage.

In some ways, the democratic type resembles the progressive type. While not supporting the revolutionary objectives of the student movement, the democratic type recognizes that student protest has achieved some positive changes in the university system. Some in this group even believe that the student movement on the whole has been beneficial, awakening the previous generations to "truths" which they seemed to have forgotten. Concerning the goals for universities in their country, they are not hostile to a university which provides a forum for the critical analysis of national life and acts as a vanguard of change in the society. Like the progressive, the democratic type is in favor of an effective supranational government and views favorably the limitation of nuclear and biological arms.

The democratic type in France is most clearly representative of respondents who define themselves as apolitical. They are likely to be in engineering or business and the arts. Parents have either a university or a secondary school education. Students still living with their family tend to be found in this group, as well as women students.

Type III, Progressive

The progressive, more than the democratic, is favorable toward the student movement, which is seen as an agent of change responsible for reforms at the university and for a general awakening in society. In addition, this type endorses the notion of the university as a critical forum for debating various aspects of society and as a vanguard to change society.

The progressive type is liberal and an entrenched pacifist who believes in disarmament and the elimination of nationalism, to be replaced by an effective worldwide organization. He judges racial discrimination to be a crime, and is favorable to the opening up of natural borders and the free exchange of people among countries.

The more we move toward the extreme wing of the progressives, the more we find a favorable judgment of the student movement, whose objectives and means of action are seen as democratic and as reflecting, contrary to what many people think, considerable maturity. In the struggle to transform or to replace existing institutions the progressive favors legal action more than the call to revolution. In effect, although he does not completely condemn the use of violence, sometimes judging it an effective and legitimate means of action, the progressive usually prefers less extremist solutions.

This type of student respects the freedom and the rights of each person—a respect which he feels is not always reciprocated on the part of the government. Like revolutionaries, progressive students agree that the university should become a base of political action and subscribe to the notion that one of the goals of the student movement should be to establish a common front with the workers. The most extreme students in this category think that students should leave the university for the factory in order to aid the workers in the struggle. This attitude in France especially characterizes the communists, who believe in addition that in order to eliminate capitalism, the students of the world should unite their efforts and be ready and willing to sacrifice their own happiness in order to build a new society which will assure the happiness of future generations.

The progressive acknowledges having been most influenced in his political evolution by his friends and less often, as compared to the revolutionary, by ideologists. This type, especially on its liberal wing, best describes the moderate left. Communist students split between the progressive and the revolutionary types.

Students in sciences are split between the democratic and the progressive types, the latter more often being represented by students in the humanities. The social background of these students is somewhat lower than that of the conservative and democratic students. Parents are likely to have a secondary or a primary school education. This is particularly true in the case of the mother. Students who work and those who are married also tend to belong in this category.

TYPE IV, REVOLUTIONARY

The revolutionary type may be distinguished from the progressive by his intolerance, his extreme positions, and his favorable attitude toward violence. Like the progressive, the revolutionary is fighting capitalism and the present form of government, and appears quite ready to endure sacrifices in order to construct a new society as well as to leave the university to help the workers in their struggle. But more than the progressive, the revolutionary emphasizes revolution as the only real means of profoundly changing society. He is more favorable to the destruction of the political system, whatever the consequences. He does not think that a revolution would have an adverse effect on any progress already achieved or would result in a more repressive society. Society as it now is seems to him to have more negative than positive aspects. Today's freedom is for him only an illusion.

Like the conservative, but for obviously different reasons, the revolutionary does not favor free elections and does not think that the student protest movement has resulted in an improvement in the university. As to the first point, he only sees a "masquerade" rather than true democracy. As to the second, he believes that only a revolution can effect the changes needed to transform a bourgeois institution into a base of proletarian culture.

The revolutionary accords to politics a predominance in his life. Vis-à-vis violence he is rather positive, and considers it as a means which is both legitimate and effective for rapidly realizing valued goals. This extreme attitude can be summarized by the dictum "no freedom for the enemies of freedom," since he refuses the right of expression to certain groups viewed as "reactionary." This type of student is also against elected assemblies and discussions with the administration at the university, believing that other types of action (e.g., strikes, boycotting of classes, occupation of buildings, destruction of goods, physical attacks on teachers, etc.) are more useful in obtaining the desired goals. It may be noted, however, that the most extreme attitudes are relatively rare.

The revolutionary type in France best typifies the anarchists and, to a lesser degree, the far left. Revolutionary students are likely to study social sciences and to live on their own. The social background of the students is the lowest compared to the three preceding groups, their parents being likely to have only a primary education. Finally, more men than women belong to this category.

In conclusion, when we look at the distribution of political tendencies and then more generally at the sociopolitical ideology of French students, it is important to emphasize the differences introduced by the intensity dimensions (axis 2). For instance, the center does not represent a middle ground or a category for students who do not know exactly where they fit on the political spectrum. On the contrary, the center is linked to an attitudinal cluster shared by rightist students. The intensity of political involvement is what principally distinguishes the students of the right from those of the center. Those in the center are relatively moderate in their views and more tolerant toward the student movement and toward reforms which will tend to improve the present sociopolitical system in the direction of more equality and justice. Yet they are strongly against any radical changes and violence.

On the other hand, the political groups which do reflect ideological ambivalence and a heterogeneity of attitudes are the apoliticals and the moderate left. Their position near the origin of axis 1 (ideological dimension) indicates the absence of clear-cut attitudes toward the status quo for apoliticals and for those of the left toward radical changes in society.

Apoliticals express above all else the desire to remain outside of politics and the rejection of sectarianism and violence. This neutrality, however, reflects a relatively positive attitude toward society in general. On the other hand, the moderate left is composed of students unhappy with society but desiring progressive change inside the system. This group is especially characterized by its tolerance and its favorable attitudes toward disarmament, the opening of borders, and the establishment of a supranational organization capable of working effectively at a worldwide level. Thus students who identify themselves on the left appear in the majority of cases to do so in order to express their dissatisfaction with the status quo rather than to support a revolutionary ideology.

Among the revolutionaries there is, on the general ideological level, little difference between those who define themselves as communists, anarchists, or on the far left. Yet the anarchists, judging from our results, are somewhat more radical than the communists or others of the far left. The views which best characterize the communists are that people should destroy the present form of government; join in a common struggle of students and workers; work for an international, revolutionary organization of students; and replace the present bourgeois university by a proletarian culture. Those on the far left differ little from the communists in these respects, although they give more support to the use of violence.

The anarchists are clearly distinguished by their extreme position. They are most likely to favor violence in all its forms, especially at the university, and to wish to destroy the present system even without knowing what will replace it.

Finally, men appear to be much more involved politically than are women in terms of the intensity dimension. This last finding corroborates the notion that in general women are less interested in politics than men. We find the same situation in most of the countries studied, except in the United States, where feminist movements were already in existence at the time of our study.

ITALY (FIGURE 8.2)

We find on the whole the same typological relationships in Italy as in France. Yet the proximity between the political tendencies in the two countries is slightly different.

Figure 8.2.   ITALY

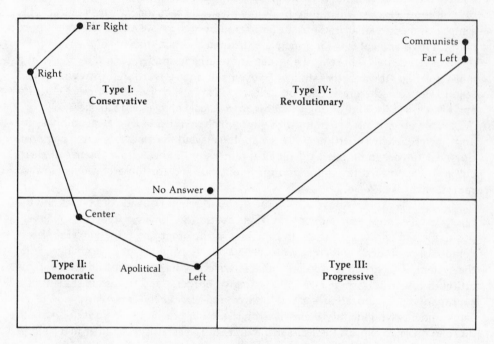

We can see that the political spectrum is much larger than in France, indicating a wider ideological gap between the two extreme tendencies, far left and communist on one side and right and far right on the other. In particular may be noted in this country the extremism of attitudes and opinions of all these as opposed to the moderate groups (center, apolitical, and left).

The distribution of the different political tendencies along the two axes shows that rightist students (including the far right) appear in the upper part of the first quadrant, which represents the *conservative type*, that is, the most favorable to expressions of nationalism, nonlimitation of armaments, and acceptance of racial and religious discrimination.

The students of the center, the apoliticals, and those on the left appear in the *democratic type* (quadrant II). However, it should be noted that students of the center are clearly situated on the conservative side of the ideological axis (axis 1) whereas apolitical and leftist students are situated near the origin of axis 1. This indicates that the latter two are heterogeneous and/or ambivalent in their orientations toward conservatism and transformationism. This situation indicates that in Italy students of the center have a general ideological orientation similar to those of the right and the far right. Yet they differ clearly in the intensity of their attitudes. They appear more moderate, tolerant, and open to reforms. They condemn violence in general as well as all forms of action which can disrupt studies at the university. This group shows the most positive attitude toward society.[9]

Apolitical and moderate left students do not constitue homogeneous groups, yet most tend to favor the status quo rather than radical changes in their society. Their position in the quadrant representing the democratic type indicates an attitude of tolerance. They are in favor of internationalism, freedom of expression, and a university which acts as a vanguard of change in the society. While recognizing the positive aspects of the student movement, they condemn, like those in the center, violence in general and most of the activites undertaken on university campuses. They remain rather skeptical about the liberalizing effects of a revolution, which might result in another system just as repressive as the present one.

It is striking to note that in Italy no political group appears in the third quadrant, that of the *progressive type*. Both communist and far left students are typified by the *revolutionary type*, radical both in their attitudes toward changes and in their political involvement.

In Italy, communist and far left students are situated at the extremity of both the ideological axis (1) and the intensity axis (2). This indicates that, in contrast to the situation in France, students of the far left as well as the communists are much more politically active and favorable to changes than students of the moderate left. There is in this country, as compared to France, a larger gap between the moderate left— which is closer to the center—and the communists and far left, both of which are characterized by the extremism of their opposition to the status quo.

Certain positions are held in common by the far right, the far left, and the communists, such as acceptance of violence as an effective means of action, and also a shared desire to destroy the present system even without knowing what will replace it. Also all three groups oppose elections based on universal suffrage. Thus there appears to be a virulent activism in this country, more than in any other, on the part of the conservatives as well as of the revolutionaries. Those in the center, those on the left, and the apoliticals are opposed to this activism.

The distribution of sociological groups demonstrates that university disciplines have little influence on political orientation. There is only a slight preponderance of the conservative type in engineering, business, and arts and letters, and of the progressive type in law and the social sciences; medicine is found among the progressive and the democratic types; and the revolutionary type appears most frequently in the sciences. As in all the countries studied atheism is linked to the revolutionary type, whether it is practiced in the family or is a personal choice of the student.

Conservative and moderate students were influenced by their parents' political views, and remain close to their parents, both emotionally and morally. In contrast, the revolutionaries were more influenced by their friends and their peers, and feel that their political orientation is quite different from that of their parents.

Finally, even more clearly than in France, women in Italy seem much less engaged in politics than do men. There is an obvious preponderance of men in the revolutionary type.

---

[9]We must recall that this category of *center* includes students who identify themselves as Christian Democrats. It is therefore not surprising to find among them approval of existing institutions.

SPAIN (FIGURE 8.3)

In Spain as in Italy, the political spectrum is wide as compared to the other countries. However, this is more marked for the first (ideological) dimension (axis 1) than for the second (intensity) dimension (axis 2).

Figure 8.3. SPAIN

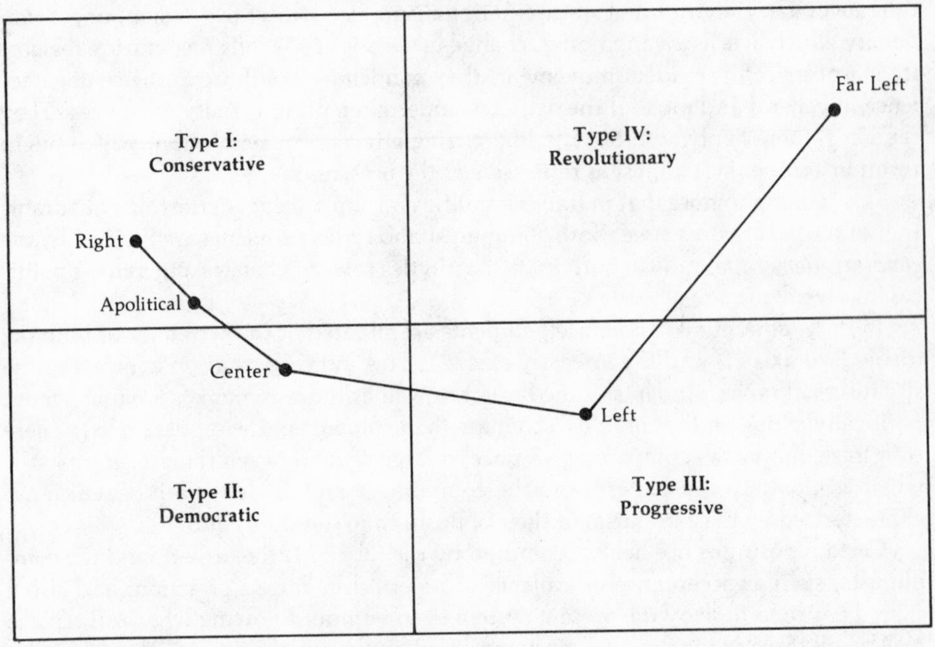

NOTE: No data were available for the small group giving "no answer."

The shape of the graph indicates that the various political groups differ in these countries much more in terms of ideology than in terms of political involvement. The rightist and the apolitical students, even though they are situated at the extremity of the conservative end of the ideological dimension (axis 1), still remain close to the origin of the intensity dimension (axis 2). This indicates a conservative outlook but a low involvement in political matters. This same relatively low involvement also characterizes those who identify themselves with the center or the left. This may be explained by the fact that in Spain, an authoritarian rightist regime was in power at the time of the study. Opposition to the status quo, which may induce an intensity of political involvement of rightists living in liberal countries, was not aroused. As expected, the rightist students are the most conservative, followed closely by the apolitical. This group in Spain appears also in the quadrant representing a conservative attitudinal configuration. This is unlike the situation in many other countries, where apolitical students appear in the quadrant representing a democratic orientation.

Thus it may be noted that the self-definition of apoliticism implies more or less an acceptance of the particular point of view of the actual government.

The center in Spain, which appears in the quadrant representing a democratic type, is quite similar to the right and the apolitical. However, these students are less optimistic in evaluating their society and are against all forms of violence.

Unlike the left in France and in Italy, where it appears near the center of axis 1 (ideological dimension), half-way between the conservative and the transformationist poles, the left in Spain is clearly on the transformationist side. This location indicates that in Spain students of the left represent a homogeneous group, clearly distinct from and antagonistic to those favorable to the status quo.

Differing from the left in France and in Italy, the left in Spain definitely favors changes and is quite distant from the more or less conservative ideology. Judging their society negatively, these students favor political changes, certain forms of student protest, and agree that the university has an important role to play in realizing these changes. Unlike the students on the far left, however, they do not favor extreme methods of action, such as violence and all that it entails. We find again, as in the other countries, that these students are characterized by tolerance and an orientation toward disarmament, the elimination of nationalism, and the establishment of a supranational government. The far left, in contrast, is clearly radical, and demonstrates a more intense emotional involvement.

The results indicate that the split in Spain between those who accept the status quo (the right, the apoliticals, and the center) and those who reject it (the left and the far left) is clearer than in the other countries studied to this point.

When we look at the social characteristics of the students in Spain, we find first that, as in other countries, religious beliefs are closely related to political orientation. Atheism goes with revolutionary ideology. Second, the relation between university discipline and political ideology is not clear. That is, we do not find types of students who may be definitely categorized by the kind of studies they pursue. There is, however, a tendency for students in sciences, engineering, business, medicine, and the arts to favor the status quo more than do those in the humanities, law, and the social sciences.

Students whose parents had attained the highest levels of formal education tended to adhere to the status quo more than did others. In particular, those whose mothers had studied at the university were more conservative, as were also those who did not have to work outside in addition to attending the university. Conversely, those who did not live with their parents and those who worked outside the university were more favorable to change.

We should note the difference in Spain between the youngest students (under 21), the most politicized and receptive to extremist ideas, and those who were older (over 24), much more moderate and more likely to endorse universalist ideals (worldwide government, the elimination of nuclear and biological arms, the decline of nationalism). Finally, women in Spain have more favorable attitudes toward their society than do men and on the whole are more conservative. Other sociological characteristics did not emerge as significant.

AUSTRIA (FIGURE 8.4—see page 260)

The distribution of political groups in Austria shows that three groups—the apoliticals, the right, and the center—may be distinguished from one another only by their degree of political involvement, since all three are fairly close to the conservative end of the ideological axis. In Austria, as in Spain, and in contrast to the situation in the other countries, those who define themselves as apolitical are rather similar in their political attitudes to the rightists. Both of these groups are characterized by their negative reaction vis-à-vis the student movement. It is striking that in this country few of the students in any group endorsed the notions of armaments and nationalism, even among the conservatives. In this respect, Austrian conservatives differ substantially from those in the other countries. As for student demonstrations, the conservative type in Austria reports never having participated in these activities and expresses no desire to do so.

The center in Austria is found in the second quadrant (democratic type). These students are not *a priori* against all protest movements and would be ready to participate in them, although they condemn violence and any action which threatens the freedom of others, such as strikes, occupation of buildings, and interruption of classes. They do not support the idea of a revolution, which, according to them, would ruin progress already achieved in their society. They are completely opposed to the idea of destroying the present form of government.

Those on the left are found in the third quadrant (progressive type). In this group we find the same universalist and liberal attitudes which characterize students on the left in the other countries. They are most favorable to the student movement in its common struggle with the workers and other students around the world to transform society into a more egalitarian institution. They are also anxious to see the teaching system become more democratic. Yet, compared to the students on the far left, they do not endorse extremist methods.

Those on the far left fit precisely the revolutionary type (fourth quadrant). They endorse the use of violence and other extreme methods to achieve their ends, such as

Figure 8.4.   AUSTRIA

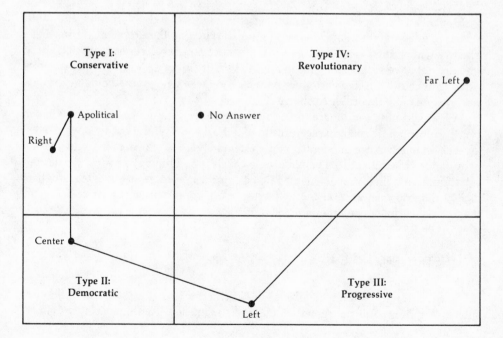

the destruction of the present system even without knowing what will replace it and the use of the university as a base for political action. As in some other countries, those most in favor of violent means are least in favor of using spokesmen, elected assemblies, or any other kind of "compromise" to reconcile opposing opinions in the university.

As for parents' educational background, conservative students tend to come from relatively well-educated families, and those who are more intolerant in their opinions and more critical of society more frequently come from less well-educated families.

With regard to university disciplines, the conservative type is more likely to be found studying engineering, business, or law. Those in arts and letters are more frequently of the democratic type, while those in sciences and the social sciences compose the progressive type. Students in medicine, in contrast to the situation in all the other countries, seem more critical of their society and appear in the revolutionary type.

Students with a job and living outside of the family unit, as in other countries, tend to be more favorable to change (transformationist). Younger students appear more conservative than older ones, who are more progressive but also more moderate in their political involvement. Finally, men seem more involved in politics and favorable to change than women. Other sociological characteristics did not emerge as significant.

GREAT BRITAIN (FIGURE 8.5—see page 262)

Here we find a polarization in the distribution of the political groups. Those on the right, the apoliticals, and the center constitute one pole, while anarchists, the far left, and the communists constitute the second pole. The left is about half-way between the two.

On the intensity-of-involvement axis, only the right emerges as endorsing extremist views. At the opposite end, the left shows the least degree of political involvement. The other political groups are fairly close to the center of axis 2 (intensity). This indicates a moderate posture of all groups with the exception of the right in expressing either a conservative or a transformationist orientation. Rightist students fit the conservative type of the extremist variety. They oppose the notion of the university as a critical forum and as an avant-garde for social change; they refuse to condemn racial discrimination, are against the elimination of atomic weapons, and do not recognize any positive aspects of the student movement.

The apolitical students appear also in the quadrant representing the conservative type but are less extremist. These students are characterized by their antirevolutionary attitude and their condemnation of violence.

The students of the center belong to the democratic type. They reject all illegal actions at the university, but do not reject *a priori* the usefulness of the student movement.

The left appears in the third quadrant (progressive type) and, as indicated above, is about midway between the right and the far left. These students would like to see the elimination of nationalism and of atomic armaments and the beginning of a supranational form of government. On the other hand, they are ambivalent about the elimination of capitalism and, compared to the more radical groups, are not favorable to a revolution or the total destruction of the present political system.

The communist and the far left students, also of the progressive type, are in favor of destroying the actual political system and of making the university a place amenable to leftist activities. The students should unite in a common struggle with the workers and form an international revolutionary front.

Figure 8.5.   GREAT BRITAIN

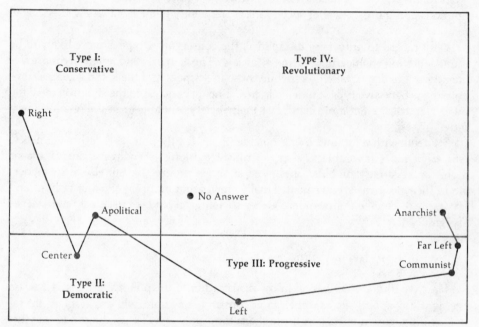

The anarchists appear in the fourth quadrant (revolutionary type). Yet, in contrast to other countries, they are relatively moderate in their prorevolutionary attitudes. Few of them accept violence or illegal action at the university, condemn their society, or subscribe to the notion that freedom of expression should be limited.

The conservative type seems to predominate among students in engineering and business, while the democratic type is found more frequently in the humanities. Students in the sciences are divided between the conservative and democratic types. Law students seem to be of the progressive type. Those studying medicine are the most conservative and the most politically involved.

Once again women are clearly more moderate than men, less politically involved, and more in favor of the status quo. Students living with their families are much more conservative than those who live on a university campus or have independent living accomodations and those who hold jobs outside of the university.

THE UNITED STATES (FIGURE 8.6)

In the United States few students endorse a revolutionary ideology. Those who do are relatively isolated and marginal compared to the mass of students who are favorable to the status quo.

Students who define themselves as on the right are clearly represented in the first quadrant (conservative type) and have rather extremist views; these include a nationalist attitude, condemnation of the student movement, and rejection of use of the university as a political and critical forum.

Students of the center and/or defining themselves as belonging to the Democratic party are situated in the second quadrant representing the democratic type. They are rather conservative but more open and more tolerant than those on the right. They are against all prorevolutionary attitudes and endorse capitalism but also accept protests and are critical of their society.

Figure 8.6. UNITED STATES

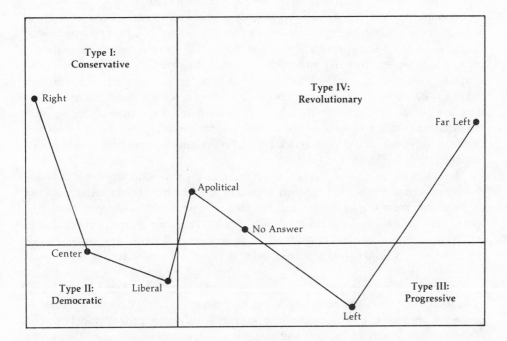

Liberals are also found in the democratic type. Their attitudes about society and politics are closer to those in the center than to those on the left. Like the center and the right, these students judge American society as positive on the whole and very liberal. Thus they remain profoundly attached to existing institutions and to the capitalist system. As for political actions they regard as acceptable at the university, only the use of spokesmen and of elected assemblies are favored, while violence in any form is condemned. They have a more positive opinion of the student movement than do students in the center. The liberals are also more favorable than are those in the center to the notion of the university as critical of society, a vanguard for social change. More than students in the center, the liberals condemn all acts of violence and of revolution. Like the left, they are against the arms race and nationalism, and favor the establishment of a supranational government.

Leftist or socialist students in the United States are closer to the far left on the ideological dimension and closer to the liberals on the intensity dimension. They are situated in the third quadrant representing the progressive type. The left is the group most in favor of student protest. In addition to the use of spokesmen and elected assemblies, leftists endorse confrontation and public demonstrations as valid types of action. Few of them believe, however, that student protest should lead to a complete destruction of the system. As in other countries, we find in the United States that students on the left care about freedom of expression and have ambivalent attitudes regarding violence, illegal acts, and revolution.

We must note a particularity in this country as regards the apolitical students, who are situated near the center of the ideological axis but high in intensity. In contrast to what might have been expected, this group of students is politically involved. This is apparent in the adoption of attitudes which seem extreme—the condemnation of the student movement; the rejection of the idea of a worldwide government; the desire to abolish elections based on universal suffrage; restriction of the freedom of expression for certain groups; and, more radically, the acceptance of violence. These students' general outlook on society is quite negative.

Perhaps they are "apolitical" because they reject all existing political parties. Some of those students seem close to the ideology of the right, others close to that of the far left. The group apparently includes those students who manifest a real antipoliticism, rejecting the party system as it exists in the United States and refusing to adopt a given ideology, as well as those who find "refuge" in neutrality, through either ignorance or disinterest in politics, implicitly accepting the status quo. This issue is especially pertinent in the United States where, at the time of this study a strong counterculture existed, one of whose major themes was apoliticism or antipoliticism. The events at the Woodstock Festival represented a striking example of this tendency.

The last political group, the far left, represents the revolutionary type. It is distinctly isolated from the other groups, including the left. In particular, the far left is distinguished from the left by its high emotional content and its acceptance of violence in realizing the goals of the revolution—destruction of the government; changing the bourgeois university into a base for proletarian culture; a very negative evaluation of society; and denial that freedom of expression is characteristic of the present system.

The university disciplines of the students appear more related to political ideologies than to the intensity of the students' involvement. There is a predominance of conservative students in medicine, the sciences, law, engineering, and business, while students in arts and letters and social sciences are relatively more inclined to adopt radical attitudes in favor of change. Students in art clearly belong with the progressive type.

Students who do not work are more conservative than those who do. The level of formal education of the parents appears to be related to the degree of political involvement of the students. Those whose parents received little formal education appear more intolerant and sectarian in their attitudes than those whose parents attended a university. These latter are more liberal and moderate in their opinions.

Finally, unlike the finding elsewhere, women in the United States on the whole tend to take more radical positions than do men. The radicalism we see among female students in the United States may be connected with the growth of the feminist movement, which, when this study was undertaken, was clearly more important and influential there than in other countries.

AUSTRALIA (FIGURE 8.7)

Differences in attitude among Australian students are minor compared to other countries. The responses are not widely distributed, but are clustered near the center of the axes, except for the far left students.

The conservative type is composed of three groups—the right, the center, and the apoliticals. The right is somewhat more extremist and conservative than the other two groups. The rightists are nationalists and do not favor the elimination of atomic weapons. They also deny any positive contribution of the student protest movement. They see the university as elitist; an institution which should remain aloof from political struggles.

Figure 8.7. AUSTRALIA

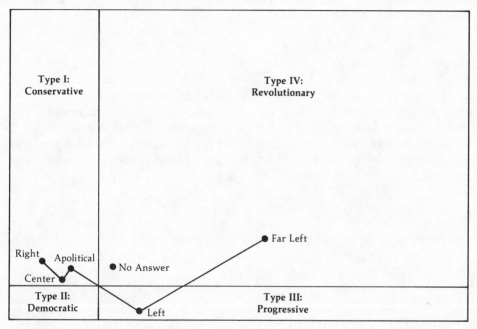

There is practically no difference between the students in the center and the apoliticals. Favorable to the capitalist system, both groups condemn revolution and any act which might question the established order. The university should remain as neutral as possible, and the student protest movement is endorsed only if it remains within the boundaries of the law. Like the students on the right, these two groups most frequently recognize the influence of their parents on their own political evolution.

No political tendency falls into the democratic type, that is, those who are moderately conservative but reformist. The left falls into the third quadrant (progressive type). As in other countries, it is characterized by a moderate anticapitalist attitude: changes should be realized by legal means rather than by violence or extreme types of action. The ambivalence of the left is characterized by the fact that these students see more positive than negative aspects in their society.

In contrast, the students on the far left, who appear in the fourth quadrant (revolutionary type) are clearly distinguishable from the other political groups. They view their society negatively and favor revolution. For them violence is seen as valid and appropriate. They are the most sectarian, since they do not accord to all groups the right of freedom of expression and believe that certain groups should be excluded from the university. At the same time, they criticize the present system for its lack of true freedom. Compared to the left in other countries—notably the United States and Great Britain—the far left in Australia is characterized by a certain adventurism in its radicalism. Indeed, the statement we used which identifies this group best is "I am in favor of the destruction of the present political system without knowing what will replace it."

Few differences from other countries appear in the distribution according to sociological groupings. Students in law and medicine tend to be of the conservative type, while those in the social sciences and the pure sciences are more favorable to change. No difference politically appears by sex; this contrasts with the findings in Great Britain and in the United States.

JAPAN (FIGURE 8.8)

It is interesting to note that the first quadrant (conservative type) does not include a single political group. This may be related to the fact that in Japan the few rightist students were combined with those of the center. The center and the apolitical are represented by the democratic type (second quadrant) and the left by the progressive type (third quadrant). The far left is represented by the revolutionary type and appears quite distant from the other groups.

Figure 8.8.   JAPAN

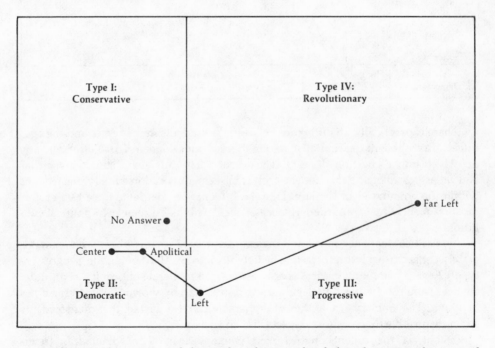

Students in the center and the apoliticals seem divided in their attitudes toward the capitalist system. Some of them favor a change in the system of government but differ from those on the left by their anti-revolutionary attitudes. These same students are opposed to any kind of liaison between students and workers or any type of international common front. They believe that the university should remain politically neutral; no action should interfere with studying. Yet they do not condemn the student movement in Japan, since they recognize certain contributions resulting from the movement, especially at the university. Those on the left share with the democrats their distaste for sectarianism, violence, or any kind of extremist activities but differ from them in accepting the use of spokesmen and of student manifestations.

Students on the left are characterized by their desire to eliminate capitalism and by their negative view of the present society. They believe that the fight against existing institutions should be conducted jointly with the workers.

The far left is distinguished from other political groups by its radicalism rather than by its extremism. In particular, these students usually support the idea of changing the university into a base for political action. They also think that only a revolution can really improve the university, replacing the existing system by a proletarian culture. They are in favor of the student movement and consider it mature and democratic in its goals. Like those on the left, students on the far left think that if the student movement has as a real objective the destruction of the present government, students should join in a common front with the working class and form an international revolutionary organization.

In contrast to the situation in other countries, although the far left in Japan believes more than the other political groups that violence is a method of effective action, it condemns the principle of violence *per se*. It also rejects other types of action which are acceptable to the far left in other countries, e.g., disruption of classes and occupation of buildings.

Extremist attitudes are rejected by Japanese students in the center and, to a lesser degree, by students on the left. Unlike the situation elsewhere, democratic groups have a negative attitude toward their society. In the center, a substantial number of students question the capitalist system; on the left, many are skeptical of the student movement.

With regard to sociological differences, older students tend to fit the conservative type, while the younger ones are either democratic or progressive, that is, moderate.

Students at the University of Todai are, on the whole, more extremist (as indicated by their position on axis 2) than those at Waseda University, yet no ideological difference (as indicated by their position on axis 1) emerges between these two universities. At Todai there are more students of the conservative and the revolutionary types, while at Waseda the students fall more frequently into the democratic and progressive categories.

Students in social sciences and in law show a tendency to belong to the conservative type. Those in business and engineering, as well as those in arts and letters, seem to be more moderate but at the same time less satisfied with the existing system in their country. The revolutionary type of student is most often found among those in the sciences.

The level of education of the parents is also related to the students' attitudes, but more with regard to the intensity of their involvement than to their ideological orientation. Students whose parents attended a university are clearly more extremist and politically involved than those whose parents did not go beyond the primary level of formal education. The latter tend to be progressives.

As in the other countries, the fact of working accompanies a more radical position, and not having a job is associated with more conservative attitudes.

The few women included in the Japanese sample are clearly of the progressive type.

NIGERIA (FIGURE 8.9)

In this country, there is less of a strictly ideological divergence between the various political tendencies than a difference in the degree of political involvement and activism. There is also, generally speaking, a rather close proximity of the various political groups on the ideological axis. In effect, although conservative tendencies differ from radical, the ideological divergences are minor compared to those in other countries. At many points, there is a certain consensus between the attitudes of the students on the right and those on the left.

Figure 8.9.   NIGERIA

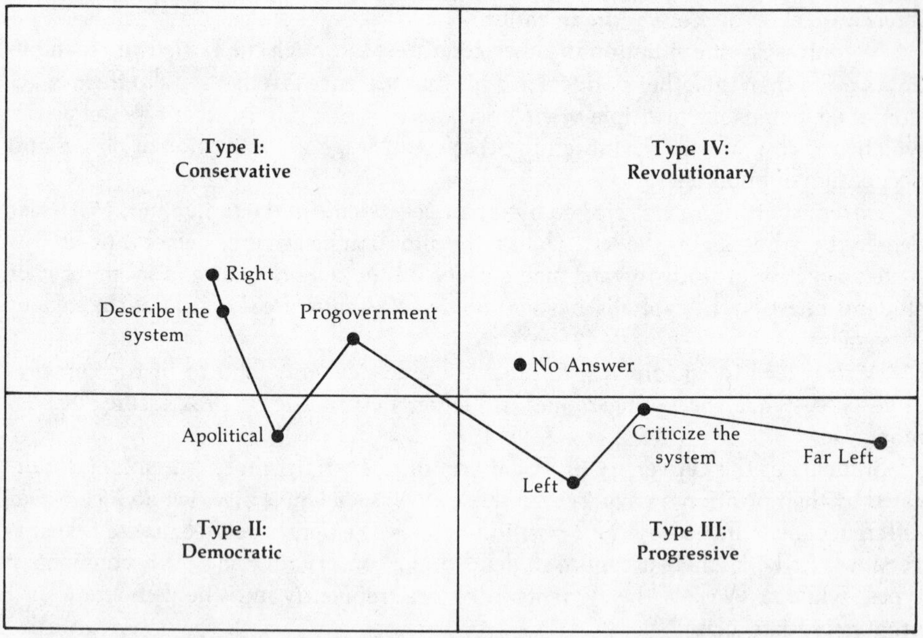

We note first the position of three groups of students who, without categorizing themselves politically, either described the socioeconomic and political situation of their country in a neutral manner (group termed "describe the system"), stated their agreement with the government and the status quo ("progovernment"), or criticized the system and the present socioeconomic situation in their country ("criticize the system").

The first group, which merely describes the government, is near the right and is included in the first quadrant, which represents the conservative type. This group and the right have very similar, conservative tendencies. They favor capitalism over other systems and oppose all student manifestations or protests which might question the status quo.

The progovernment group is also located in the first quadrant (conservative type), but its position near the center of the ideological axis indicates a great heterogeneity in the attitudes expressed. While against revolutionary movements, the progovernment students differ from the more conservative groups in their clearly less favorable attitudes toward capitalism. They are more anxious to find a new, innovative path for their country. In this regard, these progovernment students are like the students on the left.

The students who are critical of the government appear in the third quadrant (progressive type) nearer to the left than to the far left. They, like the students on the left, are somewhat less favorable to political action and to the destruction of the government than are students on the far left, who are clearly more revolutionary.

The students on the left, those who are critical of the system, and those on the far left are all the progressive type of student. These three groups condemn the capitalist system. According to them the fight should be a common one, not only inside their own country but also in solidarity with revolutionaries from all over the world. Since political activism most clearly distinguished students on the far left from those on the left in other countries, it is striking that in Nigeria no political group was found to represent the revolutionary type of student. On the other hand, in the democratic type—directly opposed to the revolutionary type and condemning political activism—we find students who defined themselves as apolitical. These students do not want to see the politicization of the university; like those on the right, they are the least ready to sacrifice themselves in order to build a new society.

The background characteristics of the students are not very significant with regard to the types formed by the two factorial axes. Field of study introduces practically no difference between the groups. Younger students are generally more favorable to change than are older students. Students who come from homes where the parents had secondary or university education are more extremist than those whose parents attained only a primary education or are illiterate. Finally, as in other countries, the absence of religious belief is closely related to student attitudes in favor of political change.

TUNISIA (FIGURE 8.10—see page 270)

The results obtained in Tunisia concerning the sociopolitical orientation of students are not comparable to those obtained in the other countries because of the omission of many items: those dealing with protest movements, politics, and types of possible actions at the university. This explains the limited display of responses on the ideological and the intensity dimensions. Yet, in spite of these limitations, the usual political continuum from right to far left can be observed. This indicates that in spite of a truncated instrument the political attitudinal range still emerges.

The resulting attitudinal types are necessarily different from those in the other countries because the more extreme political variables are lacking. The first (upper right quadrant) may be termed *nationalist*. Students in it are characterized by the following items of belief in descending order of frequency: there should be no elimination of atomic or biological weapons; nationalism should not be eliminated; the university should not act as añ avant-garde agent for social change; and elections by universal suffrage should not be abolished. This group includes a preponderance of students in the social sciences and those whose parents have had little education. No political tendency is best characterized by this type. The students who define themselves as rightists are situated between the nationalist and the activist type. This indicates a political involvement but a heterogeneous outlook on sociopolitical issues.

Figure 8.10.   TUNISIA

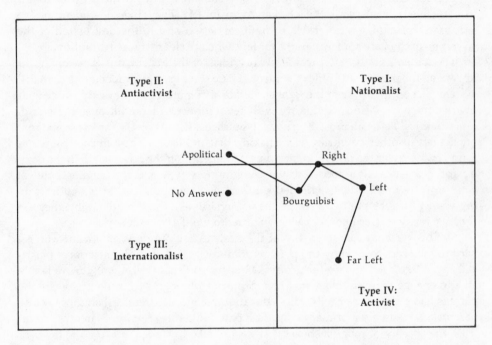

The second type of student (upper left quadrant) may be termed apolitical or *antiactivist*. This type is characterized by the endorsement of the following items in descending order of frequency: violence is not an effective method for realizing change; the student movement has not revealed truths which former generations ignored; the capitalist system should not be eliminated; the student movement is characterized by lack of maturity; violence as a principle is to be condemned; freedom of expression is present in the system; and the university should remain outside of politics.

In general, this type of student is very negative in his judgment of the student movement and has a rather favorable opinion of Tunisian society and of capitalism. These students recognize more than those in the other groups that they were influenced in their political thinking by their parents. Most of them live at home and define themselves as apolitical.

The third type (lower left quadrant), which may be called *internationalist*, is characterized by the following items: atomic and biological arms should be eliminated, nationalism should be abolished. Students in the sciences and in medicine, as well as those coming from well-educated families, tend to be internationalist.

The fourth type (lower right quadrant), defined as *activist*, is mainly character-ized by the following items: the principle of violence is not condemned; politics is an important source of satisfaction in life; the university cannot remain aloof from poli-tics; and militant students are not in the minority at the university. The student movement is seen as positive, while capitalism does not appear as a viable system. The students on the far left and, to a lesser degree, those on the left are activists.

Those who call themselves Bourguibists are ambivalent ideologically, with about half of them favorable toward capitalism. Like the apoliticals, they feel free in their society and are the least ready to make sacrifices in order to create a new society. They share with the left, however, the need for some kind of political action within existing institutions. The far left is distinguished by its strong anticapitalist attitudes, its favorable attitudes toward the student movement, and its acceptance of illegal acts.

There is relatively close proximity of all of the political groups in Tunisia, with the exception of the far left. A similar phenomenon was noted in Nigeria (and to some extent also in Australia). In the two African countries, ideological differences appear to be less clearly defined than in the West. There are students of opposing opinions sharing the same political concepts.

In conclusion, rightist, progovernment, and apolitical students are more favor-able to the status quo and the capitalist system and opposed to student activism. Students who place themselves on the left and especially on the far left usually take the opposite view. The far left is, as one would expect, in all of the countries the most radical group compared to the others. There are, however, important nuances related to each country's own sociopolitical situation. The far left in Anglo-Saxon countries is less radical, less extremist, less ready to have recourse to revolution in order to change the status quo, than is the case elsewhere.

In all the countries studied[10] there exists a political continuum ranging from the right or extreme right to the far left in the same order. This range appears even in those countries where the corresponding political parties do not exist officially. These results provide empirical proof of the accuracy of the political scale used in the present study.

Thus we see that in all countries studied (except Tunisia) the most extreme politi-cal tendency on factor T (transformationism) is represented by the far left, including the communists and anarchists in France, Italy, and Great Britain. On the other hand, the most extreme political tendency on factor C (conservatism) is always rep-resented by the right. There is proximity between the right and the center in all of the countries, which indicates a relative homogeneity of general views between these two political groups. The leftist or socialist tendency appeared in all countries except Italy on factor T (transformationism), but its position close to the center of the ideo-logical axis (Austria, Japan, Australia, Great Britain, France, and Nigeria) denotes at the same time a real moderation in attitudes in comparison with the far left, as well as a certain heterogeneity in ideas and opinions.

In the United States and in Spain, the left is closer to the far left on factor T (transformationism) than in most other countries, which indicates a similarity of viewpoints on many political questions. On the other hand, in Italy the position of the left on factor C (conservatism) indicates that this political tendency has more in

---

[10]Except in Tunisia.

common with the center than with the far left or the communists. We note, however, its proximity to the center of the ideological axis which indicates, as in the other countries, moderate attitudes and a certain heterogeneity of opinions of students in this group.

Finally, those who define themselves as apolitical have, nonetheless, political attitudes. Their ideas are close to those of the right in Spain and Nigeria, of the center in Japan, Australia, Austria, and Great Britain, and of the left in Italy, France, and the United States. In this last country, the liberals, who constitute a separate category, appear politically closer to the Democrats and to a lesser degree to the Republicans than to the left. This indicates that their opinions are rather conservative. This last observation is particularly important, as in numerous polls in America, people who call themselves liberals are often considered as being on the left.

Chapter 9

Summary: Conclusions and Implications

It is difficult to write a brief and at the same time adequate summary of an investigation conducted in eleven different countries providing a mass of complex data that do not easily lend themselves to simple recapitulation. In a sense, most of the preceding chapters are themselves summaries of the findings, and it may therefore seem pointless to attempt a summary of these summaries. It does appear to be worthwhile, however, to present an overview of the contents of this volume, indicating what has been attempted and what may be regarded as having been accomplished, what our data have established and what remains to be done in the future. The contents of this chapter will therefore be presented in five sections dealing with (1) the limitations of the investigation, including an autocritique of the general approach and of the methodology; (2) the advantages and special contributions which we have offered and the lacunae we have tried to fill in this important research area; (3) the conclusions which appear to be justified, and their relation to the theoretical formulations in the existing literature and to popular impressions regarding the attitudes and the behavior of students throughout the world; (4) the implications that may legitimately be drawn as to the student movement in general, its nature and its consequences; and (5) suggestions which emerge regarding the student movements of the future and the research that might be encouraged with a view to increasing our knowledge and understanding of a phenomenon which shook the world.

Limitations and Criticisms

Mention has already been made of certain limitations in this study and of possible criticisms which might be directed against it. These may be summarized as follows:

a. Reference is made to "youth culture," but the study is restricted to "student culture." There are two aspects of this criticism, both of them justified. In the first place no data were obtained from young people who were not students. Nonstudents were left out partly for reasons of convenience, but also because the "problem" as seen by the outside world was one of *student* unrest, of *student* protest and occasionally of *student* violence. Second, the study did not include those among the students who had left the university, the dropouts, the alienated, the proponents of the counterculture, the hippies, the flower children, the provos, and all others who, for one reason or another, were attempting to build their own different life in their own nonuniversity climate. This study involved only those who had remained within the university. Although the questionnaire included many items related to and stimu-

273

lated by the content of the counterculture, those who provided the answers were not the most extreme representatives of this tendency, for obvious reasons. The study was, indeed, limited to those at the time attending a university. It is to be hoped that future research will be extended to nonuniversity youth.

b. A second major possible criticism refers to the deficiencies in our sampling procedure. We were, of course, conscious of this problem from the outset, and aware of its implications. One friend and colleague, a distinguished American psychologist who was asked to apply the questionnaire in his own university, refused on the grounds that he could not guarantee to obtain a representative sample; he added that a poor sample was worse than none at all. Our difficulty was due in part to the fact that we had such limited funds at our disposal that we could not hope to obtain an ideal, truly representative sample in so many countries. The problem went deeper, however. In certain countries, and even in certain universities, it was impossible to obtain a complete list of students from which we might choose our sample according to recognized statistical criteria. This was the case, for example, at the University of Paris. What we did as a consequence, after consultation with several experts in this field, was to obtain a varied rather than representative sample— varied in terms of university discipline, the kind of university attended, sex and social status, and political orientation. In some countries, however, as in Yugoslavia, Nigeria, and Tunisia, all our subjects came from one university; in the others a number of different universities were included.

In the case of some countries (as is indicated in the text), a comparison of our sample with the distributions found by major polling organizations gave us a certain degree of assurance that we had not done too badly as far as sampling was concerned. In any case we have placed more stress on the comparisons of groups of differing political orientation, where we feel we are on safer ground, than of national samples as a whole. With regard to the latter we present our results as hypotheses, or at the most as probabilities, in the hope that future research will be able to make a more adequate "representative" test of our findings.

c. The problem of translation, or of equivalences in meaning of the questions applied and the connotations of the terms employed, is exceedingly complex, and our study is open to criticism in this respect. We did not undertake the kind of double translation, for example, from English into Japanese and back again into English, which is so often advocated. Our technique was rather to work from the beginning in several languages, with colleagues who accepted the inclusion of a particular item in the questionnaire only if they thought it could be applied successfully to their students. The native languages of this original group of colleague participants included English, French, Italian, German, Slovene, and Portuguese. Pilot studies were then conducted to iron out any difficulties. As colleagues from other countries joined the enterprise, more languages were added, for example Spanish and Japanese, and in those cases we relied on extensive discussions and on care and caution exercised locally. We feel that the inner consistency of our results gives evidence of the success obtained by this procedure. There were a few cases of misunderstanding, however, which we have identified in the text.

Exact and faithful translation obviously does not always mean exact equivalence of meaning. The political terms "left" and "right," for example, are easily translatable, but "left" in the United States is not the same as "left" in France or Italy. We did find differences between left and right in all countries, and always in the same direction, but not always to the same extent. It is for this reason that we have laid stress on situational factors in each country, explainable only by taking into account the specific historical factors which are responsible for the present political structure.

d. We used a questionnaire, and there are many among our colleagues who would feel that in dealing with such complex attitudinal issues we might have learned more through personal interviews, preferably in depth, or through more systematic participant observation. Here we made the deliberate choice of an extensive rather than a more intensive study. We did have a number of preliminary interviews, individually and in groups, with students who spoke freely and often with passion about the situation within and outside the university as they saw it; these interviews of course helped us in the formulation of our own questions. Our critical survey of the published research in this field and the theoretical formulations of the meaning of the student protest convinced us, however, that generalizations had been based on too few cases and on a geographically too limited sample. We concluded that we could best make a contribution through a study of a sufficiently large number of cases in a variety of different national and regional settings. We are firm believers in the value of intensive techniques, but we feel that the method we chose can also make a real contribution. We would like to think that some of the issues we have raised may suggest future topics of research of a more intensive nature.

Specific Contributions

We have already indicated what we regard as the major specific contribution of the study. To the best of our knowledge, ours is the first, and probably the only, investigation which has attempted to get answers to the same questions from students in a large number of different countries. (If we are mistaken in this claim, we hereby present our apologies to those colleagues whom we have slighted.) This enabled us to discover whether statements made about *"the* students" but based on research within one country would apply equally well to students elsewhere. It may be that we were somewhat too ambitious. Presenting and analyzing data from eleven different countries (plus three others where the relatively small number of respondents limited our analysis) not only resulted in considerable delay in preparing this report, but also created difficulties in presenting the results as clearly and as readably as we would have wished. We believe, however, that this extension was worthwhile, since it supplied us with sufficient variety to test our hypotheses more fully and with greater confidence.

A second contribution, in our judgment, arises from the fact that our rather lengthy and complex questionnaire made it possible for us to go considerably beyond the usual presentation of results. We were able to describe a number of interrelationships, indicating the degree of correspondence among the answers to a number of different questions.

In addition, our central focus on the political self-identification of our respondents brought the student's position into relation with a whole series of opinions and attitudes. Our focus was not exclusively, or even mainly, on activists (or the far left) but on the whole range from far left to right. It seemed to us that an understanding of the situation in each country required us to consider the total pattern rather than concentrate only on those who have attracted attention because of their activist or revolutionary involvement.

Some Conclusions

We shall make no attempt to review at this point all the conclusions (or at least probabilities) which seem to us to emerge from our data. Instead we shall rephrase, in terms of questions, a number of the issues which we identified in the literature, and see to what extent they are borne out by our data.

a. Is there (or was there) a universal, or at least international, culture common to the students of the world? In part, but in part only. It is not easy to determine whether or not a "culture" exists; it is never present to the same extent or with the same qualities in all the members of a particular society. We felt, however, that one reasonable criterion would be that 50% or more of the respondents agreed with the particular attitude or cultural item under consideration. We found that the majority of our respondents, for example, were against racism and urged that nationalism be abolished. There were exceptions, however: nationalism was supported by those from Nigeria and Tunisia. In all countries except Australia and the United States, 50 percent or more were in favor of the elimination of capitalism. (This question did not apply in Yugoslavia.) On the other hand, drugs (at least marijuana) were looked upon favorably in the United States but not elsewhere. There is in general much less interest in political activity in the United States than in other countries, and the plans of American students for the future are much more likely to be concerned with private issues such as occupational careers and the family. A positive attitude toward the university and satisfaction with what it has to offer are much more common among Anglo-Saxon (and also Nigerian) respondents than elsewhere; the Anglo-Saxon students also show a more marked tendency to recognize good aspects of their society in general. On many issues, as our results have indicated, the differences among countries are striking.

On almost every issue there are such marked differences associated with political position as to indicate that variations within a nation are at least as important as variations among nations. The far left, usually regarded as the political base for radical activists, is everywhere in the minority. In the Anglo-Saxon countries, this group constitutes an even smaller minority than elsewhere, and also is much less extremist in its political views than the far left, for example, in France, Italy, Spain, or Japan. For all these reasons (and many more examples could be given) we feel justified in concluding that the idea of a single, pervasive youth culture, even if restricted to the case of students, is not supported by our data.

b. Is there a conflict of generations? The position represented by a positive answer to this question usually takes on a Freudian flavor, with the conflict phrased in terms of a slightly modified Oedipus complex. We have already indicated our doubts about a theory which presumably has universal implications and yet applies to only a small minority of students, the activists. In our own investigation we used a relatively simple and superficial approach, asking our respondents how close they felt to their parents on a number of dimensions, and we realize that no psychoanalysts would accept our results as constituting a refutation of their thesis. At the same time we are struck by the fact that so many students express a feeling of closeness to their parents rather than conflict. As already indicated, we were impressed also by the extent of disagreement among different groups of students; in other words, we mostly saw an *intra*-generation conflict rather than one between generations.

c. Are those on the far left attempting to put into effect ideas held by their liberal, well-to-do, well-educated parents? This is one of the striking conclusions reached in some of the American studies. Our data do not contradict this finding as far as the United States is concerned, but in other countries, such as France and Italy, students on the far left are more likely to come from poorer, less well-educated families. This is one issue in connection with which the extension of the investigation to a number of different countries helps to clarify and limit an otherwise too facile generalization. We must add that in general, even in the United States, those who feel closest to their parents are usually on the right rather than on the left of the political spectrum.

d. Are students on the far left more frequently found in the social sciences than in other disciplines? Our data provide moderate support for an affirmative answer to this question. The analysis which we undertook indicates that in a number of countries students in the social sciences show a definite tendency to express views that are clearly to the left of center. In some countries there is no evidence of such an association. In no country, however, is the reverse relationship found; that is to say, there are no countries in our sample in which the social sciences are associated with rightist political tendencies.

e. Do students on the far left usually identify with any particular religious orientation? In earlier studies in the United States they apparently tended to be found among Jews, liberal Protestants, and atheists. In our cross-cultural study, a very large proportion of them are nonbelievers or atheists, with a negative attitude toward religion in general.

f. Is there any evidence as to whether the attitudes identified in 1969–70 have persisted to the present day? Our 1977 study was limited to two countries, France and the United States, and to a small (approximately 100 respondents in each case) but varied sample; we present these new results with considerable caution. It is striking to note how little change there has been in general. In the United States we find a small but definite move toward the right; in France there is a slight increase in the moderate left at the expense of the center. There is still considerable support for the "here and now" philosophy which is part of the counterculture, and in France a greater tolerance regarding the use of marijuana.

Some Implications

We have already given reasons, which we hope will be regarded as adequate, for our emphasis on the importance of cross-cultural comparisons. Social scientists throughout the world are theoretically aware that generalizations from research in one area and in one culture are unwarranted and often dangerous, but they frequently forget! We know of no better way of overcoming this danger than by developing and applying techniques that can be used in other cultures. At the same time we have described some of the difficulties we encountered in developing a research instrument that would have the same meaning in different cultures.

These were not the only problems. Our colleague from Brazil was very helpful in the early planning stages, but we found it impossible to apply the questionnaire in that country in view of the political situation there. The questionnaire was used in Tunisia but only after deleting a number of items which were regarded as too sensitive. In Yugoslavia, although we were under the impression after our preliminary meetings that agreement had been reached, it was found impossible to apply the same political categories as elsewhere; this in turn made impossible many of the comparisons we wanted to draw. These problems are indicated in the text. They made our life difficult, but not enough to discourage us from using the considerable amount of material that remained.

Perhaps because of our concern with the mass of detail at our disposal, we did not develop any adequate theory of the nature of the student movement in general. Our feeling was that we first needed more data, and in the light of our results we have been able to draw certain implications regarding the prevalence of youth culture, the characteristics of the protesters, the conflict of generations, and so forth. We would like now to make an attempt to go a little further.

Those students who defined themselves as on the left, and particularly on the far left, were in general the most negative about their society, the university, and their parents. They were the ones who were most disturbed by what they saw as the injustices of the present system, and the most eager to do something about them. The student movement gave them a sense of power, a feeling that something could after all be accomplished. This was frequently mentioned by those who participated, either as leaders or as followers, in the various student manifestations. The radicals were always a minority, but when they were joined by others as a consequence of confrontation with the police or in order to protest unpopular government actions (the Vietnam War, pollution, etc.), these others also participated in this sense of power. This was a heady, exhilarating experience, and undoubtedly gave to many students the feeling that they now represented a group to be reckoned with.

This feeling did not die with the apparent end of conflict in 1970. There has been a whole series of events in many countries in more recent years, some even contributing to the toppling of the government in power, in which students played an active role. In some cases the trouble has arisen in relation to the specific situation in the university, such as the raising of fees for foreign students (Great Britain) or building on an area where students had been killed (Kent State University in the United States); in others it has been more general, expressing discontent with the government's actions and also with the difficulty of finding adequate jobs after graduation (Italy). Whatever the specific cause, the movement depended on a consciousness of power, student power. This is perhaps the major heritage of the "events" from 1966 to 1970.

In many cases the students have had, and continue to express, legitimate grievances. They have also protested, and continue to protest, against injustices to others (as in the case of racism), dangers to society (pollution), and the excesses of nationalism. Rarely have adults given to these problems the attention they deserve. In these respects, the elders may learn from the young; there is need for an "ascending education" in which students do some of the teaching.

Future Research

We present now a few suggestions regarding the kinds of research which in our judgment would deepen our knowledge in the general area of student attitudes. Some of these have already been indicated.

1. Extension of research to youth outside the university in order to discover what is specific to students.
2. An intensive study of individual cases in several countries, together with participant observation of student activities.
3. Methodological improvements with regard to sampling and translation.
4. Inclusion of more detailed knowledge about the particular situation in each country—its social, economic, and political history—in order more fully to understand the range and frequency of the expressed attitudes.
5. A comparison of the attitudes of students with those of their own parents. Our data on this point come entirely from what students themselves said about their closeness or distance from parental values. Granting that their definition of the situation is itself important, it would be of value to determine to what extent the definition of closeness or distance is shared by the parents.
6. Perhaps most important, a study of the degree of persistence or change in student attitudes over time. There have been opinion polls, particularly in the United States, which have asked the same or similar questions at various intervals; these are certainly welcome, but we are convinced that such trend studies should be based on information more complete than those usually associated with polls. Our own 1977 study was conducted with this in mind, but as we have already indicated, our samples are too small for the results to be entirely convincing. Trend studies might in our judgment be fruitfully applied in two ways. First, the same questions might be asked at intervals of samples of students from the same countries and as far as possible the same universities. This would answer more adequately some of the questions we have raised. Are there changes in the attitudes of successive generations of students with regard to their society, the university, politics, nationalism and internationalism, their parents, and so forth? Second, it would be at least as interesting to study the changes in the attitudes over time of the respondents in the original study. Would negative reactions, for example, against racism, nationalism, and capitalism persist into later life? Would the passing of the years move the respondents who reacted negatively to these issues toward a more conservative "Establishment" position? This application of what has been called the "panel" method might make it possible to predict a little more accurately from the results obtained today what changes we should expect in the near future.

A Final Comment

If we are correct in our emphasis on legitimate grievances, on the one hand, and on the phenomenon of student power, on the other, should we expect clashes in the future, with a possible revival, at least in some countries, of a student movement? Predictions are almost always difficult if not dangerous, but both history and today's newspapers indicate that we should expect clashes, although they give us no definite clues as to when or where. Can we prepare for this possibility in any constructive manner?

At the time of the major confrontations in the late sixties, it looked to some people as if society had been divided by age into two opposing camps. There was even talk of "generationism" comparable to racism, with negative stereotypes and prejudice directed by the young against their elders and vice versa. (It was forgotten by both sides that "youth" might frequently be a matter of temperament and personality rather than of years, and also that the conflict was by no means universal, but was restricted to a minority.) Social scientists have shown that something can be done about racism; not enough to eliminate the problem, but at the local level sometimes capable of reducing the severity of the conflict. Certain instances of industrial disagreement have also been controlled, to the satisfaction of both sides, as a result of the intervention of social scientists. The high hopes raised by Kurt Lewin through the development of "action research" have not been realized, but there are more than occasional successes to its credit.

Have we learned anything from the applications in other fields to justify the hope that something can be done in connection with "generationism" as well? One thing is certain: no problems were solved when student violence was met by counterviolence. Can we develop techniques of dialogue or communication which might help? Are there any "superordinate goals," common to both generations, related to the fundamental problems of society, realizable only by joint action, to which we can appeal? This has occasionally been accomplished in connection with issues within the university. Can it be extended more widely?

What can the social sciences contribute in the way of specific solutions to these practical problems?

We are convinced that some degree of opposition between generations is inevitable. The attitudes of the young and their criticisms—sometimes justified, sometimes exaggerated—present a challenge to all those concerned with the understanding of social issues and with contributing to the solution of social problems. We express the hope that social scientists will respond to this challenge and will aid in the development of specific approaches which will lead to cooperation rather than confrontation in the future.

Appendices

A Short Description of the University System and of the Student Movement in the Different Countries

This international research included eleven countries, which may be classified by their geographical location into four main groups:

1. Five European countries
   a) France, Italy
   b) Austria, Great Britain
   c) Spain
2. One socialist country in Europe, Yugoslavia
3. Two African countries
   a) Tunisia
   b) Nigeria
4. Three other countries
   a) In America, the United States
   b) In Oceania, Australia
   c) In Asia, Japan

We present here a short description of the university system and of the student movement in each country. While these brief sketches are limited, they do allow us to underline specific problems for students in their own nation. This description applies to the situation at the time this investigation was conducted, 1969–70.

Europe

COUNTRIES WITH A REVOLUTIONARY TRADITION

FRANCE

There was already a student movement at least in terms of the expression of a collective identity around the year 1900. The National Student Union of France (l'Union Nationale des Etudiants de France, or UNEF), created in 1907, was one of the first organizations specifically for students, but until 1945 it dealt mainly with the university and its structure. However, in 1936, during the era of the Popular Front (le Front Populaire), violent confrontations occurred in the Latin Quarter between the students on the right and those on the left. These clashes involved a large part of the student world.

After World War II, which left France extremely divided politically and the French people extremely politicized, the National Student Union entered the arenas of society and of politics. The first student strike of national proportions, in 1947, was organized in order to improve the general living conditions of university students. Although various political tendencies were part of the National Student Union, the left was particularly influential.

The Cold War in the early 1950s drained power away from the left in the National Student Union, as conservatives and neofascists became more influential. It was only in 1956, at the time of the elections for the National Assembly, that the left composed the majority nationally and in the Student Union.

The Algerian War, from 1956 to 1961, marked a turning point for this organization. In effect, the Student Union played an important political role in the regrouping of the various workers' unions in order to force the government to negotiate—which eventually ended in the independence of Algeria. This war provoked a profound awakening of the political consciousness of the members of the Student Union and influenced their subsequent actions. Since then this union has not ceased its opposition to the government—an opposition which has often taken the form of violence. At the same time, however, internal dissension grew between the "orthodox" communists and the groups on the far left, which were composed of Trotskyites and Maoists. These extremist groups were no longer clandestine and their ranks multiplied.

This "degeneration" of communism, to use the term of Duprat (1968), provoked a considerable departure of the "ultras" of the Communist party, as they sought out more extreme movements which were seen as more likely to reply to their needs.

The explosion of May 1968 marked the end of this first phase. Since this date the student movement has taken an original form which broke away from the traditional student organizations. The students became an autonomous political force in their own right. Unlike the situation in other countries, such as Italy or West Germany, the French student movement initiated a general social revolt. "Awakened by the violence of the police against the students, many Frenchmen felt the need to participate in the general protest of the students" (J. Minces, 1970, p. 154). Yet the French student protest movement did not really innovate any new forms of action, except in the case of certain groups of anarchists. The action taken, according to Minces (1970), was an imitation of previous revolutions, the copy of actions taken in other countries (Italy, Japan, West Germany, the United States).

If the themes of the "conflict of generations" and of the "counterculture" often appeared in Anglo-Saxon countries as tied to the student movement, in France as in Italy it is more correct to speak of a crisis in the university due to the archaic nature of its organization. All observers underlined the nonadaptation of the university to contemporary society. A contradiction existed between the "liberal" orientation of the university and the social and economic needs of the country. The university as an institution had not really been greatly modified since the end of World War II, while the composition of society and the proportion of the student population had changed vastly. For example, as in many industrialized countries, the number of

French students doubled in less than ten years. This fact alone changed the meaning of advanced studies. In the past, entry of students into advanced university studies almost automatically insured access to the elite. Now, either many graduates could not find work or they were underemployed. Thus the French university in 1968 was truly in a state of organizational crisis, as Touraine (1972) and others have pointed out.

The change in university training from that of an elite to that of a wider population, rather than augmenting the chances of the lower classes, only raised the absolute number of students who were not "inheritors" of the system, as Bourdieu and Passeron (1964) demonstrated in denouncing the illusion of the democratization of the university system. In fact, not only were the chances of access to higher education a function of social class, but the functioning itself of the university favored those who were favored and disfavored those who were disfavored.

Whatever the selection criteria, the dropout rate in the French universities was very high. We need only look at the statistics of those who failed or who dropped out to see that they were the highest in Europe (cf. Bisseret, 1968; Delage, 1967; Poignant, 1967).

The so-called neutrality of the university was put into question. The university was denounced as an institution regimented by the values and models of the bourgeoisie. Bourdieu and Passeron treated the university as a fundamental, ideological apparatus which determined the behavior of those who frequented it.

ITALY

Italy, like France, is a country of strong political traditions, with a Communist party which has become more and more influential, as the recent (1976) elections have proved. The Italian Communist party is the largest in Europe outside of the East European countries. Anti-Stalin in nature and tradition, the party has always favored theoretical research in the political domain.

Unlike the French, the Italian Communist party did not take an antagonistic position vis-à-vis the student movement, but always encouraged a dialogue with it. As Rossanda suggests (1971), the Italian working class has always been characterized by a combative spirit and was affected by the student movement when it exploded.

The student movement in Italy was born in a context of social and political conflicts, which themselves became more acute due to the growth of a mobile proletariat and of hostile emigrants moving from the south to the north and from rural environments to the cities. This imbalance in the social fabric was exploited by the party on the far right, the Italian Social Movement (il Movimento Sociale Italiano, or MSI). This party obtained 4.5 percent of the votes in the 1968 elections, promising work to the unemployed, a better standard of living to the lower classes, and order to the middle classes. The effects of this party were not negligible; its frequent and violent battles with groups on the far left contributed both to growing social tension and to the hardening of the leftist groups' positions.

The student protest in Italy occurred on three planes. On the university level, the students complained of the lack of contact with their professors, of the quality of their teachers, of failure to provide education for the masses, and of the lack of job opportunities. Nationally, the students criticized the institutions of what they regarded as a corrupt and irresponsible system. They were hostile to the model of representative democracy, such as that of the United States, and to the model of

Soviet communism, both of which, according to them, represented another form of imperialism. More generally, the students rejected the values of modern society. In addition to traditional criticism of a political nature, the student movement raised the issues of authoritarianism, the "neutrality" of culture, repressive tolerance, etc. All of these were somewhat similar to issues which emerged at Berlin, Nanterre, and Berkeley.

While the student protest movement was not new in Italy, it gained real influence in 1967, especially in Trento, Venice, and Pisa, and then spread throughout the country in 1968. Turin and Rome became centers for the student protesters. Beginning with purely structural demands for changes in the university, the students then attacked the politics of the government, which, according to them, was accomplishing nothing. Higher education in Italy, even more than in France, was considered archaic, based on hierarchical structures which were rigid, if not medieval. As in other countries, the number of students had doubled in ten years and therefore overburdening outdated university systems. We must also note the existence of a large number of students rather specific to Italy—students "fuori corso" (not in courses), who, aged between 28 and 30, were still at the university.

The catastrophic state of the university and what the students considered the lack of good faith of administrators concerning university changes favored the growth of the student movement and of revolutionary groups.

COUNTRIES WITH A "SOCIAL-DEMOCRATIC" TRADITION

GREAT BRITAIN

In all of the Anglo-Saxon countries, the revolutionary political tradition is weak, with no real leftist, Marxist heritage. In Great Britain the Labor party is pragmatic and seeks above all else "to resolve antagonistic conflicts by the integration into capitalism of partial reforms" (Brau, 1968, p. 116).

The Communist party has very little influence, as its members are few. This situation gave to the rebellion of young people a rather special flavor: it was more anti-institutional than truly a politically oriented phenomenon. The few student manifestations before 1967 were directed against the war in Vietnam and against the use of atomic weapons. The most remarkable peace marches occurred in 1963. In 1964 there appeared violent groups like the "mods" and the "rockers," who started riots in Clayton, Margate, and Brighton. Finally, about 1966 an atmosphere often described as one "of madness" took hold with the advent of Carnaby Street, miniskirts, and pop music, introduced by the Beatles and the Rolling Stones. These events suggest a cultural, esthetic, and artistic revolution, which is not specific to students. It was only from 1967, with the affair of the London School of Economics discussed below, that we can speak of a truly student protest movement. Comprised of many diverse ideological groups, the movement transformed diffuse criticisms into a systematic attack against the university system and capitalist society. Still, these actions were undertaken by a minority; student activism was never as strong in Great Britain as it was in many other countries of Europe.

As in France and Italy, there occurred a rapid growth in the student population. Before World War II, 2.7 percent of young people in the same age bracket were students; in 1967 this percentage had risen to 11 percent. As in other European countries, Great Britain's university system was not equipped to handle this rapid increase. The explosion in numbers created a need for more professors; it was also pointed out that they were often aided by inexperienced assistants. The students also complained of the low intellectual level of instruction, a devaluation of scholarships relative to the cost of living, and a general crowding of all university buildings.

Blackburn (1969) describes this phenomenon as a "new poverty." Although the state financed higher education, industry gained more and more power at the universities, creating, modifying, and even directing entire departments as a function of the economic needs of supply and demand.

In Great Britain, as elsewhere, there was also the major problem of employment. Students, who constituted a group of the "elite," no longer received the same social advantages. The diploma, for them, ceased to represent, as noted Jones, Barnett, and Wengral (1967), an assured guarantee of a job on the level of their accomplishments.

Finally, the adoption of the binary system, as proposed by the government's Secretary for Teaching and Sciences Crosland in 1965, provoked a certain malaise. In effect, this system ended with two sorts of higher education: two-thirds of the students remained within the "traditional" model, receiving a liberal arts education; the remaining third of the students obtained a truly professional education which was highly specialized and financed by local authorities. The students in the second category considered themselves as second-class students, as the "poor relatives" of the others. Their training was, according to them, overly specialized.

Insufficiency of resources, poor working conditions, the influence of industry, and the binary system represent the sources of the principal student demands, expressed by the National Union of Students. In addition to these criticisms, we must note the actions of some students in regard to the occupation of the Suez Canal, the struggle against racism and colonialism, and, more internationally, the efforts of the Campaign for Nuclear Disarmament. It remains true, however, that agitation at the universities in Great Britain had a basis which was less politically motivated than in other European countries. Indeed, student demands, except for those concerning movements for peace, concerned primarily the university.

The first student manifestation, in 1967, occurred at the London School of Economics. This event had a true political character. Students proclaimed the existence of "student power" and rejected the notion of *in loco parentis*. In addition, they wanted to create a free university, with student control of the content of instruction. These students saw the university as an institution of social criticism. The university itself, its ideology, and its role in society were questioned.

While not as widespread as in other European countries or in the United States, student protests erupted in 1968. Although the National Union of Students and the movements on the left, especially the Radical Students' Alliance, agreed with regard to concrete questions relating to the university system, there was also a transformation in the perspectives of the student movement in Great Britain due to foreign student movements, such as that of the National Student Union in France and of Students for a Democratic Society (SDS) in West Germany. New tactics, such as occupations of buildings and sit-ins were practiced, both in order to question university and governmental policies and to express the students' disapproval.

The revolutionary Socialist Students' Federation was also founded in 1968. Yet this and indeed most of these groups on the left reflected the concerns with regard to the university system rather than truly political perspectives, due to the lack of a revolutionary heritage (Blackburn, 1969). The student revolt in Great Britain remained an affair of a small minority, more or less restricted to the domain of the social sciences, who questioned their society and the nature of their own education. In general, the student movement in Great Britain seemed more similar to the counterculture movement of certain leftists in the United States than to student movements in countries having a long Marxist tradition.

AUSTRIA

The student protest movement in Austria was only a marginal phenomenon, despite the political past and the proximity to West Germany, where student manifestations were among the most violent.

In 1970 the People's party, which for twenty years had the majority in Parliament and directed a rather conservative government, lost in the general elections to the Socialist party. This party formed the first socialist government in Austria since World War II. In spite of this change, however, Austria did not undergo any political crisis of major consequence. The new government continued to practice a brand of prudent reformism.

The student movement of the far left, aligned to that of West Germany, denounced this "bourgeois" reformism. At the same time, student demands reflected some of the same themes as elsewhere, particularly that of the overpopulation of the universities. But really large student demonstrations did not occur: "it seems that the students on the right in Austria, who for more than a century have dominated university life, remain intact and entirely control political activities in the universities" (Markovits and Freund, 1973, p. 1).

The student protests were limited to the University of Vienna, which is the most important Austrian university and the most liberal and progressive institution in the country. It appears reasonable to say that the conservatism of the students and the rejection of politicization by official organizations were the primary blocks to activism of the masses.

SPAIN, A COUNTRY WITH A HISTORY OF AUTHORITARIANISM

In comparison to other European countries, the student rebellion in Spain had a rather specific character. Young people in Spain, until very recently with the restoration of the monarchy, grew up knowing only the regime of Franco. Opposing political parties were not able to function, except clandestinely.

In 1950 the working classes began to protest, especially in the Asturias and in Catalonia, where the students supported them. After 1952 a certain cultural renaissance occurred. The general level of higher education made important advances. People spoke again in veiled terms of Marx and of social classes in courses on philosophy, law, sociology, and economy. Students and intellectuals became more and more conscious of the need for political action. "You must make politics, unless you want politics to be made against you," said the poet Antonio Machado.

The strikes of miners in the Asturias and in Leon during the summer of 1963 marked an important step in the struggle against the Franco regime. The violent repression of these strikes, ignored by the press, was denounced in a letter signed by painters, poets, academicians, authors, actors, editors, and professors from all over the world. This affair seemingly influenced the students and contributed to their op-position to the government. An atmosphere of revolt arose in Spanish universities, where the protest extended to political issues.

After serious riots with the police, in 1958 the Spanish Student Union obtained some freedom and became more liberal, but the government took away from this or-ganization most of its power and responsibility. At this time many illegal and clan-destine groups of students and professors were formed. Although the government tried to defuse these groups by playing on the apparent liberalization of the Spanish Student Union, it failed, as it did also with the creation of an official union, whose elections the students boycotted. The illegal groups grew in importance and influ-ence, especially the Democratic Spanish University Federation (Federación Universi-taria Democrática Española) and the Spanish Democratic Union (Sindicato Español Democrático).

The student movement reacted strongly against the dictatorship, claiming the right to freedom of expression as well as amnesty for political prisoners and de-manding the closing of American air bases in Spain. Given the structure of the uni-versity and the political system the rights of students and those of many other groups in society were not respected. In this sense, it was everyone's duty to unite with the forces opposing the government which were fighting for a true democracy in Spain.

Faced with a government closed to all dialogue, the protesting students con-cluded that "we know that it will be possible to destroy it only through violence" (*Democracia Popular*, January 1968).

The two centers of rebellion were Madrid and Barcelona, but the revolt spread to other universities. Groups of Trotskyites, Maoists, and Guevarists began to be ac-tive during this period. The struggle against the war in Vietnam and against the American presence in Spain intensified. Student agitation grew, resulting in the crea-tion of a university police force.

While much of the criticism concerned politics and policies, as in other countries, the students also attacked the university system for its antidemocratic nature, with less than 1 percent of the children of workers enrolled as students.

The structures of instruction were judged as out of date and the allotted budget as insufficient. Moreover, the lack of jobs constituted an important problem.

In general, the student movement in Spain seemed similar to those which devel-oped in Latin America, rather than to those in Europe or in the Anglo-Saxon coun-tries. Two major orientations guided the movement. For some it was a question of creating the first conditions for an armed battle on Spanish soil, while for others it was necessary to try to undermine Franco's regime by a common struggle of the stu-dents and the workers.

YUGOSLAVIA, A SOCIALIST COUNTRY IN EUROPE

The protest movement in the socialist countries of Europe has, as we would ex-pect, a different nature than that in the countries in Western Europe. In contrast to the situation in many other countries, students are not asking for a change in the re-gime of their country. In none of the socialist countries is a return to capitalism or a "liberal," social—democratic type of socialism contemplated. Rather, the students desire to improve the present system in fighting against bureaucracy and the power of the party, which sometimes has turned away from the Marxist ideal. Also, the students claim the right to factual information and freedom of expression; in these demands they are supported by a large percentage of the intelligentsia of their country.

Yugoslavia is certainly in many respects the most liberal country of the socialist bloc. The country is still undergoing important economic difficulties, and there are marked tensions among the country's different nationalities, languages, and cultures. Moreover, the notion of "self-rule" for the workers often serves, as Perlman notes (1970), as a "rationalization for a bureaucracy which is technocratic and commercial, having succeeded in concentrating in its hands riches and power created by Yugoslavian workers" (p. 267). Thus inequalities multiply.

Yugoslavia, like Czechoslovakia and Poland, experienced student agitation. Its students, much more than their counterparts in these other countries, seem to have had information about student movements in other countries. Not only were they interested but they felt concerned. The sit-in organized by the students of Ljubljana to protest the imprisonment of young high school students in France is one example of their knowledge. Another is the letter published in the review *Students* in April 1968, which was signed by many students in philosophy, opposing antisemitism and the repression of intellectuals in Poland. (*Students*, 1968). These students also protested against the war in Vietnam and against militarism.

Unlike student movements in the West, which generally oppose at any given moment their respective governments and the values they represent, the protesting students in Yugoslavia share the ideology of their government. They desire only that the social and political programs of their country be truly implemented or partially modified. They denounce the insufficiencies of their government's economic policies and also social inequalities, demanding more democracy. They criticize their elders for having betrayed, in some ways, the socialist revolution.

The University of Ljubljana (included in our study) and the University of Belgrade were the two major points of student protest in Yugoslavia. The protests became rather important by 1968 and remained so thereafter. It is striking to see that in the Republic of Slovenia, characterized by a high degree of economic development, there was the most lively political and university protest.

At the university, the students demanded the right of "self-rule" and, as *Students* (1968) indicates, wanted to establish with their professors "a modern program," substituting discussion for lectures in most of their courses. The students also believed that access to education was not very democratic. For example, in Ljubljana only 35 percent of the students were children of workers and of peasants, whereas these groups comprised 80 percent of the population of Slovenia. The youth of Ljubljana still suffered from the fact that their presence at the university depended on their parents' wealth and influence.

The students realized that university reforms could not be separated from more general problems concerning their socialist country. As a student editorial reported, "There can be no reform at the university if there is no reform in society at large, because we cannot separate the university from the ensemble of other social institutions" (*Susret*, June 1, 1968). It is striking to see here, as elsewhere, a criticism of the university and political systems which leads to more general criticism of society. We find again the idea and hope for the creation of a nonalienating society and the elaboration of a nonalienating culture.

TWO AFRICAN COUNTRIES

Problems raised by student movements in African countries are radically different from those of industralized countries. First, colonization has had important consequences on political institutions and on the university and educational system. The content of teaching is often poorly adapted to the country and based on a European model. The level of literacy is low; only an elite reaches as far as secondary or higher education. Culturally there is a hiatus between the "traditional" masses and the "modern" elite. There is conflict between Western models, suggested by some, and traditional tendencies, revitalized by the national movements of independence.

Student agitation rarely reaches outside the university or the secondary school. Students here more than elsewhere are a privileged group and therefore are the elite of the country.

TUNISIA

Independent since 1956, Tunisia is often considered both in Africa and in the West, as a "successful" developing country. It is seen as democratic, liberal, secular, and even socialistic (Palmiery, 1969). The middle classes, which abandoned the traditional socioreligious structure during colonization, assimilated technical methods and Western culture, thus producing the middle-level workers in modern Tunisia.

The old Destour, a movement of the upper middle class, asked only for more participation within the colonial context. The Neo-Destour, created by Bourguiba in 1934, appeared as a more radical protest movement, advocating changes in the economic and political structures of the country.

Tunisian socialism, which was also called "Bourguibist realism," stresses realism and progress rather than ideology. Socialism, Bourguiba wrote in describing his first four-year plan, "is not a frozen ideology, elaborated in an ivory tower or immobilized by dogmatism."

In the late sixties socialist reforms were introduced aiming to accelerate the development of cooperatives in agriculture, business, and industry. Many small businesses were closed as a result and a wave of unemployment occurred followed by an increased emigration to France. The reforms were considered a failure. Impatient with the slowness of economic development the population became restive and popular protest appeared in endemic fashion.

Impatient with the slowness of economic development, the population became more restive. Popular movements appeared in endemic fashion. University manifestations, begun in 1966, became more violent. The opposition began to develop a political character. The major workers' and students' unions took positions of protest. A new radical opposition was organized around the Groupe d'Etudes et d'Action Socialiste Tunisien, also called "Perspective." This group, founded in 1960 in Paris, had a Marxist tendency but refused to align with the Tunisian Communist party or with Trotskyist cells. University manifestations in December 1966 and the repression, which followed led this group to specify its objectives more fully. The general intensification of the protests (1967–1968) resulted in stronger and stronger action by the government. There were four deaths in 1971–72, all of high school or university students.

The governmental repression, which surprised the student as well as the nonstudent world, was judged as vain and led to the fall of Ben Salah. The group "Perspective" was, for all practical purposes, dissolved in 1968.

If the sociopolitical situation of the country contributed to student discontent, the state of the university system also played an important role in the student protests. As in the other countries studied here, but perhaps even more strikingly, the number of students grew rapidly in ten years. For example, the University of Tunis registered 2,000 students at its creation in 1960 but had grown by 1968 (according to Lang and Lang 1972), to nearly 8,000. Lang and Lang (1972) also report: "In its present state, the university reunites in the long run traditional Islamic studies and establishments which continue the part of the colonial heritage. They are, consequently, strongly influenced by tradition and French educational models" (p. 18).

To this duality between two linguistic and cultural modes is added the problem of students who feel the need to study abroad; in many cases the value of Tunisian diplomas is questioned. Tunisia did not succeed in training a sufficient number of technicians and engineers. Because of the lack of the necessary educational structures, many students were sent abroad, the majority to France, and some never returned to their own country. Another problem arose because of the prestige accorded to students who had studied abroad. This led many of the Tunisian elite to choose to study in France rather than in Tunisia. Thus students at universities in Tunisia feel like "poor relations" and believe that they do not have the same status and consideration as those who study in France.

We also find an important disparity between rural and urban areas and another in terms of the socioprofessional background of the parents. As Lang and Lang note (1972):

> While students come from all over Tunisia, they are never geographically representative. The major cities like Tunis, Sousse, and Sfax contribute more than their part, in general because secondary schools have long been established in these regions. Habitually, even students born in isolated regions come to the university from an urban milieu rather than a rural one. Thus, in a country essentially rural and where agriculture is the main industry, only one quarter of the university students come from a rural background. Given these circumstances, it is not surprising that many Tunisian students, like those in other countries, are disproportionally recruited from the upper and middle classes of the country p. 60].

Finally, students in Tunisia, like their counterparts in Western countries, feel uncertain about their professional future. This slogan was often repeated during the protests: "With or without education, we have no future." These various factors of discontent at the university level and at the social level maintain strong tension among the students. Sporadically, there are student manifestations and strikes which force the government to close the universities.

NIGERIA

Before the military came to power in 1966 and banished all parties and abolished all elections, Nigeria had some twenty-seven political parties, of which the most important were the Northern People's Congress, Action Group, and the National Convention of Nigerian Citizens.

The educational system of the country, as is often the case in former colonized countries, remained structured on the model of the colonial power. In the 1960s, half of the Nigerian leaders and functionaries had received their primary or secondary education in a mission school. In higher education the British influence was even more apparent. In 1970, 10,000 students were registered in the country's five universities.

The University of Ibadan, where our study was conducted in Nigeria, is the oldest (founded in 1948) and the most prestigious in the country. Its goal was to provide the country with qualified personnel capable of taking over the control of the administration. Thus the first generations of graduates had access to the very highest positions. As numbers grew, this situation changed.

Traditionally, wealthy families preferred to send their children to schools abroad, a situation which has facilitated access to the university for capable students of humble backgrounds.

We must note that the University of Ibadan retained strong ties with the British universities until 1963 in all matters pertaining to curriculum and examinations. This situation represented a source of prestige for this Nigerian institution, but was also a source of anxiety for the students. Its very rigid system of examinations, its university norms, and its more and more restricted nature led many students to look for success in foreign universities. Once their studies were over, many returned as professors or as assistants. Students at the university complain that even if their university is the best in their country, the diploma they receive does not have the same prestige as that received abroad. Thus the students at Ibadan raise as issues the poor quality of the student-teacher relationship and the devaluation of their diplomas.

In a general way, the emphasis given to education, as Ojetunde suggests (1969), resulted on the individual level in a weakening of family ties and the attenuation of the relationships with the traditional milieu. The rupture with the parents was born of the conflict between the ambitions of the young and the incapacity of some parents to offer their children higher education. The older generation lost some of its authority and often became hostile toward the young people. This alienation of educated youth in relation to their family, which corresponds to what we call elsewhere the generation conflict is, according to Ojetunde (1969), stronger in Nigeria than in the United States. In effect, the dissolution of the family is reinforced by life styles of young people influenced by Western norms, while the family unit remains often poorly educated (in the Western sense) and traditional.

Although the relationships between the "moderns" and the "traditionalists" are in conflict and many young people are dissatisfied with their education, no rebellions occurred in the universities until 1950, at Ibadan, and May 1968, at Ife.

The revolt in 1950 at Ibadan was caused by the installation of barbed wire around the dormitories, which was to stop late-night sorties by the men and the unauthorized visits from women. The dormitories were occupied, automobiles were overturned and burned, and the sacking of the vice-chancellor was demanded. Public reaction at the time was very hostile to the students, who were seen as a privileged few, "the tax-payers' suckers," and "the pampered adults." The university itself was viewed as "the multi-million-dollar baby." After the expulsion of five students, peace returned to the campus.

In May 1968, a violent revolt occurred at Ife, which was important in that it happened under a military regime and martial law was evoked. The university was closed for three weeks. The students were protesting against the poor relationships between themselves and the university administration. They demanded the right to assemble freely in order to participate in social activities.

At the time of this study, the students, mainly at Ibadan, were not rebelling violently against the university. Their actions were limited to peaceful demonstrations and sit-ins. The students were much more demanding with regard to national politics. Any declaration or act of a minister or of a member of government which was judged unfavorably by the students could provoke confrontations between the students and the police. Such confrontations did not occur at the university itself.

The student revolt was not limited to the university. There was rebellion of students on the high school level which, according to Ojetunde, was directed against authority itself (i.e., the state). For this author, both the high school and university students' revolts resulted from acculturation and the rejection of traditional values. These rebellions were directed more against the government than against the universities, not because the students were politically conscious and involved, but because this was the only battlefield acceptable to the general population. The government was seen as responsible for the lack of job openings.

The political and university situation of the country and the specific character of the nonorganized protest of young people make it impossible to speak of a student movement in the same sense as in other countries.

Three Other Non-European Countries

THE UNITED STATES OF AMERICA

The origin of the recent student movement in the United States was the birth of the Free Speech Movement (FSM) at Berkeley during 1964–65, but it was only with the intensification of the war in Vietnam that the movement became widespread. The students were directly affected by the draft. They borrowed many of the tactics previously employed in the civil rights movement. As numerous American authors have noted, the civil rights movement was certainly a major precondition for student activism against the university system.

The civil rights movement greatly affected the consciences and the political awareness of American students. Unlike students in Latin America or in some European countries, students in the United States have been shown (Goldsen et al., 1960) to have been in the past relatively passive about politics and not very politically engaged.

In 1968 the revolt at Columbia University marked the beginning of a large student movement which was to affect many universities in the country. The crisis at Columbia had two precipitating causes. First, the university planned to take over the use of part of a "people's park," which the university owned but which was used by members of the black community, in order to build a gymnasium there. Second, Columbia was participating in the research of the Institute of Defense Analysis (IDA), financed by the Pentagon, and the Students for a Democratic Society (SDS) organized a campaign against the school's participation. This underlined the interrelationship between life at the university and the military-industrial complex in the United States.

Unlike the student movements of other countries, which began at the universities and then branched out to criticism of the government, the American student movement received its initial impetus from the students' sensitivity to certain general problems—first the civil rights movement, then the Vietnam War. Attacks against the educational system were only a minor aspect of the motivations of the students. A poll conducted in 1968–1969 showed that only 13 percent of American students regarded their educational system as fundamentally dissatisfying and as requiring complete change. The majority of students believed that the system was excellent or needed only minor modifications.

However, if American students do not suffer from an outdated university system, they do criticize the impersonality of their universities. In the United States, the university no longer caters to an elite, but educated about 40 percent of young Americans at the time of this study. This transformation of the liberal university into the industrial university, described by Kerr (1963) as "the passage from the university to the multiversity," created many problems. It is apparently the source of alienation for many students: "The multiversity is a confusing place for the student. He has difficulties establishing his identity and finding a feeling of security" (Kerr, p. 45). The students suffer from anonymity and complain of being "treated like IBM cards": "I am a human being; please do not fold, tear or mutilate."

The student movement, born out of the civil rights movement, became a strong force of opposition to the war in Vietnam, and these two themes—ethnic discrimination and the war—formed the basis of other kinds of criticism, such as the presence of United States Reserve Officers Training Corps offices on university grounds and the conducting of research for military ends. Yet the malaise at the university was probably in the case of many students a reflection of a wider dissatisfaction with the national government and the American way of life.

The increased demands for profound, structural changes at the university between 1965 and 1970 were due more to political protests and to the radicalization of the student body than to university conditions per se. In 1971 Lipset and Schaflander showed that the demonstrations at Columbia in 1968 were clearly tied to the existence of preexisting groups, heavily involved in activist politics, and had little to do with actual university problems. According to Schnapp and Vidal-Naquet (1969):

> the revolutionary students became aware of the fact that the university is an apparatus, that this apparatus is an instrument of power. Exteriorly, this institution functions like an apparatus of production. Interiorly, however, its function is political and social oppression. When their studies are completed, the students are forced into society [p. 38].

In the *Ramparts* issue of June 11, 1968, Tom Hayden, one of the leaders of the American far left at the time, expressed this idea in more direct terms: American students want either a university which is independent and new and reacts against the course of American society or no university at all.

This denunciation of the role of the university in modern society is common to all student movements. But in contrast to the situation in other countries, the new American left could not look for support among the working classes, which are in general politically and rather passively conservative. Moreover, the openness of the American political system offers more opportunity to deal constructively with student demands.

OCEANIA: AUSTRALIA

After World War II Australia elaborated a vast policy of immigration with the goal of having a working force capable of exploiting and developing the resources of the country. As Short (1970) explains, this policy resulted in a population which was very diversified in terms of national origin. The most numerous were Europeans; Australia was known for its discrimination against non-Europeans. This policy has become more liberal, but there are few citizens from Asia or Africa. On the other hand, exchange students from these two regions are relatively numerous (12,500 in 1966, according to the Australian Universities Commission), and while not completely accepted, they do represent a means of awakening Australian citizens to realities beyond their own country.

The Australian political system is modeled on that of Great Britain. Its originality resides in the federal division of functions between the national government (the Commonwealth) and the regional (state) governments. In this respect, the system resembles that of the United States. Two principal political parties exist: the Labor party and the Liberal Country party.

As in all countries, the demand for higher education has grown more rapidly than the infrastructure, creating a problem of overpopulation at the universities. "From 1946 to 1956 the number of male students grew by 38.6 percent; the number for women decreased by 18.1 percent. The following decade saw these percentages multiply to 147 percent for the men and 390 percent for the women . . ." (Short, 1970, p. 292).

The government made a significant effort to deal with this explosion of numbers. In 1961, 62 percent of the students received financial aid, compared to 49 percent in 1956. Since 1970, however, the government has placed more emphasis on so-called colleges of advanced education, where the instruction is technical and specialized.

Australia did experience some student protest, especially in 1968, but never knew the violence of destruction and riots with the police. Largely influenced by foreign student movements, particularly that in America, the protest of Australian students focused on civil rights and welfare for the aborigines, the war in Vietnam, the draft, and university reform.

The impact of the student movement in Australia is difficult to determine. A study conducted in 1969 at the University of New South Wales by the Students' Union showed that 16 percent of the students interviewed had never taken nor would take part in a political demonstration, while 24 percent thought they would do so if the cause were judged worthwhile. On this basis Short (1970) established a profile of the members of the student protest movement:

> In any university the number of activitists is obviously very small. The real thrust is given by students in research and the young members of the university personnel. Support comes from a larger group, sincerely interested in the questions raised or who, in certain cases, join the group "for kicks." The thesis of the new radicals at the head of the movement seems to be revolution rather than reform, and the method used is confrontation rather than reasoning. According to some, the goal is to create a situation where all authority is rejected (allowing) a period of flux, during which the new society might emerge [p. 305].

ASIA: JAPAN

What has been called the "giant leap" of Japan since 1955–56 has brought about a whole series of problems in the social and economic domains, which were being felt by the people of Japan at the time of this study. Discontent appeared in the lives of manual workers, whose salaries were low and who, as a consequence of specialization, found their labor monotonous. The peasants also suffered from having to leave their land for the cities in order to survive. Finally, many intellectuals, mainly on the left, criticized the internal and external policies of their government. They were especially hostile to Japan's position regarding the war in Vietnam and the problem of Okinawa. Some students were disturbed not only by governmental policies but also by the living conditions and the level of instruction at the university.

We found the political situation in Japan characterized by three major factors. First, the conservatives continued to dominate the political scene at the time of this research. Second, the two-party system seemed precarious and in part unreal; in fact, since the 1960s it has appeared realistic to describe the country as having a two-party system with the same party always in power, the Liberal Democrat party (the Jiyu-Minshuto), and a secondary party, the Socialist party (the Shakaito). Third, there has always been in the Japanese mind much uncertainty about party affiliation and about the very concept of a party; to belong to one constitutes only a formal procedure. The average Japanese does not think in terms like "liberal" or "socialist" the same way an average British or American voter does.

It is impossible to speak of the students without mentioning the large movement known as the Zengakuren. Zengakuren is the abbreviated form of Zen Nihon Gekusei Jichikai So Rengo (the Japanese Federation of University Students' Governments), established in 1948 under the direction of the Communist party. The Zengakuren counted 300,000 members when it was founded, including 75 percent of the student body. In 1967 the organization had 700,000 members. At first, the Zengakuren had as its principal objective the improvement of student life and the university system, but rapidly other policies became prominent.

First, there was a split-off of the Trotskyites in 1950 at the time of the peace treaty and security pact between Japan and the United States. It was in 1960, however, that the rupture between the communists and the rest of Zengakuren was consummated with the revision of the security pact between the two powers.

The Zengakuren then divided into three groups: (1) the Minsei, a pro-communist group with direct ties to the Communist party in Japan; (2) the Sampa Rengo, the alliance of three anticommunist factions; and (3) the Marugaku, the Marxist League of Japanese Students, which is also hostile to communists. Each of these groups was itself divided into subgroups. In 1968 the Minsei included 69 percent of the Zengakuren. It continues to be concerned with problems associated with the university.

The most active group is the Sampa Rengo. It violently rejected any idea of political compromise or attempts at negotiation. According to the students in this group, the Japanese Communist party is reactionary. The Sampa Rengo saw itself as the avant-garde of the revolutionary force which would destroy the sociopolitical system. The thirteen subdivisions of this group at the time of our study rarely joined together, but were mutually antagonistic and hostile. The first appearance of the famous helmets and clubs in 1964 occurred during a confrontation between these groups. The protest movements at the universities were at the same time directed against the university as an institution and against the economic and political situation of the country.

The Kokusai Bunka Shinkokai, or Japan Cultural Society (1970) published a report on education in Japan which, after describing the situation before World War II, gives an account of the various reforms introduced and the problems which they raised. Before the war, higher education had as its primary goal to develop the country and to help move it into the ranks of the industrialized nations. It was nationalistic, pragmatic, and elitist. The university system was transformed and democratized after the war. The reforms tried to reduce the multiplicity of systems by unifying them, in order to give more people access to the university. Education was to become more democratic. It was a matter no longer of providing only a professional, specialized education, but of providing a liberal education, based on critical thinking and a wider view of society.

Students' protests were directed against both the form and the content of their education. The division of studies into two cycles (one or two years of general education followed by two or three years of specialization) aroused student discontent.

The quality of instruction varies from department to department in the same university and from university to university. In fact, the attempt to unify the different institutions of higher education was a failure. The national universities, financed by the government, have the capacity to conduct costly research and to offer many courses. They thus attract the most gifted students. Their prestige is generally higher than that of private universities. The budget of the latter depends largely (46 percent in 1961) on students' fees, as few subsidies come from the government. These universities accept as many students as possible. They concentrate their efforts in literature and social sciences and reduce the number of professors to a minimum. This last factor creates a numerical imbalance between professors and students: Japan also is confronted by the phenomenon of student overpopulation—or teacher underpopulation.

University authorities hope that the state will give them greater financial assistance yet at the same time respect their autonomy. The students reject this notion in that it implies the participation of the government and thus the possible control of the universities.

The autonomy of the university, the variations in quality among the various institutions, the difference between the public and the private schools, and the qualitative and numerical relationship between students and their teachers all remain unresolved problems in Japan. These criticisms have been recognized by official organs of the government, in particular in 1968, by a Special Commission of the Ministry of Education (cf. *Japan Times Weekly*, November 9, 1968, p. 8).

The growing control by the government during the war and the repression of progressive and Marxist teachers after defeat intensified the feelings of hostility and of distrust of the students toward their government. The notions of liberalism and of antinationalism persisted after the reforms. Students felt more and more concerned by political problems and social dilemmas and frequently joined radical movements.

These concerns were manifest from the creation of the Zengakuren in 1948. This movement quickly became known for its involvement in national and in international problems. For example, it acted against the "Red purge" of Japanese professors by the occupying Americans in the early fifties, against the installation of American bases on Japanese soil, against nuclear experiments by the Americans and the Soviets, and especially against wars, such as the one in Vietnam. These activities were estimated to involve 800,000 participants, mobilizing both students and workers.

Some authors, like Fuse (1970), explain this radicalism, the spectacular violence of the students, and their wide-ranging criticism of society by concern over lack of status. According to him, the distribution of status and of power has become a crucial problem in the wealthier societies of the postindustrial era—more important than the class struggle and the redistribution of wealth. Students, like the urban pro-letariat—which explains their cooperation—belong to groups with low status and thus no defined powers of negotiation. Thus they choose violent means and illegal methods to obtain their objectives.

In Japan the student protest movement and its activities, during the dozen years preceding this study, were characterized by latent dissatisfaction, fermenting over many years, directed against the university and, more generally, against society.

Factorial Analysis of "Correspondences"

A. Description of the Method

What do we mean by a "correspondence"?

A correspondence would exist between set I of individuals or variables, and set J of questions or observations if elements i of I and j of J are associated in a pair (i, j).

For example, in France table P on I × J is defined for the 94 variables of a political nature on the questionnaire, as follows:

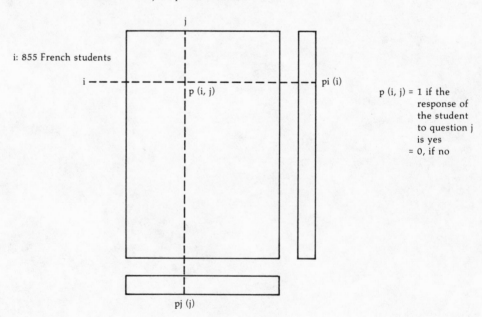

j: 94 political variables

i: 855 French students

p (i, j) = 1 if the response of the student to question j is yes
= 0, if no

The marginal elements of table P are defined:

$$p\,j(j) = \sum_{i \in I} p(i, j) = \text{number of times students i of I replied yes to question j,}$$

$$= \text{"weight" of question j,}$$

$$p\,i(i) = \sum_{j\epsilon J} p(i, j) = \text{number of times student i replied yes to the questions,}$$

$$= \text{"weight" of subject i.}$$

Each individual i of I may be described by a line on table P, by a series of 94 zeros or ones (94 replies to political questions, for example).

Each question j of J may be described similarly by a column on table P; for the French sample of 855 subjects, by a series of 855 zeros or ones.

There are, then, two possible geometric representations:

$\mathbb{R}^n$ (where n = dimension of I = 855)
p points j (where p = dimension of J = 94), each having 855 components,
or
$\quad\quad\mathbb{R}^p$ (where p = dimension of J = 94) n points i, each having 94 components.

The cluster of p questions (replies by n individuals) is then figured in a large-dimensioned space.

The goal of the analysis is to reduce the dimensions of this space by projecting the cluster of points onto a subspace, so that the distances between the points are most faithful to the distances between the elements themselves.

The distance utilized in analysis of correspondences obeys the following axioms:

a. The distance between two i of I subjects grows smaller as the profile of lines representing them is more alike; if these lines have an identical profile, the distance is nonexistent. Whatever j of J is,

$$\frac{p(i, j)}{p\,i(i)} = \frac{p(i', j)}{p\,i(i')} \quad\longrightarrow\quad d(i, i') = 0.$$

b. If two columns (corresponding to two questions) having identical profiles are added in a third column, the distances between subjects are unchanged:
Whatever i of I is,

$$\frac{p(i, j)}{pj(j1)} = \frac{p(i, j2),}{pj(j2)}$$

and if j1 and j2 are replaced by j0 so that

$$p(i, j0) = p(i, j1) + p(i, j2)$$

then d(i, i') is unchanged, whatever i and i' are.

In $\mathbb{R}^p$, the distance between two i and i' individuals will be

$$d2\,(i, i') = \sum_{j=1}^{p} \left| \frac{1}{pj\,(j)} \left(\frac{P(i, j)}{pi(i)} - \frac{p(i', j)}{pi(i')} \right)^2 \right|$$

and in $\mathbb{R}^n$, the distance between two j and j' questions will be:

$$d2\,(j, j') = \sum_{i=1}^{n} \left| \frac{1}{pi(i)} \left(\frac{p(i, j)}{pj(j)} - \frac{p(i,j')}{pj(j')} \right)^2 \right|$$

To reduce the dimensions of the space, the principal axes of inertia of the point cluster are determined in decreasing order from the "moments of inertia" called "proper values." These axes, along which the cluster is most elongated, are called "factorial axes." The origin of the axes is at the cluster's center of gravity. The axes are orthogonal. The projections onto these axes of subjects i and of questions J are called *factors.*

It is, then, in the space of the extracted factors that the cluster is projected. The representation of the cluster on the plane of factorial axes 1 and 2 is the best plane representation of the cluster.

To evaluate the importance of each j point in the determination of each axis, the *absolute contribution* of j is calculated:

$$CA(j\alpha) = pj(j) \times F\alpha^2(j)$$

contribution to the axisα; where $F\alpha(j)$ is the value of the projection of j upon the axis or factor α of j.

Finally, to see to what extent an axis may be represented by a question, a "quantity" called "relative contribution" is calculated, which is the correlation between the factor and the question (COS^2).

As it is tedious when judging the interpretation of an axis to consult the lists of coordinates of points with the help of lists of contributions on the listings, a program allows for the graphic representation of the cluster on the projection planes of axes 1 and 2, 1 and 3, etc.

The computer produces, with the help of a tracer[1], a card upon which the factorial cluster of points for the set of individuals and the factorial cluster of points for the set of responses are simultaneously projected on the plane plotted to the axes taken two by two.

An essential aspect of the methodology adopted[2] is the ability to obtain simultaneously the distribution of the attitudinal variables and the "identifier" variables.

This method permits a global view of the general orientation of a given group, not only upon one question, but upon a set of associated questions. Each identified group is represented on the original graphs[3] by a point. This point is the projection of the center of gravity, or barycenter, of the responses of the given group. That is, a point is projected which represents the mean weight of responses of all individuals connected to a given identifier. Thus, for instance, the point representing the political identifier "left," projected in the plane of axes 1 and 2, will reflect the average position in this plane of the set of students defined by this identifier, etc.

B. Classification and Coding of Replies

REMARKS ON THE CODING OF REPLIES

For certain questions (Example: question 8 on the questionnaire), the scale of replies contained five levels:

Extremely important, very important, fairly important, not very important, and unimportant.

---

[1]BRUME Program, developed by G. Thauront (1973).

[2]Thanks to a formula for the reconstitution of data in terms of factors, it is possible to introduce variables in the analysis—for example, in our analysis, the identifiers—as *supplementary elements*, that is, not directly intervening in the calculation of factors. This permits their inclusion without disturbing the values of the factors over the other elements, whose probable position we wish to know, if they were integrated onto the data tables submitted to analyses. Thus, projection of these supplementary variables allows them to be placed on the graphs and distribution with regard to the other attitudinal variables on the factors extracted by analyses, to be seen.

[3]As explained before, we cannot present the graphs in this publication, because of the difficulty to reduce their size without being prejudicial to their clarity.

This scale was reduced to three levels, the question then giving rise to three items:

If the student replied "extremely important" or "very important," his response will be 100.

if he replied "fairly important," his response will be 010.

If he replied "not very important" or "unimportant," his response will be 001.

For certain questions, the type of responses proposed was the following (example: question 13 on the questionnaire):

Agree totally, quite agree, quite disagree, totally disagree, and no opinion.

The question then gives rise to three items:

The student does not agree;
his response will be 10.

The student agrees;
his response will be 01.

If he expresses no opinion,
his response will be 00.

The "no answers" to the questions were assimilated with no-opinion responses and coded as 0.

Thus a table of zeros and ones was submitted to analysis. Each row on the table represents the set of responses of one student, and each column represents the set of responses of the students of the country concerned to one question.

IDENTIFIERS

1. Male
2. Female
3. Place of study
4. Type of university (in USA only)
5. Humanities
6. Social sciences
7. Sciences
8. Medicine
9. Law and economics
10. Architecture, fine arts
11. Engineering and business
12. Single
13. Married
14. Lives with the family
15. Lives on campus
16. Lives independently
17. Father's education primary
18. Father's education secondary
19. Father's education university
20. Mother's education primary
21. Mother's education secondary
22. Mother's education university
23. Works

24. Does not work
25. Believer
26. Nonbeliever
27. Father believer
28. Father nonbeliever
29. Mother believer
30. Mother nonbeliever
31. Extreme right (Italy)
32. Right
33. Center
34. Liberal (USA)
35. Left
36. Communist (France, Great Britain, Italy)
37. Extreme left
38. Anarchist (France, Great Britain)
39. Apolitical
40. No answer

In Nigeria there was also:

Criticizes the government
Describes the situation of his country

ATTITUDINAL VARIABLES: SOCIOPOLITICAL OPINIONS

1. Chosen
2. Not chosen } Politics as a source of satisfaction

3. Agree
4. Disagree } Overthrow the present government

5. Agree
6. Disagree } The student movement reflects great immaturity

7. Agree
8. Disagree } Student protest has improved the university

9. Agree
10. Disagree } Only a political revolution can change the university

11. Agree
12. Disagree } Destroy the present system without knowing what will replace it

13. Agree
14. Disagree } A revolution would destroy current progress

15. Agree
16. Disagree } Establish a common student-worker front

17. Agree
18. Disagree } The student movement represents a minority

19. Agree
20. Disagree } Destroy the bourgeois university and replace it with a proletarian culture

21. Agree
22. Disagree } Coordinate the efforts of students worldwide toward a revolutionary goal

23. Agree
24. Disagree } The educational system maintains discrimination

25. Agree
26. Disagree } Violence is legitimate for attaining valid goals

27. Agree
28. Disagree } No limit on immigration

29. Agree
30. Disagree } Democratic goals of the student movement

31. Agree
32. Disagree } Democratic means of action of the student movement

33. Agree
34. Disagree } A revolution today would lead to a new repressive regime.

35. Agree
36. Disagree } The student movement has revealed truths to older people

37. Agree
38. Disagree } Go to the factories to help the workers in their struggle

39. Agree
40. Disagree } Discrimination is a crime

41. Agree
42. Disagree } Supranational government

43. Agree
44. Disagree } Violence is an effective form of action

45. Agree
46. Disagree } Abolish universal suffrage

47. Agree
48. Disagree } Eliminate biological and nuclear weapons

49. Agree
50. Disagree } Eliminate nationalism

51. Agree
52. Disagree } Violence as a political means is to be condemned

53. Agree
54. Disagree } Freedom of expression and of the press exists in our political system

55. Agree
56. Disagree } Sacrifice of the present generation for future generations

57. Agree
58. Disagree } Capitalism should be eliminated

59. Agree
60. Disagree } The university should serve as an avant-garde to change society

61. Agree
62. Disagree } The university should critically analyze national life

63. Agree
64. Disagree } The university should be a place for study, as independent as possible of politics

65. Agree
66. Disagree } The university as the base of leftist political action

67. Agree
68. Disagree } Action within elected assemblies

69. Agree
70. Disagree } Negotiations and directive interviews with the administration

71. Agree
72. Disagree } Demonstrations and marches

73. Agree
74. Disagree } Picketing

75. Agree
76. Disagree } Strikes, boycotting classes

77. Agree
78. Disagree } Interruption of classes

79. Agree
80. Disagree } Occupation of buildings

81. Agree
82. Disagree } Destruction of files and property

83. Agree
84. Disagree } Attacking administration and faculty members

85. Freedom (of speech only) for all political groups
86. Freedom of expression and action for all political groups
87. Varying freedoms for various political groups

88. Friends
89. Parents } Groups that influenced own political development
90. Ideologists

91. Good
92. Bad } Overall, society is:

93. Good
94. Bad } Overall, the student movement is:

Questionnaire

THE STUDENT AND SOCIETY
-=-=-=-=-=-=-=-=-=-=-=-=-

The role of the student in modern society is becoming
a world-wide major issue. This international survey is
a contribution to this topic, and is conducted under
the auspices of the International Social Science Council,
a non-governmental organisation which includes representatives of the various social science disciplines. The
countries in which the study is being conducted include:
Australia, Austria, Brazil, Canada, Colombia, France, the
German Federal Republic, Great Britain, Italy, Japan,
Nigeria, Switzerland, Tunisia, the United States and
Yugoslavia.

The students participating in the study have been drawn
from different types of universities, covering a broad
range of disciplines.

By completing this questionnaire you will help us to discover how students in different countries see their role
in society, and the values that are important to them.

All the information given will be treated as strictly
confidential and will be used purely for research purposes.

Given the international character of the survey, you will
probably find alternatives that do not fit exactly your
point of view. Try, however, to answer them. In any case,
there is a final page marked "Comments" where, if you wish,
you may add your observations.

Thank you very much for your cooperation.

PERSONAL BACKGROUND *

1. Age: .... years   Sex: Male ☐   Female ☐

2. Which educational establishment do you attend? ....
   ....

3. Which degree, diploma or certificate are you studying for? ....
   ....

4. What is your major subject(s)? ....
   ....

5. How many years of university study (counting this year) have you
   completed or nearly completed? ....

       As a full-time student   Number of years
       As a part-time student

6. Are you married?   Yes ☐   No ☐
   If you are married, how many children do you have? ....

7. Do you live:
       — with your family?
       — in a dormitory?
       — Other? (please specify)

---

* For statistical purposes

8. When you have finished your studies, do you plan to be engaged in a specific occupation?   Yes ☐   NO ☐

If you answered YES, which of the following requirements would be important to you in your choice of occupation? (please check the appropriate column for each requirement).

	Highly important	Very important	Somewhat important	Of little importance	Of no importance
8.1. Enable me to look forward to a stable, secure future.					
8.2. Give me an opportunity to do something useful for others.					
8.3. Provide me with a chance to earn a good deal of money.					
8.4. Give me a chance to exercise leadership.					
8.5. Give me social status and prestige					
8.6. Give me a chance to influence the policy of my government.					
8.7. Keep me out of a vast bureaucracy.					
8.8. Avoid any position that contributes to the strengthening of the capitalist system.					
8.9. Allow me to be a free person avoiding long range commitments.					
8.10. Leave me many free hours to do what I want.					

9. When you will have finished your studies, how easy do you think it will be to find the kind of work you would like? (please check one box)

Very easy	Relatively easy	Slightly difficult	Very difficult	Impossible

10. To what extent is the education that you are now getting relevant to your occupational goals? (check one box under the term which you think appropriate on the following scale.)

Not at all relevant	Slightly relevant	Moderately relevant	Quite relevant	Extremely relevant

11. a. At the present time most men and women live together in small family units. Some possible alternative ways of living are given below.

Please check the alternative which you think would be most probable in the year 2000.

1. ☐ The present form of marriage will persist.

2. ☐ Marriage will persist but will be accompanied by even greater liberty regarding extra-marital sex, for both men and women.

3. ☐ Legal marriage will be replaced by free union.

4. ☐ Marriage will persist but families will live together communally with other families.

5. ☐ Men and women will live togecher communally, without marriage.

6. ☐ Other (please specify): ....
....

b. Of these different alternatives, which one best defines the kind of life you would prefer to have? (please quote the appropriate number from 11.a above).
☐

c. Which of the alternatives best defines the kind of life you expect to have? (please quote the appropriate number from 11.a above).
☐

12. Which three of the following activities do you expect will give you the greatest satisfaction in life?

(Put the number "1" next to the activity from which you expect the greatest satisfaction, a "2" next to the second and "3" next to the third).

Make three choices only.

☐ Your career

☐ Your family life

☐ Your leisure or hobby

☐ Your participation in political affairs concerning your country

☐ Your participation in activities at an international level

☐ Your religious beliefs and activities

☐ Other (please specify): ....

13. A number of opinions which are often expressed, are given below. How much do you agree or disagree with each of these opinions?

(Please check the appropriate column for each statement. Keep in mind the situation in your own country).

	Strongly agree	Slightly agree	Slightly disagree	Strongly disagree	Cannot answer
1. There can be little doubt that technology has been a force increasing the sum of human happiness.					
2. The present differences between social and moral values of youth and the older generation are far greater than in the past.					
3. One of the goals of the student movement should be the destruction of the present form of government.					
4. The student movement usually reflects a considerable degree of immaturity.					
5. The student protest in general has led to the improvement of the university.					

(question 13 continued)

	Strongly agree	Slightly agree	Slightly disagree	Strongly disagree	Cannot answer
6. Effective change in the university could only be achieved by a political revolution.					
7. In our society today, buying and selling constitute the values accepted by the majority of the people.					
8. I am in favour of destroying the present political system even without knowing what will replace it.					
9. The technological revolution has been used more to oppress than to liberate.					
10. One of the goals of the student movement should be to establish a common front among students and workers.					
11. The militant students are only a small minority.					
12. A revolution in this country now would destroy the progress which is currently being made toward improving society.					
13. The university as a bourgeois institution should be destroyed.					
14. Students throughout the world should co-ordinate their efforts toward a revolutionary goal.					
15. The present educational system maintains social discrimination.					
16. Violence by students, when used to reach valid goals rapidly, is legitimate.					
17. Immigration to this country should be unrestricted.					
18. The student movement is essentially democratic in regard to its goals.					
19. The same standards should be used concerning the sex life of men and women.					
20. The student movement is essentially democratic in regard to its means.					

(Question 13 continued).

	Strongly agree	Slightly agree	Slightly disagree	Strongly disagree	Cannot answer
21. Abortion should be an individual choice without legal restrictions.					
22. A revolution which would succeed in overthrowing the present government would sooner or later lead to a new repressive regime.					
23. In an ideal society work and play would be indistinguishable.					
24. The student movement has revealed truths that the older generation had previously not recognized.					
25. The family is a universally oppressive institution.					
26. Students should leave the university for the factory in order to help the workers in their struggle.					
27. Middle class morality destroys the spontaneity of individual experience.					
28. In our society today, the conflict of generations is acutely felt.					
29. In our society, women as a group are oppressed.					
30. Any discrimination against a person because of his race, religion or colour should be considered a crime.					
31. All censorship should be abolished.					
32. Women can improve their position only by organizing protest movements.					
33. An effective world-wide government should be established.					
34. Contraceptive devices should be made available to all.					
35. Violence is the most effective form of action capable of producing profound social changes.					

(Question 13 continued)

	Strongly agree	Slightly agree	Slightly disagree	Strongly disagree	Cannot answer
36. Popular elections should be abolished because the majority of people cannot be trusted to decide what is good for society.					
37. All biological and atomic weapons should be destroyed.					
38. Nationalism should be eliminated.					
39. Restrictive measures should be taken against the use of marijuana and hashish.					
40. Men and women should have equal access to positions of highest political responsibility.					
41. The role of religion in society should diminish.					
42. Violence as a political technique is, in general, to be condemned.					
43. Restrictive measures should be taken against the use of L.S.D.					
44. Freedom of expression and freedom of the press represent true achievements of our political system.					
45. In order to build a new society, the freedom and happiness of the present generation must be sacrificed for that of future generations.					
46. Capitalism should be eliminated.					

14. The following are possible goals for universities in your country, at the present time.
(Check the appropriate column to indicate whether or not you agree with each goal).

	Strongly approve	Approve	Disapprove	Strongly disapprove	No opinion
1. To act as a vanguard of change in our society.					
2. To advance technology in response to the economic needs of the country.					
3. To advance fundamental research regardless of immediate practical applications.					
4. To furnish training in highly specialized skills.					
5. To fill the manpower needs of government and business.					
6. To provide a forum for the critical analysis of all aspects of national life.					
7. To stimulate the personal development rather than the technical competence of the students.					
8. To provide a place of learning and investigation as free as possible of political involvements.					
9. To provide a basic general education and appreciation of ideas.					
10. To provide the student with a means to higher income and status.					
11. To open all the universities to anyone who wants to attend, without selective admission.					
12. To conduct research for government and industry within the university.					
13. Allowing students to pursue their own interests without having to concentrate on one field of study.					

(Question 14 continued)

	Strongly approve	Approve	Disapprove	Strongly disapprove	No opinion
Opening the university only to students who wish to study seriously.					
Eliminating all grading of students by faculty.					
To be a base for radical political action in the larger society.					

e following are types of actions which students have taken in different universities.
lease check the appropriate column to indicate whether or not you approve of
ch action).

	Always acceptable	Often acceptable	Acceptable in restricted circumstances	Never acceptable	No opinion
Working through student representatives.					
Directly petitioning and meeting with administrative officials.					
Demonstrations and marches					
Picketing and blocking access to university facilities.					
Striking or boycotting classes.					
Disrupting classes.					
Sit-in and occupancy of buildings.					
Destroying records and property.					
Physical attack on members of the faculty who disagree.					
Physical attack on members of the administration.					

16. Where will the student movement be 5 years from now in your country?

(Put the number "1" opposite the alternative which you consider the most probable, a "2" opposite the second most probable).

Make 2 choices only.

☐ It will be seriously weakened by the reaction of the conservatives

☐ It will be torn by internal dissension

☐ It will be larger and more powerful

☐ It will spread to the workers

☐ It will disappear temporarily but will be revived at a later date

☐ Other (please specify): ....
....

17. Can you say whether or not the following factors have played a role in the student revolt in each one of these countries?

(Answer by YES, NO or DON'T KNOW in each box)

	France	USA	Great Britain	Italy	Germany	Japan
1. Poor university system						
2. Authoritarianism of teachers						
3. Lack of employment possibilities for college graduates						
4. Political discontent						
5. Socio-economic discontent						
6. Crisis of civilisation						
7. Foreign conspiracy						
8. Conflict between the generations						
9. Inspired by agitators						
10. Other (please specify):						

....

....

....

18. How would you describe your own political position?

   ....
   ....
   ....

19. Approximately what percentage of university students do you think
    would share your general political orientation?

    (Please check the appropriate alternative):

10% or less	25%	50%	75% or more

20. To what extent do you feel free to express your political point
    of view within your university?

Completely free	Relatively free	In between	Relatively restricted	Not at all free

21. Please check the column which you think corresponds to the degree
of freedom of expression that each of the following groups should
be allowed in your university

	Should have no freedom of expression	Should have entire freedom to express their opinions verbally	Should have entire freedom to express their opinions even through actions
Anarchists			
Communists			
"Gauchistes"			
John Birchers			
Maoists			
Nazis			
Socialists			
Other (please specify):			

....

....

....

....

22. Which of the following has most influenced your own political development?

    (Please check one box only). (Please specify when appropriate):

    ☐ Students: ....

    ☐ Friends: ....

    ☐ Parents: ....

    ☐ Young people in general: ....

    ☐ Teachers: ....

    ☐ Politicians: ....

    ☐ Authors: ....

    ☐ Journalists: ....

    ☐ Political associations: ....

    ☐ Political leaders: ....

    ☐ Other (please state): ....

23. Please check the appropriate column for each of the following terms according to how close you feel to your parents:

	Very close	Reasonably close	Distant	Very distant	Don't know
In emotional terms					
In moral values					
In political outlook					

24. Would you please state briefly if there are any differences between you and your parents concerning the following points

	Yes	No	Specify
Leisure			
Religion			
Achievement			
Individualism			
Creative pursuits			
Importance of the present moment			
Sexual experiences			
Money			
Communion with nature			
Arts			
Drugs			
Other (please specify):			

....
....
....

25. What is your father's occupation ?

....

Please state his rank or grade (e.g. foreman or manager, etc.)

....

26. What is your mother's occupation?

....

27. To which level were your parents educated?

	Father	Mother
. Primary school		
. Secondary school		
. University		

28. Every society has its good and bad features. In this society would you say the balance is on the good or the bad side?

(Please check one box)

28.a)   Good [ ]   Bad [ ]

28.b) What are the 2 best features, as you see them?

1.:..

2.:..

28.c) What are the 2 worst features as you see them ?

1.:..

2.:..

29. a) Try to imagine a society of which you really approve.
       What are the 3 most important elements of such a society?

    1.:...

    2.:...

    3.: ....

   b) Could this society be realised?

                    Yes ☐   NO ☐

     If YES, in what way? : ....

     ....

     ....

     ....

30. a) Every university has its good and bad features. In your university,
       would you say the balance is on the good or the bad side?

       (Please check one box)

                    Good ☐   Bad ☐

   b) What are the 2 best features, as you see them?

     1. : ....

     2. : ....

   c) What are the two worst features, as you see them?

     1. : ....

     2. : ....

31. Are you a member of a student organisation? (Please check one box)

                    Yes ☐   No ☐

    If YES, please specify the organisation: ....

    ....

32. a) Every student movement has its good and bad features. For the student movement in your country as a whole, is the balance on the good or the bad side?

   (Please check one box)

   Good ☐   Bad ☐

   b) What are the 2 best features, as you see them?

   1. : ....

   2. : ....

   c) What are the 2 worst features, as you see them?

   1. : ....

   2. : ....

OPTIONAL QUESTIONS

33. Do you work outside your studies?

   Yes ☐   No ☐

   If YES, are you engaged in

   . full-time work?

   . part-time work?

34. a) What are the religious affiliations of you and your parents?
   (Please check the appropriate boxes)

	Yourself	Father	Mother
Catholic			
Jewish			
Protestant (please state denomination)			
No religious affiliation			
Other (please specifiy)			

34. b) In religious terms, are you or parents believers?

	Yourself	Father	Mother
Yes			
No			

35. What is your nationality? ....

<u>Note</u>: The Yugoslav questionnaire was somewhat modified, and included a number of questions specific to the Yugoslav situation. These questions are indicated in the text.

References

ABRAMS, P., LITTLE, A. "The young voter in British politics." *British Journal of Sociology,* 16, 1965.

ALMOND, G. A., VERBA, S. *The civic culture.* Princeton, N.J.: Princeton University Press, 1963.

ALZON, C. *La femme potiche et la femme bonniche.* Paris: Maspero, Cahiers Libres, 1973.

ARIKPO, O. *The development of modern Nigeria.* London: Penguin African Books, 1967.

BELL, D. "Columbia and the New Left," *The Public Interest,* 13, 1968, pp. 61–101.

BENZECRI, J. P. *L'analyse des données,* vols. 1 and 2. Paris: Dunod, 1973.

BETTELHEIM, B. "The course and nature of student unrest." Paper presented to the Special Subcommittee on Education of the House Committee on Labor and Education, March 1970.

BIRNBAUM, N. *The crisis of industrial society.* New York: Oxford University Press, 1969.

BISSERET, N. "La naissance et le diplôme." *Revue Francaise de Sociologie,* 9 (1), 1968, pp. 185–287.

BLACKBURN, R. "A brief guide to bourgeois ideology." In Cockburn, A., Blackburn, R. (eds.), *Student power: Problems, diagnosis, action.* Baltimore: Penguin, 1969, pp. 163–213.

BOUDON, R. "Crise universitaire et participation." *Cahiers de l'ISEA,* IV (9). Geneva: Librairie Droz, September 1970(a).

BOUDON, R. "From one university to another." *Youth and Society,* 2 (2), December 1970(b), pp. 141–175.

BOURDIEU, P., PASSERON, J. C. *Les héritiers: Les étudiants et la culture.* Paris: Editions de Minuit, 1964.

BRAU, J. L. *Cours, camarade, le vieux monde est derrière toi! Histoire du mouvement révolutionnaire etudiant en Europe.* Paris: Albin Michel, 1968.

BRAUNGART, R. G. "SDS and YAF: A comparison of two student radical groups in the mid-1960s." *Youth and Society,* 2 (4), 1971, pp. 441–458.

BROCHIER, J. J., OELGART, B. *L'internationale étudiante.* Paris: Julliard, 1968.

BURN, B. Article in *The Times Higher Education* supplement, London, January 1972.

COCKBURN, A., BLACKBURN, R. (eds.). *Student power: Problems, diagnosis, action.* Baltimore: Penguin, 1969.

COMITE ETUDIANT POUR LES LIBERTES UNIVERSITAIRES (CELU). *Pour rebâtir l'université.* Paris: La Table Ronde, 1969.

CONVERSE, P. E., DUPEUX, G. "Politization of the electorate in France and the United States." *Public Opinion Quarterly,* 26, 1962, pp. 1–23.

CONVERSE, P. E., SCHUMAN, H. "Silent majorities and the Vietnam War." *The Scientific American,* 222, June 1970, p. 22.

COOPER, D. *Death of the family.* London: Tavistock, 1971.

DAHRENDORF, R. *Class and class.conflict in industrial society.* London: Routledge & Kegan Paul, 1959.

DAVIS, K. "The sociology of parent-youth conflict." In Coser, R. L. (ed.), *The family: Its structure and functions.* New York: St. Martin's Press, 1964, pp. 455–471.

DELAGE, C. "Orléans: La naissance d'une université," cited by Boudon, R., in "From one university to another," *Youth and Society,* 2 (2), December 1970.

Democracía Popular, Ljubljana, January 1968.

DENITCH, B. "La nouvelle gauche et la nouvelle classe ouvrière." *L'Homme et la Société,*16, April-May-June 1970, pp. 43–54.

DUPRAT, F. *L'internationale étudiante révolutionnaire.* Paris: Nouvelles Editions Latines (Collection "Points de Vue"), 1968.

EGGINTON, J. *Observer Review,* November 1971.

ENGELS, F. *L'origine de la famille, de la propriété privée et de l'état.* Paris: Costes, 1931.

EYSENCK, H. J. *The psychology of politics.* London: Routledge & Kegan Paul, 1954.

FARNSWORTH, D. "University psychiatrist looks at campus protest." *Psychiatric Opinion,* 6, 1969, pp. 6–11.

FEUER, L. S. *The conflict of generations.* New York: Delacorte Press, 1968.

FINLEY, D. J., SIMON, D. W. "Self and nation." *Youth and Society,* June 1972, pp. 427–439.

FISCHER, E. "Les voies de la révolution: La nouvelle gauche et l'ancienne." *Politique Aujourd'hui,* October 1970, pp. 3–10.

FISK, T. "The nature and causes of student unrest." In Crick and Robson (eds.), *Protest and discontent.* London: Penguin, 1970, pp. 78–85.

FLACKS, R. "The liberated generation: An exploration of the roots of student protest." *Journal of Social Issues,* 23 (3), 1967, pp. 52–75.

FLACKS, R. "Social and cultural meanings of student revolt: Some informal comparative observations." *Social Problems,* Winter 1970, pp. 340–357.

FRIEDAN, B. *The feminine mystique.* New York: Dell, 1963.

FRIJDA, N., JAHODA, G. "On the scope and methods of cross-cultural research." *International Journal of Psychology,* 1 (109), 1966.

FUSE, T. "Le radicalisme étudiant au Japon." *L'Homme et la Société: Sociologie et Contestation,* 16, 1970, pp. 241–266.

Gallup Poll on College Students, 1971.

GEZI, K. I., KRUSCHKE, E. R. "Law-abidingness among conservative and liberal students." *Education,* 91, Milwaukee, November-December 1970.

GILLESPIE, J. M., ALLPORT, G. W. *Youth's outlook on the future: A cross-national study.* Garden City, N.Y.: Doubleday, 1955.

GLASER, B., STRAUSS, A. *The discovery of grounded theory.* Chicago: Aldine, 1967.

GOLDSEN, R. K., ROSENBERG, M., WILLIAMS, R. M., SUCHMAN, E. A. *What college students think.* Princeton, N.J.: Van Nostrand, 1960.

GOMBIN, R. "Les grands ancêtres." *La Nef,* (Paris) 48 (7), 1972.

GOODE, W. J. *World revolution and family patterns.* New York: Free Press, 1963.

HANCOCK, A., WAKEFORD, J. "The young technicians." *New Society,* 5, January 1965.

HOLLINGSHEAD, A. B. *Elmtown's youth.* New York: Wiley, 1949.

HOLTZMAN, W. H., et al. *Personality development in two cultures.* Austin: University of Texas Press, 1975.

HOOK, S. *Academic freedom and academic anarchy.* New York: Cowles Book Co., 1970.

HOWARD, J. R. "The flowering of the hippie movement." *The Annals,* 382, 1969, pp. 43–55.

HYMAN, H. H. *Political socialization: A study in the psychology of politics.* New York: Free Press, 1959.

JACOB, P. *Changing values in college.* New York: Harper, 1958.

Japan Times Weekly, November 9, 1968, p. 8.

JONES, G. S., BARNETT, A., WENGRAL, T. "Student power: What is to be done?" *New Left Review,* 43, May-June 1967.

KAHL, J. A. "Educational and occupational aspirations of 'common man' boys." *Harvard Educational Review,* 23, 1953.

KELLER, S., ZAVALLONI, M. "Ambition and social class: A respecification." *Social Forces,* 43 (1), 1964.

KENISTON, K. *The uncommitted: Alienated youth in American society.* New York: Harcourt, Brace, 1965.

KENISTON, K. "The sources of student dissent." *Journal of Social Issues,* 23 (3), 1967, pp. 108–137.

KENISTON, K. *Young radicals: Notes on committed youth.* New York: Harcourt, Brace, 1968.

KENISTON, K. "Moral development: Youthful activism and modern society." *Youth and Society,* 1 (1), September 1969, pp. 110–127.

KERR, C. *The uses of the university.* Cambridge, Mass.: Harvard University Press, 1963.

KLINEBERG, O., ZAVALLONI, M. *Tribalism and nationalism among African students.* Paris: Mouton, 1969.

KLINEBERG, S. "Parents, schools and modernity: An exploratory investigation of sex differences in the attitudinal development of Tunisian adolescents." *International Journal of Comparative Sociology* (mimeo), XIV, 1974.

KOKUSAI BUNKA SHINKOKAI (Japan Cultural Society). *Higher education and the student problem: Current social problems,* Report no. 1, 1970.

KORTE, C. "Pluralistic ignorance about student radicalism." *Sociometry,* 35 (4), 1972, pp. 576–587.

LANCELOT, A. *Les attitudes politiques.* Paris: Collection Que Sais-je?, 1969.

LANDE, A. "Les anarchistes." *La Nef* (Paris) 48 (7), 1972.

LANG, K., LANG, G. *Student, university and society* (mimeo). State University of New York at Stony Brook, 1972.

LEARY, T. *Politique de l'extase.* Translated by Sisley, P. Paris: Fayard, 1973.

LEFEBVRE, H. *Critique de la vie quotidienne.* Paris: L'Arche, 1945.

LERNER, G. "The feminists: A second look." *Columbia Forum,* 13 (3), 1970.

Libro bianco sul movimento studentesco. Rome: Edizione Galileo, 1968.

LIMPUS, L. *Liberation of women: Sexual repression and the family.* Boston: New England Free Press, 1970.

LINDSEY, J. K. "Fitting response surfaces with power transformations." *Journal of the Royal Statistical Society,* vol. 21, 1972.

LIPSET, S. M. "University students and politics in underdeveloped countries." *Comparative Education Review,* 10 (2), June 1966, pp. 132–162.

LIPSET, S. M. "Students and politics in comparative perspective." *Daedalus,* Winter 1968, 97 (1), pp. 1–20.

LIPSET, S. M., SCHAFLANDER, G. M. *Passion and politics: Student activism in America.* Boston: Little, Brown, 1971.

LYONNS, G. "The police car demonstration: A survey of participants." In Lipset, S. M., Wolin, S. (eds.), *The Berkeley student revolt.* Garden City, N.Y.: Doubleday, 1965, pp. 519–529.

MARCUSE, H. *Eros and civilization.* Boston: Beacon Press, 1955.

MARCUSE, H. *One-dimensional man.* Boston: Beacon Press, 1964.

MARCUSE, H. *La fin de l'utopie.* Paris: Editions du Seuil (Collection "Combats"), 1968.

MARCUSE, H. *An essay on liberation.* Boston: Beacon Press, 1969.

MARKOVITS, A., FREUND, M. *Politics and attitudes: An analysis of a survey of Viennese students* (mimeo), University of Vienna, 1973.

MEAD, M. "Social change and cultural surrogates." In Kluckhohn, C., Murray, H. A. (eds.), *Personality in nature, society and culture.* New York: Knopf, 1948.

MEAD, M. *Culture and commitment: A study of the generation gap.* Garden City, N.Y.: Doubleday, 1970.

MENDEL, G. *Crise de générations: Etudes sociopsychanalytiques.* Paris: Petite Bibliothèque Payot, 1969.

MERTON, R. K. *Social theory and social culture,* revised ed. New York: Free Press, 1957.

MINCES, J. "Réflexions autour du 'Journal de la Commune Etudiante.'" *L'Homme et la Société,* 16, 1970, pp. 149–159.

MITSCHERLICH, A. *Vers une société sans pères.* Paris: Gallimard, 1969.

MURY, G. *La société de répression.* Paris: Editions Universitaires, 1969.

MUSGROVE, F. "University freshmen and their parents' attitudes." *Educational Research,* 10, 1967.

MUSGROVE, F. "The problem of youth and the structure of society in England." *Youth and Society,* 1 (1), September 1969, pp. 38–58.

MYERHOFF, B. "New styles of humanism: American youth." In McEachern, A. W. (ed.), *Youth and Society,* 1 (2), December 1969, pp. 151–178.

NILES, F. S. *"The influence of parents and peers on adolescent girls."* Unpublished doctoral thesis, University of Manchester, 1968.

"Nous sommes en marche." Tracts presented in SCHNAPP, A., VIDAL-NAQUET, P. (eds.), *La commune étudiante: Textes et documents.* Paris: Editions du Seuil, 1968.

OJETUNDE, J. *Student revolt in Nigerian institutions of higher learning* (mimeo). Paris: E. Hess, 1969.

PALMIERY, M. C. "La Tunisie en crise." *Politique Aujourd'hui,* October 1969, pp. 97–109.

PARSONS, T. "Youth in the context of American society." In Erikson, E. H. (ed.), *Youth: Change and challenge.* New York: Basic Books, 1962.

PERLMAN, F. "Naissance d'un mouvement revolutionnaire en Yougoslavie." *L'Homme et la Société,* 16, 1970, pp. 267–286.

Perspectives décennales de 1961–1971. Tunis: Secretary of State for Information, 1960.

PETKOVIC, R. "Que veulent les jeunes en colere?" *Revue de la Politique Internationale,* Belgrade, May 1968.

POIGNANT, R. "Education dans les pays du Marché Commun." Cited by Boudon, R., in Cahiers de l'ISEA 4 (9), 1970.

President's Commission on Campus Unrest. *Campus Unrest.* Washington: Government Printing Office, 1970.

Ramparts, June 11, 1968.

REICH, W. *Sexual revolution.* New York: Farrar, Straus & Giroux, 1969.

RILEY, N. W., MOORE, M. E. "Adolescent values and the Reisman typology: An empirical analysis." In Lipset, S. M., Lowenthal, L. (eds.), *Culture and social character.* New York: Free Press, 1961.

ROKKAN, S., VIET, J., VERBA, S., ALMASY, E. *Comparative survey analysis.* Paris: Mouton, 1969.

ROSSANDA, R. *Il manifesto: analyses et thèses de la nouvelle extrême-gauche italienne.* Paris: Editions du Seuil, 1971.

ROSZAK, T. *The making of a counter-culture.* Garden City, N.Y.: Doubleday, 1969.

RUDD, F., RUDD, E. *New students' politics at Essex* (mimeo). University of Essex, 1968.

SCHNAPP, A., VIDAL-NAQUET, P. (eds.). *La commune étudiante: Textes et documents.* Paris: Editions du Seuil, 1969.

SHORT, L. N. "Youth in Australia: A survey of background and problems." *Youth and Society,* 1 (3), 1970, pp. 289–308.

SMITH, B. M., HAAN, N., BLOCK, J. "Social psychological aspects of student activism." *Youth and Society,* 1 (3), March 1970, pp. 262–288.

SOMERS, R. H. "The mainspring of the rebellion: A survey of Berkeley students in November 1964." In Lipset, S. M., Sheldon, S. W. (eds.), *The Berkeley student revolt.* Garden City, N.Y.: Doubleday Anchor Books, 1965, pp. 549–550.

"Sondages." *Revue Française de l'Opinion Publique,* 4, Institut Français d'Opinion Publique, Paris, 1968, 1970, 1972.

STEPHANE, A. *L'univers contestationnaire ou les nouveaux chrétiens.* Paris: Petite Bibliothèque Payot, 1969.

STOETZEL, J. *Jeunesse sans chrysanthème ni sabre.* Paris: Plon, UNESCO, 1953.

Students, (Belgrade) 4, April 1968.

Susret, (Belgrade) May 15 and June 1, 1968.

THAURONT, G. "L'analyse des correspondances." In Benzecri, J. P., *L'analyse des données,* vol. 2. Paris: Dunod, 1973.

TIANO, A. *Le Maghreb entre les mythes.* Paris: Maspero, 1963.

TOURAINE, A. *Le Monde,* March 9, 1968 (a).

TOURAINE, A. *Le mouvement de Mai ou le communisme utopique.* Paris: Editions du Seuil, 1968 (b).

TOURAINE, A. *Université et société aux Etats-Unis.* Paris: Le Seuil, 1972.

TRENT, J. W., CRAISE, J. L. "Commitment and conformity in the American college." *Journal of Social Issues,* 23, 1967, pp. 34–51.

TRIANDIS, H. C., VASSILIOU, V., VASSILIOU, G., et al. *The analysis of subjective culture.* New York: Wiley, 1972.

TROW, M. Study done for the Carnegie Commission. 1970.

UNEF. "De la misère en milieu étudiant." *Etudiants de France* (special supplement to no. 16), Association Fédérative Générale des Etudiants de Strasbourg, 1967.

UNESCO. *Rapport sur la jeunesse.* Fifteenth General Conference of UNESCO, October-November 1968.

UNESCO. "Youth in contemporary society." *Youth and Society,* 1 (1), September 1969, pp. 5–37.

UNESCO and OECD. *Access to higher education,* 4 (annex), Vienna, November 1967.

VANEIGEM, R. *Traité du savoir-vivre à l'usage des jeunes générations.* Paris: Gallimard, 1967.

WESTBY, D. L., BRAUNGART, R. G. "Class and politics in the family backgrounds of student political activists." *American Sociological Review,* October 1966, pp. 690–692.

White Paper on Higher Education. Tokyo: Ministry of Education, 1964.

WRIGHT, D. S. "A comparative study of the adolescent's concepts of his parents and teachers." *Educational Review,* 14, 1962.

WRIGHT, M. C. *Power, politics and people.* New York: Ballantine Books, 1963.

YANKELOVICH, D. "A Fortune survey." In *Youth in turmoil* (adaptation of a special issue of *Fortune*). New York: Time-Life Books, 1969, pp. 31–46.

YANKELOVICH, D. *The changing values on campus*. New York: Washington Square Press, 1972.

YANKELOVICH, D. *The new morality: A profile of American youth in the 70's.* New York: McGraw-Hill, 1974.

ZAVALLONI, M. "The comparability of indicators in cross-cultural attitudes surveys." *Social Science Information,* 7, 2, 1969, pp. 93–100.

Index